SUFFERING *in the* ARMY *of* TENNESSEE

SUFFERING *in the* ARMY *of* TENNESSEE

A Social History of the Confederate Army of the Heartland from the Battles for Atlanta to the Retreat from Nashville

Christopher Thrasher

VOICES *of the* CIVIL WAR
Michael P. Gray, Series Editor

Knoxville / The University of Tennessee Press

The Voices of the Civil War series makes available a variety of primary source materials that illuminate issues on the battlefield, the home front, and the western front, as well as other aspects of this historic era. The series contextualizes the personal accounts within the framework of the latest scholarship and expands established knowledge by offering new perspectives, new materials, and new voices.

First Edition.

Library of Congress Cataloging-in-Publication Data

Names: Thrasher, Christopher David, author.

Title: Suffering in the Army of Tennessee : a social history of the Confederate Army of the heartland from the battles for Atlanta to the retreat from Nashville / Christopher Thrasher.

Other titles: Voices of the Civil War series.

Description: First edition. | Knoxville : The University of Tennessee Press, [2021] | Series: Voices of the Civil War | Includes bibliographical references and index. | Summary: "Generally, volumes in the Voices of the Civil War series are edited diaries, letter collections, or journals by a single soldier or civilian. In Christopher Thrasher's unique contribution to the series, *Suffering in the Army of Tennessee*, the author draws upon diaries, letters, newspapers, memoirs, official reports, and genealogical sources to capture from as many points of view as possible the experiences of ordinary soldiers in the Army of Tennessee from the Atlanta Campaign to the end of the war. In addition to extensive primary documentation, Thrasher provides context for understanding how events developed from 1864 to the total collapse of General John Bell Hood's forces. While volumes have been written on the Atlanta Campaign or the Battles of Nashville and Franklin, no previous historian has constructed what amounts to a sweeping social history of the Army of Tennessee"— Provided by publisher.

Identifiers: LCCN 2021019298 (print) | LCCN 2021019299 (ebook) | ISBN 9781621906322 (hardcover) | ISBN 9781621906339 (kindle edition) | ISBN 9781621906414 (pdf)

Subjects: LCSH: Confederate States of America. Army of Tennessee—History. | Soldiers—Confederate States of America—Social conditions. | United States—History—Civil War, 1861-1865—Social aspects. | United States—History—Civil War, 1861-1865—Campaigns.

Classification: LCC E607 .T57 2021 (print) | LCC E607 (ebook) | DDC 973.7/13—dc23
LC record available at https://lccn.loc.gov/2021019298
LC ebook record available at https://lccn.loc.gov/2021019299

To my wife, Barbara Thrasher.
I could not have written this book
without her love, patience, and support.

CONTENTS

ILLUSTRATIONS

Maps

Tables

FOREWORD

More than one Civil War historian has contended that the great conflict was won and lost in the Western theater. The Army of the Tennessee had its origins in 1861, earned its official title in 1862, and became the main Confederate fighting force west of the Appalachian Mountains for the rest of the war. Commanders like Albert Sydney Johnston, P. G. T. Beauregard, Braxton Bragg, Joseph E. Johnston, and John Bell Hood headed this prodigious fighting force. These generals led troops who undertook campaigns in the strategic river systems that stretched to the Mississippi, and much has been written about the engagements they participated in. For example, Wiley Sword, Thomas Connelly, Peter Cozzens, and Andrew Haughton have all investigated battles and the soldiering in the Army of the Tennessee, from its rise to its fall. Besides battles and leaders, historians have also concentrated on the "common soldier" in all theaters of the Civil War. The pioneering work of Bell Wiley gave birth to a field that prompted future scholars—Reid Mitchell, James McPherson, and Peter Carmichael just to name a few—to continue providing insightful analysis in untangling motivation, mood, and these soldiers' daily activities. Especially noteworthy with regard to this book, Larry Daniel's 1991 *Soldiering in the Army of Tennessee* is social history combined with a comparative methodology in the Eastern theater, affording excellent insights into soldier discipline, religion, sacrifice, and comradeship from the "bottom up." According to Daniel, cohesion from beneath drove the Western Confederate army, unlike its counterpart. He contends that the Army of Northern Virginia had a consistent command structure, headed by R. E. Lee, offering more of a hierarchical leadership model that started with him alone on top. Daniel provides a provocative thesis, but might leave some readers wanting a more micro-campaign level exploration to prove it. Such an in-depth campaign history has indeed been published, but this one was about the Eastern theater, rather than the West. J. Tracy Power's *Lee's Misérables* details the common soldier of the Army of Northern Virginia from the Wilderness to Appomattox. Until now, an exhaustive, campaign history with deep primary source documents on the Army of Tennessee had not been written.

Much fighting of the Confederate Army of Tennessee occurred near or along the river, and although the unit was officially named after the state, it left indelible marks along the Tennessee River's banks. Meanwhile, a Union army also was christened after the Tennessee River; the naming of both sides' armies demonstrated how control of the state and the important river system it contained were vital objectives for both the Federal and Confederate governments, with overall conquest leading to the grand prize of the Mississippi. It was also along the Tennessee River, where so much fighting took place, that the author of *Suffering in the Army of Tennessee* grew up. From adolescence, Christopher Thrasher lived and breathed the local history of northern Alabama and its further outreaches. During his upbringing, he had little choice but to notice the army's paths. On fishing trips with his grandfather, before the elder pointed out places to cast in the Tennessee's muddy currents, he also pointed to the fighting remnants that were left behind, such as bullet scars in buildings. Christopher Thrasher grew up in the war's shadows, ultimately crystallizing these experiences into *Suffering in the Army of Tennessee.*

This undertaking is an exhaustive campaign and social history, bringing the voices of so many contemporaries into a deep interpretation of this army. Where the trajectory of this book differs from previous volumes in Voices of the Civil War series is that it does not contain letters or diaries from one, two, or a few contemporaries. Rather, Thrasher deserves to be called both an author—the work comprises a full-length narrative—and an editor—it is interwoven with an "army" of primary source materials that include the voices of common soldiers, officers, and civilians—from letters to diaries, postwar accounts, to official reports. Also threaded into the story are the memories of these participants, as Thrasher's discerning editorial pen analyzes postwar documents and explores the authenticity of battle reports of the day. In his eight chapters, Thrasher's engaging prose blends drama with evaluation, as he takes the reader along with the Army of Tennessee through campaigning from Atlanta to the end at Nashville. Thrasher documents experiences from the tedium of camp life to the horrors of battle; from going to church to pursuing less than noble occupations, such as falling into alcohol abuse and consorting with unsavory civilians. Thrasher's insightful interpretation notes that the soldiers of the Army of Tennessee had a "duality" in their roles, from the suffering undertaken by themselves in campaigning, to the plying of suffering on others, as their war machine ran on and on. The ebbs and flows of battle threatened to undermine the ethos of Southern masculinity, as the soldiers' personalities were in conflict with both "a desire to destroy and the desire to protect," and Thrasher argues persuasively that this most basic psychic conflict complicates "the traditional perception of the ragged Rebel." Finally, Thrasher affirms that "This work bears the title *Suffering in the Army of Tennessee*, because suffering was the most common theme in primary sources about this campaign, particularly in those produced by Confederate soldiers." Consequently, inspection reports and other primary sources demonstrate a dearth in the troops' clothing, gear, and food; yet, contemporary records also reveal other soldiers were "remarkably well armed with most of the weapons, accouterments, and ammunition needed by a mid-nineteenth century army."

Thrasher's understanding of the Army of Tennessee's campaign is no less impressive than his use of primary sources. He sets the stage with Federal movements from Chattanooga toward Atlanta, with siege on the city. There are dramatic civilian insights, analysis of the removal of Johnston to be replaced by Hood, and how Confederates reacted to these dramatic changes. The battles of Peachtree Creek, Atlanta, Ezra Church, Jonesborough, and the ultimate evacuation and fall of Atlanta, are all detailed. Utilizing desertion records as well as other key indicators, Thrasher finds that historians have often fallen short in their interpretations about apparent Southern setbacks (Peachtree Creek, Atlanta, and Ezra Church, for example), whereas Confederate morale actually seemed to surge as revealed in some of their writings during these battles. Thrasher delves into Confederate counteroffensives in Georgia and Allatoona, then fighting through Alabama and the surrounding area. He also describes the Army of Tennessee's entrance into Alabama, its movements around Gadsden to Guntersville, with guerilla war that ensued with "Tories" and "Bushwhackers." The reader follows the entrance of Nathan Bedford Forrest and 3,000 of his troopers, the battle of Decatur in October of 1864, a respite at Muscle Shoals on the banks of the Tennessee, and the Battle of Florence, as well as encampments—with details about politics, generalship, romance, desertion, and (always) suffering, especially from parasitic infestation that caused bleeding sores on many.

From Alabama, the army moved into the rich resources of Tennessee, the so called "land of plenty," so the soldiers might relieve their suffering; Hood also doubled down by promising his soldiers not only could they feed off the countryside, but he would fight on advantageous ground so they would be less at risk. Operational movements stretched from east Tennessee to central Missouri, focusing on Spring Hill and Columbia, highlighted by an amphibious assault. Stories of stealing, food, tobacco, a snowfall that intrigued many, and a variety of spirits (reflected in both moods of men and the alcohol they drank) are imbibed by the reader, before preparing for the historic Battle of Franklin.

Three miles south of Franklin, at Winstead Hill, Forrest ran into Yanks as Hood prepared for the momentous engagement. Infantry formed into battle lines, on the "soft and beautiful November day." The editor draws on various sources, from a young fighting man that turned into a history professor, to other foot soldiers, and staff officers. Union artillery crashed into darkness like fireworks wrote one onlooker, and the next day's hardest fighting was relatively brief, but nonetheless inflicted large casualties, especially on the Southern side, despite Hood's optimistic written reports. The Army of Tennessee also suffered the casualties in high-ranking generals, which also punctuated this loss. The last three chapters of the book look at Nashville—the siege, the battle, and the Rebel retreat. From December 1864 into the new year, taking Nashville was critical because of its infrastructure and roads, rail lines, and rivers. The cost was again high for the Army of Tennessee, which suffered irreparable damage. More importantly, this story ends there because while there was some fighting in 1865, in the words of Confederate soldier Robert Bevier, the Confederate Army of Tennessee "ceased to exist" after the retreat from Nashville." Thrasher believes "This does not denigrate the men who participated in the final stand, but it does emphasize the fact that there was a fundamental change after the Battle of Nashville." He concludes that "Considering the dramatic differences between postwar memoirs and contemporary accounts, and clues within some of the memoirs, it seems likely that the disastrous battles of Franklin and Nashville shaped the postwar memories of many men." So Thrasher concludes his story "on the banks of the Tennessee River for several reasons. It was the end of a campaign and therefore a convenient place to end the story." Fitting, in that the genesis of this project, from his upbringing to where his book began, was also its ending.

Michael P. Gray
East Stroudsburg University of Pennsylvania

ACKNOWLEDGMENTS

If I have accomplished anything in life, it is only because people have been nice to me. For anything worthwhile within these pages, I give all credit to my benefactors. Every flaw is entirely my own.

I express my gratitude to archivists and librarians, too numerous to mention, who helped me at archives across the country. In the words of my dearly departed friend Jim Sanderson, archivists are "the keepers of the treasures." I am grateful for all the wonderful people who keep the treasures safe.

I thank Scot Danforth, Michael Gray, Alex Mendoza, and the entire team at the University of Tennessee Press for their help in transforming a very rough manuscript into a finished book.

I appreciate my dear friend Gene Barnett who taught me everything I know about the Confederate cavalry.

I am grateful to my colleagues Chuck Argo and Abby Hanks who provided comments on several versions of this manuscript and helped me improve my writing.

I reserve my deepest thanks for my parents, David and Theresa Thrasher. From the moment of my birth, they indulged my curiosities, encouraged me to fall in love with learning, and convinced me that the answers to life's mysteries lay within the yellowed pages of long-forgotten books.

INTRODUCTION
Suffering in the Army of Tennessee

The most destructive war in American history had all but destroyed the South by 1864. In September, Union forces won a series of hard-fought battles, captured the charred ruins of Atlanta, Georgia, and occupied the most vital crossroads in the region. Typically, armies retreat in the aftermath of defeat, but the battle-scarred defenders of the southern heartland were anything but typical. In desperation, the Confederate Army of Tennessee bypassed the victorious Union forces in Atlanta, avoiding Union strength and searching for the invader's weak underbelly somewhere far to the north. At first it seemed just crazy enough to work. The rebels captured scattered federal garrisons, feasted on captured provisions, and crushed nearly every man in blue who dared defy them. For a while, the plan worked just well enough to worry Union commanders. After a short stretch of successes, fortune turned its back on the army of the heartland. Stiffening Union resistance along the Tennessee River forced the rebels to search for a crossing far to the west, eating up precious time, the one commodity they could least afford to waste. By the time the rebels entered Tennessee, a mighty blue host blocked the roads north. On November 30, 1864, the rebels discovered entrenched federals at Franklin, Tennessee. With little hesitation, the men in gray unfurled their banners and flung themselves at their opponents. The rebels captured the position but paid for the ground with six thousand irreplaceable men. Unable to puncture the heavily fortified city of Nashville, Tennessee, a few miles to the north, the Confederates dug in and waited for the winds of favor to turn in their direction once more. Fortune never came their way, but a reinforced Union army did, sweeping the Army of Tennessee from the state that gave them their name on December 15 and 16, 1864, forever shattering the last remnants of what had once been the famed army of the heartland and ensuring federal victory in the western theatre.

Numerous writers have weighed in on this momentous campaign, but their works leave an opening. In his famed memoir, Co. Aytch, Sam Watkins lamented "the histories of the Lost Cause are all written out by 'big bugs,' generals and renowned historians." Watkins believed that, despite his humble station in life, he too had a story worth telling and wrote one of the most enduring personal accounts of life in the Confederate Army of Tennessee. In the decades since Watkins published his work, authors have produced an endless stream of material on the Civil War including some excellent books on this campaign. However, most of the writing is still produced by and focuses on the "big bugs," rather than ordinary people. An astute reader can see the flickering ghosts of ordinary men in the great campaign narratives; a quote from a nameless private, a comment on the army's morale, or even a footnote from some mostly ignored diary. Ordinary Confederate soldiers deserve a more prominent place in the story.

This is an unconventional book. It is neither a story of a single participant nor is it a typical campaign narrative. Sam Watkins wrote a great book, but he told the story of only one man, and this work tries to fill in the gaps with stories from other soldiers. This book is a grand overview of the campaign like Wiley Sword's *The Confederacy's Last Hurrah*, but if Sword's book is a photograph, this book is a photographic negative of that same image. The pictures are similar but reversed and highlight different aspects of the image. Sword told stories of the "big bugs," and this work shares tales from the men in the ranks. Derek Frisby wrote what might be the best brief history of the campaign, *Campaigns in Mississippi and Tennessee, February–December 1864*, for the Center of Military History. While Frisby did great work, his book is only sixty-seven pages long and as a result lacks much of the detail present in this book. Although produced nearly half a century ago, Thomas Connelly's *Army of the Heartland* and *Autumn of Glory* remain two of the finest overviews of the Confederate Army of Tennessee. This book takes inspiration from Connelly's work while focusing more narrowly on the fall 1864 campaign and drawing on resources that only came to light long after Connelly's work appeared on bookshelves. Like the works of Alex Mendoza, this book details the suffering of soldiers in the Army of Tennessee, but while Mendoza focuses on the early phases of the war, this book examines the final stages of the conflict. This book borrows its social history focus from Larry Daniel's *Soldiering in the Army of Tennessee*, which provided fascinating insights into the ordinary soldiers of this army, but while Daniel gave a brief snapshot of these men throughout the war, this is a far more detailed account of soldiers on a single campaign. J. Tracy Power's *Lee's Miserables* is an outstanding history of ordinary soldiers in Virginia, and this work provides a counterpoint focused on the men who fought across Georgia, Alabama, and Tennessee. The Eyewitness to Battle series of books, particularly the volumes dedicated to the battles of Franklin and Nashville, do an excellent job of explaining battles in the words of actual participants. Unlike those books, this work covers the often-ignored weeks of boredom as well as the moments of terror that punctuated life in the army.

Telling the stories of common soldiers is not easy. The research for this work began with an examination of the scholarly literature on this campaign to gather a sense of the overall themes. Traditional primary sources, including diaries, letters, and newspaper accounts produced during the war, provide the foundation for this book, but it also draws on official reports, genealogical resources, and even statistical information. The work also draws heavily on postwar memoirs and articles in *Confederate Veteran*. Postwar accounts are prone to bias. In comparison to letters and diaries produced during the conflict, they may overdramatize soldiers' wartime experiences or exaggerate their suffering. However, they are still valuable sources from actual participants, particularly when used in combination with sources produced during the conflict. To tell the story of many men, the work allows as many men as possible to speak. This book does not provide a seat at the general's table, where a single officer speaks and others listen. Instead, it offers a place in the ranks among an army marching through the darkness, where many muttered voices grumble, argue, and joke as obscured faces slip past the listener in the night. The work builds on existing scholarship but provides several important new insights.

This work bears the title *Suffering in the Army of Tennessee* because suffering was the most common theme in primary sources about this campaign, particularly in those produced by Confederate soldiers. The life of a Confederate soldier during this campaign was difficult in ways that the people of the present will probably never fully appreciate. Many members of the Confederate Army of Tennessee were aware that they possessed a dual role as both the victims and the cause of suffering. Confederate soldiers struggled with difficult conflicts on this campaign. Officers were torn by a desire to protect their men and an obligation to send those men to their deaths in an effort to achieve victory. Soldiers realized their presence inflicted pain on southern civilians even as they tried to protect them from the Union army. Combat veterans loathed the sight of young boys and old men in the ranks, while they lamented the army's dwindling numbers. Soldiers struggled with their desire to go home, where they could protect their families, and their duty to remain in the army, where they could defend their nation.[1] The appearance of a conflicted southern masculinity stuck between competing desires provides additional support for Ted Ownby's excellent work, *Subduing Satan: Religion, Recreation, and Manhood in the Rural South*.[2]

This work complicates the traditional perception of the ragged rebel. The Confederate soldiers who took part in this campaign were not barefoot scarecrows carrying squirrel rifles nor were they as well supplied as their Union counterparts. Inspection reports and other primary sources indicate that most Confederate soldiers on this campaign lacked the clothing, camp equipment, and food they needed. However, those same primary sources

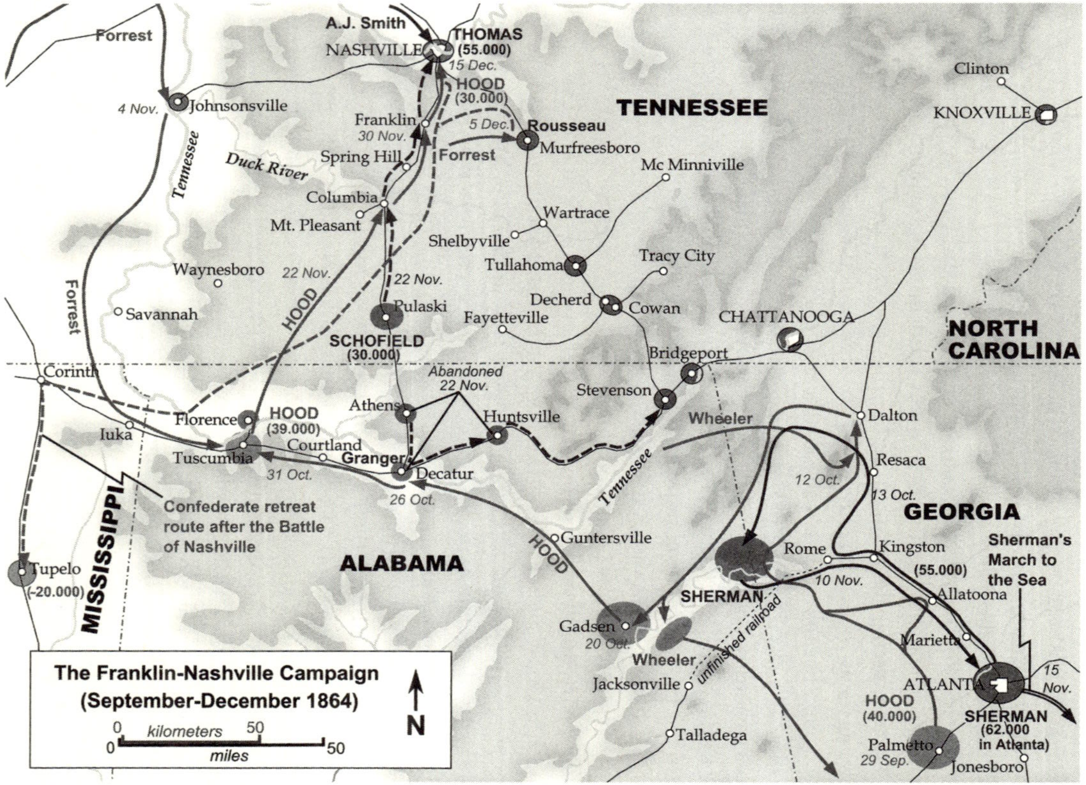

Map 1. Franklin–Nashville Campaign. Map by Hal Jespersen, www.cwmaps.com.

also suggest that the men were remarkably well armed with most of the weapons, accouterments, and ammunition needed by a mid-nineteenth century army. They had little of what they needed to live but almost everything they needed to fight. In the words of one observer who commented on another rebel army, Confederate soldiers were "a lean and hungry set of wolves."[3]

Finally, this work demonstrates that many men remained with the doomed campaign because they did not feel it was doomed. Up until the last few days of the campaign, many Confederate soldiers believed that victory was only one good fight away. A shocking number of southern soldiers preferred the danger of headlong assaults to the safety of trenches. While less prevalent in postwar memoirs written with the benefit of hindsight, many contemporary accounts indicate that morale climbed on the offensive and plummeted on the defensive. Even the horrific Battle of Franklin, which many scholars believe destroyed the army, increased many men's morale. Many Confederate soldiers found the cold, hunger, and boredom of the defensive works outside of Nashville more demoralizing than suicidal charges.[4]

1

"WE HAV [*SIC*] TOOK OUR STAND HERE"

The Battles for Atlanta

> We hav took our stand here I think and hope. I don't see any chance for peace. some says it will end but I cant think so. I can tel you they hav fought very heard hear in places for the last 2 weeks and killed lots of men . . . The yankies slip up on us some times . . . but dont make a great eal by it I warn you . . . Mother I am a heep hearder hearted than I ought to be but I hav seen so many men killed and wounded till I dont care for it no more than if it was a chicken. I do want to go home so bad I cant rest well.[1]
>
> —Angus McDermid, 29th Georgia Infantry

Preparing for the Campaign to Defend Atlanta

As the winter turned to spring in 1864, the forty-five thousand starving and poorly clothed men of the Confederate Army of Tennessee prepared for the upcoming campaign. Confederate troops under the command of General Joseph Johnston joined forces with their native soil to transform the difficult terrain between Union-occupied Chattanooga, Tennessee, and Confederate-held Atlanta, Georgia, into an attacker's nightmare. James Maxwell began his military career as a University of Alabama cadet in 1861, but by 1864 he was a sergeant commanding an artillery crew in Lumsden's Artillery Battery. The dark-haired, slightly built young man explained that men dug in since experience had long ago convinced them that "a very small ditch would reduce the number of causalities by a very large percent." Facing a seemingly unstoppable blue menace with vastly superior numbers, the rebels would need every advantage their shovels could provide in the upcoming campaign.[2]

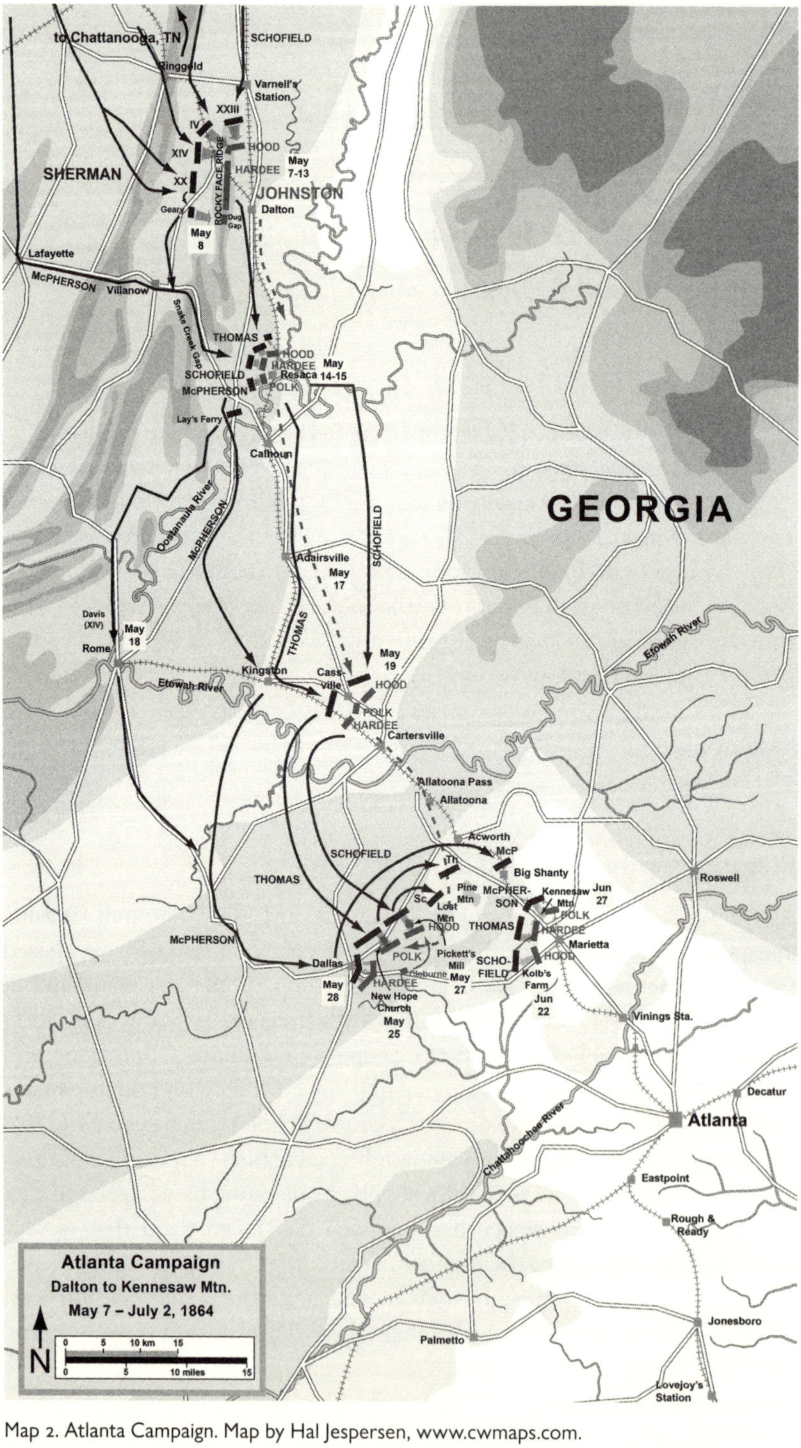

Map 2. Atlanta Campaign. Map by Hal Jespersen, www.cwmaps.com.

The Union Offensive Begins

On the first day of May 1864, General William Tecumseh Sherman opened the spring campaign with orders that sent his 110,000 well-equipped, blue-clad soldiers southeast from Chattanooga, Tennessee. John Jackman of Kentucky's Confederate Orphan brigade noted in his diary that "we are again on the war path." Union soldiers quickly encountered rebel handiwork. General Sherman complained "the whole country is one vast fort" consisting of "fifty miles of interconnected trenches" that were studded with abatis [obstacles made of sharpened branches that functioned like wooden barbed wire fences] and carefully prepared artillery positions. Confederate soldiers took pride in the fact that "wherever Sherman went, he was faced by rifle pits." John Porcher of the 10th South Carolina Infantry claimed that on at least one occasion men of his regiment refused to dig in "because the line was badly placed." They promised to defend the ground but had no desire to exhaust themselves digging trenches in a poorly chosen location. General John Bell Hood, commanding a corps at that time, threatened to shoot the men if they refused to dig. Porcher's account does not reveal if the men dug or Hood shot anyone, only that the fighting continued.[3]

The Confederate forces made a series of desperate stands at Dalton (May 7), Resaca (May 14), Adairsville (May 17), Kingston (May 18), Cassville (May 20), and Dallas (May 25–28). Kentucky soldier John Jackman claimed the men greeted calls to give battle with "loud cheers" because they were "anxious to fight." The rebels achieved their greatest victory at the Battle of Kennesaw Mountain on June 27, when Sherman hurled his troops at entrenched Confederate positions. In the battle 1,999 Federals were killed and wounded out of their 17,733 engaged troops. These were much higher losses than the 270 killed and wounded rebels out of 17,301 who were engaged. John Hagan with the 29th Georgia Infantry believed "we have in evry case whipped the enemy & I beleave they will be retreating in a few days." Time proved Hagan wrong. Tattered gray scarecrows slowed but could not stop the relentless blue steamroller that moved ever closer to Atlanta in the summer of 1864. General Sherman explained, "we gain ground daily, fighting all the time." His objective was the city of Atlanta.[4]

General Sherman grew frustrated as he tried pushed his army forward over "difficult" terrain consisting of "dense overgrowth and short, steep ridges of flinty stone" in a series of engagements that he considered not real battles, but "one universal skirmish extending over a vast surface." Summer rains of lukewarm water slowed movements, turning roads into mud and making an already difficult campaign even more unpleasant for everyone involved. John Bennitt, a surgeon with the 19th Michigan

Infantry, concluded that "soldiering" on the campaign was "rather hard business."[5]

In spite of the setbacks, some Union soldiers remained upbeat. Dick Harris, a native of Knoxville, Tennessee, serving with the 3rd Tennessee Union Infantry, informed his father that, while several of his friends were killed or wounded in recent fighting, he was unharmed and "ready for them again." Harris assured his father that "the boys are all well and in fighting spirits." He optimistically predicted that the rebels would offer no further resistance north of Atlanta.[6]

Atlanta in Danger

The Army of Tennessee proved incapable of stopping the advancing foe in the spring of 1864, and the Confederacy's leaders began to worry that Atlanta might fall. On June 28, 1864, Governor Joseph Brown of Georgia wrote an urgent letter to Confederate president Jefferson Davis, arguing that Atlanta was as important to the Confederacy as the heart was to the body, urging the president to send more troops, and warning "we must hold it." President Davis responded quickly, agreeing that Atlanta was vital and arguing that he had already done everything in his considerable power to protect Atlanta. He pointed out that Confederate forces protecting the city were outnumbered by a smaller margin than any other Confederate army and suggested that the ongoing cavalry raids by General John Hunt Morgan and General Nathan Bedford Forrest would weaken Sherman's advance. Governor Brown replied to President Davis several days later, openly doubting that raids by Forrest into Mississippi and Morgan into Kentucky would do anything to deter Sherman's drive towards Atlanta. He concluded that Davis was making serious mistakes and predicted the fall of Atlanta "may prove fatal to our cause." For all of Brown's criticism, Davis had few options as the Army of Tennessee retreated towards Atlanta.[7]

President Davis and Governor Brown were very worried about the potential fall of Atlanta, but many soldiers did not share such concerns. J. P. Austin, a member of the 9th Kentucky Cavalry, claimed that the city was in no danger and that the army was perfectly capable of withstanding an indefinite siege. W. P. Chambers, a twenty-five-year-old schoolteacher turned sergeant in the 46th Mississippi Infantry, explained that, while the army was losing ground to the Union forces, rebel morale was at all-time high because they were losing far fewer men than their opponents and felt confident that the process of attrition would eventually wear down the invaders. C. T. Hardman of the 6th Alabama Cavalry informed his wife that "the troops are all in fine spirits and are confident of their ability to defend themselves."

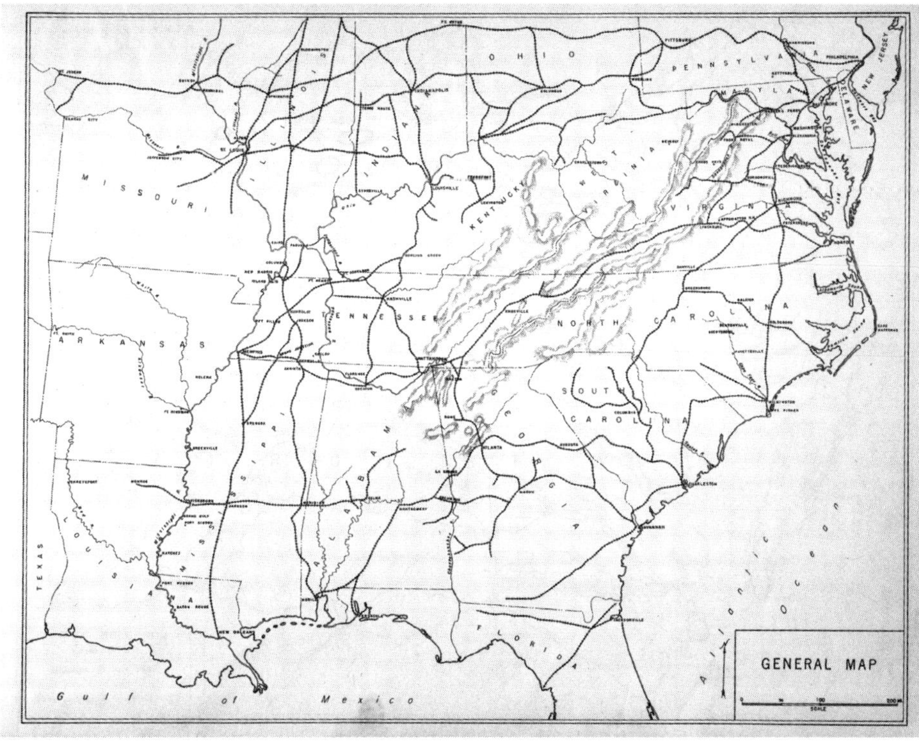

Map 3. Major Railroad and River Transportation Routes Used during the Civil War. United States Military Academy. Department of Military Art and Engineering, Vincent J. Esposito, and Matthew Forney Steele. *Civil War Atlas to accompany Steele's American Campaigns* (West Point, N.Y.: 1941). Library of Congress.

Andrew Neal of the Marion Light Artillery was "in fine spirits" and predicted that soon Johnston would spring his trap, forcing the Union army to flee north. Henry Reddick of the 1st Florida Infantry was just happy to have rations and appreciated Johnston because he "looked after the commissary much better" than the army's previous commanders.[8]

While many soldiers had absolute confidence in their commander, an increasingly vocal faction of soldiers was unhappy with Johnston. J. N. Wyatt of the 12th Tennessee Infantry explained in a letter that "there is some dissatisfaction with Gen. Johnston for retreating so much." Thomas Hardin of the 37th Georgia Infantry told his wife that he might die soon because General Johnston was allowing the Federals to advance "without any hindrance." Hardin described Johnston's work as a failure that would lead to "carnage." Joel Murphree, a thirty-seven-year-old merchant turned

Panoramic view of city of Atlanta from the top of the Female Seminary, extending from the Medical College on the southeast around by the south to a point on Peach Tree Street, October 1864. Library of Congress.

quartermaster sergeant with the 57th Alabama Infantry, admired Johnston but felt that the army could not retreat forever and worried that another "retreat will demoralize the army." Some of the men were already demoralized. R. W. Banks, serving in the 37th Mississippi Infantry, claimed that under Johnston "the army grew smaller in numbers and weaker in spirit."[9]

Dissatisfaction led to desertion. Large numbers of Confederate soldiers deserted to the Federals. During May and June 1,141 Confederate soldiers deserted into Federal lines, an average of 142.5 per week. Federal soldiers reported that most of these deserters wanted nothing more than to get back to their homes that lay behind Federal lines. Other former rebels became civilian workers for the Union military, simultaneously strengthening the Union while weakening the Confederacy. Many more men undoubtedly deserted and went home without turning themselves over to the Federals.[10]

The men who remained understood that many of their comrades were deserting to the Federals rather than continuing the fight, which diminished the morale of the men who remained. Private Celathiel Helms, a member of the 63rd Georgia Infantry, told his wife that Confederate officers "are fearful that all their men will go to the Yankees." Confederate surgeon Junius Bragg told his wife that since "desertion is the order of the day, I think we had better quit and go home." Captain Hugh Black, a two-year veteran in

command of a company in the 6th Florida Infantry, gave his wife a long list of men from his unit that had deserted and confessed that "I think that it will stand me in hand to go and make peace with the Yankees."[11]

The Army of Tennessee Enters Atlanta

As a warm rain fell, bathing filthy men in tepid water, the Army of Tennessee fell back into Atlanta in the second week of July 1864. The weary veterans took little notice of intermittent small arms fire that punched through the rain drops as Yankee skirmishers nipped at their heels. Sergeant John W. Sparkman of the 48th Tennessee Infantry described Atlanta in his diary as "a very nice little city." Robert Jarman of the 27th Mississippi Infantry was just a few weeks shy of his twenty-fourth birthday when he entered Atlanta. The thickly bearded university student turned infantrymen believed that "the men were all very glad" to enter Atlanta because they had been on active campaign for several months and "we needed some rest." Kentucky cavalryman J. P. Austin recalled Atlanta as looking less like a city and more like a fortress consisting of "a network of redoubts and rifle-pits." While some men seemed pleased to come into town, others like Alabamian Joel Murphree worried that Atlanta's importance would ensure that a disastrous battle would be fought at its gates.[12]

The Army of Tennessee sought to defend Atlanta, but they may have caused more suffering than they prevented. Many southern civilians were deeply distressed by the approaching armies, having hoped that the Army

Private Thomas Kitchen, Georgia Regiment. Library of Congress.

of Tennessee would defeat the invaders somewhere far to the north. Watson Landingham, serving as a clerk to General John Bell Hood, was conflicted about the Confederate army's presence in Atlanta. He was dedicated to the Confederate army, but he realized that the rebel troops were hurting many of the southern civilians they were dedicated to protect. He informed his mother that the army's presence caused "considerable alarm" to Atlanta citizens, many of whom fled the city in a panicked frenzy that he considered more terrifying than combat. New Jersey–born Confederate soldier Hiram Williams had similarly conflicted feelings. The northern-born Confederate was a loyal member of the Army of Tennessee, but he noted the pain that his comrades caused to southern civilians as he described rebel soldiers taking blankets and food from empty houses, as well as "pillaging everything" by tearing down artwork, shredding women's clothing, and scattering books in often repeated scenes that "made my heart sick to see such wanton destruction." Alabamian John Crittenden told his wife, "if you could be here and see the ruin that has come upon this part of the country you would be astonished. I have known our own soldiers to go to a farm and destroy everything on the place." Robert Patrick of the 4th Louisiana Infantry witnessed a woman give drinks of fresh milk to soldiers passing near her farm, but the men were not content with generous gifts. They stole all her chickens, grain, and even tore down fences so they could more easily graze their horses on her land. Patrick concluded, "I do not think the Yankees are any worse than our own army." Patrick was clearly upset by his army, which was supposed to protect Atlanta but was hurting the people they vowed to defend.[13]

The Army of Tennessee that fell back on Atlanta consisted largely of determined veterans, but the war was beginning to fatigue even the most ardent Confederates. Angus McDermid, a twenty-year-old farmer who joined the 29th Georgia Infantry in 1861 when he was only seventeen years old, wrote a letter home to his mother in Berrien, Georgia, explaining that "the last month of has bin very heard, I never hav seen sutch tite times in my life." McDermid was conflicted when his seventeen-year-old brother Ansel joined the army. He felt "sorrow," but his sadness was tempered by a grim determination that even boys "must stick up for their rites." Elbridge Littlejohn, a member of the 10th Texas Cavalry since early 1862, informed his wife that he was suffering from "constant diarrhea and fatigue." He prayed for an end to the war, since "I was never as tired of anything in my life." Veteran officer Lieutenant Joel E. Ruffin of the 50th Tennessee Infantry lay in an Atlanta hospital, which he described as a horrific place filled with gangrene and death. Ruffin believed 90 percent of Confederate surgeons should be executed for gross incompetence. John Coleman, a wealthy merchant who joined the 3rd Texas Cavalry in 1861, told his sweetheart back in Texas he was suffering from an illness that only a change of climate could repair. He told her that while he did not typically approve of "fast women," she could "flirt with all the boys if that will cheer you any"

Enoch Hooper Cook Jr., Pvt, Co. H, 38th Alabama Infantry. Library of Congress.

since he felt confident "you will not go too far." He assured her that the war would end in 1864 and that he would then return home to marry her. Captain Hugh Black, a veteran company commander in the 6th Florida Infantry, also believed that the conflict was almost over. Writing home to his wife that the Army of Tennessee had "done their best and last," he argued that there no "use in the army trying to do anything more." Georgia militiaman Benjamin Hunter lamented everything he had sacrificed to serve the Confederacy and told his wife he wanted to come home. Thomas Hardin of the 37th Georgia Infantry stood at a crossroads between a desire to go home and enjoy comfort and a competing desire to do his duty. Ultimately, he remained with the army because "my life is not my own." He accepted death and trusted on God for eternal salvation.[14]

Once in Atlanta, Confederate soldiers enjoyed a brief period of relative rest before the armies settled down to a siege. J. N. Wyatt of the 12th Tennessee Infantry explained in a letter to a friend, "the men are taking advantage of the quiet to rest and prepare themselves for the coming fray, for a battle seems inevitable." Some men supplemented their rations by picking delicious blackberries that seemed to grow everywhere around the town, and men attended religious services for the first time in many months. The Confederate mail system, which was unpredictable on its best days, finally caught up with the troops in Atlanta, and Charles Roberts, a Mississippian in Stanford's battery, wrote his wife to report that he received priceless letters from her after a long absence of news from home. Members of the 4th Louisiana Infantry purchased a jug of whiskey in Atlanta and "had a jollification." Other men picked perfectly ripe apples and devoured them eagerly. Georgia infantryman Angus McDermid became "as fat as a hog" from stuffing his belly with potatoes. He also enjoyed the feel of a new pair of shoes on his feet.[15]

Confederate soldiers traded items across the lines to the Yankees and eagerly devoured every newspaper they could acquire. Officers tried and failed to end the trades of tobacco for coffee across the lines. Alabama soldier John Crittenden enjoyed the brief respite, but he disliked the inevitable conversations between opposing soldiers because the Yankees "tell such extravagant tales," claiming that they had 175,000 men in their army and more reinforcements on the way. Crittenden did not believe the Federal claims, but some men did and became demoralized. Crittenden was torn between a duty to follow orders, which would help men avoid the demoralizing "extravagant tales" told by Union soldiers, and the desire to obtain precious luxuries like coffee. He finally justified the forbidden trade by pointing out the exorbitant prices charged by southern merchants. Thomas B. Cox, a native of Alabama who served in the 6th Mississippi Infantry, felt that "the

E. H. Rennolds, 5th Tennessee Infantry, from *A History of the Henry County Commands.*

Americans" in the Union army were friendly fellows who sympathized with the Confederates and shared their desire for a rapid end to the war. On the other hand, "a great number of the Federal soldiers were foreigners and Negroes and seemed to care for nothing except the pay they were to get." Larry Johnson of the 16th Tennessee Infantry enjoyed the time he spent chatting with Federal troops and wished that "this brother love could have prevailed" and ended the war.[16]

The Confederate army's leaders tried to end the illicit interactions. E. H. Rennolds of the 5th Tennessee Infantry noted in his diary that General Otho Strahl "is calling all who have held communication with the Yankees to a strict account." General Hood demanded immediate execution for any soldier found trading with the enemy, although it is unclear if anyone actually suffered that penalty. It is possible that Confederate commanders forbid informal truces at least in part because Federal troops used these moments as opportunities to provide rebels with Union uniforms they could wear to more easily slip through the lines and desert to the Federal army.[17]

The relative peace and quiet of informal truces did not last long, as the siege of Atlanta began in earnest. Men hated the "everlasting sharpshooting" that soon began to annoy everyone while giving neither side an advantage. Risenar Etter watched his brother die from a bullet fired by a Union sharpshooter. The Tennessean railed against the "inhuman enemy" who took his only brother from the world and prayed that God might save him

Unidentified soldier in Confederate uniform and C.S.A. belt buckle with cartridge box and percussion cap box. Library of Congress.

from a similar fate. By July 19, Union forces had cut off the roads between Atlanta and Mobile, Alabama. This prevented Hiram Smith, serving with the engineers, from keeping in touch with his friends in that city, "which does not please me at all."[18]

Men sought to defend Atlanta by building earthworks and returning fire, but their efforts were hampered by severe shortages of tools, weapons, and ammunition. According the official Confederate regulations, every fifteen infantrymen should have possessed two spades, two axes, two pickaxes, and two hatchets, but the men had far fewer tools. Alabamian James Maxwell took pride in Confederate ingenuity, observing that while Union soldiers possessed far more tools, rebels without shovels used tin plates and bayonets to build trenches that were every bit as good as the ones produced by their northern counterparts. James Nisbet, an infantry officer from Georgia, lamented the fact that the Army of Northern Virginia had high quality equipment, while the Army of Tennessee limped along with the leftovers. J. P. Austin later remembered that though the men suffered from shortages, "the boys took to the trenches as ducks to water."[19]

The civilians of Atlanta suffered as well as the soldiers. Colin Dunlop described the city as a burning husk of its former glory, where the shops were all boarded up and civilians suffered from illnesses as they hid from artillery fire in caves. William Sloan went to visit friends in Atlanta and discovered once-proud ladies living in a dirt pit under their house. During his visit, a lady left the shelter and went into the house with plans to obtain food. As she entered the domicile, a shell plowed through the house and sent it crashing down on top of her. Somehow, she survived. In an effort to ease the suffering of Atlanta's civilians, hungry soldiers gave up one day of their rations to the city's poor. Stuck between the desire to ease the suffering of civilians and the competing desire to maintain their strength so that they could punish their enemies, these men decided that helping civilians was the more important duty. Jesse Henderson proudly wrote in his diary that the men gave up their rations of their own free will, without being coerced by the officers.[20]

Johnston Removed from Command

Johnston's popularity declined as his promised victory never materialized, and by July the army's rank and file was divided in roughly equal numbers between Johnston's supporters and his opponents. President Davis hesitated to replace Johnston, because he understood the importance of stability to the army, but the situation grew increasingly desperate with every passing day. Military experts, most influentially General Braxton Bragg, urged Davis to remove Johnston. Civilian leaders joined the chorus of calls for Johnston's removal, and Davis received an endless stream of "delegations, petitions, and letters" demanding Johnston's immediate dismissal. On July 16, Davis sent Johnston a final telegram, asking how Johnston intended to repel Sherman's drive on Atlanta. Johnston responded with a vague plan to wait for a moment when the Confederate forces could "fight to advantage." Shocked by Johnston's apparent apathy in the face of catastrophe, President Jefferson Davis sent a telegram on the evening of July 17, 1864, that relieved General Joseph Johnston and made General John Bell Hood, then serving as a corps commander, the new commander of the Army of Tennessee.[21]

Johnston and Hood were wildly different men. Johnston was a fifty-seven-year-old Virginian and Hood a thirty-three-year-old Kentuckian turned Texan. The Confederate diarist Mary Chesnut described Hood as a tragically heroic figure with a "sad Quixote face, the face of an old crusader" and eyes that shone with a "fierce light." Both Hood and Johnston were West Point graduates who had served in the United States Army, but while Hood had worn blue for less than a decade and never risen above the rank of first lieutenant, Johnston had served for more than thirty years, eventually becoming a brigadier general. Both had served in the Confederate army from the start of the war and both were wounded in action, but while Hood had enjoyed a meteoric ride from captain to army commander in less than three years, Johnston began his Confederate service as a leading general.[22]

The greatest difference between Hood and Johnston was undoubtedly their approach to war. Johnston focused on the defensive. To his admirers he was "a master of defensive tactics" that made his opponents pay dearly for every step forward. To his critics he was a timid man who refused to fight. Hood's focus on the offensive and his well-deserved reputation as "among the most aggressive of the Confederate commanders" made him Johnston's polar opposite. To his supporters he was "the Gallant Hood," who never hesitated to lead his men to glory. Hood's critics argued that he was an aggressive bully with an insatiable bloodlust. When President Davis asked, General Robert E. Lee praised Hood as "a good fighter, very industrious on the battlefield" and noted, "I have a high opinion of his gallantry, earnestness, and zeal." Still, Lee did not fully endorse Hood's promotion, famously referring to the battered soldier as "all lion" and "none of the fox."[23]

Many accounts written with the benefit of hindsight reported that the army was outraged and demoralized by Johnston's replacement. Lot Young of the 4th Kentucky Infantry later recalled that "we had unbounded confidence in General Johnston." Arkansas soldier George Rozell remembered Johnston as "the greatest military genius and strategist the war produced on

Private Thomas McCreary of Co. E, 3rd Kentucky Regiment. McCreary is wearing a jacket that was probably produced at the Columbus Depot. Library of Congress.

either side" and claimed Hood's promotion was "disastrous." In one of the most famous memoirs of the war, Sam Watkins of the 1st Tennessee Infantry recalled that in response to Hood's promotion "five men . . . marched off, and it was the last we ever saw of them." Watkins argued that these men were hardly isolated cases and that they were representative of "the sentiment of the Army of Tennessee at that time." According to a postwar discussion, when General Patrick Cleburne heard of Hood's promotion, he replied only "oh hell, oh hell." In an 1893 account, Lieutenant Colonel R. H. Shotwell of the 35th Mississippi Infantry claimed the army was depressed by Johnston's removal. Perhaps no writer was more critical of Hood than Claude Hadaway, a member of the 54th Alabama Infantry since 1861, who argued that Hood's promotion was "the death knell of the Confederate cause."[24]

In contrast to the negativity of postwar accounts, many contemporary accounts expressed indifference or even some level of support for Hood. Texan cavalryman Elbridge Littlejohn respected both General Johnston and General Hood but stated that "it is believed by all if Gen. Hood had been in command of the army all the time the fight would now have been over with." Archie Livingston of the 3rd Florida Infantry noted in a letter that Hood was "a good officer" who he hoped would blunt the Union offensive. Georgia infantryman John Hagan loved Johnston but was filled with hope that Hood would win a great victory. Mississippian Charles Roberts criticized his comrades for their "blind and childlike confidence" in General Johnston. Not every Confederate soldier even found the change of commanders worthy of comment. Risenar Etter kept a detailed diary during this time with daily entries, but he made no mention of the change in army commanders.[25]

Perhaps the most interesting comparison comes from a rare incident of a common soldier who provided both contemporary and postwar accounts. E. H. Rennolds recalled in his postwar memoir that the men responded Johnston's dismissal with "sad faces and downcast eyes." He claimed that the men realized that, while Johnston had been cautious, Hood would be launch aggressive assaults that the army was ill prepared to carry out. As a result, "the excellent morale of the army was destroyed," as a sudden dread of "desperate fighting and consequent disaster settled down on the hearts of all." In contrast, E. H. Rennolds's diary entry written the day of the change stated only that "Gen. Johnson [SIC] issued an order saying he was ordered to turn the command over to Gen. Hood" and "all are stounded at it."[26] While it is true that these accounts do not exactly contradict each other and that Rennolds's postwar memoir might provide nothing more than an accurate elaboration of the brief note recorded in his diary, it might also be possible that the subsequent disasters he witnessed under General Hood colored his memory.

Considering the dramatic differences between postwar memoirs and contemporary accounts, as well as clues within some of the memoirs, it seems likely that the disastrous battles of Franklin and Nashville shaped the postwar memories of many men. In a 1930 account, Alabama infantryman R. A. Lambert claimed that Hood's promotion was "a very cold, wet blanket" on the army. He suggested that the subsequent battles of Atlanta, Franklin, and Nashville proved that the soldiers were right to doubt Hood. Robert Dacus, serving with the 1st Arkansas Mounted Rifles (dismounted), provided a long, rambling condemnation of Hood's promotion and then lamented "how different things went and how disaster after disaster overtook our army after General Hood took command subsequent events will prove." Irving Buck, General Patrick Cleburne's assistant adjutant general, argued that the men who doubted Hood's abilities were correct, "as events quickly demonstrated," and saw the change of commanders in literary terms, referring to Hood's promotion as "the beginning of an Iliad of woes." Tennessee cavalryman George Guild claimed that when Hood took command, the men made "direful" predictions that "were proved in so brief a time afterwards." Claude Hadaway denounced Hood's promotion, sarcastically asking his readers "did the battle of Franklin, Tenn., show the wisdom of the change?"[27]

Even after the war and the tragedies of the 1864 campaign, some soldiers remembered Hood fondly. Frank Anderson, who served as one of Hood's couriers, described Hood as "a born gentleman" who "never failed to salute a courier" and typically "had a kind word for him." In Edward McMorries's postwar account of his service with the 1st Alabama Infantry, he refused to address rumors of Hood's misconduct since "Gen. Hood was incapable of either falsehood or impropriety." When two of Hood's daughters attended a reunion of Confederate soldiers held in Atlanta, Georgia, in 1898 (Hood died the year before in a yellow fever outbreak), soldiers lined up to greet them and praise their departed father as a great commander.[28]

Even if Johnston was more popular with the troops in July 1864, popularity is hardly the best metric for evaluating a commander. Johnston had failed to stop the blue juggernaut that was barreling down on the essential city of Atlanta. Thomas Hardin believed that General Johnston allowed the Federals to advance on his home state of Georgia "without any hindrance." Johnston later claimed that he spent the summer of 1864 preparing for the perfect moment, drawing Sherman into a trap that would have reversed the course of the war. However, it is unclear if Sherman would have ever walked into a trap, if Johnston could have sprung one, or if Sherman would even have cared. Johnston's most successful encounter with Sherman was probably the Battle of Kennesaw Mountain on June 27, 1864, in which Sherman launched a frontal assault against the Confederate defenders. The battle was a tactical defeat for Sherman, but it did nothing to thwart the Union army, which simply flanked the Confederate army and moved one step closer to Atlanta. In the words of the historian Thomas Connelly, "Johnston's standing was based more upon what he allegedly could have done if he had been given the opportunity than by any real achievement." After the war, Sherman dismissed discussions of Johnston's plans to trap him by suggesting that any such trap would only have lengthened the war without changing its outcome. This was hardly postwar bluster. In June 1864, Sherman explained, "I begin to regard the death and mangling of a couple thousand men as a small affair, a kind of morning dash—and it may be well that we become so hardened." In a letter to General Ulysses S. Grant written on August 7, 1864, in the midst of the Atlanta campaign, Sherman expressed support for Grant's aggressive tactics: "let us give those southern fellows all the fighting they want, and when they are tired we can tell them we are just warming to the work." Clearly Sherman planned to take Atlanta, even at an awful cost. It is not clear what, if anything, Johnston or any other Confederate general could have done to stop the men in blue.[29]

Edgar W. Jones, a veteran who joined the 18th Alabama Infantry in 1861, provided a more balanced critique of the change in commanders than most observers. He noted that, while many soldiers were quick to criticize Davis for replacing Johnston with Hood, "the criticisms were unjust" since Johnston's "falling back movement could not go on forever." Clearly, "something had to be done—something different." Jones acknowledged that putting Hood in charge might not have been the best choice, but "nobody knows."[30] Jones was correct. There is no evidence that Johnston would have saved Atlanta or that the Confederacy could have long survived without the vital transportation and manufacturing center. Something different had to be done. It was unclear on July 17, 1864, if Hood was the right man for the job, but everyone believed that he would do things very differently than his predecessor, and he wasted no time in proving the accuracy of that expectation.

Within hours of Hood's promotion, a Union spy slipped out of Atlanta and informed Sherman of the change. Sherman asked General John Schofield, Hood's former classmate at West Point, about Hood. Schofield had little in common with the rank and file of the Confederate army, but he agreed with their assessment that Hood "was bold even to rashness." According to another account, Schofield went even farther, warning Sherman, "he'll hit you like hell, now, before you know it." While Sherman was pleased by the prospect of encountering a commander who would fight in the open, unlike Johnston who entrenched at every opportunity, he urged his men to be cautious since Hood could choose the time and place of battle. On

July 19, Sherman ordered a continuation of the flanking movements that had already proved so successful in the campaign.[31]

The Battle of Peachtree Creek July 20

Late on July 19, scouts informed Hood that the Union Army of the Cumberland had crossed Peachtree Creek, roughly three miles north of Atlanta, but that the Union Army of the Ohio and the Union Army of the Tennessee were still on the north bank. Hood believed that Sherman's position straddling the creek presented an opportunity. The newly appointed army commander decided to organize an attack for the afternoon of July 20. He would concentrate General William Hardee's and General Alexander Stewart's corps against the Army of the Cumberland, crush the exposed Federals, and turn Sherman's right flank before additional Union troops could cross the creek. General Benjamin "Frank" Cheatham's Corps and Georgia State Troops would take up entrenched positions across from the Federal left flank, which would block the Union Army of the Ohio and Army of the Tennessee if they tried to circle around and catch the rebel assault columns from behind.[32]

The plan, with its emphasis on concentrating superior forces against an isolated portion of a larger enemy force, was good, but executing the plan was a different matter altogether. Hood failed to immediately inform his subordinates of his plan and gave them insufficient time to prepare for the battle. Limited scouting and the area's heavily wooded hills delayed the Confederate attack, making coordination nearly impossible. While a more experienced set of commanders might have overcome these difficulties, Hood's promotion, the death of General Leonidas Polk several weeks before, and political infighting among various factions of officers caused confusion within the Confederate command structure and made careful adherence to the battle plan even more difficult.[33]

Poor planning, confusion, and difficult terrain all caused delays. The attacks that should have begun at 1:00 p.m. did not commence until almost 4:00 p.m. Although the Union forces did not anticipate an attack, they dug trenches because by this time veteran soldiers of both the North and South were aware of the defensive power of fortifications and constructed them at every opportunity. The delay of a few hours ensured that, instead of catching Union soldiers in the open as they crossed the creek, the Confederate forces would collide with an enemy securely anchored behind breastworks.[34]

J. P. Cannon of the 27th Alabama Infantry later recalled that, just before the assault commenced, General Stewart gave the men of his corps a rousing speech, urging them to "assault the enemy in his works" and destroy him at all costs since "the fate of Atlanta" depended on their attack.

The men were troubled since "it is a fearful thing to charge an enemy in his works," but "feeling that it had to be done, we nerved ourselves up to point to do our whole duty." The divisions advanced in columns since "we could have never have gone through that tangled mass of timber and brush in line of battle." Once beyond the worst of the woods, the men formed in line of battle, while Union skirmishers peppered them with bullets. Cannon heard an order of "fix bayonets, forward, double-quick, march." The men poured forth like a dirty gray avalanche, "raised the old rebel yell and rushed the works." The Union lines responded to the yell with noise of their own in the form of the "roar of musketry and the thunder of cannon; grape and canister and minnie-balls" that "mowed great gaps in our ranks," but the survivors keep running "until it seemed a hand-to-hand conflict was inevitable." In the moments before the gray-clad ranks reached the Federal lines, "our boys began to waver and soon the line fell back under cover of a little hill." Still determined to win the day, the men reformed and charged again, once again failing to reach the Union lines.[35]

The 66th Georgia Infantry formed into a line of battle as part of Steven's Brigade in Walker's Division of Hardee's Corps. Their left flank rested along the Peachtree Road. James Nisbet, commanding the regiment, pointed out that there was a gap on his men's left. He argued that the error should be corrected before the men continued their advance, but his concerns were overruled, and he received an order to charge. Nisbet was a veteran officer who learned his trade at horrific battles including Antietam, Fredericksburg, and Chickamauga. Nisbet was caught in a conflict between a duty to protect the men under his command and the obligation to follow the orders that might damage the enemy, even at awful cost. He knew the danger of charging towards a determined enemy while his flank dangled in the air and the suffering that the attack could inflict on his men, but he also knew that almost every victory was bought at a terrible cost. Like so many other officers before and after him, Nisbet followed the orders that sent him into danger and led his men forward at a run.[36]

Robert Dacus and the 1st Arkansas Mounted Rifles (dismounted) "went into the charge believing we should do as we had done in every engagement for the past two months, drive everything before us." At first their confidence seemed well founded; they pushed the Federals out of their first line of breastworks, captured a Union position, and paused to regroup. They were then disheartened to realize that the Union soldiers who fled from the first line had taken up a much stronger position in a secondary line where they joined large numbers of Federals who were already in place.[37]

The 5th Tennessee Infantry advanced near the center of the fighting. At around 4:00 p.m. they came within a short distance of the Federal lines and charged. Lieutenant J. W. Howard took the lead, grabbed his cap off his head, and waved it wildly "leaping the fences like a deer." Next, "we charged up to within about sixty or seventy-five yards of the enemy's works and halted in a ravine and sought protection behind trees." They waited, unable to advance or retreat as successive units piled on top of them in a confused morass. Caught between Union and Confederate lines with nowhere to go, the Tennesseans watched helplessly as bullets tore into flesh, maiming friends and strangers.[38]

It was about 4:30 when R. M. Collins and the 15th Texas Cavalry (dismounted) moved out into an open field in sight of the Union lines on the Confederate right. The Union troops "greeted us with a terrific fire of shot and shells," but most of the ammunition flew harmlessly over the heads of the rebels. When the Texans came to a farmer's fence, they grabbed it, pulled it out of the ground with a single movement, and threw it down. At that moment, an artillery shell burst in the Confederate ranks.[39]

The 66th Georgia Infantry charged, driving in the Federal skirmishers, and then slammed into Union breastworks, which the Confederate commanders claimed did not exist. The 66th Georgia and 1st Georgia Infantry Regiments captured the Federal breastworks to their front, but they had no support on their left flank. Union soldiers took advantage of the weakness, pouring a murderous fire into the front and left flank of the Georgians, who somehow stood the ground until their brigade commander, General Clement H. Stevens, rode in and ordered the men to fall back. Before the men could obey the order, a bullet pierced the general's head and killed him. The Georgians retreated as ordered, carrying the body of General Stevens and some of their wounded as they withdrew to their own lines.[40]

On the Confederate left, W. R. Bell took his place with the 14th Mississippi Infantry. He witnessed a Confederate artillery crew firing on a Federal battery on the opposite bank of Peachtree Creek. Their efforts were hampered by a tree that stood in their way. W. R.'s brother obtained an axe from somewhere and began chopping the tree down while most men sought cover from the bullets and artillery shells that filled the air with screeching metal. W. R. became enraged by his brother's carelessness and angrily pulled him down to the ground. An instant after the brothers hit the dirt, a Union artillery shell crashed into the tree, showering the brothers with splinters. W. R. looked at his brother and screamed over the thunder of battle, "where would you have been if I had not pulled you back?" His brother yelled back that he did not care if he lived or died.[41]

In the face of overwhelming opposition, members of Stewart's Corps fell back to cover, where they regrouped to try again. Immediately in front of the 27th Alabama stood a three-gun Union battery, supported by masses of entrenched blue-coated infantry. For their third assault, the rebels focused on those cannons and somehow drove the Yankees from the field, capturing all three pieces of artillery and the flag of the 33rd New Jersey Infantry. Secure within the Federal trenches, the Alabamians planted a rebel flag on the breastworks, convinced that they had won the day.[42]

T. J. Walker of the 9th Tennessee Infantry was near the center of the attack. He later remembered that, in spite of the men's personal hatred of Hood, the men "rushed to the charge with their old-time enthusiasm, although to all appearances it seemed to be rushing into the very jaws of death, for we were repulsed with fearful loss." Unable to break the Federal lines, Walker and his regiment retreated rather than suffer annihilation.[43]

James Nisbet and the 66th Georgia Infantry retreated to the main Confederate lines, absorbing enemy fire and taking casualties as they withdrew. Nisbet later recalled, "never was I under a heavier fire than there." As the bullets ripped into southern flesh, he became convinced that "I would certainly see my Valhalla that day."[44]

Amongst the ranks of the 27th Alabama Infantry, celebration at their breakthrough turned to shock and sorrow as the rebels failed to dislodge the Union troops on their right. The Federals launched vigorous counterattacks against the rebels, who had enjoyed a limited breakthrough. Bullets thudded into gray-clad bodies from the front and the right flank forcing the rebels to retreat "sorrowfully . . . mourning the loss of so many of our friends" but "thankful that we had escaped." The Alabamians left the Federal cannons they had briefly captured behind but took the flag they captured from the New Jersey regiment as a souvenir of their limited success.[45]

When the 66th Georgia Infantry returned to the main Confederate lines, they encountered the Mississippians of Lowery's Brigade advancing towards the Federals. The Georgians told their comrades from Mississippi that the Union troops were entrenched behind a line of heavy breastworks. General Mark Lowery, known as the "preacher general" for his civilian profession, insisted that the men were mistaken, that "General Hood informed me that they had just crossed the creek." In an effort to convince General Lowery, the Georgians advanced once more, driving away the Federal scouts that had pursued them and exposing the fortified line occupied by the rest of the Union forces. Shocked and dismayed, General Lowery ordered all the men in his vicinity to fall back rather than launch a suicidal attack. The order to withdraw came too late for many men. The 66th Georgia lost roughly one-fourth of their troops in the failed assaults.[46]

When a shell burst amongst the dismounted 15th Texas Cavalry, R. M. Collins felt an impact and crumpled to the ground. After a quick examination, the lieutenant realized that the shell had ripped through his "gray Georgia jeans pants" and sent a chunk of shrapnel through his left thigh. The veteran officer had seen such wounds before and concluded that he was a dead man. With no hope of survival but a desire to live long enough to "repeat all the prayers" he could think of, he tried to slow the bleeding with a compress while four men put him on a stretcher and moved him to the rear. The fire continued unabated during the evacuation, but Collins did not care since he had already conceded that he was about to die. The stretcher-bearers delivered the Texan to a field hospital where, much to his shock, the surgeon described the wound as "an ugly one, but not necessarily fatal." Chloroform was in short supply, so four men held Collins down while the surgeons "went into the ugly wound with probes and fingers," searching for the Yankee lead and Georgia cloth that resided somewhere within his leg and eventually removing a deformed chunk of metal and fiber from the Texan's thigh.[47]

Robert Dacus and the 1st Arkansas Mounted Rifles (dismounted) stared across the field at the second line of Union fortifications as the sun began to fall. As darkness covered the battlefield, the regiment withdrew into the trenches they occupied before the battle. Dacus concluded, "we had made a desperate charge, lost many of the best men in our corps, and accomplished nothing."[48]

Lieutenant Thomas Flynt and the 6th Texas Infantry moved into supporting positions for the main Confederate line that afternoon. Thankfully, that place in the line had protected them from the worst of the carnage suffered by many other units. Although in reserve, the Texans suffered from Union artillery fire that killed two men and wounded fifteen.[49]

When night fell, the fighting tapered off. The battle was mostly over, at least for the day, but the occasional bullet still rang through the air. Handfuls of Confederate survivors stuck between the lines faced a question of remaining in a place of uncertainty between the opposing armies or searching for a better position under the cover of darkness. Most of Confederates between the lines slowly withdrew through the moonlight and eventually found places of relative safety within the main Confederate lines. An unknown number of men probably lost their lives to the bullets that still occasionally flew between the lines. George Bost of the 4th Arkansas Infantry was amazed that he had somehow survived the fight and thanked "the kind providence of an all wise God" for his survival.[50]

Despite his dislike of the army's new commander, J. P. Cannon blamed the defeat on common soldiers. He was angry that the men of Hardee's Corps had failed to obey Hood's orders and take the Federal positions at all cost. Cannon felt that the men of Stewart's Corps had done their duty and that Hardee's men could have done far more to win the day. Cannon argued that if Hardee's men had simply done as instructed, the rebels would "have driven the enemy across Peachtree Creek."[152] He did not acknowledge any differences in the unique physical circumstances of terrain or enemy resistance faced by Hardee's and Stewart's men. He attributed the different result entirely to what he saw as the failure of Hardee's men to do their duty. The soldiers of Stewart's Corps "literally obeyed his orders," and Hardee's Corps did not. Like many Confederate soldiers, he seemed to feel that manly determination could overcome all odds and that failure was the result of moral rather than physical weakness.[51]

Hood's plan failed. In the battle 18,832 Confederate soldiers hurled themselves against 21,655 Yankees. The Army of Tennessee killed and wounded roughly 1,600 invaders but lost about 2,500 men of their own. The piles of dead and wounded did nothing to change the steady movement of the Union armies as they encircled Atlanta. As the rebels retreated to their pre-battle positions, the blue noose tightened around Atlanta. Robert Patrick believed that "if Hood follows up the policy inaugurated yesterday, we will either drive the enemy back or we will go up the spout ourselves." Many years later, Kentuckian Lot Young wrote that histories of Peachtree Creek suggested "a prominence in excess of the facts." He felt it was actually "a straggling, haphazard kind of hide and seek affair, magnified into a battle."[52]

The 66th Georgia marched back into Atlanta with orders to join Walker's Division and take up positions along the McDonough Road. Exhausted by the battle and subsequent march, the men were allowed a brief rest among the ruined houses, ignoring the occasional shells that fell in the distance. While they relaxed, a young solider snacked on a piece of hardtack (a small biscuit that looked something like a half-inch thick, three-inch square saltine cracker). A parrot, probably a pet that had escaped from a wealthy household, said, "give poor Polly a cracker." The youthful rebel was clearly confused, having probably never heard of, much less encountered, such a creature. The exasperated soldier turned to his comrades and said, "Gee Whilkens, boys, damned if the world hain't coming to an end! Even the birds are talking and begging for bread." He next turned his attention to the parrot, proclaiming, "Sure you are a might smart bird, and I'm sorry for you, but you go to hell! This is the first cracker I've seen for two days."[53]

The Battle of Atlanta July 22

Despite the failure at Peachtree Creek, Hood still believed that he could drive the Union forces away from Atlanta with a vigorous assault. Army commanders typically sought to anchor their flanks against natural obstacles, but General Joe Wheeler's cavalry scouts discovered that the left flank of Union Army of the Tennessee under General James McPherson rested

Civil War battle scene at the Atlanta Cyclorama in Atlanta, Georgia. Library of Congress.

"in the air" and was therefore vulnerable. Hood ordered Hardee's Corps to make a fifteen-mile march on the evening of July 21 and attack the left flank of the Union forces at dawn. Hood hoped that once Hardee turned the Union flank, Cheatham's Corps could assault the center, crushing the Federal forces between them. Stewart's Corps, heavily engaged in the Battle of Peachtree Creek, would remain in Atlanta and protect the city in case of an unexpected movement by the Federals. While the Confederate infantry and artillery of Hardee's and Cheatham's Corps prepared to strike the exposed Union left flank, Wheeler's cavalrymen sprinted around the Union lines to the northeast, where they hoped to capture Federal supply wagons, left unguarded at Decatur, Georgia. Speed and surprise were essential. To succeed, the rebels needed to strike the Federals before they realized that the attack was underway or had time to fortify. Hood was trying to replicate the great victories of General Thomas "Stonewall" Jackson at the battles of Chancellorsville and Second Bull Run. It was a reasonably good plan, but General McPherson had served with Hood before the war and anticipated the attack. He shifted units to counter the Confederate advance. Rebels marched towards Federals waiting to spring a trap.[54]

Robert Jarman and the 27th Mississippi formed a skirmish line in front of the Georgia militia, a group Jarman found "very amusing." In contrast to the battle-hardened veterans who prided themselves on traveling light, members of the militia all carried "bed quilts and pillows and packs large enough for a mule." While they waited for the order to move forward, the veterans killed and devoured an old bull.[55]

The difficult terrain broke up the Confederate lines and damaged the organization they would need in the fight to come. Thomas Flynt and the 6th Texas Infantry advanced through a dense forest near the Flat Shoals Road, roughly in the center of the Confederate line. The difficult terrain made it nearly impossible for the Texans to keep their place in line. Units became confused and disoriented as they marched towards the enemy. James Nisbet, commanding the 66th Georgia, received orders to advance even when he pointed out that the regiment's left flank was exposed and therefore vulnerable.[56]

At around 1:00 p.m., Richard Beard and the rest of the 5th Confederate Infantry formed in a line of battle. General Patrick Cleburne, commanding their division, told the men "to move forward, and turn neither to the right nor to the left until we were within the enemy's breastworks." At that moment, Beard heard a burst of artillery fire from the rebel lines that "announced too clearly that the ball was about to open in good earnest." The sound of firing placed the men into a state of "excitement," and they moved forward at a run.[57]

William Ritter and the 3rd Maryland Artillery kept up a steady fire on Union positions. They had little hope of inflicting serious damage on the prepared Union forces, but they tried to distract the Federals from the Confederate infantry attacks. The gunners from Maryland made little impact. Most of the Union soldiers on the receiving end of their barrage were hardened veterans who had been under fire before.[58]

The Confederate attack quickly bogged down as they assaulted prepared Union troops who sheltered in defensive positions within the nearly impassable terrain. When T. J. Walker, his friends, and the 9th Tennessee Infantry encountered the Federal lines, they realized that the Union forces were one step ahead of them. Instead of an unprotected flank, the rebels viewed a well-prepared foe, secure behind three lines of breastworks. The regiment received orders to attack, and "our lines moved forward at double quick." A battery of Confederate artillery got a cannon stuck between two trees in the dense woods. Henry Reddick and other infantrymen from Finley's Brigade tried to push it out. The Floridians pushed with all their might as Union artillery poured shells into their position, killing both men and horses. Thomas Flynt and the 6th Texas Infantry lost contact with other units in the dense forest near Flat Shoals Road. Union troops turned their exposed flanks and forced the Texans to retreat.[59]

Observers far from the front lines heard the sounds of battle in the distance. John Sparkman enjoyed a place of relative safety with the army's wagons, but the echoing thunder of artillery and gunfire told him that a major battle had begun. He predicted that "here Hood will rise or be ruined." The veteran Sparkman knew the importance of morale and lamented, "I wish the men had more confidence in him."[60] While it is certainly true that a soldier's confidence matters, the Confederate soldiers rushing into battle that day faced obstacles that were more physical than psychological.

As Hardee's infantry struck Federal positions near Atlanta, Wheeler's horsemen assaulted the Union wagon trains in Decatur, Georgia. The troopers were tired of the siege, eager for action, and, according to Wilbur Mims of the 3rd Alabama Cavalry, approached "this chase like school boys in a game." The rebel horsemen routed their adversaries, but the teamsters and their guards managed to take most of their wagons with them as they left town.[61]

Captain Richard Beard and the rest of the 5th Confederate Infantry advanced through a forest littered with tangled brush on their way to the Federal left flank. The rebels captured a line of Federal skirmishers without

Battle of Atlanta, depicting death of Gen. James B. McPherson, July 22, 1864. Lithograph by Kurz & Allison, created ca. 1888. Library of Congress.

firing a shot and kept moving forward, where they stumbled across a wagon road. A man who Beard later learned was General McPherson, commander of the Union Army of the Tennessee, galloped down the road with his staff trailing behind. McPherson had just left a meeting with General Sherman and was conducting a personal reconnaissance of the fighting. At the time, Beard had no idea who the blue-coated officer was, but Beard knew that the man must be at least a corps commander, based on nothing more than the large collection of officers who surrounded him. Beard recalled seeing a look of apparent shock on McPherson's face as he suddenly realized that he was only a few feet from the Confederate line of battle. Although no words were spoken, Beard raised his sword as a signal for McPherson to surrender. In response, McPherson "raised his hat as politely as if he was saluting a lady" and then wheeled his horse to the right, dashing off at a gallop. According to Beard's later account, Corporal Coleman, standing near Beard, raised his rifle and fired a single shot that penetrated McPherson's back and ripped through his heart, killing him instantly and sending him tumbling to the ground. A flurry of additional bullets flew towards McPherson's fleeing staff. Beard approached McPherson, lying dead in the dirt, and asked a wounded Union officer for the name of the dead man. The officer replied, "Sir, it is General McPherson. You have killed the best man in our army."[62]

Lot Young was with the Orphan Brigade of Kentucky on the Confederate right. It quickly became clear to the men in the ranks that "there was a lack of understanding and cooperation of movement, coupled with almost insurmountable obstacles that might have been avoided." Despite the frustration and confusion of a poorly planned assault, the men from Kentucky pressed ahead.[63]

Around noon, the 33rd Alabama Infantry in Cheatham's Corps advanced in a line of battle on the Federal works. They marched up the Flat Shoals Road towards the ninety-degree angle where the Federal lines shifted northeast. After advancing for some distance, they charged and captured a line of poorly constructed Union breastworks, capturing men, gun, accouterments, and even an ambulance. The rebels pursued the Federals until they came to Sugar Creek at the point where it diverged west, and the attackers paused to fill their canteens.[64]

Overwhelming Union firepower forced the 6th Texas Infantry to withdraw but did not break their spirits. The Texans still had plenty of fight left in them. After falling back and reorganizing, the 6th Texas Infantry surged forward once again. They joined the attack of Govan's Brigade near the Flat Shoals Road close to the center of the Confederate line and rushed forward with the men from Arkansas.[65]

As the 66th Georgia Infantry advanced on the Union lines, they passed through a marsh fed by Sugar Creek, overgrown with underbrush and briars. The regiment lost cohesion as they picked their way through the thick vegetation, taking casualties from enemy fire as they walked. When the Georgians finally emerged in the clearing beyond, they discovered that the Federals were much closer than anticipated. Barely forty yards away, the blue-coated members of the 39th Ohio Infantry poured a volley of minnie balls into the disorganized Confederates. While most of the rounds sailed harmlessly overhead, the men from Ohio gave the Georgians no time to react and rushed into the gray ranks, demanding their surrender. Forced to select between death and capture, many men, including James Nisbet, surrendered. When a Yankee lieutenant expressed surprise at Nisbet's stoicism in the face of capture, Nisbet replied, "I have captured thousands of your men, since the war commenced." The Georgian had played the game for years, and he accepted that he was now on the losing end of the contest.[66]

The Confederates' brief pause allowed the Federals to reorganize along a secondary line of much stronger works on the crest of a hill running east to west. After filling their canteens from Sugar Creek, the 33rd Alabama and W. E. Preston charged uphill into a wall of bullets, getting to within thirty yards of the Federals before they collapsed to the ground, exhausted, and sought to return fire without exposing themselves. Preston later recalled that "one of the regiment wandered about among us with a minnie ball in his forehead and a knot of brains as big as a hen's egg over the hole." As the man wandered through the midst of battle, "occasionally we could hear another ball strike him, which he did not appear to mind, and we not caring, thinking the sooner he died the better."[67]

Despite the overwhelming odds against an assault into strong defensive lines, for a moment it looked like the Confederates might just win the day. Confederate forces pushed Union troops back from their front lines, and they paid a heavy price as they lost ground. The 9th Tennessee Infantry drove the Federals out of the first and then the second line of their trenches, inflicting terrible losses on the defenders who scattered to the third and final line. The Tennesseans thought that their desperate attack might break the Federal lines. Alexander Spence and other members of the 1st Arkansas Infantry enjoyed a similar moment of success as they penetrated the Union trenches. Once within the Federal lines, Spence and his comrades got busy "killing a good many Yankees with bayonets."[68]

As James Nisbet and the other Confederate prisoners moved towards the rear, a Union enlisted man with a thick German expressed his desire to bayonet them. The young Union lieutenant in charge of escorting the rebels to the rear threatened to kill the soldier, and for a moment it appeared that one of the men in blue was about to die. A Union captain came along, smacked the disobedient enlisted man with the flat of his sword, and ordered him to leave the rebels alone, which put an end to the standoff. A moment after the rebels resumed their movement to the rear, General States Rights Gist's Brigade of South Carolinians attacked the Union lines near the Confederate prisoners. The rebels and their guards took cover in a ditch, waiting to see who the prisoners would be when the smoke cleared. Eventually, the firing tapered off, revealing that the Union lines remained intact, and the rebels resumed their march to the rear.[69]

The 5th Tennessee Infantry pressed their advantage. They drove the Federals from the "half-finished rifle pits" of the advance line and into the more substantial breastworks to their rear. After pausing to reform their ranks, the Tennesseans advanced up a hill where they clearly saw the Union infantry behind "a low line of earthworks." As they came within range, the Yankees opened fire, bullets tore into flesh, and Tennesseans passed from this world on the forest ground.[70]

As the Federals fled to their third and final line of defensive works, T. J. Walker, serving as the color bearer for the 9th Tennessee Infantry that day, followed them. The intense firing tossed clouds of dense smoke into the air, filling Walker's nostrils with the acrid sting of sulfur and obscuring his vision. Like a blind man, Walker groped forward through the darkness with only the physical presence of his comrade Tom Estes on one side and his brother Roe Estes on the other to ensure that Walker was not alone. When Tom was struck dead by enemy fire, Walker kept going, convinced that someone would fill the gap momentarily. Somehow, Walker made it to the third line of Federal works. As soon as he planted the colors on the breastworks, a bullet punctured the head of Roe, sending him face first into the Union trench. A Union soldier demanded Walker's surrender. Before anyone could react, a little breeze pushed the smoke aside, and Walker realized that he could not see another rebel in any direction. Walker and the Roe brothers had made the assault completely on their own, and only Walker remained among the living. Instead of surrendering, Walker picked up the regiment's flag and ran "at the rate of a mile a minute" until he found comfort among the rest of his regiment, still occupying the second line of Federal works.[71]

W. E. Preston and the rest of the 33rd Alabama quickly realized that, while one group of Federals kept up a steady fire on them, another detachment was slipping up around their flank. Union soldiers ordered the rebels to surrender, and many of Preston's comrades complied, but, as Preston later explained, "I was not obeying Yankees when I had good legs." He ran through a gap in the Union trap and rejoined other Confederates rallying in a line of trenches that Union soldiers had occupied at the beginning of the battle. He was pleased to escape the trap and enjoyed the relative safety of his new position.[72]

James Maxwell, with Lumsden's Alabama Artillery, watched from alongside his cannon while the Georgia militia assaulted the final line of Union trenches held by the battle-hardened veterans of Blair's XVII Corps. The militiamen obeyed the order to charge, "but the result was the mere sacrificing of some of the old men's lives to no advantage." Maxwell later recalled, "seeing some of these old citizens being borne past on litters affected all the old war-torn Confeds." The Alabamians appeared more upset by the suffering of these strangers than the suffering of their own friends. Maxwell and his comrades "were used to seeing veteran Confederates wounded and killed, but old graybeards, in citizen's clothes, was something new." He appears to have felt an internal conflict when he saw those old men die. It was one thing for a vigorous young man to lose his life while achieving an important objective, but he and his friends were repulsed by the pointless deaths of men who should be home enjoying the protection of the army, not dying in a hopeless struggle to help it. The long-serving rebels were angry, since "we could not see where it was at all possible for them to help us at all." Bitterly, Maxwell remarked, "we could do better without their help."[73]

The 5th Tennessee Infantry had outrun the rest of the line and stood exposed without support on either flank. In the confusion, a cluster of men advanced to within fifty yards of the final Federal line, where they took cover and waited for reinforcement. After a few minutes, they realized that nobody was going to join them, so they crawled on their bellies through tall weeds, leaving their dead comrades behind them. The regiment's surviving officers decided that the offensive was futile and ordered the men to return to their lines at the double quick.[74]

Angus McDermid watched several of his friends die in a hail of gunfire that left him wounded but alive. Somehow McDermid stumbled across a stray horse and mounted up to flee, but "they shot it out from under me and that hurt me some." McDermid did not specify the nature of his injury, but whatever happened did not extinguish his determination to return to his own lines. Once again on foot, McDermid struggled back to safety.[75]

Late in the day, Hosea Garrett, a lieutenant with the 10th Texas Infantry, once again led his men in another assault on the final line of Union trenches. The rebel forces were disorganized and scattered. Garret recalled, "I suppose that there was not more than half a dozen men with me." He blamed the failed assault on exhaustion caused by the long march into battle. Forced back by superior enemy numbers and firepower, Garret ordered his men to withdraw, which he claimed "was the first time the 10th

Regt. ever failed to accomplish anything." The failure to achieve the unit's objective appears to have bothered Garret more than the loss of life.[76]

Remnants of the 33rd Alabama congregated in trenches occupied by the Federals at the start of the battle, strengthening the position by using their bayonets to deepen the holes, adding head logs, and waiting for the men in blue to counterattack. While the rebels waited, someone discovered that a captured Federal ambulance contained a ten-gallon jug of medicinal whiskey. The officers rationed out the precious liquid, giving each man about one fourth of a pint. While a few men sold or gave away their shares, most drank it eagerly. The anticipated counterattack never came and when night fell, the men withdrew to the lines they occupied before the start of the battle.[77]

After the battle concluded, Thomas Key, commander of Key's Arkansas Battery, witnessed a conference between Generals Hardee and Cleburne in which they discussed giving up the ground they had captured in the battle. While the generals chatted, the men gathered "small arms, ordnance wagons, and other implements of war." Key gazed out over the battlefield that night, and "the pale faces of the dead men seen beneath the mellow rays of the moon gave the scene a ghastly and unearthly appearance." When the sun rose, "began again the work of death." Key knew no name for the battle, so he simply called it "the battle of the 22nd of July."[78]

Most modern historians regard the Battle of Atlanta, or "the battle of the 22nd of July," as a Confederate defeat, much like Peachtree Creek. Roughly 36,934 rebels engaged 32,422 Union soldiers. As with Peachtree Creek, the Confederates suffered far more than their northern counterparts. About 7,000 Rebels were killed or wounded, as opposed to 1,989 Union soldiers who suffered the same fate. Lot Young lamented that among the dead and wounded were some of the best officers and enlisted men from his unit, the famed Orphan Brigade of Kentucky. Young found the losses particularly devastating because those men died "without any tangible results." Suffering that accomplished nothing seemed to bother him far more than suffering that purchased victory, even at a horrific cost. The Kentuckians were not alone. The battle had caused terrible losses to the Army of Tennessee and failed to blunt the Union advance.[79]

When the Army of Tennessee pulled back to its breastworks around Atlanta, they left many of their wounded behind. W. J. Worsham and other soldiers from Tennessee volunteered to remain in the field hospital and care for their friends, even though it meant certain capture. Worsham and his comrades who remained behind appeared to place a greater value on easing the suffering of their wounded friends than on avoiding the horrific suffering of a Union prison camp. When the Union army took possession of the hospital, they allowed Confederates working in the hospital to remain. For nearly a week, Worsham cared for the wounded of both armies. When all the wounded men he knew were dead or well enough to be sent to prison camps, Worsham quietly slipped away through the lines and rejoined his comrades in Atlanta.[80] Somehow, he had managed to ease the suffering of his friends while also protecting himself from the ghastly fate of a prisoner of war.

With Hood's plan to drive the Federals from Atlanta a failure, the Army of Tennessee returned to their trenches. Union sharpshooters fired at any rebel who exposed himself, often killing or wounding careless men. According to T. J. Walker, after the Battle of Atlanta, "the whole army had to lie under cover night and day, because of the continuous shower of balls." The men tried to avoid exposing themselves and consumed their meager rations in holes covered with dirt. One evening, Walker was the last to enter the pit for dinner. As he stepped down, a Federal bullet hit him in the chest, knocking him down on top of the dinner table. Indifferent to death of a comrade but consumed with hunger, a soldier screamed out, "Confound the luck! Why couldn't that damned Yankee bullet have struck him before he entered the door so that he wouldn't have fallen on the table and ruined our dinner!" The men pushed what they assumed was a corpse out of the pit, rescued their food from the dirt, and only then did they discover that

Chevaux-de-frise on Marietta Street; photographic wagons and darkroom beyond, Atlanta, Georgia, 1864. George N. Barnard, photographer. Library of Congress.

Walker was badly stunned but very much alive, since the bullet had struck the sewing kit that he kept in his chest pocket.[81]

July 24 was the Sabbath, supposedly the day of rest, but "soldiers know no Sabbath," and even on the Lord's Day "arms are being used, and the heavy guns are firing upon Atlanta." Teamster John Sparkman said nothing about his own hunger in his diary on July 24, but he lamented the suffering of the animals he cared for. He was unhappy that the army's draft animals "have been without corn for two days." On July 26, General Hood sent virtually all noncombatants, including quartermasters, cooks, and clerks, to the front lines. Two days later, Hood ordered men to the Peachtree Creek battlefield to recover guns and ammunition.[82]

W. E. Preston of Company B, 33rd Alabama Infantry, provided one of the most comprehensive accounts of the Confederate infantry trenches. The areas in front of the trenches were protected with abatis, which were sharpened tree branches that acted like wooden barbed wire. The trenches themselves were "good deep ditches with a step in the front inside of the ditch, upon which we would stand to fire under the head log." Head logs were horizontal beams that stood over the front edge of the trenches and provided men with a narrow slit between the dirt below and the wood above, through which soldiers could fire their rifles in relative safety. After firing their rifles, men would step backwards off the step and into the

View from casemates Confederate fort-D, looking north, Atlanta, Georgia. Library of Congress.

bottom of the trench, where they could reload completely hidden from direct observation by the enemy. The relative safety of those trenches came at a price. Brush roofs over the trench shielded men from the worst of the sun, although it did nothing to keep out the rain, which collected in the bottoms of the trenches.

The Confederate artillery occupied somewhat different positions than the infantry. Cannons could not be easily lowered into nor extricated from trenches. Therefore, the artillerists lived behind earthen walls that were between ten and fourteen feet thick and tall enough to allow the men to stand erect behind the walls without exposing themselves. The dirt for the walls came from deep ditches dug outside the walls. These ditches often filled with water and acted like moats in front of the fortifications. Artillerymen lived most of their lives aboveground, unlike the infantrymen who sheltered below. As a result, infantrymen constantly worked to drain the water from around their positions, since it often made their shelters unbearable mud pits. In contrast, Confederate artillerymen were happy to have water fill the ditches outside their works and put another obstacle between them and the Yankees. Like the infantrymen, artillerists sought protection from the sun under arbors made of branches and even strung blankets, which sheltered them from the worst of the rain. Men of every branch of service dug pits some distance behind the breastworks to use as toilets and surrounded the area with brush to provide men with privacy.[83]

The trench lines evolved during the siege. The initial lines were built by slave labor before the Army of Tennessee came to Atlanta. At the start of the siege, the rebels slept on the open ground behind the trench line, but as the fighting wore on, the Federal fire intensified. Several men were killed and wounded while sleeping in the open. As a result, infantrymen began sleeping in the trenches. These were uncomfortable places to sleep, but discomfort was preferable to death. When the Union army's fire became so intense that men could not even walk to the rear for water or ammunition without risking death, the men built traversing trenches to that they could walk all the way to the rear without exposing their heads above the ground. Men confined to life below ground initially kept small fires burning in the trenches at night, until they discovered that increasingly attentive Union observers could occasionally spot the light. With this realization, evening fires were forbidden, and men spent their nights shivering in the mud. Eventually, Union gunners constructed improved positions that allowed them to throw shells into the Confederate trenches from multiple angles. With no other way to protect themselves, rebels absorbed the punishment and prayed for salvation.[84]

The Battle of Ezra Church July 28

On July 27, Sherman renewed his flanking movements. This time he turned his attention west and ordered the Federal Army of the Tennessee, now under the command of Hood's old West Point classmate General Oliver Howard, who replaced the deceased General McPherson, to cut the Macon and Western Railroad. Hood's scouts quickly informed him of the move, and he determined to try and intercept the Union advance. Hood sent Lee's Corps westward to occupy the key crossroads near Ezra Church, build breastworks, and block the Federals. Stewart's Corps was supposed to swing around and launch an attack on the Union right flank and rear. Hardee's Corps would remain within Atlanta's defenses. As with the battles of Peachtree Creek and Atlanta, the plan was reasonably good and bore the obvious influence of Hood's mentor, Robert E. Lee. However, the problem came when the army attempted to carry out the plan.[85]

Edward McMorries and the 1st Alabama Infantry in Stewart's Corps marched at the quick time towards their left, where they found a road along the edge of the woods. For an hour they rested, hoping for a cool breeze that never came to stir the air and cool their sweating bodies. The men were then ordered forward. As they approached the battle, men heard the increasingly loud and unmistakable sounds of small arms fire. They also saw an ominous stream of ambulances, taking mangled Confederate bodies to the rear. At 2:00 p.m., they formed into line at one end of a pasture and stared at the Federal infantry a quarter of a mile in their front. The blue-coated men sheltered in a thickly overgrown oaken forest on the opposite side of the pasture. McMorries noticed that the Alabamians and Mississippians of Cantey's Brigade stood on a hill to the right and slightly forward of the 1st Alabama. Cantey's men absorbed Federal fire, neither advancing nor shooting back, and seemed to be waiting for the 1st Alabama to move forward so that they could advance together. When McMorries and the 1st Alabama moved forward, the Union infantry poured fire into them. In response, the Alabamians sped up to the double quick, leaving behind a trail of dead and wounded comrades in their wake. The regiment advanced over a level plain and took shelter when they came to a ravine. By the time they arrived in the ravine, Cantey's Brigade had disappeared. A short distance to their front, two lines of Federal infantry stood securely behind breastworks. For half an hour, the rebels in the ravine waited for reinforcements or orders to push forward. While they waited, Union troops poured a heavy fire into the gray ranks, killing and wounding many members of the regiment.[86]

Stephen Lee's Corps was supposed to build breastworks and wait, but General Lee thought he saw an opportunity. In an effort to seize the initiative, he abandoned his orders to entrench and wait. He launched a rapid assault against entrenched Federals. The results were as predictable as they were tragic for the men who died that day. Starke Oliver and the 24th Alabama Infantry advanced through an open field and encountered Union troops strongly fortified on the crest of a hill. The Alabamians charged up the incline. The Federals responded with an intense fire. The fire did not stop the rebels. They kept running forward until they got within thirty steps of the men in blue, when the units on the flanks of the 24th Alabama gave way and left Oliver and his men absorbing fire from three directions.[87]

As Robert Jarman with Lee's Corps moved forward, a bullet slipped right past him and shot his friend J. S. McRea in the shoulder. A short time later another bullet whizzed by and hit a member of his company in the chin. Despite the obvious danger, Jarman retained his place in the front rank and kept moving forward.[88]

The artillery batteries holding Atlanta kept up a steady fire on the Federal positions around Atlanta. Confederate detachments burned several houses between the lines that Union troops were using as shelter. Blue-clad gunners responded by sending shells crashing into Atlanta, which killed soldiers and civilians indiscriminately.[89]

Lee's Corps continued their attacks. Austin Smith of the 4th Louisiana Battalion of infantry advanced as part of Lee's Corps on the Confederate left. With a rush, the Louisianans penetrated the Union breastworks. Smith captured the flag of a Federal artillery unit. It was a small victory, if only a symbolic one. In the face of intense flanking fire, Starke Oliver and the 24th Alabama Infantry withdrew. They reformed with the rest of their brigade two or three hundred yards away from the Federal breastworks. After a brief rest to catch their breath and reorganize, the entire brigade advanced once more. This time they managed to occupy a small crest, where they piled fence rails up for protection.[90]

After waiting for what seemed like an eternity, the 1st Alabama Infantry received orders to withdraw. The Federals showed no mercy, keeping up a heavy fire and inflicting numerous casualties on the rebels as they crossed the open ground on their way back to their own lines. Once they returned to the main Confederate line, the men were reformed and sent against the Federal lines again. Just like before, the rebels made it to the ravine but were caught unable to advance further and eventually received the order to retreat over the open ground under heavy fire.[91]

As the sunlight faded into evening, the fighting died down, and men traded the battlefield for the even more gruesome realities of the field hospital. During the final retreat, Edward McMorries's friend Bryant Brooks, a twenty-one-year-old "picture of vigorous manhood" was struck in the

The surgeon at work at the rear during an engagement. Wood engraving, Winslow Homer, 1862. Library of Congress.

chest by a Federal bullet. McMorries helped his wounded friend to the field hospital three hundred yards behind the Confederate front lines. Hospitals were supposed to be places that alleviated suffering, but Civil War hospitals were often places of misery rather than comfort. The hospital "was more distressing than the battle." In the center of the hospital was "a crude operating table" under the trees, which was surrounded by wounded men in every direction for fifty yards "lying on the ground in agonizing groans." As he sought an open place where Brooks could rest, McMorries saw "blood-stained litters" which "were leaning about against the trees, and over all, a few tallow candles cast their dim and flickering light." Eventually McMorries brought a surgeon to examine Brooks. The doctor "examined the wound, beckoned the assistant surgeon, both made a hasty examination" and without a word, both doctors walked away "the surgeon merely shaking his head negatively at me." Brooks died the next day.[92]

The Army of Tennessee proved incapable of pushing the Federals away from Atlanta, and the siege tightened. General Sherman claimed that he never felt a moment of worry during the battle, and the attacks raised the morale of his troops, since it convinced them that the rebels were willing to throw their lives away in useless assaults with little hope of success. In contrast, General Hood believed that "if all the troops had displayed equal spirit, we would have been successful." He, like many Confederate soldiers, saw defeat as a moral failure of men who failed to do their duty rather than a physical failure of men who tried their best against overwhelming odds. However, the large numbers of Confederate casualties cast doubt on Hood's explanation. At the Battle of Ezra Church, 12,594 Union soldiers engaged 14,150 Confederates. The losses were remarkably one-sided, with only 559 Union dead or wounded, but about 4,100 Confederates suffering the same fate. Robert Patrick believed that Hood's strategy "would do well enough I think, if we had plenty of men, but this is not the case."[93]

In spite of the fact that many modern historians consider the battles of Peachtree Creek, Atlanta, and Ezra Church as Confederate defeats, many Confederate soldiers saw them as victories and felt an improved sense of morale. General Hardee stated in his official report that the Battle of Atlanta was a "decided success." R. W. Banks agreed with his friend Colonel E. A. O'Neal of the 26th Alabama Infantry, who stated, "we whipped them," and "Army in good spirits, and confidence in General Hood unabated." Although John Sparkman was initially worried by Hood's promotion, after the battles of Peachtree Creek and Atlanta, he recorded in his diary that "the troops are beginning to have as much confidence in Gen. Hood as they had in Gen. Johnston" since "retreating I think is done." Artilleryman Andrew Neal believed that, under Hood's leadership, the army "has twice whipped the flanking columns." Robert Jarman claimed that many Union troops surrendered after the Battle of Peachtree Creek, since Hood clearly intended to fight. John Crittenden "was struck by a ball on the right arm sufficient to disable me for the time" at the Battle of Atlanta, but the wound did not dampen his pride in the way "we drove two lines of battle from their works with only one line," capturing Federal artillery and prisoners. Crittenden's pride in the successful attack appears to have meant more to him than his personal suffering. He predicted that the rebels would "not leave enough of them to tell the tale" in the next battle. Arkansas soldier Alexander Spence informed his parents that the men "regretted the removal of General Johnston but are now perfectly satisfied with Gen. Hood." The men grew to love Hood because "they know he will fight." These accounts are unsurprising since Confederate soldiers throughout the war often took joy aggressive attacks, even costly ones, believing "there was no glory to be gained from fighting out of a hole in the ground."[94]

With men in short supply, the Army of Tennessee began taking steps to stretch its manpower. Hood dismounted Roddy's Cavalry Brigade and ordered it into the trenches with the infantry. While the shift did not bode well for the Confederacy's long-term survival, men in the 27th Alabama Infantry were pleased that they could visit with friends and neighbors in the cavalry who they had not seen since before the war began. The reunions mostly took place underground, since "bullets from the skirmishers are flying around promiscuously." The 3rd Alabama Cavalry was able to keep its horses, but the men were forced to spend time in the trenches, a duty that free-spirited cavalrymen loathed. Hood issued orders that every soldier except for artillery gunners must carry a musket at all times, to ensure that every man was always ready to defend the lines.[95]

Hood temporarily gave up on aggressive assaults, and the Army of Tennessee retreated behind its breastworks. Thomas Warrick told his wife, "we are confined to the ditch all the time." Even the best-made trenches offered only so much protection for men like the four unlucky members of the 30th Tennessee Infantry who were badly wounded when a Federal shell fell directly into their ditch. Elbridge Littlejohn wrote home to his wife on August 7, explaining that "it is next to impossible to hear anything at all except the constant firing of artillery" and "small arms which are waiting to fill up the intervals between the artillery." Men became dulled to the danger, ignoring the noise even as "occasionally some our men get shot." He then listed his friends who were killed or wounded. An Alabama soldier identified only as "J" wrote that "the sound of small arms to me has become monotonous." While other men were discouraged, he was adamant that "I am determined not to do anything that is inconsistent with my duty, and, through God's assistance, I intend doing that to the letter."[96]

Rebels suffered from hunger in their ditches. Stephen Jordan, a member of the 19th Tennessee Cavalry, confessed in his diary that he became so desperate to feed his horse that he resorted to stealing green corn, which he hoped to never do again. Alabama cavalryman Wilbur Mims found his time in the trenches "tedious." He loathed the inaction and the lack of food. Elbridge Littlejohn told his wife that he was starving to death, dreaming of going home to Texas, where he imagined they "are all living finely" eating "watermelons, vegetables, peaches," and wishing he was there "to help you eat some of the good things." T. G. Baker ate better than most as he lay in the hospital, suffering from typhoid fever, which he contracted after he quenched his thirst on the Ezra Church battlefield with water from a stagnant puddle. Nurses fed him syrup and bread, which he later claimed was the best food he ate during the war.[97]

One of the most descriptive accounts of life in the Confederate infantry trenches around Atlanta came from Newton Davis, an officer in the 24th Alabama Infantry regiment. He was thirty-five years old in 1864, a light-haired, blue-eyed man who stood 5 feet 9 inches tall and had served in the army since 1862. On August 9 he wrote his wife a letter from an army field hospital, where he sought medicine for an unspecified illness. Davis explained, "the enemy still keeps up a continual shelling of our lines," which forced the men "to remain in the ditches," a position the veteran officer concluded was "the most unpleasant position we have had yet." He considered it "very disagreeable" to be confined to the trenches, where they were "exposed to sun and rain." The constant rain turned the dirt into mud and made the men "look like they had been wallowing in the road" with "red dirt sticking all over them." Despite the filth, men dared not leave the trenches if they could help it, since "firing is very heavy day and night," and as a result, "we have some men killed and wounded every day." He felt that the Federals were preparing to attack, and he anticipated that "it will be a bloody fight."[98]

Members of the Army of Tennessee grew depressed. According to Edward King of the 1st Georgia Infantry, "the soldiers are all worn out." Angus McDermid told his mother on August 7 that his brother and many of his friends were dead. His letter indicates that it was taking a heavy toll on the soldier. He told his mother, "I am a heep hearder hearted than I ought to be but I hav [*sic*] seen so many men killed and wounded till I don't care for it no more than if it was a chicken." McDermid was tired of the war, writing, "I do want to go home so bad I can't rest well." He explained, "my poor brother staid in the survis till he died and I intend to do the same," even though his commitment was unique since "there is lots of our men deserting right here now every day and lots a saying they will go." On the morning of August 14, Sergeant W. P. Chambers was cooking breakfast when "occurred the saddest event of the whole campaign." While the men cooked, Chambers' friend, Stephen Robertson, was struck by a single minnie ball fired from the Federal lines a long distance away. The bullet struck him in the arm and tore through his body, coming to rest just above his left hip. Robertson screamed, "lay me down!" and, after his friends tried to make him comfortable on the ground, he muttered incoherently for a while, at one point yelling "want to live!" and sometime later screaming "my poor family!" He then died and was laid to rest nearby. Hiram Williams "never saw so many wounded men in the same length of time before" and observed that the army's morale was falling fast. Alabama infantryman Samuel King Vann wrote home to his sweetheart and future wife Nancy Elizabeth Neel on August 17, 1864, to explain that "I hear a ball pass by me every syllable I make" and since beginning to write the letter "there has been two men shot through the body right here in camp." He concluded "O! how awful are the times up here" and begged for her to write him letters, which would be "the only comfort." Richard Wharton was tired of the army and "very impatient to leave." Kentucky soldier Lot Young heard the Federal bands play "Dixie," which he thought they did "to taunt us."[99]

The Federals camped around Atlanta suffered but also enjoyed luxuries that were unavailable to the rebels. James Nisbet, taken prisoner in the

Battle of Atlanta, was shocked to see merchants selling luxuries including lemonade, beer, and even ice cream to the Union soldiers. The idea of ice cream on the hot summer's day amazed rebels, who considered themselves among God's most fortunate few if they could "get a sufficiency of corn-bread, fat meat, sorghum and rye-coffee."[100]

Perhaps the greatest benefit enjoyed by Federals was that they, unlike their gray-clad counterparts, could escape the horrors of battle more easily. Both the Union and Confederate armies drafted soldiers. However, under the updated Confederate Conscription Law of February 1864, "all white men, residents of the Confederate States, between the ages of seventeen and fifty, shall be in the military service of the Confederate States for the war." For the Confederate soldiers of 1864 and 1865, who lacked the wealth or social connections required for an exemption, practically the only options were desertion, surrender, or a fight to the death. In contrast, Federal men were only conscripted for a maximum of three years. This often disrupted the army, sending men home at the worst possible times, but it did provide a light at the end of the tunnel. Frank M. Millican, a Union soldier from East Tennessee serving with the Federal army, was sick of the war by 1864 and informed his sweetheart that he hoped to receive a discharge and find good paying work in Illinois, far from the battlefield. It is unclear if Millican ever escaped the horrors of war, but many Union men like him were able to return to civilian life while the war raged on, an option that was all but unknown to those who wore the gray.[101]

Despite the hardships of Confederate camps and relative comforts of life in the Union, fewer Confederate soldiers deserted to the enemy in August. In May and June, months of retreat under General Johnston, an average of 142.5 Confederate soldiers deserted to the Federals per week. During July, when both Johnston and Hood commanded for part of the month, an average of 183 men deserted to the Union army per week. In August, a month marked by aggressive attacks under General Hood, an average of only 141 Rebels deserted to the enemy each week. Union soldiers reported that most Confederate deserters wanted nothing more than to return to their homes behind Union lines and only approached the Federals to get home. As the Federals tightened their stranglehold around Atlanta, the men in blue ensured that ever larger numbers of men could only get home by passing through Union lines, but fewer rebels deserted to Federal authorities.[102] While the limited information is insufficient to provide a definitive answer, it is at least possible that most Confederate soldiers believed that Hood might lead them to victory.

The hope of eventual victory was little comfort to civilians who suffered in the battle. John Porcher watched a woman wash clothing while her children played, as shells flew nearby. Artillery officer Thomas Key noted in his diary that on the night of August 4, "every five minutes through the whole night one or two 20 pounder guns threw shells into the city." These shells struck houses, "exploding amidst families, killing women and children." Although a battle-hardened veteran, the suffering of women and children upset Key and led him to describe Sherman as "inhuman" and "ungentlemanly." Arkansas infantryman Alexander Spence wrote that "several ladies have been killed" by Union artillery. In desperation, civilians dug ever deeper into the red Georgia clay and lived like burrowing animals.[103]

On August 20, two Union artillery batteries opened an intense fire on Lumsden's Battery from emplacements between six hundred and eight hundred yards away. Captain Lumsden was "determined to give them as good as they sent." In a flash, the men sprang into action "hammer and tongs" as they began firing all four of their guns. The veterans moved with clockwork precision. There was no conversation and no superfluous words because numerous battles had pushed them beyond the need for chatter. The only sounds were the thunder of cannons and between rounds the commands of "by hand to the front!" "Ready!" "Fire!" "Load!" The commands were repeated flawlessly by each crew roughly every minute. The Union gunners were not intimidated and kept up a steady fire against Lumsden's Battery, eventually destroying one of the battery's guns with a round that shredded the muzzle. George Little, a member of the battery, later explained the awful disadvantage faced by Confederate batteries when they dueled with their Union counterparts: "the Yankee three-inch rifle was a dead shot at any distance under a mile." He claimed, "they could hit the head of a flour barrel more often than miss, unless the gunner got rattled." In contrast, the men of Lumsden's Battery used "smooth bore 12 pounders," which could "sweep the earth" when firing anti-personnel rounds at close range but were at a tremendous disadvantage in long-range artillery duels. After a brief firefight, General Hardee, commander of the corps, ordered Lumsden's battery to cease fire. He explained that Union troops had nearly cut the Confederate supply routes to the south, and, as a result, the artillerymen must conserve their ammunition. With the fight over, the men took stock and realized that they had suffered no deaths and only a single injury. While bringing up ammunition from the rear, a veteran named Lane was struck by a shell that ripped the toes off one of his feet. Despite the wound, the artilleryman kept up his work without comment, since he "hoped some of his cartridges might pay the enemy back for his loss."[104]

In response to the Federals probes of August 20, Jabez Cannon and the 27th Alabama Infantry received orders to scout the area to their front and locate the Union lines. The regiment marched through thickly forested terrain for about five miles before emerging into a cornfield and encountering a large column of Federal troops marching down a road. Cannon claimed they "looked like Sherman's whole army." Both Union and Confederate forces were surprised to see each other, but Union veterans instinctively went into action putting the outnumbered rebels into "a mighty hot place." Initially, "we were holding our own, under the circumstances," but then the Union forces sent a brigade around the Confederate flank, to prevent any hope of retreat. Confederate officers saw the trap slamming shut and ordered an immediate retreat that turned into a footrace between the opposing forces. Cannon later recalled that, for once, the failure of the Confederate logistics system worked to the men's advantage, since gray-clad men with nothing except the clothes on their backs and rifles ran much faster than their blue-coated counterparts weighed down with full knapsacks.[105]

Unable to prevent the tightening stranglehold on the city, soldiers in the Army of Tennessee worked to improve their fortifications. Hiram Williams described August as a time of "building forts and fortifying generally." The engineers were typically considered noncombatants and rarely went into

Federal troops in Confederate fort, Atlanta, Georgia, 1864. George N. Bernard, photographer. Library of Congress.

battle like their comrades in the other branches, but in the city of Atlanta, nobody was safe. Williams and his crew were hard at work when a Union battery opened fire on a random afternoon. Many men dove for cover, but Williams, "believing that one place was as good as another," kept working. J. R. Wooten, a friend of Williams, sheltered behind a tree, but a solid shot flew past Williams and struck Wooten. The ball hit him in the left hip, tore off his right thigh, his left arm, and his right leg below his knee. The horrible wound killed him quickly but not instantly. Williams and the men of his unit who buried Wooten took small comfort in the knowledge that he, unlike so many of the men around Atlanta, received a proper resting place.[106]

Fortifications could provide only limited protection from gunfire and virtually none from the weather. Edgar Jones lived under the constant threat of death by the Federal sharpshooters, who looked for every opportunity to kill rebels. When he spread his blanket on a tree branch near his place in the trenches, it "got eighteen holes shot through it." Men often died without warning when they inadvertently stepped within sight of Union troops. The constant and seemingly random gunfire was more than some men could bear, and on at least two occasions Jones witnessed men expose themselves and dare the Federals to kill them. Both times, the Union soldiers obliged. Richard Wharton noted in his diary that a steady stream of wounded men flowed from the trenches to the hospitals.[107]

Men defending Atlanta worried about their loved ones far from the city who were increasingly threatened by Union raiders. The Confederate government often urged men to join the army in order to protect their loved ones, and many volunteered for service in order to fulfill that duty. This worked as long as the Union forces were kept an arm's length from the homes of soldiers but broke down when Federal forces penetrated the southern heartland. This presented Confederate soldiers with a difficult dilemma. In his diary entry dated August 24, Thomas Key noted alarming reports of slaves rising up against their masters as Union soldiers rampaged across the Confederacy. George Miller, a member of the 8th Confederate Cavalry Regiment, wrote home to his wife, explaining that his father had decided not to evacuate his slaves from the farm near Talladega, Alabama, since there was almost nowhere left where they would be safe from Union forces. Hosea Garrett heard that, in Mississippi, "some of our men found some of their wives tied to stakes and dead" at the hands of Union soldiers, who also "cut the throat of every wounded man they came across." Garrett hoped for divine retribution: "I can't believe that God will let such a people go unpunished." The same raids that threatened his loved ones also interrupted communications lines, making men even more desperate for news. George Higgins of the 45th Mississippi Infantry wrote home to his wife, begging for information and lamenting the fact that the mail deliveries from Mississippi were so infrequent. Confederate soldiers may have felt a conflict between protecting their individual families and protecting the Confederacy. As the Federal armies pushed ever deeper into the South and put more southern families in danger, the bonds between the Confederate soldier and the Confederate nation began to dissolve. Many Confederate soldiers became deserters, not because they were cowards, but because they decided that their greater duty was to protect their families.[108]

Sherman Withdraws August 25

On the evening of August 25, the Union army withdrew from their trenches around Atlanta. Artillery officer Thomas Key refused to allow the dreaded invader to move in peace, and "these loud-mouthed gun wagons made the night hideous with their bass voices." With grim satisfaction, he noted that his battery "no doubt caused many bluecoats to fall in the cold embrace of death." He was convinced that their disappearance meant "the scales have turned in favor of the South, and the Abolitionists are moving to the rear toward their own homes." George Athey of the 22nd Alabama Infantry believed that the Federal disappearance was a trick. Hiram Williams noted in his diary that "nearly all the boys think they are retreating and are highly elated with the idea." Williams replied to his comrades with a retort of "All Bosh!" He believed that the disappearance was "some new stratagem" that would provide Hood with a great test in which "he will either make for himself a name that will live or he will be remembered only to be derided." Williams predicted that the crippled general would fail. John Sparkman, of the quartermaster's department, reported that the southern citizens and soldiers were happy the Federals were gone but that they worried about where they went and what would happen when they got there. On August 27, William Watson and Company E of the 53rd Tennessee Infantry regiment received orders to move out in the morning and leave their blankets behind, an order that clearly indicated that the officers anticipated a very rapid march in response to Sherman's disappearance.[109]

The Battle of Jonesborough, August 31–September 1

Sherman sent six of the seven Union corps encircling Atlanta on a wide swing around Confederate trenches along the western fringe of Atlanta to cut the Macon and Western Railroad, the Army of Tennessee's only surviving rail link with the rest of the Confederacy. Sherman believed that if he could cut that line, he would force Hood to evacuate the city. Hood realized

Sherman's objective and sent Hardee's Corps and Lee's Corps of his army under command of General Hardee, the army's senior general, to assault the Federals, keep the line open, and save Atlanta. Hood, not realizing how many Union troops were on the move and fearing that it might be a diversion, remained in Atlanta with Stewart's Corps and the Georgia Militia to defend the city if it was attacked directly.[110]

On August 31, Colonel William B. Wood of the 16th Alabama Infantry commanded the brigade typically known as Lowrey's. The brigade took a place on the left, southern edge of the Confederate assault. W. E. Preston and Company B of the 33rd Alabama Infantry were sent out as skirmishers in front of the rest of the regiment. The skirmishers located Union infantry behind a line of breastworks, with artillery in support. With the enemy in sight, the entire regiment rushed their opponents, taking the line of breastworks and capturing two cannons. Lieutenant Colonel Dunklin took a moment to gleefully hug each of the cannons, which he called "black devils," before pressing the charge forward onto the second line of Union breastworks.[111]

Edgar Jones and the rest of the 18th Alabama Infantry knew that a battle had begun on the morning of August 31 because they heard the "roar of arms" before they received any orders. The regiment was part of Holtzclaw's Brigade of Clayton's Division in Lee's Corps. The Alabamians were moved

Unidentified Confederate soldier with an Enfield rifle and carrying a cartridge box on a waist belt. Library of Congress.

to several portions of the battlefield before they received orders to charge Union troops occupying breastworks on the crest of a small hill. Almost as quickly as the order to charge was heard, it was countermanded, and the men retreated in disorder, carrying as many of their wounded as they could.[112]

The 20th Tennessee Infantry and Captain James Cooper began advancing towards the enemy at 2:00 p.m. as part of the second line near the center of the assault. They passed through a patch of pine trees, taking fire from Federal artillery as they advanced, drove in the Union skirmishers, and walked into an open cornfield. The Union troops poured an intense fire that forced the Tennesseans back to the relative safety of the woods. After the battle was over, "we learned that that they were armed with sixteen shooters." More specifically, Henry Rifles, brass-framed, lever-action carbines firing a .44 rimfire cartridge. The rifles were an incredible leap forward over the single-shot, muzzle-loading Enfield rifle muskets carried by the men of the 20th Tennessee.[113]

At 3:00 p.m., E. H. Rennolds, along with the 4th and 5th Tennessee consolidated Infantry regiments, advanced as part of the second line near the center of the assault. They "met a murderous fire of grape shrapnel and musketry." Separated from the rest of their brigade and faced with a merciless barrage of fire from the Union lines, the men conceded defeat and withdrew, carrying their dead and wounded with them to the rear.[114]

Also at roughly 3:00 p.m., Robert Magill and the 39th Georgia Infantry formed into a line of battle. A cannon to their left opened fire as the signal to move forward, and the attack began. Magill recorded in his diary that "not one in a hundred believed it would accomplish anything," but even though they believed the attack was futile, the men "moved forward in splendid order through an open field."[115]

After breaking through the first line of Union trenches, the 33rd Alabama Infantry smashed into the enemy's second line. The fight was intense, but when their officers realized that the Federal lines were held by fresh troops and that the regiment had advanced way ahead of the rest of the corps, the Alabamians were ordered to retreat to avoid encirclement and capture. After returning to the main Confederate line and replenishing their ammunition, the Alabamians were ready to renew their assault but were ordered to extend their line to cover for other units that were being withdrawn farther to the rear.[116]

Hiram Williams, who spent most of his time with the engineers, finally went into direct combat on August 31, although his unit avoided the worst of the fighting as part of the second line near the center of the assault. As his company approached the already heated battle, Williams laughed at a young lieutenant who went into battle "carrying a musket and a teakettle." When an artillery shell burst nearby, he tossed down the gun and ran for his life. When another shell burst, he tossed down the tea kettle, and the men did not see him again until the battle was over. Williams recorded thinking, "thank God, I have stronger nerves than that." The men charged the Union lines without their fearful officer, "only to be repulsed with heavy loss." Williams considered the attacks "a useless waste of human life." He condemned "the wholesale butchery" and called for the commanders who authorized the assaults to suffer eternal damnation.[117]

Lieutenant William McMurray of the 20th Tennessee Infantry realized that the attack was stalling in the face of overwhelming Union firepower. In desperation, the twenty-one-year-old officer sang out a verse of "The Home-Spun Dress" in hopes that it might encourage his men:

> And now, young men, a word to you
> If you would win the fair,
> Go to the field where honor calls
> And win your lady there.
> Remember that our brightest smiles
> Are for the true and brave,
> And that our tears are all for those
> Who fill a soldier's grave.

Any encouragement the men might have felt was destroyed when a bullet struck McMurray's arm, sending him to the ground and ending his serenade.[118]

As night fell on August 31, the soldiers of the blue and the gray began kindling fires. Both armies built breastworks as darkness approached, barely one hundred yards apart from each other. Men who had sought to kill each other just an hour before enjoyed an informal truce, collecting firewood from the same piles of wood and filling their canteens from the same stream. When the men of the 19th Tennessee Infantry realized that they had few axes or shovels, enterprising men walked into the Union camps, borrowed tools, and returned them when they were done.[119]

Some men enjoyed a brief moment of rest as the fighting died down, and they converted Georgia soil and trees into defensive positions. Lieutenant Francis Fleming took a moment to write a letter to his mother back home in Florida. He told her that he was dodging enemy fire but comforted her with assurances that he and his comrades were building breastworks that would keep them safe.[120]

Johnny Green and the 1st Kentucky Infantry worked more urgently than Fleming. The Kentuckians were given "a few picks & spades & axes," along with instructions to "work for dear life." The men felt intense pressure to "erect some defense to enable us to keep the yanks at bay." If the Kentuckians could somehow keep the men in blue at arm's length for a just a little while longer, the rest of the Army of Tennessee might escape the rapidly tightening circle around Atlanta.[121]

Confederate soldiers soon made use of their defensive positions. After building a reasonably strong line of trenches, W. E. Preston and the 33rd Alabama Infantry occupied a single line, "not quite touching elbows," and watched while a mass of Federal infantry approached. The defenders were veterans and "being in a single file we knew each man had to do two men's work." The Federal line seemed unstoppable, absorbing Confederate minnie balls and ignoring the dead and wounded that trailed behind them. Preston later recalled, "we never had Yankees in the ditch with us. However, when they got within ten or fifteen paces of us, we did not know whether they could get in our ditch or not." Johnny Green reported that the Union artillery "began to shell us, but we could not stop." The veterans from Kentucky knew that only entrenchments could give them a chance at holding out against overwhelming odds. The artillery fire became so intense that a large tree nearby "was cut down by cannon balls." A shell then hit the stump and rolled into a half-completed ditch. The fuse sizzled and was sure to explode in a moment, when Walker Nash returned from the rear with a bucket of water. Without pausing, he dumped the water on the fuse and saved the lives of several men in that ditch. The rebels kept working on their trenches until "the enemy's first line charges upon us." In an instant, they dropped their tools in favor of their guns. A volley of rebel bullets slammed into the Federal attackers and then the men in gray "go at them with charged bayonets." The counterattack was short lived. The Kentuckians quickly returned to their lines when they saw "four solid lines of battle advancing across a wide field against us." A few days later, Arkansas soldier Alexander Spence told his parents that he was unhappy about the Federal's advance but "had the pleasure the other day making two Yankees bite the dust and got me a fine hat."[122]

The Army of Tennessee had kept their lifeline to the south open for the moment, but their inability to decisively defeat the Union forces meant that it would not remain open for very long. The Confederate forces paid dearly. Roughly 23,811 Confederate soldiers took part in the battle and 1,725 were killed or wounded. In comparison, only 179 of the 14,170 Union soldiers who participated were killed or wounded in the battle.[123]

Ruins of rolling mill and cars of Hood's ordnance, destroyed by rebels on evacuation of Atlanta, 1864. George N. Bernard, photographer. Library of Congress.

The Evacuation of Atlanta

General Hood knew that the Federal army might cut the final road out of Atlanta at any time and capture the entire Army of Tennessee. Rather than lose both the army and the city, Hood decided to evacuate Atlanta and at least save his army. Johnny Green hated to lose Atlanta but knew that Hood could save the army or the city, not both. Men including Andrew Neal agreed that "the preservation of the Army is infinitely of more importance than Atlanta." When darkness fell on September 1, the Army of Tennessee began withdrawing from Atlanta.[124]

The rebels destroyed most of the supplies they could not take with them. W. P. Chambers and the 46th Mississippi Infantry were pulled off the firing line and sent to destroy an army supply depot. He was appalled, having "never witnessed such wholesale destruction of property before." Chambers estimated that his regiment alone destroyed six million dollars' worth of supplies, including guns and ammunition. The Mississippians did not destroy everything, helping themselves to anything they wanted, including brand new English rifles. Alabamian John Scott lamented the loss of huge quantities of supplies, including "one hundred and twenty box cars loaded with ordnance." In a letter written the previous month, Scott had expressed some confidence in Hood's abilities, but now the infantryman mockingly asked, "and what think you of the young Napoleon who promised to accomplish so much?" Almost twenty years later, W. E. Matthews still remembered that evening. He could never forget the hellish light created by a burning city and the noise of explosions caused by the destruction of precious gunpowder. Georgia staff officer George Adair claimed that the fires burned so brightly that "I could count the hairs in the horse's tail" as the animal pulled his wagon. Mississippi infantryman R. N. Rea watched civilians by the roadside cry as Confederate soldiers evacuated. It is not clear if they cried because the army was leaving or because the fires that the rebels started were turning their once glorious city into ashes.[125]

W. P. Chambers felt the retreat "was exceedingly slow." Soldiers shared the road with "men, women and children, and all sorts of vehicles with all sorts of loads, trying to get away from the abandoned city." The flames of a burning Atlanta provided the refugees with light and the explosions of abandoned ammunition depots broke the silence. They marched all night and only made six miles. As the sun came up, the Mississippians formed a line of battle to keep a scouting party of Federals at bay. The bluecoats withdrew, and the retreat resumed. After twenty-five hours of continuous marching, Chambers fell asleep, flopping to the ground in the middle of the road and only waking when a horse's foot struck his face. Realizing that he must rest, even though it meant allowing his regiment to march on, Chambers found a comfortable spot beneath a roadside apple tree for a much-needed nap. He caught up with his regiment entrenched near Lovejoy's Station several days later.[126]

Over thirty years after the fall of Atlanta, Mrs. Ellen McCord recalled the retreating soldiers who wandered past her family's home near Atlanta in early September 1864. She remembered one young boy who stopped to get a drink at her well. He was clearly very sick, "had neither coat nor blanket only a dirty haversack," and through his delirium he revealed that he had been a patient in one of Atlanta's military hospitals before the fall of the city forced him onto the road south. Although "he was neither bright nor attractive," Mrs. McCord felt a maternal impulse to care for the boy, so she brought him into her home and called in a doctor, who diagnosed the youthful rebel with typhoid fever. For weeks he lay in bed and "muttered about shooting men and sometimes he talked of people we supposed to be his friends at home." Eventually he recovered and left Mrs. Ellen McCord for his home in south Alabama. Sometime later, she received a letter from the young man, explaining that he had arrived safely at home and promising to come and help her on her farm once the war ended. She never again saw or heard from the youth but said, "I often feel glad that I helped save the life of one Confederate soldier."[127]

The Fall of Atlanta

When Atlanta fell, the Confederacy suffered a horrendous loss. George Templeton Strong, the famed New York lawyer, reported that Gettysburg might have been Confederacy's "high water mark," but the fall of Atlanta was its "last chance." Joseph Brown, governor of Georgia, agreed, referring to Atlanta as "probably the most vital point to our success" that had fallen to Union forces up to that point. Numerous newspapers proclaimed that the fall of Atlanta greatly enhanced Lincoln's chances for reelection. Almost everything needed by the Army of Tennessee had been produced in or traveled through Atlanta, and now it rested securely in Union hands. When the Confederate army left Atlanta, they destroyed twenty-eight train car loads of ammunition in addition to large quantities of artillery, small arms, machinery, clothing, medicine, and food. General Hood, for all his faults, was aware of precarious state of his army in September 1864, noting immediately after the fall of Atlanta that "Sherman is weaker now than he will be in future, and I as strong as I can expect to be."[128]

The Confederacy had lost one of its most vital cities but saved its second most dangerous field army, which still posed a potent threat to the victorious Federals. The Army of Tennessee consisted of at least 23,000 infantry and artillerymen, mostly battle-hardened veterans. The artillery had lost much of its equipment but still boasted 124 cannons, most of which were the excellent 12 pounder Napoleons prized by Union and Confederate gunners, with roughly 106 rounds of ammunition per gun. Confederate cavalry, including 7,000 under General Forrest and another 4,500 under Joe Wheeler, raged across Mississippi and Tennessee, cutting supply lines and defeating most of the Federal troops they encountered.[129]

General Sherman realized that Confederate forces in the region remained dangerous, taking threats seriously, condemning officers who sank "into a condition of idleness," and working tirelessly to prepare for inevitable Confederate counterattacks.[130] The Army of Tennessee had lost battles, but the war was far from over, and like a wounded animal, it remained dangerous. The question was: what would it do next?

2

"SUCH MEN WILL NOT BE CONQUERED"

The Counteroffensive in Georgia

> I see around me such distress and my heart sickens at the destruction of life and property on every hand, in the army and out of it. I see grey hairs and helpless infancy driven from home, penniless almost friendless. I see the strong man cut down without a moment's warning or left a cripple for life. I see the poor solider as he toils on, sustained by the hope of better days and by the love, he bears for those far away. I saw but yesterday the Captain commanding his regiment barefoot. Such men will not be conquered.[1]
>
> —Thomas Deavenport, 3rd Tennessee Infantry

Retreat from Atlanta

The Army of Tennessee was in full retreat. The fires of a burning Atlanta bathed the sky in a hellish ochre hue, lighting the way for a shattered army meandering down country roads. Starving scarecrows in dirty rags adorned with blood-stained bandages carried little more than rifles and the bodies of comrades who could walk no farther. The sporadic thunder of exploding ordnance provided their only marching music. The Army of Tennessee was battered and defeated but remained defiant. According to James Lanning of the 25th Alabama Infantry, the army was "not in fighting order at this time." The rebels would fight again, but first they needed to regroup in the countryside near Lovejoy's Station, Georgia, roughly twenty-five miles south of Atlanta.[2]

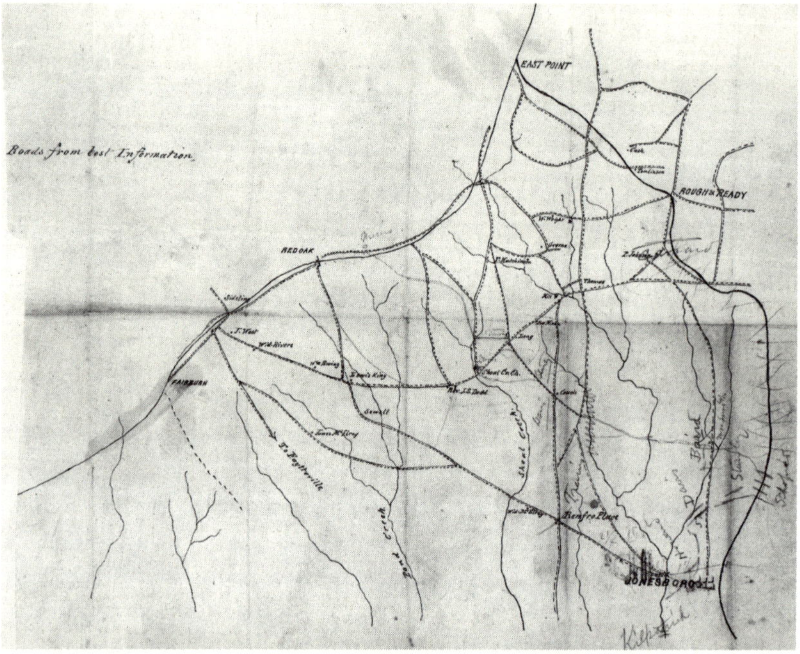

Map 4. Country northwest of Jonesborough, Georgia, August–September 1864. Shows troop positions and names of commanders annotated in pencil. Library of Congress.

Soldier Dissatisfaction with General Hood

Many members of the Army of Tennessee were understandably unhappy with General Hood. According to Arkansas soldier Alexander Spence, many troops, especially the Georgians, were "much discouraged." Kentucky soldier Johnny Green claimed, "the boys with dejected spirits say you would have never have caught Genl Joe Johnston in this trap." Alabama rebel J. P. Cannon believed that, while Johnston "would probably have given up Atlanta," he would have held it longer and inflicted greater losses on the Federals while suffering smaller losses to his own forces than General Hood had. Cannon explained that, while the men still respected Hood as a "brave and gallant officer," his promotion had been "a fatal mistake" for the Confederacy. W. P. Chambers argued that the men had never approved of Hood's promotion and that the loss of Atlanta intensified their dislike of the general. Georgia staff officer George Adair believed that "there seemed nothing left but to surrender." Captain Adam Whetstone of the 53rd Alabama Mounted Infantry believed Hood's failures of command had transformed the army into a "pitiable sight." Veteran soldier Charles Roberts informed his wife "the fall of Atlanta has killed Hood as a general, unless he makes some brilliant and successful move upon the enemy before the campaign is considered closed, which I think is very improbable."[3]

The Army of Tennessee was demoralized. Tennessean Risenar Etter noted in his diary that "there is much dissatisfaction" in the army. Alabama soldier John Scott informed his sweetheart that "we are all down with the blues" as a result of losing Atlanta and that thoughts of what might come next "causes many a heart to throb with fear." In a letter written several days letter, he described himself as "completely disgusted." Tennessee infantryman Larry Johnson considered the fall of Atlanta a fatal blow and, as a result, believed, "our collapse was a mere matter of time." In response to a rumor that Hood planned to retreat farther south, Georgian George Athey told his father, "we have lost grown anuff all reade." Texas artilleryman James Douglas told his wife that he wanted to get home and that, if he couldn't get a furlough, he would resign. Waves of demoralized Confederates offered to take the oath of allegiance to the Union in exchange for promises that they would be exempt from the draft.[4]

The demoralization led to serious breakdowns in discipline. According to Robert Jarman, his regiment, the 27th Mississippi Infantry, and the 24th Mississippi Infantry refused to drill. When officers ordered the 29th and 30th Mississippi to arrest the men who would not drill, the 34th Mississippi also refused to drill, and the 29th and 30th Mississippi refused to act against the other regiments. The standoff ended when the officers conceded, allowing the men to rest for several days. Robert Patrick, working as a clerk to General Edward Walthall, heard J. F. Conley, colonel of the 29th Alabama Infantry, accuse Charles Morris, lieutenant colonel the 29th Alabama Infantry, of cowardice. Morris responded by beating Conley "over the head with a big stick in great fashion." Patrick gave no indication that Morris suffered any punishment for assaulting a superior officer, only recording his own belief that "Conley was an old reprobate anyhow and I wish Morris had given more than he did."[5]

Despite the obvious problems caused by the fall of Atlanta, some southerners suggested that loss of the city meant little. Confederate nurse Kate Cumming reported that "I hear few regret the loss of the city." She said that "even Georgians" did not miss Atlanta because "they say it was the most wicked place in the world." The *Chattanooga Rebel*, published by this time in Griffin, Georgia, mocked the northern press for taking pride in Atlanta's capture. The article provided a detailed explanation of why the loss of Atlanta was insignificant, pointing to the time, money, and labor the Federals expended to capture the city, which they destroyed in the process. A writer for the *Wilmington Journal* in North Carolina claimed that loss of Atlanta "was no disaster" since Hood never intended to hold the city forever, only to delay the Federal advance while punishing the Yankees. Once the Army of Tennessee accomplished these objectives, they withdrew from the city, leaving the Union army to occupy a worthless shell of a town. A writer for the *Yorkville Enquirer* in South Carolina shared reports that Sherman's army in Georgia was melting away because the enlistments of thousands of soldiers were expiring and the men refused to reenlist. This fact supposedly ensured that the Union invasion of Georgia was over, at least for the near future. The *Daily Dispatch* in Richmond claimed that the shoe was now on the other foot and that the Yankees would find their stay in Atlanta just as disagreeable as the Confederate army did. In reality, Union soldiers felt understandable joy at their success, enjoying new homes among "surplus houses."[6] It is unclear if Confederate newspapers published inaccurate claims as part of a calculated effort to maintain Confederate morale or out of authentic miscalculations, but either way they promoted the idea that the loss of Atlanta meant little. Confederate soldiers, with their keen interest in the news, were undoubtedly aware of this point of view, even if they rejected it.

Many Confederate soldiers worried about their loved ones in greater peril from a victorious Union army with few remaining barriers to the Confederate heartland. Thomas Warrick of the 34th Alabama Infantry worried about his family, predicting that triumphant Federals would destroy much of the South, including his home in Coosa County, Alabama. Charles Roberts, a soldier from Oxford, Mississippi, informed his wife, "I can bear the losses I have sustained during this war without a murmur, but I do feel impatient and outraged when they make my wife and children subject to the alarm and inconvenience." He planned to remain in the army but advised his wife to encourage a young relative to seek an exemption under the "fifteen negro law" which allowed overseers supervising at least fifteen slaves to avoid the draft. If that failed, Roberts suggested that the young man should volunteer for state service that would allow him to remain close to home and avoid many of the horrors of war. The Confederate army's failure to repel invading Union armies once again forced Confederate soldiers to face the stark choice between their duty as soldiers for the nation and their duty as guardians for their private families. Some Confederate soldiers became deserters when they decided that their greater duty was at home.[7]

The crumbling Confederate mail system increased men's worries. Alabama soldier James Lanning's internal conflict played out in his diary when he was unable to get news from home. He asked himself of his "dear lonely wife and sweet little daughter; do they think of me?" In the next line, he reassured himself that, even though he had not heard from them, "they think of me often." Samuel Vann told his sweetheart that, before getting

Alabama troops at camp, Pensacola, Florida. Library of Congress.

a letter several weeks after the fall of Atlanta, "I almost come to the conclusion that you had forgotten me entirely." Stouten Dent, commander of Dent's Alabama Battery, tried to comfort his wife, explaining, "as a general rule when you do not hear I am all right. Bad news travels fast and should I be killed or wounded in any fight you would hear it very quickly." Dent was incorrect. Civil War casualty reports were notoriously slow, incomplete, and inaccurate.[8] By September 1864, this fact was very widely known. Dent may have lied in a feeble effort to comfort her, and she appears to have allowed his attempt at deception to pass without comment, perhaps because she wanted to believe, even though she must have known better.

The Army of Tennessee Rests Outside Atlanta

Despite the problems they faced, rebels enjoyed some much-needed relaxation. Sergeant James Crane of the 66th Georgia Infantry assured his parents that "I have passed through the dangers of battle safely." He set up a camp and expected "to stay some time." George Higgins informed his wife, "we are having quite a rest." According to J. P. Cannon, the men spent the first few days of September "resting, washing, and cleaning up generally." He described the men as grateful for "the first wash day we have had for four months." Although James Maxwell was a wealthy man who always carried large quantities of cash with him, he and his comrades went into a Macon store, stole all the tobacco Maxwell could stuff down his shirt, returned to camp, got drunk with some strange women, and even "kissed" one who "did not like that sort of kiss." Sadly, Maxwell did not explain what he meant by "that sort of kiss."[9]

A few of the men appeared cautiously optimistic. W. H. Henderson of the 7th Texas Infantry told his parents that he was "in as good as spirit as ever." While that might seem odd under the circumstances, Henderson explained that he was committed to "live in hope," indicating that Henderson was intentionally choosing to remain upbeat in spite of the tragic setback. Thomas Deavenport, a chaplain in the 3rd Tennessee Infantry, admitted that "we have been compelled to give up much of our country" but he was "not discouraged," even though "there is some discontent in the army." Unsurprisingly, the minister placed his faith in God and praised the almighty for his safety.[10]

W. E. Preston and the rest of the 33rd Alabama Infantry camped on an old battlefield. The Alabamians were unsure of when the skirmish had transpired or which units were involved, but the lack of dead horses convinced them that it had been an affair of infantrymen alone. The Federals must have won that day because their dead lay in neat graves, but the rebels remained where they fell or rested in shallow graves that did not fully cover them. Preston later recalled, "we would sometimes see a hand" or a portion of an arm or leg. Dogs and other animals dug up corpses and feasted on putrefying human flesh. Eventually, even the jaded veterans of the 33rd Alabama could not stand the sight of rotting human bodies, and they took it upon themselves to rebury every exposed corpse.[11]

A steady stream of civilians visited the army. Mississippi infantryman Robert Jarman remembered that two prominent men from the surrounding countryside toured the camps. After conversing with Jarman and his comrades, the soldiers invited the men to stay for dinner. The civilians only accepted after the Mississippians assured them that they had plenty to eat. Jarman explained to his reader, although probably not to the regiment's guests, that the men were in a rare state of plenty because, the day before, men from the regiment had captured a beehive and a large hog from Union scouts, who had presumably taken the provisions from southern civilians. Jarman's slave Rafe obtained biscuits with butter from an unidentified source and cooked the entire feast to perfection, convincing the visitors that the Army of Tennessee was well fed.[12] Jarman appears to have found the deception quite amusing and does not seem to have considered the possibility that the civilians returned home and encouraged their neighbors to resist the army's calls for support on the basis that the men were feasting on pork, honey, and biscuits.

Many men discussed politics in their leisure time. By September 8, the men were aware that McClellan was the Democratic nominee for president. C. T. Hardman of the 6th Alabama Cavalry told his wife, "you must cheer up," since "we have seen a good many Yankee papers and all of them are advocating peace." Stouten Dent was less optimistic, observing that Lincoln "plays his cards very adroitly" and would use the capture of Atlanta to help ensure his eventual reelection. He predicted that, if Lincoln was reelected, the war would continue and suggested that if McClellan won, he might also demand unconditional surrender. The despondent artilleryman concluded, "darling I cannot see the end of this thing."[13]

Religious revivals swept the Confederate camps. According to George Higgins, the men in the camps south of Atlanta enjoyed the quiet sermons of preachers, concluding, "it appears to us that we now have peace." Jesse Henderson believed that the men were more religious than the army's high command and claimed that if the generals would embrace the lord, "what a different effect it would have upon the army." Stouten Dent told his wife that he enjoyed the revivals and that, if not for his faith in God's approval for the Confederate cause, "I would be entirely disheartened." J. P. Cannon approved of the revivals since "they certainly need it." Cannon's decision to say, "they need it" rather than "we need it" provides a possible insight into how one infantryman felt about his comrades. The American Bible Society of New York aided the revival with the delivery of fifty thousand Bibles to the Confederate Army of Tennessee.[14] No surviving records indicate if the Yankees underlined the sixth commandment.

At least one Confederate soldier entertained impure thoughts during religious services. Robert Patrick noted in his private diary that he attended Sunday school, "where I saw a very pretty girl about 14 years old." While that might seem like an innocent comment, the twenty-eight-year-old Patrick went on to reveal, "she had the largest boobies for a girl of her age that I ever saw." This was hardly an idle observation. Patrick was sad when he got orders that sent him away from the area, since "if we were to remain here any length of time I should use every exertion to make her acquaintance certain."[15]

One of the most detailed descriptions of these religious services came from the diary of Arkansan Thomas Key:

> Last night I witnessed one of the sublimest sights that it is the fortune of man to behold. As the hidden sun tinged the clouds with the lingerings of his glory, the beautiful and love-inspiring moon smiled as sweetly and kindly as if there were no war, and the fall breeze was just at that temperature that renders everything comfortable. My footsteps were directed toward the spot where holy and devout men met to praise God. The hymn was being sung, and as I approached the stand the throng bowed in

> humble reverence before its Maker. The uncertain light from the flickering torches made it impossible to distinguish one individual from another, the reflection of the fire lamps revealed the rich leaves of the sturdy oak, the clustering hickory, and the form of the towering poplar, while the forest was vocal with katydids whose chirrupings were interspersed with the croakings of the frogs. Mingled with these were the voices of devout men at a distance making sweet melody, the chopping axes, the rattle of the military wagons, the neighing of horses that had sniffed the breeze of war under their brave and heroic riders, while from still further in the distance came the sweet and soul-enlivening harmonious airs from a brass band. But above all arose the earnest voice of the minister pleading with God for the souls of men and the deliverance of this troubled and downtrodden country from the relentless foe. As the minister pronounced the word "Amen," hundreds of manly forms, whom I recognized as the sunburned veterans of Cleburne's division and who had fought their hundredth battle and bowed to none but God, arose from their knees. I have not the language to convey even a faint idea of the grandeur of this scene, which is so imprinted and lithographed upon my mind that time alone can obliterate it. It can be felt but not described.[16]

Key cleared found the scene impressive, although there is no indication that he joined the worshipers.

The Shrinking Army of Tennessee

The Army of Tennessee was shrinking. Hood claimed that he had only lost around 5,000 men (from 44,495 effective troops to 40,403) between July 31 and September 20, 1864. Many historians are critical of Hood's claims, arguing that he had actually lost as many as 15,000 men and by September 1864 could muster something closer to 33,000 or even as little as 23,000 effectives. The Georgia Militia left the army on September 12, which removed soldiers at a time when the army could little afford any further losses. Newton Davis of the 24th Alabama Infantry told his wife that most regiments had lost more than half their men since the campaign for Atlanta began. In desperation, General Hood ordered all white teamsters, except for men in the ordnance department, to rejoin their combat units and instructed "negroes to be used in their stead." Confederate nurse Kate Cumming reported that many soldiers who were sent home to heal never returned to the army.[17]

The supply problems that had plagued the Army of Tennessee since its inception continued in the camps outside Atlanta. Thomas Warrick did

Unidentified Confederate soldier in an Overcoat. Library of Congress.

not have a coat but considered himself lucky to have everything else he needed. Cavalryman C. T. Hardman asked his wife to try to make him an overcoat, which he needed for the cold weather. Although an officer with greater resources than many men, Newton Davis informed his wife that all of his clothing was "nearly worn out," and the overcoat he would need for the cold nights ahead was "gone up completely." Charles Roberts, with the quartermaster department, told his wife that the soldiers were suffering largely because "we destroyed considerable quantities of government stores in Atlanta." Stouten Dent told his wife that he would ask her to come and see him, but even as an officer and battery commander, "I have no tent." The men of the 1st Alabama Infantry realized that the army was unlikely to supply the men with what they needed, so several men traveled to central Alabama to obtain clothing from the men's friends and families.[18] For more information on the supply problems experienced by the Army of Tennessee, please see the appendix in this book.

If the Confederate government had kept up with the men's wages, it would have allowed men to purchase more of their own provisions, but cash payments were as unpredictable and meager as every other category of supplies in the Army of Tennessee. Hood urged President Davis to pay the army immediately, but payments remained irregular at best. William McLeod of the 7th Florida Infantry noted that the men finally received wages from government on September 23, presumably a very happy moment for men in need of life's most essential goods.[19]

The men were hungry and unhappy with the limited amounts of food they were able to acquire. Newton Davis lamented the monotonous diet of "beef and bread for dinner and bread and beef for supper," as he fantasized about his mother's home-cooked meals. Stouten Dent told his wife, "the principle objection is the want of something to eat." Even when Dent obtained food, it consisted entirely of poor quality beef and nearly inedible flour. J. P. Cannon was amused when Governor Brown of Georgia asked the Army of Tennessee to observe a day of "fasting and prayer" since "we have been fasting most of the time for two years, but I am afraid not enough prayers are associated with the 'fast' to avail much."[20]

Hungry men fanned out across the countryside to buy food with their limited funds. Risenar Etter walked more than thirteen miles in search of food, eventually purchasing half a bushel of potatoes for five dollars. Charles Roberts was pleased to buy potatoes and sorghum from nearby farms. However, he was angry that farmers raised their prices, asking five dollars for a three-pint canteen full of sorghum when they had charged the same price for a gallon jug before the army moved into the area. At these prices, most men could afford little food, since privates in the Confederate army, when they were paid, received only eighteen dollars per month after their June 9, 1864, raise. Men were so bored with their monotonous rations of bread and beef that they spent all of their meager funds on food. Men paid five dollars each for chickens, honey and butter both went for five dollars per pound, and cowpeas, also known as black-eyed peas, were purchased for one dollar per quart. The men accepted the "enormous prices," since the sellers were mostly poor people with large families of barefoot children. James Maxwell always kept several hundred dollars handy and bought anything he wanted. After purchasing provisions, he and his friends "slept whilst the darkies cooked."[21]

Not every soldier paid for supplies. According to John Sparkman, "the soldiers are acting badly stealing etc." A member of General William Quarles's Brigade stole $45,000 of currency and vouchers in the middle of the night, helped himself to an officer's horse, and slipped away before anyone realized what had happened. W. P. Chambers noted widespread theft by hungry soldiers, some of whom preferred stealing to any other method of acquiring supplies, even when they had money. Robert Jarman was supervising a group of men building breastworks when two soldiers named Allen and Butler explained that they had spotted several unwatched sheep nearby. They told Jarman that, if he would excuse them from duty for a little while, they would gladly slaughter the animals and bring Jarman a portion of the meat. Jarman agreed, but when the men returned, they had no meat. They explained that what they thought were sheep lying in a field were the discarded skins of cows that some other regiment had killed. It became a great joke among the men for the rest of the campaign, so that whenever anyone in the regiment saw a discarded cowhide, they called out for Allen and Butler to fetch them some mutton.[22]

Civilians Evacuated from Atlanta

On September 7, 1864, General Sherman ordered all civilians to leave Atlanta because "Atlanta is no place for families or non-combatants." In his memoirs, General Sherman explained that he gave everyone, white and black, the choice to either move south, travel north, or to remain with the Federal army if they could find work with the military. Newton Davis told his wife the civilians were "robbed of their household furniture, jewels, and servants before being sent into our lines." Davis did not explain and may not have known if the stolen "servants" were actually slaves, who found freedom with the Federals more appealing than continued servitude to their former masters. General Hood acknowledged the policy of giving all the inhabitants of Atlanta a choice, but he made no comment on the freeing of slaves, instead lambasting Sherman's policy of forcing civilians from their homes as "ingenious cruelty."[23]

The exodus enraged Confederate soldiers who, like General Hood, denounced the move as cruel and illegal. Thomas Deavenport described the forced exodus of women and children as "heartless cruelty" and evidence that "there seems to be no deed too base or cruel for a Yankee." Charles Roberts felt "embittered against all of them, both those that have been in and are in the army and those that remain at home and without a word of objection." Thomas Key felt outrage at the "equalization of the whites and blacks under Sherman." As an example of the problems caused by "equalization," he noted that "a big black negro man" offered a white woman ten dollars if she would spend the night with him. Key did not reveal if she accepted the offer, but he did record in his diary that "the thought of such an occurrence arouses every nerve in my body for vengeance."[24]

Rumors filled the camps and the men were electric with speculation. Some men spread rumors that troops from the Army of Tennessee might go to Virginia. John Scott informed his sweetheart that he heard rumors that the army would either flank Sherman or counterattack him directly in Atlanta. E. T. Eggleston of Cowan's Mississippi Battery noted in his diary that the men were uncertain and concerned by Hood's secrecy.[25]

The New Offensive Begins to Take Shape

The Army of Tennessee stood at a difficult crossroads. Typically, defeated armies withdraw, but John Bell Hood was anything but typical. General Hood would lead the Army of Tennessee north, assault Federal supply

Brothers Captain John M. Raines of Co. C, 2nd Tennessee Cavalry Regiment, and Private Thomas ("Thadde") Raines of Co. E, 5th Tennessee Infantry Regiment, 1862. Library of Congress.

lines, and try to force the invaders to assault the Army of Tennessee on ground of Hood's choosing. Hood later claimed that he only acted after meeting with the army's leading generals and receiving their unanimous support. He admitted it would be a difficult campaign but urged the men to bear it cheerfully.[26]

Numerous observers later criticized Hood's plan, but many soldiers supported his plan at the time. D. W. Sanders, serving on General French's staff, explained that army faced a difficult problem, that every other plan for defending Georgia had already failed, and that, as a result, Hood coolly weighed his options and made the best possible decision. Corps commander General Alexander Stewart endorsed Hood's concept for the campaign. He noted in his official report, "after the fall of Atlanta the condition of the army and other considerations rendered in necessary, in my judgment, that an offensive campaign should be made in the enemy's rear." General Stephen Lee, commanding another corps, reported, "it was my opinion that the army should take up the offensive." He believed the army should look for "favorable opportunities" for "striking the enemy." Major James Bates of the 9th Texas Cavalry told his mother that "the opinion prevails here generally that Sherman will be forced to evacuate Atlanta immediately." C. Irvine Walker of the 10th South Carolina Infantry claimed, "the spirits and hopes of the army rose" when they learned of Hood's plans for a new offensive. Henry Clayton, commanding a brigade of Alabamians, informed his wife, "the troops are delighted at the idea of an advance and in most excellent spirits." George Hager reported that his regiment, the 2nd Tennessee Cavalry, was in "high spirits" with thoughts of returning to their homes in Tennessee.[27]

Southern journalists also supported Hood's plans. A writer for the *Edgefield Advertiser* in South Carolina assured southerners that, while Atlanta had fallen, "our army is unwhipped and unconquerable." The *Wilmington Journal* of North Carolina claimed that, by September 22, the Army of Tennessee was in a far better position to defeat the Federals than it was during the battles for Atlanta. In a later issue, the same paper reported rumors from Richmond that the Army of Tennessee would soon act with "crushing effect." The *Daily Dispatch* of Richmond published a correspondent's claims that, during his visit to the Army of Tennessee, he found the men and their commanders were "cheerful," "brave," "patriotic," and prepared to strike the Federals through "a novel and unexpected channel." A Georgia correspondent for the *Western Democrat* of Charlotte, North Carolina, predicted that the Army of Tennessee would take advantage of Sherman's arrogance and give him a nasty surprise.[28]

Union leaders realized that the Hood's new offensive posed a serious threat. General Sherman conceded that the Confederate forces could cut off his supplies at will and expressed frustration at his inability to obtain detailed information on Hood's plans. The worried general reinforced Union garrisons in Tennessee and braced for the worst. President Lincoln was concerned that Hood might win a great military victory that could prevent his reelection. In public, General Ulysses Grant dismissed the danger, but in private, he expressed concern. Grant acknowledged that if he were in Hood's position, he too would have gone on an offensive to the north. Years later, Grant confided, "I was never so anxious during the war as at that time" because "so long as Hood was on the loose the whole west was in danger."[29]

President Jefferson Davis and an entourage of staff officers and politicians traveled to Georgia after the fall of Atlanta. On September 23, Davis spoke to a crowd at Macon, Georgia, and delivered a speech that was subsequently published in the *Macon Telegraph*. The Confederate president acknowledged that the loss of Atlanta was a tragedy but assured his listeners that "our cause is not lost." He predicted a reenactment of the Napoleon's defeat in Russia, in which a victorious army pressed too far into enemy territory only to meet defeat at the hands of dedicated civilians and skilled cavalry. Davis explained, "two-thirds of our men are absent," most of which were "absent without leave." He offered forgiveness to men who returned promptly and argued, "if one-half the men now absent without leave will return to duty, we can defeat the enemy." Davis endorsed Hood's offensive strategy and promised to do everything in his power to support it. When General Grant heard of Davis's optimistic predictions that Sherman would fail just as Napoleon failed in Russia, he sarcastically asked, "who is to furnish the snow for this Moscow retreat?"[30]

Members of the Army of Tennessee gave President Davis a mixed reception. General Hood was happy to see Davis and claimed, "some brigades received the President with enthusiasm." He also admitted that other units "were seemingly dissatisfied" and called out "give us Johnston," a sentiment that embarrassed and upset Hood. According to Robert Bevier of the 5th Missouri Infantry, President Davis told the men that General Hood was a commander "who has struck in the cause of Confederacy an honest if not a successful blow" and angered the men when he suggested that their beloved Johnston was dishonest. W. J. Worsham and C. W. Heiskell of the 19th Tennessee Infantry stated that, when Howell Cobb, the Georgia secessionist politician and Confederate general, gave a speech in support of Davis that the men felt was sickeningly sweet, a private in the regiment called out "a shell or two would knock all the sweetness out." John Porcher of the 10th South Carolina Infantry claimed that no unit cheered Davis except for members of a single battery of artillery, in which "half the battery cheered and the other half hissed them for cheering." General Arthur Manigault exclaimed, "I would hate to go into a fight tomorrow with these men." Captain Samuel Foster saw Davis's presence as a bad omen. The long-serving Texan recalled that Davis visited the army before previous defeats at Murfreesboro and Missionary Ridge. Foster cynically suggested, "he came here just after the fall of Atlanta to concoct some other plan for our defeat and display of his Generalship."[31]

As soon as the president left, the army finished its last preparations for the offensive. The army kept a close eye on the men with three roll calls per day. In the mornings they drilled by company, and in the afternoons they drilled by battalion. Jesse Henderson felt that training on Sundays "is very inconsistent for the Sabbath I do think." When the men were not busy drilling, the officers inspected them and their equipment. Robert Patrick helped gather "everything that was eatable" from the area. He acknowledged, "this is pretty hard on the natives," but stated, "this is war." John Porcher scoured the countryside for draft animals, even taking a mule from a reluctant county sheriff.[32]

The army reorganized. Fierce fighting around Atlanta battered the famed Orphan Brigade of Kentucky until it was smaller than many regiments. The army's high command sent the survivors south to recuperate and reorganize into a mounted infantry unit. Many of the rebel regiments were mere skeletons of their former selves, and the army combined many of them into units like the 4th, 5th, 31st, 33rd, and 38th Tennessee Infantry Regiments, which became a single consolidated regiment. Larry Johnson of the 16th Tennessee Infantry lamented the heavy losses that effectively destroyed his regiment and led to the consolidation of many of the best units in the army. William Yeatman was only a junior captain, but his superiors made him the newest commander of the 2nd Tennessee Infantry. John Lavender of the 4th Arkansas Infantry believed that consolidating regiments made the Confederate army stronger than the Union army, which typically formed new regiments and lost all sense of their previous organization. In an effort to ensure devotion to General Hood, President Davis ordered General Hardee, an experienced corps commander and outspoken critic of Hood, to leave the Army of Tennessee and take a new post in command of the Department of South Carolina and Florida.[33]

Confederate Cavalry Raids Led by Forrest and Wheeler

While the infantrymen and artillerymen of the Army of Tennessee prepared to move out, Confederate cavalry forces under Wheeler and Forrest continued to make life difficult for the men in blue. S. B. Barron of the 3rd Texas Cavalry joined Wade's Supernumerary Scouts, an elite unit composed of forty-one handpicked officers from Ross's Brigade of cavalry that raided deep into Union-occupied northern Georgia. On August 19, Wheeler's troopers assaulted the Federal supply depot at Dalton, Georgia, capturing large quantities of supplies, two hundred prisoners, and several hundred mules. On September 25, General Forrest led men into action near Athens, Alabama, where they burned a Federal fort, cut rail lines, and took one thousand prisoners. On the same day, Forrest's men captured the heavily fortified Sulfur Creek trestle bridge a few miles north of Athens.[34]

Most cavalrymen seemed to enjoy raiding. A. C. McLeary of the 12th Tennessee Cavalry described the men of his regiment as "a jolly set" of "boys from sixteen to twenty." William Sloan of the 5th Tennessee Cavalry saw the raids with Forrest as a grand adventure, where men abandoned Wheeler's cavalry command and joined Forrest "for the sake of a daring exploit" and where "most of the boys are drunk" from captured brandy. Charles Gore Joy of the 14th Tennessee Cavalry loved adventure but passed on the liquor, which he claimed "smelled like turpentine."[35]

At least one trooper didn't enjoy the raiding and felt conflicted by these tactics. Captain Adam Whetstone of the 53rd Alabama Mounted Infantry recalled that raiding was "distasteful to our feelings" and that "there was not a soldier present who, upon consulting his desires, would not have returned to the army." The long-serving captain, who worked his way up the ranks from corporal more than two years before, was no coward. He saw himself as a soldier, not a vandal. Whetstone did his best to support the raid because he thought it was the best way to force Sherman into the decisive field battle Whetstone craved, but he loathed every minute of the raids that he found personally distatsteful.[36]

Observers took joy in the cavalrymen's exploits. Rumor circulated that Forrest was now the supreme cavalry commander in the region, that he had launched a raid into north Alabama, and that a portion of the Army of Tennessee's infantrymen were about to unite with him for a grand raid in the Federal army's rear. Infantryman James Lanning gleefully reported every success by General Forrest and his brave cavaliers. Captain Samuel Kelley explained in a letter home that reports that Wheeler's cavalrymen had cut off Sherman's supply lines greatly improved the men's morale. A newspaper correspondent working in Georgia claimed that Forrest would undoubtedly "crush and annihilate all the force sent to oppose him."[37]

The Army of Tennessee's Offensive Begins

On September 28, 1864, the men learned that the next grand offensive would begin in the morning. On September 28, the men received three days' worth of rations. When Samuel Foster of the 24th Texas Cavalry (dismounted) heard that the army would move out in the morning, he washed his shirt and underwear. George Higgins of the 45th Mississippi Infantry informed his wife that he was "quite nervous" and expected "a long march" to begin at any moment.[38]

The Army of Tennessee began the offensive on September 29, 1864, and, initially, it looked promising. H. K. Nelson of the 41st Tennessee Infantry noted that, as the army began moving out, three ladies stood by the road singing, "I am a Rebel soldier and Fighting for My Home," and when they finished, the men responded with "the old Rebel yell," which "thrilled everyone present." On October 1, the Army of Tennessee crossed the Chattahoochee River, moving northwest away from Palmetto, Georgia. Risenar Etter was pleased to receive badly needed shoes as he headed out. E. H. Rennolds recalled that the first few days on the march were difficult, but "all are in fine spirits," perhaps because the men enjoyed "some nice grapes" that they found along the way. Robert Smith of the 2nd Tennessee Infantry recorded in his diary that "the troops are all jubilant and confident of success." E. J. Harvie, the Army of Tennessee's assistant inspector general, informed his superiors in Richmond that he would not conduct any inspections along the march and that, "when you hear from me next, I hope it will be in the heart of Tennessee, after Sherman is whipped."[39]

Confederate journalists provided their readers with uplifting comments about the start of the campaign. The *North Carolina Standard* of Raleigh reported that members of the Army of Tennessee were in "good spirits" and congratulated them on their "astounding movement." The *Daily Dispatch* in Richmond claimed that "recruits were pouring in" to the Army of Tennessee, that the army's internal feuds were over, and that the men were happy. Several days later the *Daily Dispatch* published comments from an unnamed soldier in the Army of Tennessee who claimed that the soldiers were "in the finest of spirits," acquiring between five hundred and a thousand recruits every day, and destroying Sherman's vital rail lines with amazing rapidity. The observer acknowledged that the men were receiving little to eat but claimed the men all agreed that they would be happy "with a handful of corn every day if General Hood will only keep them going forward."[40]

Regular rations were in short supply, and the men tried to live off the land. Chaplain J. H. McNeill recalled that "the sorghum was just ripening through Georgia" and the men gathered the stalks, which "we found delicious to the taste," chewing up huge quantities and leaving a trail of chewed-up chaff along the road. Years later, H. K. Nelson asked his former comrades, who were with him on that march, "do you remember, boys, how we used to charge the sorghum patches and carry with us the stalks for that delicious juice" and "how we would climb the persimmon trees and eat the fruit thereof?" Even decades after the guns fell silent, Nelson still remembered how the sour persimmons made their mouths pucker like the "whistling school teacher."[41]

On October 1 Edgar Jones and the 18th Alabama Infantry attacked a Union supply depot at Calhoun, Georgia, northwest of Atlanta. Blue-jacketed guards fled rather than fight, and rebels destroyed the railroad tracks. Hungry and poorly clothed Confederate soldiers discovered large quantities of provisions in the Union warehouses. Confederate soldiers and civilians grabbed everything they could carry and beat a hasty retreat before Union forces could return with reinforcements. Jones and several of his friends were gleeful at the discovery of a large leather belt, which the men cut into patches to repair their worn-out shoes.[42]

As the men began their advance, the rain began to pour. E. H. Rennolds complained of the rain that fell "at long intervals, night and day." Hiram Williams, a northern man turned Alabamian, noted the heavy rains and remembered that that he had encountered similar downpours when the Army of Tennessee was in northwest Georgia the previous summer. He asked rhetorically, "I do wonder if it ever stops raining here?" James Lanning explained that the rain caused suffering even when it stopped because "there is no sun to dry" clothing and blankets, and as a result, the men were always damp and uncomfortable.[43]

Members of the Army of Tennessee also noted the hardships suffered by civilians. W. P. Chambers walked through the dead remnant of a once prosperous village near Lost Mountain, Georgia, roughly thirty miles northwest of Atlanta, where burned homes and abandoned fields made it "a desolate looking spot." The Union army were not the only men who tormented southern civilians. John Battle, an artilleryman from Georgia, informed his wife that the people he encountered "say they had as soon have the yanks among them as Wheeler's men, they destroy so much." Battle's letter indicates that the Confederate forces may have sometimes caused as much suffering to their own communities as the Union soldiers that opposed them.[44]

On October 3 General Stewart's Corps assaulted a Union garrison at Big Shanty, Georgia. According to Robert Smith of the 2nd Tennessee Infantry, Union troops had heard that Confederate forces were advancing on their position but were under the mistaken impression that it was only a raid by cavalry. Although the Federals were surprised to see Confederate infantry, "they fought very well." After a brief engagement, the rebels overwhelmed the men in blue, capturing 170 prisoners. Quartermaster Joel Murphree reported that the army captured large quantities of badly needed clothing and hats at Big Shanty.[45]

The end of the battle was not the end of the conflict near Big Shanty. Robert Smith of the 2nd Tennessee Infantry explained that the battle at Big Shanty "was the first time I ever saw a Negro soldier." With seeming indifference, Smith wrote, "our boys made short work of him and left him dead near the depot." Smith's diary indicates that the battle was over long before the Tennesseans encountered the man, and Smith gives no indication that the soldier resisted. Smith did not comment directly on how his comrades felt about the man's death, but he did note in the same paragraph that he "never saw the troops in as high spirits." Perhaps inspired by the sight of former slaves in Union uniforms, "the teamster Negroes" supervised by John Sparkman began resisting his authority and gave him "trouble."[46]

In between brief skirmishes, the Confederates destroyed Union rail lines. Confederate soldiers burned cross ties and melted rails, destroying more than fifteen miles of railroad in a few days. Samuel Foster gladly supervised the twisting of melted rails into shapes the men called "Old Mrs. Lincolns Hair pins." Sergeant John Sparkman reported that the men were very successful, destroying the entire thirty-mile rail line from Calhoun to Tunnel Hill, Georgia. Sparkman may have wished that the railroad was operational rather destroyed when his wagon train attempted to cross a narrow path near Rocky Face Ridge, Georgia, and "some wagons and teams fell down a high bank." He did not reveal if any men suffered death or injury as a result.[47]

Initially, it looked like Hood's plan was working. Just as Hood had hoped, General Sherman worried about the danger to his supply lines and sent troops chasing after the Army of Tennessee. Northern newspapers expressed surprise at Hood's rapid progress, calculating the amount of supplies needed to keep an army moving and correctly concluding that the Army of Tennessee was barely surviving on meager rations. Louisiana soldier Robert Patrick concluded, "I verily believe that Sherman has been out-witted." During the first few days of October, an erroneous rumor circulated through the Confederate camps that the Union army was retreating, and some of the men took it as proof that "one of Old Hood's promises is coming to pass already." On October 4, 1864, President Davis gave a speech to the citizens of Columbia, South Carolina, in which he claimed to bring "words of good cheer" from the Army of Tennessee, which Davis assured the crowd was strong, eager, and executing Hood's excellent plans. Davis claimed, "I see no chance for Sherman to escape."[48]

Battle at Allatoona

On October 5, French's Division including Sears's Brigade of Mississippians, Cockrell's Brigade of Missourians, and Ector's (also known as Young's) Brigade of Texans and North Carolinians, collectively totaling fewer than 2,800 men, approached Allatoona, Georgia, roughly forty miles northwest of Atlanta. The small village sat in a pass through the mountains of north

Allatoona Pass, Ga., looking south. George N. Bernard, photographer. Library of Congress.

Georgia along the Western and Atlanta Railroad and contained a large supply depot for the Union army. The rebel troops knew that the depot contained "a million rations, enough to feed a hundred thousand men for two months." Hungry scarecrows in gray salivated at the prospect of filling their bellies. Roughly, 3,000 Federal troops guarded the town from a network of trench lines and fortifications.[49]

Rebels surveyed the Union positions and did not like what they saw. Ephraim Anderson, of the 2nd Missouri Infantry, noticed that the approaches to the position were heavily forested, but the Federals had felled all the vegetation surrounding their fortifications for three hundred yards and left the materiel lying where it fell. This meant that the attackers would have to pick their way through heavy woods before emerging into tangles of rotting brush and trees, all of which would slow their progress and disrupt their organization. Union skirmishers occupied rifle pits scattered throughout the piles of brush. Beyond the tangles of brush, men in blue waited within two lines of reinforced trenches. Behind the trenches, three forts sat perched on the summit of the mountain where they could support each other with interlocking fields of fire that swept the countryside in every direction. Lieutenant Colonel R. H. Shotwell of the 35th Mississippi Infantry described the forts as strong positions "constructed and roofed with hewn logs." W. P. Chambers believed that the terrain itself was enough to make any assault difficult. The addition of well-crafted lines of trenches and forts ideally positioned on the high ground seemed impregnable. Robert Bevier of the 5th Missouri Infantry noticed that the Federal forts "stood out in bold relief" as the sun rose over the hills. He knew "there will be hot work if those regiments are made up of resolute men."[50]

Fighting broke out as the sun rose. Cowan's Mississippi Battery began shelling the Union works as soon as the sun provided enough light to see. While artillerymen worked the big guns, infantrymen added the crack of rifles to the thunder of artillery. Soon the countryside echoed with the sounds of battle. After a brief bombardment, General Samuel French ordered a cease-fire and sent a courier to the Federal lines, carrying a demand for immediate surrender. The rebels waited anxiously to discover if the Federals would surrender. When the courier carrying the demand for surrender returned to the rebel lines, a soldier called out, "is it surrender or fight?" The rider did not slow down as he replied tersely, "fight."[51]

The Confederates prepared for an assault. The brigades of French's Division deployed in a line of battle with Sears's Mississippians on the Confederate left, Ector's (also known as Young's) Texans and North Carolinians in the center, and Cockrell's Missourians on the right. The artillery would remain in place and provide covering fire as circumstances allowed.[52]

Battle of Allatoona Pass, October 5, 1864. Pencil, Chinese white, and black ink-wash drawing on green paper by Alfred R. Waud.

On the Confederate left, W. P. Chambers worried that it would be a hard fight, but an unidentified officer, probably to encourage the men, dismissively told the soldiers that the upcoming assault was nothing more than a "breakfast task." Chambers replied that anyone who wanted it was "welcome to my share of the breakfast." As the line of battle formed, Chambers recalled the verse 4 of the 23rd Psalm: "Yea, though I walk through the valley of the shadow of death, I will fear no evil: for thou art with me; thy rod and thy staff they comfort me." After meditating on the Psalm, he marched forward "with God's protecting mercy."[53]

These men knew what awaited them. Experience had long ago taught the battle-scarred veterans of the Army of Tennessee that "it is seldom that a well-fortified fort is ever taken." Since the Confederate and Union forces at Allatoona were of roughly the same size, the rebels confronted difficult odds.[54] The men knew that many of them would die in the next few minutes, but they prepared to advance anyway.

On the Confederate right, one company of the 5th Missouri Infantry discarded everything except their weapons and ammunition. Quickly, the rest of the 5th Missouri followed their example. The men loaded their weapons and listened as the bugles sounded the staccato notes that told the men to move forward.[55]

Mississippi infantryman R. N. Rea looked up towards Kennesaw Mountain in the distance, where the Federal Signal Corps flashed messages to the defenders of Allatoona. He later discovered that the signalers sent the famous message from Sherman, "hold the fort for I am coming," while he watched. Holding that fort would prove easier said than done as the Confederates began their attack.[56]

Rebel infantry surged forward against Allatoona, and the artillery opened fire. The 46th Mississippi Infantry charged down a hillside within sight of the enemy's position on the Confederate left. When the rebels arrived at the bottom of the hill, they quickly reformed their lines along the Western and Atlantic Railroad and moved forward again. While the infantry advanced, E. T. Eggleston and Cowan's Mississippi Battery kept up a heavy fire, sending 202 rounds of ammunition into Federal positions.[57]

As both Union and Confederate fire intensified, David Coleman, along with the rest of the 39th North Carolina and the 32nd Dismounted Texas Cavalry, formed a skirmish line and advanced on the Federal positions. Near the center of the Confederate line, Ezekiel Hampton and the 29th North Carolina Infantry advanced through timber while Federal troops poured a heavy fire into their disrupted ranks. The thick vegetation made it impossible to see more than a few yards, and the regiment lost contact with the other Confederate units.[58]

On the left end of the Confederate line, the 46th Mississippi Infantry reformed along the railroad tracks and surged ahead, climbing a steep hill. The rebels poured over the abatis. The obstacles slowed the attack, as the men from Mississippi spent precious moments clambering over the barriers, but the abatis also absorbed some of the hell that Union defenders unleashed towards their assailants.[59]

David Coleman, the rest of the 39th North Carolina, and the 32nd Dismounted Texas Cavalry "advanced rapidly." They took apparent joy in the attack, "cheering and firing briskly" as they moved forward. The rebels drove the Federal skirmishers into their works, where the northerners were "confused and undecided what to do."[60]

When the 29th North Carolina Infantry emerged from the thick forest, they discovered that their regiment was separated from the rest of the brigade and exposed to a heavy fire from the Federal defenders. The rebels were unsure of what to do, but they understood that standing still was suicide, so the regiment surged forward at a run, coming to within a few yards of the Union lines, where they flopped to the ground to catch their breath.[61]

On the Confederate right, Lieutenant Lamb led the 5th Missouri Infantry's skirmishers in a charge. The men in blue opened fire but failed to stop the determined Missourians. The 5th Missouri sent Federals running from their rifle pits and scrambling into their trenches to the rear, where the regrouped and got ready to make another stand against the Confederate onslaught.[62]

After a few minutes of rest, Ezekiel Hampton and the 29th North Carolina Infantry stood up and rushed into the Federal trenches near the Confederate center. Once in the ditches, the fighting descended into chaos. A primal battle of fists, rocks, swords, and clubs splattered trenches with blood and sent dying men crumpling to the feet of their assailants.[63]

For a moment, W. P. Chambers and his comrades thought that they might win a glorious victory that day. The Mississippians captured Federal skirmishers and took possession of the outer ring of trenches, but then the rebels cast their gaze farther up the hill. There was a small clearing filled with tents and, beyond that opening, another line of Federal trenches remained firmly in Union hands. The Federal troops who occupied the inner line did not give the southern men a single moment to rest, sending angry swarms of bullets down the hill while the southerners gathered priceless supplies. Lieutenant Colonel R. H. Shotwell later recalled that the Mississippians came under the fire of hundreds of Union soldiers armed "with sixteen-shot Henry rifles and about a half-dozen pieces of artillery."[64]

Lieutenant Lamb and the advanced guard of the 5th Missouri took shelter and caught their breath on the Confederate right. The rest of the brigade arrived minutes later, disorganized by their passage through the obstructions. Together once again, the Missourians surged ahead, capturing more Union positions and several prisoners. For a moment, the men in gray seemed unstoppable.[65]

The North Carolinians were making progress, although at a terrible cost. After killing or capturing all the Union soldiers in the outer line of trenches, Ezekiel Hampton and the remnants of the 29th North Carolina Infantry rushed towards the second line of Federal defenses. The Union defenders stood their ground and greeted the rebels with a hail of death.[66]

On the left end of the Confederate line, someone called out "the 46th goes ahead!" Once again praying for God's divine protection, W. P. Chambers leapt into the opening, waving his hat, taking the lead of twenty or thirty men, and echoing the call "the 46th goes ahead!" Now that the Confederates were in the open, the northern men showed no mercy, killing or wounding every member of the 46th Mississippi who charged ahead except W. P. Chambers and Lieutenant R. B. Henderson. The two unharmed survivors gave up the assault and fled downhill. A flurry of bullets smashed Chambers's rifle and tore a chunk out of his right forefinger. More bullets struck Henderson, who cried out in agony, "Brother Chambers I am gone!" Chambers refused to leave his brother in Christ behind and clasped his blood-streaked hands as the men fell to the ground together. While bullets whizzed all around, the two men prayed together until another round struck Henderson, tearing through his face, destroying his brain, and striking Chambers in the shoulder, disabling his arm. Chambers lay beneath his friend's corpse while Federal soldiers counterattacked, pouring bullets into the rebels who had remained in the first line of Union trenches. Chambers looked around for a weapon, spotted a bar of precious soap dropped by a Federal soldier and several "magazine rifles," probably sixteen-shot Henry rifles. When the shooting died down for a moment, Chambers fled down the hill without taking the soap, a rifle, or anything else except his own wounded body, somehow making back to Confederate lines without further injury.[67]

On the Confederate right, the Missourians of Cockrell's brigade moved forward. R. S. Bevier of the 5th Missouri explained, "our men were met with a murderous fire of all arms" in a battle that was "one of the bloodiest and most desperate of the war." When bullets failed to dislodge the Union soldiers, "our boys rushed upon them with the bayonet." For twenty minutes a brutal hand-to-hand fight swirled around the Confederate right. Somehow, the Federals stood their ground, and the Missourians withdrew in defeat down the hill. Ephraim Anderson remembered that, as they retreated, Lieutenant Gillespie swung his sword at a Federal solider, delivering a fearsome wound and breaking his sword. The wounded Yankee became a prisoner and joined Missourians on their retreat.[68]

In the center of the line, the rebels enjoyed more success than their comrades on either flank did. What was left of the 29th North Carolina Infantry was unable to force the men in blue from their second line of defensive positions, but they refused to give up the ground they had captured from the Federals and kept up a steady fire on their opponents. David Coleman, along with the rest of the 39th North Carolina and the 32nd Dismounted Texas Cavalry, fought nearby until 2:45 p.m., when General French ordered all of his men to withdraw. The men from North Carolina and Texas reluctantly obeyed.[69]

Union counterattacks drove the rebels from the supplies they had captured, and the Federals recaptured the materiel intact, even though the Confederate soldiers had time to destroy the booty. General French later claimed, "the matches furnished would not ignite, and no fire could be procured."[70] It strains credulity to believe that veteran soldiers who frequently made fires in difficult conditions were unable to start a blaze. It is possible that Confederate soldiers did not destroy the supplies either because they hoped they might recapture them later or because men who felt hunger pains could not bring themselves to destroy the life-giving resource they craved.

Robert Bevier and the survivors from the 5th Missouri Infantry gathered just out of range of Federal small arms, near where they formed their battle lines earlier in the day. The men were widely scattered and badly mauled, but the leaders of Cockrell's Missouri Brigade wanted to try again and were prepared for another assault. General French ordered his entire command, including the eager Missourians, to retreat. French had received erroneous reports that a large force of Union troops was advancing on his rear, threatening to cut his division off from the rest of the army. A northern newspaper told their readers that the battle at Allatoona was a great victory, since it prevented the hungry Army of Tennessee from acquiring desperately needed food and an excellent defensive position, which would have allowed them to repel large numbers of Union troops.[71]

The rebels paid a heavy price for their defeat at Allatoona. Roughly, 900 Confederates died or suffered wounds in the battle, more than 32 percent of the 2,800 rebels who participated. E. T. Eggleston was pleased that, even though "we were in an exposed position" and suffered damage to one of their caissons, "thanks to God" the men of the battery "escaped without a casualty to anyone." Other units were not so lucky. Lieutenant Colonel R. H. Shotwell described the assault as an "unfortunate" and "unwise" attack that was destined to fail. W. P. Chambers did not know the exact numbers for the entire division, but he was sure that the Confederate losses were "very heavy." Chambers's wound rescued him from the horrors that other men experienced during the rest of the campaign. He found his way to a field hospital, where the surgeons determined that the wound to his shoulder was serious enough to earn him a furlough. They sent him home to Mississippi to heal, the lone survivor among his friends who joined the Confederate army at Vicksburg in May 1862.[72]

When French's Division withdrew from Allatoona, they turned their attention towards the weaker garrison at Dalton, Georgia. Along the march, French's men tore up rail lines, "demolishing cars" and "destroying everything which could be of use to the Federal army." On October 10, E. H. Rennolds recorded in his diary that "all are in fine spirits, but marching begins to tell on most of us." When the army marched through Calhoun and Resaca, "the citizens are glad to see us," which made the soldiers "buoyant and hopeful." Wilson Howell and the 25th Alabama Infantry were startled when they stumbled across a deer along the road near Resaca. The men, delighted by the prospect of fresh venison, opened fire on the animal, but it made a successful retreat into the woods before any of the men could strike the target.[73]

Despite setbacks, some rebels believed they were winning. Samuel Foster claimed that on October 7 General Hood passed through a group of resting rebels and (incorrectly) told them that the Union army was "leaving Atlanta in a great hurry." In response, the men cheered, and Hood waved his hat in reply. Foster claimed that the Army of Tennessee was "running the Yanks out of the State of Ga. without a fight" and that "This army has done wonders!"[74] Foster was either indifferent to or unaware of the defeat at Allatoona.

Visiting the Battlefield of New Hope Church

In between Allatoona and Dalton, the rebels marched through the old battlefield of New Hope Church (fought May 25–26, 1864). John Sparkman of the 48th Tennessee Infantry described the area as desolate place where fences lay in disrepair and abandoned fields grew wild. Corn grew up in random places, sprouting from kernels that had passed through the fingers and the bowels of soldiers from both armies. Simple wooden markers identified the eternal resting place of "soldiers buried a long way from home." More men would have lain under the Georgia clay, but numerous bullets directed at human flesh struck wood, forcing trees to sacrifice their lives for the men who hid behind their trunks. Artilleryman E. T. Eggleston was startled by "acres of timber killed by minnie balls." Robert Smith observed, "three fourths of the trees between the two lines" were killed by "minnie balls, shot, and shell." He made no mention of Confederate losses, only claiming, "the invaders suffered very heavily." Alabamian J. P. Cannon painted a more clinical picture of the carnage. He recalled that the men were very interested in the old battlefield and found a hill where they could see the lines of battle clearly marked by "deadened timber from one-quarter to half-mile in width." Cannon had often heard men claim that it was odd how few men died in battle, despite the massive quantities of ammunition fired by both sides. After a quick glance at the terrain, Cannon concluded that it was because "the trees between the lines were literally torn to pieces on both sides." While many trees bore scars at roughly the same height as a man, "a large majority of them" suffered damage at ten to thirty feet above the ground "proving that most of us, under the excitement, aimed too high."[75]

The weather turned cold. Freezing rains drenched E. T. Eggleston and covered him with a heavy frost while he slept. James Lanning noted in his diary that, as the men moved northward, the weather was turning cold with "plenty of frost." He concluded, "we will need good blankets as we are moving toward a cold country." Joseph Boyce of the 1st Missouri Infantry noted that the men were suffering in the freezing rain because "we were without overcoats and shoes were very scarce."[76]

The Blockhouse Between Allatoona and Dalton

Between Allatoona and Dalton, French's Division encountered another Federal garrison. Roughly, two hundred Union troops occupied a strong position consisting of a sturdy blockhouse surrounded by trenches. The Union troops refused to surrender, even though they were vastly outnumbered, so Richard Harris and the rest of Lovelace's Battery opened fired on the Federals from about four hundred yards away, using explosive shells to kill several men in the trenches. Union troops replied with rifle fire that killed several rebels. After a half an hour of rapid fire, the Confederate artillerymen sent a shell through one of the firing slits in the blockhouse and it exploded inside, killing or wounding ten Union soldiers. As soon as the shell struck, a Union officer waved a white handkerchief in surrender, and the skirmish ended.[77]

With the fighting over, the ragged men in gray turned their attention to the newly captured supplies. Harris angrily explained that his battery did not get what he felt "we were really entitled to." He seemed to believe that his battery's artillery fire had been the primary cause of the Confederate victory and that, as a result, he and his comrades should have received the best of the provisions. Harris claimed that before the gunners could claim anything, General French appeared with his staff officers and "took the lion's share of everything." Next, the infantry swarmed over the remainder and took what they wanted. Only then did the men of Lovelace's Battery gain access to the goods that remained. While the artillerymen were last in line, the supply depot was so huge that the gunners still acquired large

Unidentified African American soldier in Union uniform with wife and two daughters. Library of Congress.

quantities of "great necessaries as well as the luxuries of life that we had not seen in a long time," including coffee and cigars. Union cavalrymen harassed the rebels as they carried away supplies but made little impact.[78]

The Conflict at Dalton

On October 13 the Army of Tennessee approached the Federal garrison at Dalton, Georgia, roughly ninety miles northwest of Atlanta. General Hood demanded that the Union garrison of one thousand men surrender. He promised that, if the garrison surrendered immediately, "all white officers and soldiers will be paroled in a few days." Even though black soldiers made up most of the garrison at Dalton, Hood specifically offered terms to the white soldiers and made no mention of the black men. Hood also gruesomely threatened that "if the place is carried by assault, no prisoners will be taken." William McLeod of the 7th Florida Infantry claimed that the rebels hoisted a flag of truce but that "it was not respected," although he did not specify exactly what he meant by "not respected." Because of the perceived disrespect, men from Finley's Brigade of Floridians received orders to advance. As the infantry moved forward, Confederate field guns opened on the Federals, sending shot and shell screaming into the ranks of blue-coated men, killing four and wounding several more. The Union commander raised a flag of truce "without the firing of a gun."[79]

While the Federal and Confederate commanders both agreed to the surrender, they disagreed over exact terms. The Federal commander at Dalton, Colonel Lewis Johnson, demanded humane treatment for all the men, both white and black, under his command. Hood refused, insisting that he "would return all slaves belonging to persons in the Confederacy to their masters." Johnson threatened that "the United States Government would retaliate." He was adamant, stating, "I surrendered the men as soldiers." Hood was unimpressed, lackadaisically suggesting that Johnson could "surrender them as whatever" but once they fell into Confederate hands, Hood would do as he pleased. Johnson was unhappy but ultimately decided that an unpleasant surrender was preferable to annihilation. The disagreement between Hood and Johnson was part of a larger struggle in which the Union demanded equal treatment for all prisoners regardless of race, while the Confederacy typically insisted on classifying all black men as rebelling slaves and their officers as the leaders of servile insurrection.[80]

With the terms decided, men in blue became prisoners to men in gray. The Army of Tennessee officially reported the capture of six hundred men from "2 negro regiments" and roughly two hundred men from three companies of white soldiers, along with "some horses and a number of quartermaster's, commissary, and ordnance stores." Surviving sources all agree that the Union soldiers offered little initial resistance but present radically different accounts of what happened next.[81]

Some Confederate soldiers claimed that Union troops of African descent were happy to become prisoners. Sam Watkins of the 1st Tennessee Infantry claimed that the men he identified as former slaves "were mighty glad to see us and we were kindly disposed to them." Watkins reported that white and black men happily worked together to destroy the railroad and fabricate evidence of a hotly contested battle.[82] Even if these memories are accurate, it is unclear if a desire for self-preservation or genuine dislike of the Union army, which often discriminated against racial minorities, motivated the black men.

The Federal commander at Dalton, Colonel Lewis Johnson, claimed that the Confederates mistreated him and his men. He argued, "the treatment of the officers of my regiment exceeded anything in brutality I have ever witnessed." Johnson explained that the General William Bate began by "heaping insults upon me and my officers." Bate also instructed his men to steal shoes from the black prisoners. The Confederate soldiers ordered their now barefooted black prisoners to tear up the railroad tracks. When one man refused, he "was shot on the spot." The rebels murdered five more prisoners because they were sick and unable to keep up with the rapid pace of the march. Johnson watched helplessly as the Confederate authorities returned escaped slaves to their former owners. When the Federal commander argued that the rebels should treat free black men from Ohio and Indiana as prisoners even if the rebels forced former slaves back into bondage, Confederate officers ignored his pleas. Along the march, rebel soldiers repeatedly assaulted the prisoners, who only survived because a handful of Confederates defended the Federals.[83]

Confederate sources mostly confirm the Federal stories of mistreated prisoners near Dalton. Edgar Jones recalled, "the boys were anxious to massacre these fellows and the officers had a hard time to keep the men from falling on them." Unsurprisingly, "the negroes were greatly excited and alarmed." Jones claimed, "the officers commanding these coons looked ashamed of it." Jones believed that the soldiers were all former slaves "as far as I could ascertain" and recalled that after "disposing of these fellows we turned our faces towards Alabama." E. H. Rennolds claimed, "the Negroes were very insolent." Alabamian J. P. Cannon indicated that the prisoners seemed eager to escape and that, as a result, "we marched them all night to prevent their recapture" and handed them over to the army's provost guards near Snake Creek Gap. H. K. Nelson remembered that the men "had a picnic," gorging themselves on goodies captured at Dalton, and

Unidentified Confederate soldier wearing a knapsack. Library of Congress.

forced the "negroes" to "carry our knapsacks." Florida infantryman Archie Livingston told his brother that all of the "negroes were soon made shoeless" by Confederate soldiers who wanted the footgear for themselves or simply sought to punish their enemies. James Lanning and the 25th Alabama Infantry watched as the prisoners passed them on the road. A prisoner called out to the rebels that "he was as good as any of them and had as much authority" and punctuated his claim "with an oath." Lanning gave no indication how the Confederate soldiers reacted.[84]

Florida soldier Henry Reddick reported nothing about racial conflict at Dalton in his postwar account. He was happy to get new shoes taken from the Federal prisoners. Reddick was disappointed that the shoes were "all number elevens" and were therefore "too big for us," but ill-fitting shoes were superior to bare feet, so "we wore them just the same."[85] This anecdote raises as many questions as it answers. Why did an entire unit of Union soldiers all have size eleven shoes? Did they all have feet the same size, or were they too victims of the oddities of military supply networks? Perhaps after several decades, Reddick misremembered the details of the incident.

The Army of Tennessee Continues the Advance

Federal units pursued the rebels. The Confederate army moved westward, trying to put the Coosa River between them and their assailants. In the rush, some units crossed the river before the pontoon bridge arrived. The 27th Mississippi came to the riverbank and received orders to strip off everything below their waists, so they could wade across without damaging their clothing. Just as the men were about to enter the water, two women in a buggy appeared and viewed Johnson's entire division naked from the waist down. The men responded with a "whoop that went up along the lines" that "could have been heard fully one mile." Once a pontoon bridge was constructed, the army still struggled to cross because the falling river and strong drift broke the bridge. In contrast to the humor and frustration of other accounts, Robert Smith of the 2nd Tennessee Infantry recorded in his diary that "one of the grandest sights to be seen on a march is an army crossing a river." He explained that the crossing was even more beautiful because "several pretty young ladies" watched from the riverbank. It is not clear if they were the same women who saw the almost naked men of Johnson's Division and might have returned for a second look. Smith was happy to claim, "the majority of the citizens in this country are true to our cause" and "all seem overjoyed at our return."[86]

While the infantry crossed the Coosa River, William Sloan and the 5th Tennessee Cavalry captured a small supply depot at Tunnel Hill, Georgia, acquiring desperately needed overcoats. The coats were warm, but their blue color meant that the men would have to dye them as soon as possible to ensure that confused friends did not shoot them and enraged enemies did not execute them as spies. Sloan regarded the dying process as an easy enough chore since "nearly all of our southern women have learned to dye the blue Yankee clothing for our soldiers and they make it a very pretty brown color." The *Daily Ohio Statesmen* claimed that Federal troops abandoned Tunnel Hill as they consolidated their forces, indicating that Sloan's new overcoat may have been more of a find than a capture.[87]

Many Confederate soldiers enjoyed increasingly high morale during the October offensive. William Hardy, a staff officer in Cheatham's Corps, told his wife that the campaign was a "complete success." General Hood reported that the flood of desertions from the Army of Tennessee had dried up. As far away as Texas, Confederate journalists reported that the Army of Tennessee's morale was high and men were flocking to the colors. John Battle, an artilleryman from Georgia, predicted that the destruction of Federal supply lines would soon force Sherman's army to abandon Atlanta. James Lanning noted in his diary that "the boys all appear to be in high spirits now that the Yanks are retreating" and that the men even "hoped that peace will now soon be made." Texas cavalryman Samuel Foster claimed, "the whole army is in high spirits," and described the campaign as "fun" and a "frolic." Foster believed that the whole army shared his belief that "Jeff

Davis and Hood made a ten strike, when they planned this thing." Archie Livingston told his mother, "we are in good spirits and hope to accomplish much" as the army moved forward with "no straggling at all." A journalist in South Carolina reported that civilians and soldiers were all "fantastic with delight" and convinced that the Army of Tennessee would soon recapture Kentucky. Samuel Vann predicted "the hardest of this campaign is over."[88]

The campaign was going reasonably well, but many men still suffered. R. H. Shotwell explained that the men of his regiment, the 35th Mississippi Infantry, were so worn out by rapid marches that they started referring to themselves as "Hood's Cavalry" and responding to orders to hurry with "unchristian replies." E. H. Rennolds recalled that, when the 5th Tennessee passed through Lafayette, Georgia, roughly a hundred miles northwest of Atlanta, they discovered that "the town has been ruined by the Yankees." While the Union troops were gone, other dangers lurked nearby, and "flankers have to be placed to watch for bushwhackers." The men lived off "sorghum, potatoes, [and] apples" collected along the line roadsides, but it "was an awful hard march." Rennolds's company brought up the rear of Cheatham's Corps and found themselves "arresting a stream of stragglers and pilferers." Mumford Dixon and the 3rd Confederate Infantry guarded wagon trains from the bushwhackers and thieves who gobbled up unguarded provisions. James Lanning suffered from old injuries to his ankle and knee along the march, and he even sold a spare shirt for two dollars and a pair of pants for five dollars because "I could not carry them." His thoughts also focused on home: "if there is a place of happiness on Earth; if there is Comfort or pleasure here; that place is home—where the smiles of his dear loved ones are all his own." While he longed to go home to his family, he wrote, "I fear it will be a long time before I see them again." Angus McDermid informed his mother that he fainted from lack of food on the march from Dalton. Wilson Howell became sick along the march, but his case was hardly unique since "we had been all sick without any vegetable diet and what was known in the army as 'scurvy' that it had presided my whole system and while in this condition I don't think I had an hours sleep." His condition became so severe that the doctors sent him home to recover, which he never did, suffering from stomach problems for the rest of his life.[89]

The lack of good shoes caused increasing problems for the soldiers. The feet of most men were "nearly worn out." John Crittenden had shoes, but they may have done more harm than good since "the tops of my toes rubbed until they bled." Chaplain Thomas Deavenport watched an unidentified captain command a regiment in bare feet." Robert Jarman explained that barefoot men of the 27th Mississippi received raw beef hides from freshly slaughtered cattle and instructions to fashion the stinking skins into crude moccasins. The improvisation worked surprisingly well, for a few hours, after which the skins became hard and dry. At that point, the men threw them away until more freshly killed cattle provided them with a new pair.[90]

On Sunday, October 16, the Army of Tennessee stood near the border between Georgia and Alabama. Hood ordered the men to halt and prepare to defend themselves from nearby Union forces. Despite Hood's willingness to fight, most of his army's high command hesitated, and as a result, Hood ordered the army to move west into Alabama, planning to cross the Tennessee River at Guntersville, Alabama. Most of Wheeler's cavalry remained in Georgia to harass Sherman's forces. General William "Red" Jackson's division of cavalry would provide the army's only mounted support until Forrest's troopers could conclude their raid in Tennessee and join the Army of Tennessee somewhere in Alabama. Union forces did not pursue the rebels, and "the armies of Hood and Sherman separated as if by mutual consent."[91]

Chaplain Thomas Deavenport watched gray-clad masses leave Georgia, describing "the poor soldier as he toils on, sustained by the hope of better days and by the love he bears for those far away." He lamented the pain that these men had suffered, as well as the pain that they had caused to their friends and foes. The minister told his reader, "I cannot give the history of this campaign language to describe its suffering." Contemplating everything that the simple soldiers of the Army of Tennessee had endured, he concluded, "such men will not be conquered."[92]

3 "EVERYTHING LOOKS LIKE DESOLATION"

Fighting in Alabama

> Bettie I have undergone many hardships since I left home, I have traveled through a great deal of country. I saw some of the poorest country that I ever saw. I had no idea that there was as much poor land in North Alabama. When we got in the vicinity of the Tennessee River it was the reverse I saw there some of the richest land I have ever seen, and more of it. In some places the whole fall of the earth was cleared up I have seen some of the most handsome residences I ever saw. None of that country scarcely cultivated. Everything looks like desolation.[1]
>
> —John Crittenden, 34th Alabama Infantry

The Army of Tennessee Enters Alabama

Shuffling men in gray crossed into Cherokee County, Alabama, on October 18, 1864. The weather was cold, chilling men in threadbare rags to their core. The rocky hills of northeastern Alabama were a poor country with little to sustain the men. Rations became scarce. Men got desperate, losing what little restraint they might have enjoyed under more pleasant circumstances. They stole with little hesitation and consumed every vaguely edible thing they encountered. Hungry men suffered even more when they ran out of the tobacco they loved even more than food or warmth. In spite of the suffering, there was little time to rest. Officers pushed their men forward at an exhausting pace.[2]

The march into Alabama posed a difficult problem for Federal commanders. On October 20, General Sherman informed General George "The Rock of Chickamauga" Thomas that "to pursue Hood is folly, for he can twist and turn like a fox and wear out any army in pursuit." Sherman also rejected a static defense against the Confederate forces since "to continue to occupy long lines of railroads simply exposes our small detachments to be picked up in detail." Consistent with Sherman's typical love of the offensive, he ordered General Thomas to help him fight a war of maneuver. Sherman would lead a force south from Atlanta, while Thomas would command forces in Tennessee, Kentucky, Mississippi, and Alabama. If Hood followed Sherman, Thomas would pursue the rebels and strike them in the rear. If Hood launched an offensive northward, Thomas should "act defensively on the line of the Tennessee" and "hold Chattanooga and Decatur." Thomas had a mobile force of roughly 22,000 infantrymen, some artillery, and 4,300 cavalry troopers. He could also call on numerous small detachments guarding strategic locations across the region. Sherman warned his subordinates that Hood "is eccentric, and I cannot guess his movements as I could those of Johnston who was a sensible man and only did sensible things."[3]

The rebels were surprised and confused by what they found in Alabama. Joel Murphree of Troy, Alabama, south of Montgomery, explained, "we never know where we are going." In a letter to his wife, Newton Davis, from Pickens County in central Alabama, described the march as a "long and tedious" trek over mountains punctuated by swamps and streams. He expressed frustration at navigating unfamiliar terrain where "no one knew where we were going." John Crittenden expressed shock that north Alabama contained some of "the poorest country that I ever saw," where "everything looks like desolation." He informed his wife, "I had no idea that there was as much poor land in Alabama." Clearly, the scruffy hills of the northern part of Alabama bore little resemblance to the rich, flat river valleys in the center of the state, which he called home.[4]

It might seem odd that Alabamians were completely disoriented while traveling through their home state, but an examination of regimental histories makes it clear that the confusion suffered by Davis, Murphree, and Crittenden was probably not unique. During this campaign, the Army of Tennessee contained roughly 294 companies and batteries from Alabama, but most of these units drew their membership from areas far from the army's line of march. During the Civil War, almost all units were highly localized organizations, drawing most of their members from small geographic areas in which friends and neighbors served together. Alabama, like all states, was not a single community but rather a collection of regions that shared little more than a state government. Of the Army of Tennessee's 294 batteries and companies from Alabama on this campaign, only 48, or roughly 16 percent, came from the eight counties along the army's line of march.[5] The remainder came from other areas, mostly the central part of the state, which was far more devoted to the Confederate cause than the northern areas, where many Alabamians remained loyal to the Union. Therefore, it should come as no surprise that many of the Alabamians in the army were completely unfamiliar with the northern portion of their home state.

Confederate soldiers found time for humor along the march. Edgar Jones, a corporal from central Alabama, explained that, when the men discovered that they were headed towards Gadsden, the town's name took on a sudden importance and became the laughing refrain on the lips of countless tired soldiers, who repeatedly asked each other, "how far is it to Gadsden?" When General French saw the slow progress made by the footsore men sleeping in the road, he swore at them in an attempt to speed their march. In response, an unidentified soldier exclaimed, "O Sammy, keep your shirt on; don't burn up your shirt." French became enraged and offered fifty dollars to anyone who would identify the solider. The men responded with laughter, and the frustrated general rode away in a huff.[6]

Near Gadsden, the men enjoyed a brief period of rest and resupply on October 20 and 21. Most men were exhausted and grateful for the rest. Others were more hungry than tired and fanned out into the countryside to gather up anything edible that did not shoot back. Joel Murphree was surprised to receive mail since "mail facilities are very irregular in this section of the country." Barefooted men who had been home recuperating from illnesses and wounds caught up with the army, often posing supply problems that undercut their value as reinforcements. Quartermaster John Sparkman explained that nearly 20 percent of the men in the Army of Tennessee were barefooted when they arrived in Gadsden, but most received shoes during their brief rest near the town. Angus McDermid was not one of the fortunate recipients. He told his father, "I haint got a sine of a shoe on my foot no I dont no when I will hav."[7]

John Crittenden was one of the men who rejoined the Army of Tennessee near Gadsden. During the Battle of Ezra Church, near Atlanta, Georgia, John Crittenden suffered a severe wound to his thigh on July 28, 1864. The injury was undoubtedly painful, but his suffering was probably eased by the fact that the army sent him home to heal. Based on subsequent letters and the fact that John and his wife conceived their third child during the furlough, the homecoming was probably an enjoyable one for the wounded veteran.[8] As his leg healed, the thirty-year-old Confederate soldier was at a crossroads. He could have remained home. His brother was back on the farm with a medical discharge. It might have been easy for John Crittenden to stay with his family, claiming that his wound made strenuous activity impossible, even if the claim was fraudulent. Thousands of men in his position were sent home to recuperate and never returned to the army, but Crittenden was not one of those men, and he made what was probably a tearful farewell to his wife.

Crittenden's return to the Confederate army was difficult. On October 15, Crittenden wrote his wife from a camp near Jacksonville, Alabama, where he joined other convalescents returning to the army. In an incident that was probably common among hungry soldiers, Crittenden explained that he ate all of the potatoes and butter in the care package he was supposed to deliver to John Bryant, a soldier in his unit, on behalf of the man's family. In an effort to make amends, he told his wife to tell Bryant's family that he would pay for the missing provisions. Crittenden explained that he would have saved some of the food for his brother-in-law but that "I may not see him in a month." The hike to the camp had been difficult since "the tops of my toes rubbed until they bled." Once in camp, he learned that Union forces were nearby and had routed a Confederate cavalry force, placing the returning soldiers in mortal danger as they tried to rejoin the army. To combat the Union forces within the state, Confederate officers forced some convalescents assembling in the Jacksonville camp to abandon their quest to return to their units, formed them into new regiments, and sent them against the nearby Federals. Like many men, Crittenden was happy to fight, but he retained a strong sense of loyalty to his home regiment. He preferred to fight alongside his friends and trusted comrades, rather than strangers. On at least one occasion, he hid in the woods to avoid both the Union soldiers who would have killed him and the Confederate officers who would have prevented him from returning to his regiment. Even though he had left his wife only a few days before, he was already eager to return, explaining, "I would like to be at home so much."[9]

Near Gadsden, Edgar Jones sought a rare opportunity to visit a family member. Although he was from Jefferson County, which lay some distance to the south of the army's line of march, the corporal's sister lived just across the Coosa River, which paralleled the army's route. His commander provided him with a twenty-four-hour pass and ordered him to take his rifle and ammunition but to leave his blanket with his comrades. If Jones thought he would not need the rifle within the confines of his home state, his recollections gave no indication that he had such a feeling, and his travels quickly proved the value of retaining the weapon. When barely out of sight of the army, Jones found the roads clogged with civilians and Confederate cavalrymen on the run from Union troops. Jones was in his home state, but the chaos of war made it impossible for him to visit his family and transformed what might have been a leisurely furlough into a desperate bid to stay one step ahead of enemy soldiers. Jones gave up on seeing his sister, but he had nothing to eat, and he was separated from the army. Therefore,

"A Deserter." Pencil drawing on blue paper by Alfred R. Waud. Library of Congress.

Jones joined other men trying to return to the army. Every member of the ersatz band expressed a desire to carry Jones's rifle. The weapon provided a semblance of security from Federal troops and allowed the hungry men to kill farm animals they discovered. Eventually he returned to his regiment safely, but Jones's experience of trying to stay one step of ahead of deadly foes while in his home state was probably not unique. Other soldiers reported that the Confederate army marched under the constant threat of assault by Union cavalry.[10]

By 1864 the once peaceful hills and valleys of north Alabama had become the scene of a vicious guerrilla war. John Wyeth, a Confederate cavalryman from Marshall County, Alabama, explained that, by early 1864, his home county had become a war zone filled with regular soldiers from Union and Confederate armies as well as bands of "Tory marauders." General Gideon Pillow, working to obtain manpower for the Confederate army, estimated that north Alabama was home to between eight thousand and ten thousand deserters. Pillow claimed that most of the deserters had remained with the army only long enough to steal arms and ammunition before returning to the hills, where they formed groups that were as dangerous as "copperheads" and were "so formidable in numbers and so thoroughly armed and organized" that they essentially controlled the region. Early in 1864 a coalition of Alabama's leaders pleaded for General Joseph Wheeler's assistance, detailing a long list of violent acts committed by Unionist guerillas in Marion, Walker, and Winston counties in the northern part of the state and predicting that, if the army failed to take immediate action, "civil war in its worst forms of conflagration and murder will sweep over this county." In retrospect, this seems like an odd warning, considering the nation had been embroiled in Civil War for nearly three full years at that point. The unpredictable violence in Alabama endangered Union troops as well. Members of the 72nd Indiana Infantry dared not straggle from their line of march across Alabama since "the country was full of bushwhackers."[11]

The line between regular soldier and guerilla was often blurry. Alabamians loyal to the federal government often provided Union forces with scouts, spies, and auxiliary troops during their campaigns in Alabama. Albert Goodloe of the 35th Alabama Infantry explained that "bootlickers for Abraham Lincoln" kept a sharp eye out for Confederate forces and eagerly reported their findings to nearby Union garrisons. Confederate infantryman Risenar Etter believed the people of north Alabama were "of union sentiments." Union general Dodge reported in April 1864 that the mountains of north Alabama were controlled by bands of Unionist irregulars who were led by members of the 1st Alabama Union Cavalry Regiment, detached for duty with the partisans. Dodge's comments described men like George Ridge, a Jackson County farmer turned Union solider, who returned home to Alabama after Confederates murdered his father and brother during a political dispute in early 1864. Ridge became the leader of a band of Unionist guerrillas in north Alabama and spent the rest of war doing everything in his considerable power to make life hard for Confederates in north Alabama.[12]

The Confederate Army of Tennessee took the danger posed by Unionist guerillas seriously as it passed through Alabama. Officers enforced orders against straggling with unusual strictness. Samuel Kelley feared for his life and referred to the region as filled with "Tories and bush whackers." Mississippian G. W. Higgins informed his wife that, even though he suffered from hemorrhoids, he kept moving since "I have been compelled to march or be captured." John Porcher and three of his comrades wanted to return to their regiment after a brief period on detached duty, but they waited near Florence, Alabama, for heavily armed mail carriers to arrive, because local citizens told them that bushwhackers in the area would kill the small band of rebels if they continued on their own. Alabama infantryman Daniel Smith explained that "the mountaineers were mostly Union men, and showed no mercy to stragglers, either killing them outright or horribly maltreating them."[13]

Resuming the line of march after their brief rest near Gadsden, the Confederate Army of Tennessee moved west. Edwin Rennolds was pleased that his regiment was in the lead since "we had first chance at the luxuries of the country" and they "fared sumptuously." Members of the 6th Alabama Cavalry replaced their worn out horses with new ones stolen from Alabamians loyal to the Union. John Crittenden explained in a letter home that the area west of Gadsden was "the wildest looking country" of steep hills and small valleys. James Maxwell made similar observations, referring to the area as "piney woods" crossed by narrow, muddy roads that the men traversed with extreme difficulty. Thomas Roane of the 51st Tennessee Infantry reported, "we are doing the finest marching I ever saw from 15 to 20 miles a day with ease although many of the men are barefoot and their feet raw and blistered."[14]

A Confederate artilleryman identified only as "F. B." crossed the roads with more difficulty than most of his comrades. He had shoes when he began the march across Alabama, but they were in such poor condition that he considered them nothing more than an "aggravation." Holes in his shoes let sharp rocks slip in that caused pain until he stopped to clean out his shoes, only to repeat the process moments later. He struggled along until he stopped to help push a cannon out of a deep rut and lost a shoe to the mud. He resumed his march with one foot encased by a shoe and another barefoot until he realized that his foot without a shoe handled the mud far better than his foot still encased in the remnants of a once-proud shoe. The rebel artillerymen bid his one remaining shoe adieu and marched the next several miles in a much happier condition. F. B. would have happily marched all the way to Tennessee shoeless, but the soft mud, which initially felt nice, quickly gave way to jagged rocks, which did not feel nice at all. In horrible pain, F. B. acquired a set of moccasins made from the still bloody hide of a recently slaughtered cow. F. B. recalled the *Leather Stocking Tales* he read as a young boy and imagined himself the hero of some new epic. That night he slept the sleep of a contented soul, but when he awoke, he discovered that yesterday's comfortable moccasins had dried into constricting torture devices. In a rage, F. B. cut the worthless moccasins off his feet and condemned Cooper as a "fraud" for endorsing moccasins.[15] In fairness to Cooper, well-tanned and carefully constructed moccasins can be quite comfortable and bear little resemblance to the crudely improvised footgear F. B. and many other rebels wore along the march.

The Army of Tennessee arrived at Guntersville, Alabama, roughly one hundred miles west of Atlanta, on October 22, 1864, and prepared to cross the Tennessee River. While camped on the river bank, Hood learned that General Forrest and his cavalry were delayed in west Tennessee and unable to rendezvous with the army at Guntersville. As a result, Hood changed his plans, sending word for Forrest to join him on the south bank of the

Tennessee some distance to the west. The presence of a large number of determined Federal defenders with gunboat support probably played a role in dissuading the aggressive commander. Sherman claimed that Hood did not attempt to cross at Guntersville because Union forces in the area would have destroyed him as he crossed the river. W. J. McDill of the 9th Tennessee Infantry and many other soldiers felt surprise when Hood ordered the army to continue moving westward without crossing the river. Evidently, Hood did not explain his change of plans to the troops. In a self-deprecating reference to their monthly pay, McDill referred to his comrades and himself as "eleven-dollar generals" and suggested that questions of strategy were beyond his pay grade. Whatever the reason for Hood's change of plans, he set his sights on Decatur, Alabama, roughly fifty miles northwest from Guntersville, as the next location for a potential crossing.[16]

Decatur, Alabama, was one of the most strategically significant cities in the region. It stood at the intersection of major roads including Somerville Road running southeast, Courtland Road leading west, and the Moulton Road running to the southwest. The Decatur Road ran through the city, connecting it with Nashville to the north and central Alabama to the south. The intersection of the Tennessee and Alabama railroad running south from Nashville and the Memphis and Charleston railroad running east to west across the state had made Decatur one of the most vital rail connection points in the state, at least until Federal troops destroyed the railroad bridge across the river. Far more importantly for the rebels marching west, Decatur stood on the banks of the Tennessee River, with an established pontoon bridge across the chilly waters. Hood believed he could capture Decatur "without serious loss."[17]

The Confederate Army of Tennessee approached Decatur from the east. Stewart's and most of Cheatham's Corps took the lead in light marching order, carrying nothing except weapons, ammunition, haversacks, and canteens. Lee's Corps trailed behind in reserve. Since speed was less important to Lee's men, they marched in heavy marching order, carrying everything they owned, including blankets. A lucky few even had tents. A pontoon bridge accompanied each corps. Vaughn's Brigade of Tennesseans in Brown's Division of Cheatham's Corps briefly left the rest of the army to rendezvous with supply wagons near Blountsville, Alabama, to the south and escort them to a reunion with the rest of the army near Decatur. Not long after the rendezvous, G. W. Gordon of the 11th Tennessee Infantry watched a drunken colonel stumble in a mud hole that was about two feet wide and six inches deep. The inebriated officer wanted to ensure that nobody else suffered a similar fate, so he ordered a soldier to stand beside the hole and warn everyone to avoid it. Veteran soldiers who made a habit of plunging through icy waters and charging through walls of bullets laughed uproariously at the drunken colonel's worries and the shrugging soldier's dire warnings to avoid a six-inch-deep mud hole.[18]

The Army of Tennessee arrived near Decatur on October 26, completing a march of 135 miles in little more than a week since they crossed into Alabama. As the Confederates neared the town, supplies of food failed to keep pace, and men once again faced shortages. Elbridge Littlejohn informed his wife that "we have suffered more for the want of something on this campaign than on any previous one" but "I don't mind to do without when I know it can't be had or that the generals are doing without." General French earned Littlejohn's respect as the general sat by the roadside, gnawing on hickory nuts like a common solider. Daniel Smith recalled that near Decatur the men received no rations of bread or vegetables and only minimal quantities of beef. Thomas Warrick reported that men subsisted on half rations and lived for days on nothing more than parched corn. Members of the 3rd Florida Infantry subsisted on a few ears of corn roasted in the ashes of their campfires. Georgian Walter Clark reported that the men received meager rations of two ears of corn each. Hungry men in the 33rd Alabama Infantry jokingly encouraged their commissary sergeant to throw away his scales since they were convinced he would soon run out of things to weigh.[19]

Chaplain James McNeill and his comrades found innovative solutions to the lack of meat. He and his messmates each kept a single piece of pork that they used as seasoning when they boiled the black-eyed peas that composed most of their diet. Eventually the desire for protein overwhelmed the pastor, and he ate the tiny bit of pork that repeated cooking had turned into something the size and color of a lump of coal. The taste did not satisfy, and McNeill recalled, "I might as well have swallowed my dish rag."[20]

While many men begged civilians for food or became simple thieves, Edgar Jones and some of his friends slipped away from the army as they passed a particularly prosperous farm. The soldiers told the farmer that their general sent them to prevent hungry soldiers from stealing any of his property. With a broad smile, the farmer welcomed the soldiers, providing them with a place at his dinner table and a comfortable place to sleep. When the farmer retired to bed, the soldiers quietly stripped the house, barn, and smokehouse of supplies and returned to their camp. In the morning, the farmer discovered the theft and immediately traveled to the army's camp, found a general, and demanded a harsh penalty for the thieves. The general agreed to punish the culprits, if the farmer could identify them. The farmer could not pick out the guilty men, and the army resumed the march. Jones recalled that the army passed by while "the old man stood looking as if he could never again trust a soldier."[21]

The Battle of Decatur Begins, October 26, 1864

On October 26 the Army of Tennessee arrived on the outskirts of Decatur, Alabama. General Hood hoped to lead his troops across the Tennessee River at Decatur, but instead of a welcoming bridge across the river, the Confederates encountered a determined Union garrison with no intention of surrendering the strategic location. Charles C. Doolittle of the 18th Michigan Infantry was temporarily in command, while General Robert Granger was a few miles north in Athens, Alabama. Most of Decatur's residents had abandoned the town or been forced out by the Union army, but an eclectic collection of three thousand defenders from Ohio, Michigan, Indiana, and Wisconsin, along with Tennesseans loyal to the federal government, guarded the town, the river crossing, and large quantities of supplies. The Federals occupied a line of breastworks roughly one mile long, looping around the town and anchored on both ends against the Tennessee River. Scattered rifle pits provided additional cover for the defenders. Two well-constructed forts strengthened the lines. The forts and breastworks bristled with seventeen cannons. The defenses to the south and west were particularly strong, protected with ditches and abatis, but the eastern flank lacked such improvements and was therefore weaker. With a long and mostly level plain extending for about a thousand yards in front of the Federal positions in every direction, the men in blue enjoyed excellent fields of fire. Four Union gunboats patrolled the Tennessee River near Decatur, adding the weight of their artillery to the defense and making it nearly impossible for the Confederates to cross the Tennessee River without neutralizing the garrison first.[22]

On the morning of October 26 Colonel Doolittle sent two parties of fifty mounted scouts down the Somerville and Courtland Roads in search of the rebel army. Members of the 10th Indiana Cavalry, a green regiment that only received its horses the day before, quickly returned, claiming that they encountered the Army of Tennessee three miles down the Somerville Road. Doolittle hoped that the inexperienced scouts were mistaken. Perhaps the rebels advancing on Decatur were nothing more than a band of irregular Confederate cavalry. Doolittle decided to verify the troopers' findings personally. He mounted a horse and galloped out of town towards the location of the reported sighting. He did not get far. When barely outside the Union works, Doolittle saw five thousand Confederate infantrymen transitioning from columns into lines of battle and sending out a screen of skirmishers. In an instant, Doolittle knew that the Army of Tennessee would soon collide with his tiny garrison. He ordered men from 2nd Tennessee Union Cavalry to delay the rebels while he alerted the remainder of his command.[23]

Albert Goodloe of the 35th Alabama Infantry waded across Flint Creek south of town and began skirmishing with Federal cavalrymen, probably members of the 10th Indiana Cavalry on their initial scouting foray. The Alabamians lured the blue-coated equestrians into an ambush and "would have effectually ruined them had not about half our guns failed to fire from having been rained on so much." As the surviving cavalrymen fled for their lives, the rebels found the sudden turn of fortunes "ludicrous," and Goodloe reported, "we could not but yell them on with hearty bursts of laughter."[24]

Following Doolittle's orders, members of the 2nd Tennessee Union Cavalry sallied forth to delay the rebel advance. The Tennesseans rushed forward on horseback and opened an intense firefight with Confederate infantry as soon as they saw the men in gray. Confederate infantrymen brushed aside Federal cavalrymen, formed a skirmish line, marched to within four hundred yards of the Federal positions around Decatur, and lay down to await further orders. Alexander Spence of the 1st Arkansas Infantry realized that the Federals at Decatur were "strongly fortified and in considerable force." Isaac Shannon, a member of the 9th Tennessee Infantry detached for duty as sharpshooter and equipped with a highly accurate Whitworth Rifle, noticed a high hill commanding the otherwise level plain. He approached division commander General John C. Brown, who was preparing his men for an assault, and suggested that a team of skirmishers on the high ground might help with the attack. Brown agreed, and Shannon led a group of rebels up the rise.[25]

Tennesseans loyal to the Union bought precious time for the Union garrison, but they could not last long against overwhelming numbers. Doolittle tried to strengthen his main lines by ordering every available man of the garrison into the trenches and ordering them to hold at all costs. Confederate couriers carrying a call for surrender approached Decatur under white flags. A weaker man might have been tempted by the offer. Doolittle knew that he faced terrible odds. He had barely three thousand men to confront a mighty army. If Doolittle was tempted to surrender, he never admitted it. He refused to meet with the Confederate couriers or even acknowledge their demand. The rebels would have to pry Decatur from Doolittle's cold, dead hands.[26]

At 1:30 p.m. the Confederate infantry launched a determined assault on the Union breastworks east of town. Members of the 2nd Tennessee Union Cavalry continued to fight a delaying action, but they were horribly outnumbered and on the verge of collapse. Reinforcements arrived just in time. Battery A of the 1st Tennessee Union Light Artillery galloped up to the line and took up position in a small redoubt overlooking the Somerville Road. The gunners in blue from Tennessee quickly opened fire on the advancing men in gray from Tennessee. L. Jackson Sanders of the 30th Tennessee Infantry looked on helplessly as a single, well-placed shell removed the limbs of three of his comrades. The big guns pushed the rebels back and gave the blue-coated cavalry a much-needed boost of confidence. The horsemen reformed their lines and stood their ground.[27]

Members of Stewart's Corps shifted around the Federal positions and tried to break the Union lines due south of town. W. O. Sowell and the rest of the 35th Alabama Infantry charged forward and ran into Federal infantrymen taking cover in a grove of trees surrounding a house. The Alabamians charged through the trees, clambering over fences and pushing the Federals off the house's porch.[28]

Isaac Shannon and other skirmishers of the 9th Tennessee Infantry opened fire on the Union lines from their hilltop perch overlooking Decatur from the east. Blue-clad gunners of the 1st Tennessee Union Light Artillery responded with rapid bursts of cannon fire that veered in every direction, as if the Federals "were surprised or excited." Shannon sought cover behind an oak stump two feet high and eighteen inches in diameter. Union rifle bullets soon joined shells and "came closer and closer and thicker and thicker until the air seemed in almost a continual buzz."[29]

Under intense Confederate pressure, Federals fled from their unprotected positions in front of the house on the south side of Decatur. They fell back to a line of breastworks in the rear of the home. Confederate infantrymen launched repeated assaults on the trenches, but the line was strong, and the Federals were done running. Exhausted rebels pulled back and waited for promised reinforcements. They hoped that more men might shift the balance in their favor and allow them to penetrate the Union lines.[30]

The Confederate infantry did not have to wait for long. Lieutenant Colonel Williams, commanding the artillery for Stewart's Corps, ordered his batteries to take up positions about nine hundred yards from the Union lines and open fire all along the line. The rebel gunners, sitting in the open, had little chance against their blue-clad counterparts, who enjoyed the protection of sturdy breastworks. Union gunners did quick work, and the rebel artillerymen "suffered severely." Lumsden's Battery of Alabamians stood its ground and traded artillery fire with a Union battery until a Union three-inch shell ripped the arm from a gunner and the rebel artillerymen retreated. Members of Tarrant's Alabama Battery withdrew as well, after Union artillery fire wounded several of their men and disabled one of their cannons.[31]

The battle was not going well for the men in gray. The infantry had tried and failed to break through. The artillery was unable to punch holes in the Union line. Almost all the cavalry was far to the northwest with General

Forrest. In desperation, Hood decided to send the infantry forward again, in hopes that the third time might be the charm. It was not a popular decision. When officers ordered the 5th Tennessee Infantry regiment to prepare for an assault, "protests and muttered threats of refusal were heard among the men." General French, commanding a Confederate division of infantry, agreed with his disgruntled soldiers, believing that Decatur was not worth the blood good men were about to shed to capture it. Doolittle was an old friend of his, and French knew that he would not give up easily.[32] In spite of objections raised by men from privates to generals, the orders were final, and the rebels surged forward once more.

At around 4:00 p.m., Colonel Doolittle sent portions of the 29th Michigan Infantry to reinforce the vulnerable eastern flank of the Federal defenses between Somerville Road and the Tennessee River, just as the fighting reached a crescendo in that area. Mississippians and Alabamians of Loring's Division repeatedly slammed their bodies into the reinforced but still weakest point of the Federal line. The rebels purchased little with their blood and suffered horribly at the hands of men from Tennessee, Michigan, and Indiana, who kept up a steady volume of artillery and small arms fire from the safety of excellent breastworks. W. J. Worsham, C. W. Heiskell, and the rest of the 19th Tennessee Infantry advanced all the way to an abandoned line of three-man rifle pits in front of a Federal fort. Within the fort, Union troops kept up a steady fire, punishing the Tennesseans until they withdrew. J. M. Miller of the 20th Tennessee Infantry watched "a man being borne on a litter with the top of his head shot off by a cannon shot, leaving under jaw with chin whiskers an odd looking sight, his brains being splattered on his comrades." Most of the 9th Tennessee Infantry obeyed orders to withdraw out range of the Federals' deadly fire, but Lieutenant Ozanne stopped and climbed a tree to get a better view of enemy positions. A shell from a Union three-inch rifled gun struck the tree just blow Ozanne's feet, and he cried out, "I've seen enough." He fled to the rear as exploding shells struck the ground nearby and coated him in a layer of sticky mud.[33]

As night fell on October 26, the Union gunboat Stones River arrived at Decatur, carrying 1,300 reinforcements. Members of the 102nd Ohio Infantry, 18th Michigan Infantry, and 73rd Indiana Infantry regiments joined the defenders of Decatur. General Granger also arrived that evening from Athens, Alabama, and took personal command of the rapidly growing garrison. Lieutenant Colonel Williams, commanding the artillery for Stewart's Corps, ordered Captain Tarrant to move his battery forward and fire on Union reinforcements crossing the river, but darkness fell before the gunners could get into position, and Williams ordered them to withdraw rather than waste ammunition.[34]

A sidewheel gunboat, the USS *General Grant* was commissioned on July 20, 1864, at Bridgeport, Alabama. It destroyed 22 small boats off Port Deposit and Crow Island in October 1864, assisted in the capture of pontoon bridges at Decatur, Alabama, and participated in the bombardment of Guntersville, Alabama, on January 15, 1865. National Archives.

The fighting was over for the night. At about 7:00 p.m. General Hood established his headquarters at the Garth House, roughly two miles outside Decatur. Stewart's Corps camped southeast of Decatur, along the Somerville Road. Cheatham's Corps occupied positions within two and half miles of Decatur, due south of town. General Lee's Corps finished their destruction of nearby rail lines and pushed four miles past Somerville, Alabama, a little west of Decatur. Torrents of rain poured forth from the black sky that night. The water drenched the men in gray, who had few tents or blankets. Most men had nothing more than threadbare clothing to protect them from the icy water. The rebels tried to get comfortable, rooting around for the least drenched and least freezing patch of ground they could find. Occasionally a man would stumble into an unseen rifle pit, sink into frigid water, and "lose all his religion." The Federals were far more fortunate than their adversaries, enjoying the protection of log huts, tents, ponchos, and thick wool overcoats.[35]

October 27

A dense fog covered the valley as a hesitant sun rose on October 27. After a long night suffering under icy rains, the 1st Arkansas Infantry moved into the front lines, relieving John Lavender and the rest of the 4th Arkansas

Infantry. The drenched men withdrew to safety and warmed themselves over smoky campfires. Lavender's shoes were so wet that they almost disintegrated. His skin from his knees to his toes was pale and wrinkled from sitting in water all night. The band of the 102nd Ohio Infantry warmed up their instruments and played "Yankee Doodle." In response, a Confederate band played "Dixie." Next the Ohioans played "The Star-Spangled Banner," and the rebels responded with the "Bonnie Blue Flag." An unidentified soldier shouted out that he planned to fire. The concert ended as members of both armies sought cover. Union troops saw figures groping through the fog towards their lines and ordered them to identify themselves. They replied that they were "Cheatham's men," and the Federals ordered them to advance. When the rebels realized that they were walking into a trap, they turned and ran back towards their own lines. Union men opened fire, shooting two fleeing rebels.[36]

General Thomas in Nashville sent a flow of supplies and reinforcements towards Decatur and ordered the garrison to "defend Decatur to the last extremity." Early on October 27, more Federal reinforcements arrived, including troops from 68th Indiana Infantry, 73rd Indiana Infantry, and the 13th Indiana Cavalry, who were equipped as infantry. Federal reinforcements joined the sporadic fighting all along the line. Members of the 14th Colored Infantry walked straight into battle and immediately opened an "annoying musket fire" on the rebels. The men in gray returned the favor, killing and wounding several members of the regiment with small arms and artillery fire. William Given of the 102nd Ohio later told his wife that "we fought like tigers" because they preferred to a quick death on the battlefield to the slow hell of a southern prison camp. The Union garrison felt confident they could withstand anything the rebels might throw at them.[37]

The Confederate army kept up the pressure on Decatur, pushing forward against a Union garrison that refused to give ground. Rain storms soaked the rebels and made it impossible for men to see as they struggled to advance. Lieutenant Colonel Williams ordered Captain Tarrant to move his battery into fortifications on the bank of the Tennessee River, where they could disrupt the flow of reinforcements into Decatur. When Tarrant arrived, he found that the promised breastworks were incomplete, offering virtually no shelter from Union artillerymen and sharpshooters, who fired on them from across the river. Despite his disappointment, Tarrant ordered his gunners to hold their ground and fight it out. At 2:00 p.m. Federal troops charged Tarrant's Battery on the banks of the Tennessee River. For some unknown reason, the rebel infantry failed to support their brothers in the artillery, and the gunners were forced to retreat. After withdrawing down the river bank, the battery regrouped just as two Federal gunboats came into view. Tarrant ordered his men to open fire. Two of the three rapidly fired shells struck the gunboats, although Tarrant was unsure how much damage they caused, if any.[38]

In the face of an ever larger and continually reinforced Federal garrison, the Confederate assault stalled. Unable to move forward, the men in gray began digging into the sticky Alabama soil. Men without entrenching tools shoveled mud with tin cups in a fight to transform soil into breastworks. After several hours of labor, the rain won, and men fell asleep in muddy holes that offered little protection from Union bullets and none from the rain that refused to stop.[39]

That evening, General Pierre Gustave Toutant-Beauregard, commander of the Department of the West, which included the Army of Tennessee, arrived at General Hood's headquarters at the Garth House. Beauregard condemned Hood for the movement west, which placed additional strain on the collapsing Confederate logistical system. Hood replied that he had no choice since the Federal garrisons guarding the eastern crossings were too powerful to overwhelm. Beauregard then insisted that if the eastern crossings were impregnable, Hood should have assaulted Decatur at the earliest possible moment, rather than launching piecemeal attacks that wasted lives while leaving the Federals in control of the town.[40]

October 28

The Confederates were unable to win a conventional victory, so they got creative. Civil War armies rarely attacked in the dark, when men were as likely to kill their comrades by accident as their enemies on purpose. However, the Army of Tennessee was under tremendous pressure to capture Decatur, so they rolled the dice. At about 3:00 a.m. on October 28, Confederate forces launched a daring attack in the dark against the western end of the Federal line. Initially it looked promising. The rebels drove back confused Union skirmishers, but the men in blue quickly realized what was happening and regrouped. Confederate forces failed to penetrate the main Union line and took up positions in shallow fox holes about a hundred yards from the Federal line, a threateningly close distance. The rebels were only one good charge away from breaking the Union lines.[41]

As the sun came up on October 28, the rebels pushed forward once again. The 1st Alabama Infantry sent a line of skirmishers towards the Federal forces guarding Decatur, but the Alabamians encountered stiff resistance. One man received a mortal wound and the regiment retreated. The Federals quickly counterattacked, capturing rebel prisoners and sending uncaptured rebels fleeing for their lives. The prisoners informed their captors that Hood was determined to capture Decatur, regardless of the cost. Stewart's and Cheatham's Corps kept pushing forward from the southern and eastern edges of Decatur, while Lee moved his corps west and wedged them between Decatur and Courtland.[42]

Even with reinforcements, the Federal garrison still numbered less than five thousand men, many of them going into battle for the first time. The Confederate Army of Tennessee boasted at least twenty-three thousand men, mostly veterans. In spite of the huge disparity in numbers, as the sun rose on October 28, the Federal garrison prepared to counterattack the rebels. To bolster their meager numbers, Federal officers once again scoured the town for noncombatants to send into the front lines. General Granger ordered all of his artillery batteries within close range of the rebels to load their cannons with canister and train their muzzles on the Confederate positions. A flanking column of Union infantry slipped around the riverbank to the west in the fog, sneaking behind Confederate rifle pits. With a shout the men in blue charged the rebels from the rear, flushing them out into the open, where they ran into a barrage of Union artillery and small arms fire.[43]

The counterattack took the rebels by surprise, and the men in gray paid an awful cost. The 3rd Confederate Infantry was attempting another advance when they ran headlong into the Union counterattack. Forty surprised Confederate soldiers became prisoners. James Cooper of the 20th Tennessee barely escaped as he scurried back to rebel lines one step ahead of the Federals. William Pettus, "as brave a boy as ever fought for freedom," was struck by a musket ball that shattered his leg. Marion Harlan was laying "in a recumbent position" when "a solid cannon shot entered his shoulder and passed lengthwise through his body."[44]

At about noon the Federals launched another sortie. With a shout, 355 members of the 14th Colored Infantry poured out of Decatur's defenses and captured a Confederate battery. The 2nd Tennessee Infantry counterattacked and tried to recapture the cannon. Federals were unable to move the cannons back to Decatur, so they disabled the guns by driving spikes through the touch holes and returned to the Federal lines. Safe behind breastworks once more, the Federals took a roll call and discovered that sixty members of the regiment were killed or wounded during the brief encounter.[45]

Both the Union 14th Colored Infantry and the Confederate 2nd Tennessee Infantry who fought each other in the Battle of Decatur came from Middle Tennessee and drew many of their members from Sumner County. Before the war, most members of the 14th Colored Infantry had been slaves, and some members of the 2nd Tennessee had been slave owners. It is unclear if any former slaves killed their formers masters at Decatur, but it is certainly possible.[46]

The Federals were winning, and they knew it. The men were in justifiably high spirits. General Granger was pleased with his men's performance and felt that the counterattacks were a complete success. When General Thomas received word that the garrison had not only held their ground but had actually launched successful counterattacks against the rebels, he proclaimed that the garrison "can whip Hood's whole army."[47] By the time Thomas sent that message, it pretty much had.

The fighting died down along much of the line as rebel batteries engaged Union gunboats. According to E. T. Eggleston, his battery of artillery fired thirty-two rounds and struck the enemy vessels several times before withdrawing without causing any apparent damage to the boats or suffering any casualties of their own. General Granger reported the duel between gunboats and shore batteries somewhat differently. He claimed that the gunboats came within three hundred yards of the Confederate batteries and blasted their adversaries with double-loaded canister rounds that "it was impossible for men to withstand." A single shell from the gunboat Stones River blew up a Confederate caisson, instantly killing seventeen Confederates. The rebel gunners fled in disorder, and "many bodies were afterward found in the river."[48]

October 29

On October 29 General Hood ordered his army to begin scouting to the west in search of a less well defended crossing. Most of the Confederate army remained near Decatur, but they kept a respectful eight hundred yards away from the Federal lines. Federal gunners killed anything in gray that dared to get any closer. The men in blue listened to rebel bugles echoing in the distance and reported that they had "supplies in abundance, especially confidence." General Granger was pleased to hold Decatur, but he worried about Hood's next move. He sent probing detachments of skirmishers to gather intelligence and disrupt rebel plans.[49]

October 30

On the morning of October 30, it became clear that the Confederate army was withdrawing in defeat. Colonel Doolittle reported that "a sense of relief was entertained by all." W. J. McDill of the 9th Tennessee Infantry remained behind as part of the Army of Tennessee's rear guard and "had the pleasure of being shelled considerably." Federal troops saw the Confederates leave and advanced on the rebel's rear guards "but took care not to come to close." The Army of Tennessee was a dangerous beast, even as it walked away in defeat. Union newspapers as far away as Washington, DC, gleefully reported that the men in blue "handsomely repulsed" the Confederate assaults. Federal glee was tempered by fears that the rebels would soon strike again.[50]

Unable to push through the determined garrison, the Confederate Army of Tennessee hoped for better luck somewhere to the west. Initially, Confederate newspapers reported that the Army of Tennessee had captured Decatur and won a great victory, but they were forced to publish humiliating retractions days later. General Hood abandoned the Garth House and set up the army's headquarters twenty miles west of Decatur. Lee's Corps led the way with the exhausted men of Stewart's and Cheatham's Corps trailing behind. The army left most of the wounded behind, since they had no way to transport them. With the nonchalance of a veteran, Joel Murphree referred to the Battle of Decatur as "a little brush." However, Decatur was far more than "a little brush." A Union force, never numbering more than five thousand men, with the aid of only seventeen artillery pieces and four gunboats, repulsed the entire Army of Tennessee, which consisted of at least twenty-three thousand troops and sixty pieces of artillery. The Federals once again proved that determined defenders behind breastworks could defeat a much larger attacking force. The successful defense of Decatur also forced the Confederates to make another long detour to the west, wasting time and supplies when they could ill afford to spare either.[51]

Once again, the Confederate rank and file paid the price for a failed attack. Arkansas infantryman John Lavender believed that roughly 5,000 members of the Confederate army were killed or wounded at Decatur. Other estimates indicate that 113 Union soldiers were killed wounded or captured, while the rebels lost closer to 1,000 from all causes. E. T. Sykes of the 43rd Mississippi Infantry received a serious wound in the final day of the Battle of Decatur. There was little room in the field hospitals, but the plantation where Sykes lived as a boy was near the battlefield, so his comrades carried him there. Not long after Sykes arrived, he passed from the earth in the same room where his mother had brought him into the world.[52]

The Federals decisively defeated the Confederate Army of Tennessee at Decatur, but some rebels denied the obvious truth. In his memoirs, General Hood claimed that the fighting at Decatur was simply "a slight demonstration" intended to distract the Federal garrison. Infantryman Alexander Spence told the woman he planned to marry that, while the Federals occupied a strong position at Decatur, "we could have taken the place" and only left the Federals in control of the town because "it would have cost more than it was worth." Major James Bates told his mother that Hood "did not care to take the place." At least one Confederate journalist claimed that Hood never intended to capture Decatur, only to distract the Federals so his supply trains could move west.[53]

Out of range of Federal guns, the rebels were safe from Federal troops but not from their own empty bellies. With all hopes of crossing at Decatur extinguished, Confederate soldiers quickly turned their attention to more pressing matters. Hungry rebels melted away in an effort to find something to eat, a process that Daniel Smith called "disastrous to the discipline of the army." Many men felt "gnawing hunger" that "preyed on us," and "mounted officers had to guard their horses when fed to prevent the corn from being stolen from them." H. K. Nelson claimed that he and his comrades would never forget the intense hunger they felt as they turned away from Decatur. Alexander Spence claimed that many of the people he encountered refused to accept Confederate currency. Although Spence was quick to denounce the civilians as "Federal," and many probably were, it is also possible that even loyal rebels realized that Confederate money was nearly worthless in the fall of 1864.[54]

Near Courtland, Alabama, about twenty miles west of Decatur, Hood ordered his engineers to investigate the possibility of crossing the Tennessee River. The engineers reported that they could get the army across but that it would be difficult. Hood considered it but decided not to cross since his men were desperately short of provisions. Previously, he had assured Beauregard that his army could live off the land, but that plan was clearly not working. Hood ordered his men to keep moving west in hopes that they could obtain supplies near Florence, Alabama.[55]

As the army resumed their westward march, they observed the devastation caused by war. Alabama soldier Daniel Smith described the area west of Decatur as a "fertile country" that bore the scars of constant conflict. Almost all the buildings on numerous, once grandiose plantations were nothing more than charred ruins. Tennessee infantryman Risenar Etter noted that all of the slaves were gone except "some poor old crippled ones who could not get away." G. W. Higgins of the 45th Mississippi Infantry informed his wife that the area between Decatur and Florence was "as rich as any" but that almost all of the inhabitants were gone and nature had reclaimed the once bountiful farms. Texan Samuel Foster described the Tennessee River valley as the richest land he had seen since leaving his home in Texas but observed that fields lay fallow, chimneys marked the locations of burned down houses, and no living thing remained in the once heavily populated region. Alabama officer Newton Davis noticed that "marks of this cruel war are visible on every hand" and described the area between Decatur and

Campaign sketches. "Foraging" by Winslow Homer. Lithograph published in 1863 by L. Prang & Co. Library of Congress.

Florence as a scene of beautiful farmland that had gone to waste and ruin as the plowshare was abandoned and the sword clutched in its place.[56]

Many Confederate soldiers blamed the Union foragers for the devastation they observed. John Sparkman stated, "there is fine land here, but the Yankees have troubled the citizens so much that they have nearly all left home." E. H. Rennolds felt the devastation "makes the heart sick," but he took grim satisfaction in his belief that Union foragers "will be repaid." Thomas J. Key, who had lived near Tuscumbia, Alabama, as a young man before moving to Arkansas, recorded in his diary, "as I passed down the once beautiful valley of the Tennessee, I saw nothing except wrecks of palaces and devastated plantations." He noted that the destroyed farms provided few opportunities for foraging, leaving horses "weak and poor from their prolonged fasting." Key placed all of the blame for this destruction onto the shoulders of Union general Grenville Dodge and used a clever turn of phrase to predict that in the next life "he will not able to dodge the fiery torments that justice will heap upon his guilty soul." General Hood also noted the destruction and issued a circular to the troops pointing out the devastation in hopes of motivating the men.[57]

The Federal cavalry observed and harassed the Confederates as they moved westward. Jesse Henderson, a member of the 41st Mississippi Infantry, encountered a regiment of Federal cavalry near Courtland, Alabama. The cavalry troopers "charged our pickets" in an attempt to capture the rebel infantrymen. The Confederate pickets ran back to the main body of the army, and the reinforced body of rebels repelled the Federals, who retreated in disorder.[58]

After several days of hard marching, the army arrived on the banks of the Tennessee River near Florence, Alabama. Thomas Head of the 16th Tennessee Infantry recalled, "the march had been a long and severe one, and the men were worn out and exhausted." Tired men set up camp and enjoyed a brief rest.[59] On the banks of the river, the town of Muscle Shoals took its name from the rocky shallows in that stretch of the Tennessee River, which were populated by freshwater shellfish.

The Battle of Florence

Roughly one thousand Federal cavalry occupied Florence, Alabama, and guarded the strategic crossing over the Tennessee River. Confederate soldiers lamented that, once again, a bridge across the Tennessee River was in the possession of Union soldiers. The Confederate artillery unlimbered their guns on hills just south of the river crossings and began sending shells into Union-held Florence on the northern bank. Alabama soldiers lobbed artillery shells into an Alabama town, inadvertently endangering and quite possibly killing Alabama civilians. According to Louisiana soldier R. H. Lindsay, the Federals were "perfectly indifferent" to the approaching rebel army. John Dicks of the 4th Louisiana Infantry claimed that the Federals were unaware of the danger because "some of our men had strolled up and engaged the enemy in conversation and deceived them as to the whereabouts of Hood's Army."[60]

As shells rained down, the Confederate infantry began their assault. General Lee ordered a two-pronged attack across the roughly one thousand yards of murky water that was the Tennessee River. Members of Johnson's Division crossed over in pontoon boats. Edgar Jones enjoyed his first view of the "the beautiful city of Florence" as he stared across the muddy waters for a few moments before joining the assault on the town. Infantrymen crowded into small boats. Nobody could find any oars, so men improvised crude replacements out of scrap wood. While infantrymen rowed across the water, engineers set up a pontoon bridge for the rest of the army. To keep the approaching darkness at bay, men in every boat carried torches. Eerie flames reflected off muddy water in amber hues. James Lanning watched from the bank and reported that it was a "grand sight." Sharpshooters stood in the bow of each boat and fired their rifles as the boats advanced. R. H. Lindsay worried, "I had but little hope of ever reaching the north bank of the river with my little squad," but thankfully, "our artillery played upon the enemy with terrific effect" and "caused them to skedaddle away." Some of the artillery fire fell among the attackers as well as the defenders. A Confederate shell struck Andrew Devilbliss, a sharpshooter with the 11th Louisiana Infantry, in the back, killing him nearly instantly. As Alabamian Edgar Jones stepped onto the northern bank and prepared to assault Union positions, he noticed a Frenchman sketching the scene of men, boats, torches, and fading sunlight. The artist also caught the eye of a Confederate colonel, who carefully examined the work and expressed his approval. The colonel then offered to purchase the artwork for one hundred dollars. Writing many years later, Jones longed to see the beautiful sketch once more before he passed into the next world, but it appears he never got his wish, and the sketch seems to have disappeared forever.[61]

Safe on the northern bank, the rebels advanced on the heart of town. A civilian provided the rebels with detailed information on the Union troops in the town, allowing the Confederates to rout their opponents after a brief skirmish and leaving Florence in Confederate hands. Unlike the encounter at Decatur, where Union soldiers made a determined and successful stand, the Federals at Florence retreated after the brief engagement, finally providing the Army of Tennessee with a path across the Tennessee River. Union efforts to hold the crossing were hampered by the smaller garrison and the shallow water that gave the nearby town of Muscle Shoals its name, which made it difficult for Union gunboats to get close enough to engage the Confederates. Newton Davis suggested that the skirmish was hardly worthy of comment, claiming that only about a thousand Union troops were present and that they "all skidaddled as quick as possible" in response to the first shot from the Confederate artillery. According to W. H. Henderson of the 7th Texas Infantry, the successful capture of Florence increased the men's wavering confidence in General Hood's leadership.[62]

In contrast to the mixed reception faced by Confederate soldiers in northeast Alabama, many of Florence's residents welcomed the Confederate army with open arms. Louisiana soldier R. H. Lindsay recalled that the local civilians gave the rebel soldiers "a most royal welcome" and gave the soldiers presents, including badly needed "shirts, shoes, boots, socks, etc." Newton Davis described Florence's citizens as "carried away with excitement" as they cheered, waved, and clapped their hands with joy to welcome the gray-clad men into their city. Davis attributed the warm welcome to the suffering that Florence had suffered at the hands of Union soldiers and condemned the Federals for having "carried away" all of the "able bodied negroes," leaving nobody to work the fields. John Crittenden claimed the ladies of Florence, both black and white, poured into the streets and greeted his regiment with "rapturous applause." Crittenden seemed confused by the complete absence of black men in the town, but while he might have been unaware, many of the area's former slaves had joined the Union army, most notably the 2nd Alabama Infantry, later renamed the 12th US Colored Troops, which would play a key role in the Battle of Nashville several weeks later.[63]

Even in Florence, an area with many eager Confederate civilians, some whites remained loyal to the Union. Samuel Kelley spent an evening in the home of "an old tory who has a son in Lincoln's army." Kelley did not mention how his host felt about housing a Confederate soldier or if the civilian had any choice in the matter. James Crane of the 66th Georgia Infantry was initially pleased by the warm welcome, but he quickly detected signs of disloyalty. Many of the wealthy women wore luxury goods only available to those that did business with northern merchants.[64]

Even after they "skedaddled" out of Florence, Union soldiers remained nearby. On November 1 a Union patrol taunted Confederate forces until the rebels brought twelve cannons into action and repelled the Federals. On November 4 a handful of Union troops floated across the Tennessee River and tried to destroy the pontoon bridge, but the rebels captured them

Confederate Artillery Battery near Charleston, South Carolina, 1863. George S. Cook, photographer. Library of Congress.

before they could damage the bridge. On November 5 Union cavalrymen made an advance towards Florence along the Huntsville Road. Confederate infantry and artillery units marched out to intercept the horsemen. As the artillery roared and infantrymen advanced, the Federals broke and ran. The rebels might have won a far more decisive victory, but hungry rebels abandoned the advance to feast on crackers and syrup the enemy had left behind and to divide up abandoned Yankee blankets. At least twenty Union soldiers were not quite fast enough and became prisoners. Samuel King Vann assured his sweetheart that the overcoat, blanket, and oilcloth he captured would keep him warm during the winter and exclaimed, "I delight in fighting the cavalry."[65]

The Federals retreated whenever pressed, but they never went far, often remaining within sight but out of rifle range of Confederate troops. The Union scouts provided their superiors with a steady stream of news on the Confederate army, welcoming deserters with food, taking prisoners, and reporting on the weakness of the Confederate forces. The presence of these Union forces kept the rebels on their toes. Confederate soldiers spent much of their time near Florence on the picket line, improving lines of breastworks, and expecting another advance from the Federals at any moment. Freezing rain fell intermittently, making the men miserable as they worked. General Hood took the presence of Union soldiers so seriously that he ordered the destruction of houses that stood in the way of Confederate defenses, probably escalating conflicts between soldiers and civilians.[66]

The Army Camps Near Florence

The Confederates had a river crossing and were surrounded by grateful civilians, they but lacked the most basic supplies needed to continue their advance. The generals promised the men that they would find "ample supplies of all kinds" in Florence, but hope turned to disappointment when the men realized "no supplies were there, and no visible signs of any coming." Elbridge Littlejohn told his wife, "we are out of anything to eat." According to Alabamian Daniel Smith, men were fueled by "short rations of a miserable quality." Desperate men ate things they would have normally rejected, including parched corn so hard that it was almost impossible to chew and unseasoned greens. While chopping firewood, the men of Lumsden's Battery accidently knocked a tree onto a mule, killing it instantly. Rather than let the animal rest in peace, the artillerists eagerly butchered the beast they would have considered unfit for human consumption just a few months before. For the next several days whenever a man would eat a piece of the mule's flesh, he would "hold up his head and bray his funeral hymn." Farmer turned infantryman John Crittenden gladly reported that some of the "finest looking cattle I have ever seen" arrived from Texas, but he admitted that the small heard provided the soldiers with only a single meal. E. H. Rennolds believed the lack of food led to breakdowns in discipline, since "the men grumble at drilling on short rations." A mobile army required well-fed horses, but artillery officer Thomas Key reported that the horses were starving as well as the men. The animals would have fared better, but hungry soldiers stole the rations intended for the horses. After stealing all the food intended for the horses, hungry men ate acorns. Most soldiers lacked enough clothing, and many "had but apologies for shoes."[67]

Since the Army of Tennessee lacked the resources it needed to continue the offensive, it set up camp near Florence and waited for supplies to arrive. W. J. McDill was optimistic, telling his sister that the rail line to Florence was being repaired quickly. General Hood sent a flurry of messages alternately begging and demanding the immediate delivery of supplies, especially food, from the Confederate government. Texas soldier R. M. Collins

THE FOOD QUESTION DOWN SOUTH.
JEFF DAVIS. "See! see! the beautiful Boots just come to me from the dear ladies of Baltimore!"
BEAUREGARD. "Ha! Boots? Boots? When shall we eat them? Now?"

Editorial cartoon entitled "The Food Question Down South" and captioned "See! see! the beautiful Boots just come to me from the dear ladies of Baltimore!" Beauregard: "Ha! Boots? Boots? When shall we eat them? Now?" *Harper's* v. 7, no. 332 (1863, May 9): 304. Library of Congress.

remembered that, while the army waited near Florence, the provost guards attempted to round up reinforcements from home guard companies and hospitals. Weapons and ammunition provided the Army of Tennessee with a particularly difficult problem. While food and clothing might be gleaned from nearby farms and new men drafted from the civilian population, guns and ammunition could only come from military sources. Hood begged Colonel Josiah Gorgas, the nation's chief of ordnance, to send ammunition.[68]

Confederate authorities tried and ultimately failed to supply the army with provisions. W. J. Ross, superintendent of the Memphis and Charleston Railroad, attempted to extend a rail line to the south bank of the Tennessee River, but his work crews suffered from a lack of tools, labor, and food. In desperation, the army began impressing civilian workers to help with the railroad, but considering the Confederacy's labor shortages, it is unclear how many men they were able to round up. Hood also ordered the transfer of all wagons used for personal baggage to the supply trains. The additional wagons probably helped, but the shifting of equipment caused confusion. The *Daily Dispatch* in Richmond reported that the government delivered "large quantities of hard tack and bacon" to the Army of Tennessee, but there is no evidence that the quantities were large enough to overcome hunger. General Nathan Bedford Forrest's cavalrymen raided Union supply networks and seized everything they could for the army, in contrast to his more typical policy of destroying the majority of captured goods so that his forces could move quickly.[69]

The Confederates faced long odds when the campaign began, and success became less likely with every passing day. General Hood anticipated this problem, noting that immediately after the fall of Atlanta "Sherman is weaker now than he will be in future, and I as strong as I can expect to be." The Army of Tennessee's inability to make a rapid movement into Middle Tennessee provided Union commanders with time to prepare for the Confederate offensive and undoubtedly made the rebel advance several weeks later even more difficult. The Union assembled, fed, supplied, and trained its troops while the rebels suffered from hunger. William McMurray of the 20th Tennessee Infantry believed that Hood lost the war in the quiet camps near Florence. The delay allowed the Federals to assemble an army that "would have crushed him" even if he conducted the rest of the campaign flawlessly.[70]

Problems caused by meager quantities of food were exacerbated by poor distribution and preparation methods. During this portion of the campaign, the army typically provided each man with a meager daily ration of three-quarters of a pound of rough cornmeal and about a pound of raw beef that was more bone than meat. Rations were issued to company

The Florence, Alabama, Home of Robert Patton who fed Confederate soldiers during November 1864. Library of Congress.

cooks, who boiled the beef. Cooks mixed the cornmeal with water, formed it into pones, and "browned—not cooked" the meal in Dutch ovens. Much of the food was accidently destroyed by poorly trained cooks, leaving men with even less food. The army typically issued three days' worth of rations at a time, and the quartermasters expected the men to survive on their allotment for the three days until the next distribution. However, the small quantities meant that many soldiers ate three days' worth of rations on the first day and suffered hunger or satisfied their cravings in other ways during the next two days. The imperfect system often broke down when the lack of gristmills forced men to suffer hunger or eat raw grain.[71]

Hungry soldiers fanned out into the countryside in search of provisions. Daniel Smith claimed, "thousands at a time were scattered through the country searching for something to satisfy their hunger." According to John Crittenden, "if it was not for what we get foraging we would be compelled to suffer." In a later letter, he gave thanks for the humble pea, since "if it were not for peas I know not what we would do." Risenar Etter expressed gratitude to the old farmer who gave the soldiers three-fourths of his turnip patch. Edgar Jones received a sumptuous dinner at a stately brick mansion belonging to Robert M. Patton, a local politician and future governor of Alabama, who had initially opposed secession but accepted the will of the majority, supporting the Confederate war effort, sacrificing his fortune, and losing two of his three sons in battle. By the fall of 1864, Patton's farm was already bordering on ruin because campaigning armies had stripped the homestead of slaves and livestock. Despite his encroaching poverty, Patton fed hundreds of Confederate soldiers every day until his supplies were entirely exhausted.[72]

The army's leaders claimed that "no discontent manifested itself at any time" during the stay near Florence, but many ordinary soldiers saw things a bit differently. Thomas Key recorded in his diary that soldiers stole cattle from his friend Mr. Halsey and "committed other outrages on citizens." Tennessee soldier A. C. McLeary later recalled that boredom often led to mischief in camp. He and his comrades made a game of grabbing unsuspecting slaves, wrapping them in blankets, and then slinging them into the air while the men laughed. It was all fun and games until one of their victims landed on a tree stump and was badly hurt. The slave's master came to camp to confront the soldiers who injured the slave. McLeary and his friends responded by grabbing the old master and throwing him, just as they had thrown his slave. In an effort to keep the peace, the army's leaders sent men into the countryside to arrest any soldiers who misbehaved or were absent from the camps without permission. John Crittenden informed his wife that theft in the camps was common and reported that unknown soldiers stole his food and canteen in a series of several thefts. Soldiers stole and devoured a milk cow belonging to General States Rights Gist. They also placed the cow's head on a pole in front of the general's tent. Surviving sources gave no indication of what the culprits were trying to indicate, but severed heads are rarely used to communicate friendly thoughts.[73]

The army's feeble attempts to stop unauthorized foraging accomplished little. Men noticed the stricter discipline but continued to forage liberally. Daniel Smith claimed that many "officers, themselves half-starved, sympathized with their men" and suggested that even the strictest officers were unable to control their men since no punishment could be worse than a certain death by starvation. Many officers walked a fine line, never actually foraging themselves but looking the other way when their men disappeared and later accepting food from their men without asking questions about the mysterious provisions. These officers, and many of their men, were faced with a conflict between a desire to behave ethically and a need to eat. Captain Samuel Foster discovered that several men from his brigade had distracted a guard and stolen hogs reserved for the army's high command. Foster did not formally condone the theft, but he accepted a share of the pork and made no efforts to punish the culprits. Perhaps no participant summarized the situation better than George Little of Lumsden's Alabama Battery, who explained, "it was all contrary to military law, but soldiers were not going to sit still and starve."[74]

If soldiers had consistently paid for the items they acquired from civilians, it might have eased tensions, but this was not an option in most cases. The army failed to pay soldiers for months on end, leaving men with little or no cash. G. W. Higgins told his wife that he was unable to purchase food since "our monies is about out." Even if the army's payroll department had consistently paid the men on time, it would have meant little. The value of Confederate currency was in freefall by late 1864. Even wealth could only protect men so much; increasing shortages of essential goods meant that few supplies were available for sale at any price. According to infantryman Joel Murphree, "buying provisions with money is about played out."[75]

In spite of the hardships, Hood's decision to wait near Florence for supplies did provide the men with opportunities for rest and relaxation, which improved their morale. Soldiers and civilians mingled at plays and dances held to celebrate the army's arrival. The army's medical department treated men for wounds and illness acquired along the march. At the home of Charles Palmer and R. M. Halsey, Thomas Key enjoyed good food, pleasant conversation, and musical performances. He noted in his diary that such experiences were "seldom enjoyed by me or by any other soldier." Newton Davis accompanied his comrade Captain Oliver when Oliver's old friend Mrs. Simpson invited him into her home. John Morton, an artilleryman from Tennessee, recalled that the camps rang with cheerful songs, one of which was titled "Goober Peas":

> Sitting by the Roadside on a summer's day, chatting with
> my messmates passing time away,
> Lying in the shadow underneath the trees, Goodness
> how delicious, eating goober peas!
> Peas! Peas! Peas! Peas! Eating goober peas! Goodness
> how delicious, eating goober peas!
> When a horseman passes, the soldiers have a rule,
> To cry out at their loudest "Mister here's your mule."
> But another pleasure enchantinger than these, is wearing
> out your Grinders, eating goober peas!
> Peas! Peas! Peas! Peas! Eating goober peas! Goodness
> how delicious, eating goober peas!
> Just before the battle the General hears a row, He says the
> Yanks are coming, I hear their rifles now,
> He turns around in wonder, and what do you think he sees,
> The Georgia Militia, eating goober peas!
> Peas! Peas! Peas! Peas! Eating goober peas! Goodness
> how delicious, eating goober peas!

I think my song has lasted almost long enough, The subject's
interesting, but rhymes are mighty rough,
I wish this war was over when free from rags, and fleas,
We'd kiss our wives and sweethearts and gobble goober peas!
Peas! Peas! Peas! Peas! Eating goober peas! Goodness
how delicious, eating goober peas![76]

At least a few soldiers in camp around Florence believed that the campaign was going well. J. A. Tillman of the 24th South Carolina Infantry informed his sister that, despite newspaper accounts to the contrary, "the army is in fine spirits." He described the campaign as a string of rapid movements and great triumphs, during which the Army of Tennessee "marched 400 miles," destroyed several blockhouses, captured two thousand prisoners, destroyed forty miles of enemy railroads, and did all of this without the death or wounding of a single man of his company. He acknowledged that "we are now in a rather bad condition—everything being nearly exhausted," and reported that he himself suffered from "chills and fever." However, he and his comrades remained happy because "our enemy is in a much worse condition as he has no advantage whatever." He believed that the government would soon repair the railroads to Florence and provide the men with everything they needed. Lieutenant Francis Fleming wrote a letter to his mother in Florida stating that he still maintained hope that the Confederacy might win the war.[77]

The time spent in camp also provided men with an opportunity to reflect on the news, and perhaps no topic elicited greater excitement than the exploits of General Forrest and his cavalry. W. H. Henderson of the 7th Texas Infantry informed his parents that Forrest's men were "doing some good work for us" capturing enough shoes to equip the entire army. E. T. Eggleston of Cowan's Mississippi Battery gleefully noted in his diary that Forrest's men were destroying enemy boats and capturing tons of supplies. John Sparkman, of the 48th Tennessee Infantry was pleased to receive supplies provided by Forrest's raiders. Supplies were not always free; Robert Smith of the 2nd Tennessee Infantry noted in his diary that "Forrest's cavalry sells captured shoes at $35.00 a pair."[78]

Abraham Lincoln, perhaps the man most hated man south of the Mason-Dixon, ran for reelection on a platform of continuing the war to force the rebellious states back into the Union, and the election was a topic of constant conversation in the Confederate camps. Farmer and schoolteacher turned soldier John Crittenden predicted that the presidential election would determine the course of the war and feared that Lincoln's reelection would result in four more years of war. Artillery officer Thomas Key made a similar

Print titled "The Soldier's Dream of Home" By Currier & Ives. Library of Congress.

mention in his diary, expecting that the war would continue until the Confederacy could "conquer the peace," a feat that he feared was impossible in the face of renewed Union drafts, which Key expected to send a million more northern soldiers marching towards the Confederacy. James Lanning was even more cynical, claiming that the election was irrelevant since, in his opinion, the peace movement was a farce and the war would continue no matter who got elected.[79]

The warm welcome of Florence's civilians and the opportunities for leisure did little to cure the gnawing homesickness of Alabamians who were in their home state but still far from their homes. In the same letter where John Crittenden of the 34th Alabama Infantry expressed delight at the warm welcome he received in Florence, he also lamented the fact that he had not heard from his wife for several months and expressed his urgent desire to return home, pleadingly asking his wife, "have the babies forgotten me?" In letter dated several days later, he begged for news from home and explained that he felt like "a cast off somebody when the mail comes, and I get no letter." Samuel King Vann of the 19th Alabama Infantry informed his sweetheart that, while he noticed many pretty girls among the welcoming throngs, "none of them can withdraw my love from you." He pleaded for letters from his sweetheart, explaining that he would like to hear from her every single day. James Lanning of the 25th Alabama Infantry used his diary as a record of his repeated failures to obtain the leave of absence he so desperately wanted. He often asked himself if his dear loved ones missed him and then reassured himself, "yes, they think of me by day and dream of me by night no doubt." Thomas Warrick of the 34th Alabama Infantry wrote a letter to his wife explaining, "I Want to se you all veary Bad But ther ant no Chans to se you for I Cant Com hom." Newton Davis of the 24th Alabama Infantry was so envious of his friend Graham, a preacher, who received a furlough to attend a religious conference in Tuscaloosa, Alabama, that he almost wished he was a preacher as well. Davis concluded one letter by explaining, "the nearer I get to home the more anxious I become to go there."[80] Soldiers like Davis were caught in a difficult conflict between their duty as soldiers and their desire to return home.

Not every soldier withstood the temptation leave, and desertion became an increasingly serious problem. An official report dated November 6, 1864, listed 94,481 men as enrolled in the Confederate Army of Tennessee, yet only 23,503, or roughly 25 percent, of men were effective and present for duty. The *Jacksonville Alabama Republican* published a long-winded editorial claiming that only one-third of the Alabama men who should be with the army were present for duty. In November 1864 Lieutenant Colonel H. C. Lockhart, serving as Alabama's commandant of conscripts, estimated that between April and November 1864 alone, roughly 8,000 Alabamians deserted from the Confederate army. By November 17 the situation was so desperate that the Alabama state legislature circulated an impassioned appeal to Alabamians who were absent without leave, begging them to return to the army and promising to obtain pardons for soldiers who returned voluntarily. The camps near Florence were within a few miles of J. P. Cannon's home, and he took advantage of the relative quiet to obtain permission to leave with strict orders to return in forty-eight hours. Cannon enjoyed the visit so much that he overstayed his leave, returning nine days later, and apparently suffered no consequence for violating the terms of his leave. His officers were probably just glad he came back. Three men from Key's Battery deserted on the evening of November 6, and each man stole a horse and saddle, which transformed "disgraceful" desertion into "iniquitous" theft in the opinion of their commander.[81]

While the horse thieves may have been nothing more than criminals intending to return home, it is also possible that they planned to join the Union army. Confederate deserters from many units flowed into nearby Federal camps and provided the Union army with information. The Union actively encouraged men to desert from the Confederate army, providing deserters with exemptions from conscription, civilian jobs, and cash bonuses. These policies reveal that Union authorities realized that it was far cheaper to hire southerners than to kill them. James Lanning recorded his diary that, on November 12, a Confederate soldier who had deserted and joined the Union forces near Florence was captured in the act of trying to destroy the Confederate pontoon bridge and was executed by firing squad. Desertion was crippling the Confederate war effort.[82]

New recruits could have helped counterbalance the problem of desertion, but few materialized. Confederate manpower was simply exhausted by the fall of 1864, and there was no realistic hope that significant numbers of reinforcements might join the ranks. Andrew Hill, a sergeant in the 16th Alabama Infantry, noted that his brother John joined the army as it passed through Alabama but that he did so "contrary to my advice." Hill did not indicate why he told his brother to stay away, only that he urged his brother to avoid military service. Florida soldier Archie Livingston told his sisters that the situation was so desperate that he supported "arming the negro." He admitted that it would be an unpopular move, but "I am in for anything for success." Livingston failed to appreciate how right he was. General Patrick Cleburne, a famed division commander in the Army of Tennessee, also suggested arming slaves, faced stern opposition, and may have been passed over for promotion as a result. President Davis was outraged by the idea of arming slaves and believed that even discussing the idea was "injurious to the public service." General Howell Cobb realized, perhaps better than most, what was at stake when he pointed out, "if slaves will make good soldiers our whole theory of slavery is wrong."[83]

The supplies that Hood hoped would arrive failed to materialize in sufficient quantities, and, by the first week in November, the situation was getting desperate. Robert Smith noticed the Tennessee River was "rising and falling so much that it is impossible to finish the bridge." Heavy rains had swollen rivers and made it impossible to get beef cattle to the men. Federal troops noticed Confederate attempts to transport supplies across the river and became increasingly proficient at cutting off this tenuous logistical thread during November.[84]

As the weather grew colder, the men suffered for lack of clothing and shoes. Robert Smith cursed the mule that "tore up my fine English overcoat." Infantryman W. J. McDill ended a letter to his sister because "my hands are so cold I can barely write." Risenar Etter noted that many men were "barefooted and have not pants." According to J. W. Preston, some men were forced to wear primitive moccasins, which were poor substitutes for shoes. G. W. Higgins told his wife that soon he too would wear the primitive moccasins, unless she could send him a new pair of shoes. E. H. Rennolds acquired some soap but was unable to get his clothes clean. He dreaded the possibility of a winter campaign since "I am almost barefooted and badly prepared for winter." R. M. Collins recalled that the men were "poorly clad" so they dug shallow holes in the ground and "spooned" to share body heat. When even shared bodies could not provide a comfortable temperature, men gave up on sleep, rekindled their campfires, and spent the night smoking, cracking jokes, and cursing their luck. The lack of clean clothing caused many of the men to suffer from mange, a debilitating skin disease caused by parasites that caused hair loss and bloody sores.[85]

Some of the men predicted that the Army of Tennessee would remain near Florence during the winter rather than force poorly supplied men to march north into the cold. Captain Samuel Foster believed that the army would advance a few miles into Tennessee and set up winter quarters. Stouten Dent informed his wife of his plans to build a winter hut so that he could entertain visitors from home. According to Elbridge Littlejohn, General Hood revealed plans for a brief raid into Tennessee, after which the army would return to Florence for the winter. Littlejohn was pleased with the idea of making only a brief foray north because "the weather will be getting very cold and we are ill prepared to withstand it," since the men had "few blankets and no tents." James Lanning was adamant that "we will soon be in winter quarters." While many soldiers thought it was more prudent to remain near Florence for the winter, Hood disagreed. The battered army commander possessed a well-deserved reputation as a gambler, and many historians have portrayed Hood's advance into Tennessee as an ill-advised bet against long odds.[86] However, Hood and his army had few choices. Setting up a winter camp near Florence was a terrible idea.

Unidentified Union Cavalry Trooper. Library of Congress.

The area around Florence was a place of conflict, not safety. North Alabama was a war zone crawling with northern troops and Alabama unionists who kept up a constant pressure on Confederate forces in the area. Robert Jarman explained that, while camped near Florence, "nearly every day or night for part of the time had skirmishing with the Federal cavalry." In a letter dated November 10, John Crittenden described the Union cavalry as an ever-present menace, constantly probing the Confederate lines and only withdrawing when the rebels made a determined thrust towards them. In order to return to the army after an extended leave, Samuel Kelly of the 30th Alabama Infantry had to cross territory dominated by "Tories and bush whackers." On November 8, three Union regiments of infantry and another of cavalry advanced on Florence, and Ross's Brigade of Texas cavalry blocked their path. After a sharp engagement, the Federals withdrew but only after inflicting "some loss" on the rebels. Federals constantly picked up Confederate prisoners, who provided Union commanders with accurate reports about rebel forces.[87] There is no reason to believe that Union soldiers and their Alabama supporters would have suddenly changed course and allowed the rebels to enjoy a peaceful winter.

The Confederate forces near Florence lacked enough supplies, and the situation was getting worse, not better. The rebels were hungry, barefoot, and lacked essential equipment. By late 1864 the Confederate Army of Tennessee simply did not have adequate horses, wagons, or railroads to transport essential supplies, even if these supplies had been available somewhere in the Confederacy, and there was no reason to believe that the army could acquire them while remaining near Florence.[88]

The army had clearly overstayed its welcome, devouring what little food surpluses the local civilians had and causing conflicts with even their most ardent supporters. On November 10, Thomas Key noted that the water level of the Tennessee River was rising to the point that it was difficult to cross, a fact he predicted would further exacerbate the army's already tenuous position. His prediction proved accurate several days later. On November 13, the army attempted to send men, artillery, and cattle across the river. The cattle became frightened for some unknown reason, stampeded, and drove men and materiel into the water, drowning several soldiers who were unable to swim in the cold water. E. H. Rennolds observed that the rain "washes away bridges as fast as they can be built." According to Daniel Smith, in the days before the Army of Tennessee resumed its march northward, "all the army had chronic diarrhea and all were hungry." Newton Davis worried that the nights were turning colder and wetter, leaving men "too cold to sit up and too wet to lie down." Sufficient quantities of blankets and tents could have kept the men reasonably comfortable, but the army had very few of these essential items. A Federal prisoner estimated that less than 10 percent of rebels had blankets. John Crittenden claimed that even a "negro" tended to get better food than he and his Confederate comrades received. Crittenden concluded that "I am seeing now about as hard a time as I have seen during the war." In desperation, Crittenden asked his wife to try and send food. He predicted "serious results" unless the supply situation improved.[89]

The Confederate army could have retreated, but to retreat without fighting a major battle would have demoralized the army and wasted precious time. The Confederacy was dying and could not afford to sit idly while the Union became stronger and it became weaker. A soldier from South Carolina was even more blunt, claiming, "the Confederacy is on her way up the spout."[90]

Some soldiers were eager to resume the march northwards. William Hardy, a staff officer in Cheatham's Corps, believed that the time was right since Sherman's march south from Atlanta left the rebels with an open road to Nashville. James Cooper claimed, "everyone was sick at heart with the delay," even though they were "on pretty short ration" and suffering in the cold. W. H. Henderson of the 7th Texas Infantry told his parents that the camps were filled with rumors that the advance would soon resume and that he wished "God speed the day when we will start." At least one newspaper mocked Hood for doing nothing in north Alabama while Sherman devoured Georgia. In the words of Edgar Jones, "the only hope for us was that when we got further from the border line dividing the two armies that things would be more plentiful." Infantryman John Crittenden preferred to remain near Florence, but he admitted that many men were anxious to move north, where they believed Confederate sympathizers were eager for the army's arrival and prepared to supply them during the winter. Desertion was already a major problem in the army, and a retreat would have only exacerbated the situation. Confederate prisoners claimed that Hood moved north, at least in part, because his men promised they would desert rather than retreat. John Scott informed his sweetheart that the men expected "long marches, short rations, and hard fighting" but were willing to "endure anything and meet the enemy anywhere," secure in their belief that "we are going to whip Sherman badly." According to Mississippian G. W. Higgins, the men were anxious to resume the dreaded march since "they all know that they will have it anyhow."[91]

The long-awaited arrival of General Forrest and his cavalrymen raised the army's morale in the days before they resumed the march to the north. Infantrymen and artillerymen from Tennessee serenaded General Forrest, and the famed commander "responded in a very encouraging speech." The newly arrived Forrest became the commander of all the cavalry in the Army of Tennessee and began reorganizing the horse soldiers for the march northwards.[92]

A week before the rest of the army renewed their advance, Newton Cannon and other specially selected members of the 11th Tennessee Cavalry traveled north. Operating in small bands of six men each, they gathered intelligence, destroyed railroad tracks, tore down telegraph lines, ambushed Federal soldiers, and in general did everything in their power to make life difficult for the Union defenders of Tennessee.[93]

General Forrest's presence may have raised the infantry's morale more than it should have. The celebrated general brought only three thousand troopers to the area around Florence. He took command of an additional two thousand already there. The rebel cavalrymen were fresh from raids in Tennessee and Mississippi, which damaged the Union forces but also exhausted the rebels and their equipment. Forrest admitted that "my men and horses were much jaded." Perhaps because of their poor condition, the celebrated horsemen were unable to protect their own wagon train, much of which fell into Federal hands.[94]

On November 15, 1864, General Hood proclaimed that November 16 would be a day of "fasting and prayer" and encouraged every member of the army to attend worship services. Samuel Foster attended church on

St. John's Episcopal Church, Tuscumbia, Alabama. The building was first used in 1852. Library of Congress.

November 16 with roughly seven hundred soldiers, all of whom were quiet and attentive. Thomas Key also attended religious services and reported, "the building was thronged to overthrowing with soldiers." John Crittenden attended church that morning and thought of his wife, suspecting that she was also worshiping the Lord near their family farm in Tallapoosa County, Alabama. The sermon Crittenden heard was from the Apostle Paul's letter to the Ephesians, chapter 5, verse 1. Although he did not quote it in his letter, the verse states, "Be ye therefore followers of God, as dear children." In closing, Crittenden wrote, "Let me hear from you as soon as possible. I am as ever your affectionate husband."[95]

The Army Marches North

After several attempts to resume the march north were canceled due to bad weather, the Army of Tennessee began leaving Alabama and moving towards the state from which it took its name on November 20, 1864. John Young of the 7th Tennessee Cavalry claimed that the order to cross the Tennessee River "brought more joy into the Tennessee troopers than any other occurrence of the war." At 6:54 a.m. the sun rose through heavy clouds. It was a "cloudy, ugly, morning." The sky was dark, and the "rain was incessant." The men marched through icy mud "the consistency of gruel." A tenuous pontoon bridge snaked across the frigid Tennessee River. Isaac Shannon's legs no longer carried him reliably, so the talented sharpshooter rode a mule towards the bridge until a sentinel informed him that only officers could ride across the fragile bridge. Shannon was stuck on the south side of the river until division commander John Brown intervened, personally leading the mule and its rider across the bridge. Samuel Foster described it as "the longest pontoon bridge I have ever seen." Before pressing northward, he stopped on a high bluff to watch the rest of the army cross. One and a half miles long, the bridge lay just barely on top of the river, and from a distance it appeared the men were walking on water. A band led each brigade; the infantrymen marched in columns of four, following the musicians. Foster could tell that Florence had once been a beautiful city, but "war's destroying hand has been here and left its mark." Many of the once proud houses were charred ruins. A light dusting of snow christened starving soldiers as their bare feet shuffled across the frozen ground. As they marched north, Edward McMorries of the 1st Alabama Infantry cast a parting gaze over his right shoulder and saw a few ladies by the roadside, waving farewell, which was nice enough except they were crying. He believed, "their tears revealed that we were without any hope of success."[96]

4

"BY SOME MISUNDERSTANDING"

Spring Hill and Columbia

> We reached Spring Hill, twenty miles, about sundown, and found our advanced troops engaged with a small force of the enemy, in a short line of rifle pits. By some misunderstanding among the generals no attack was made, and night closed in upon us. All through the early part of the night the Federals could be heard passing along the pike only a few hundred yards away.[1]
>
> —E. H. Rennolds, 5th Tennessee Infantry

The March Begins

After a long delay in Alabama, the Army of Tennessee crossed the Tennessee River near Florence and resumed its advance northward towards Tennessee. Hood planned to get into the rear of General John Schofield's Union forces located at Pulaski before they could withdraw behind the Duck River. Aware that windows of opportunity were closing quickly, Confederate officers demanded strict discipline and a rapid advance. Officers told the men not to straggle or do anything that might delay them for even a moment. To ensure that these orders were enforced, officers assigned the most trustworthy men to the provost guard, with full authority to punish anyone who failed to keep up. Hood told his men that they were on a rescue expedition to save their friends and families from "the grasp of the despoiler." The commanding general promised the men that Tennessee was "a land of plenty." General Hood also assured his men that they would not fight unless they enjoyed equal numbers and excellent ground. Samuel Foster took comfort in this promise since "we could always whip an equal number of men with the choice of the ground, and every man felt anxious to go on under these promises."[2]

Forrest's cavalrymen led the way, with the infantry and artillery following close behind. Newton Cannon and his compatriots from the 11th

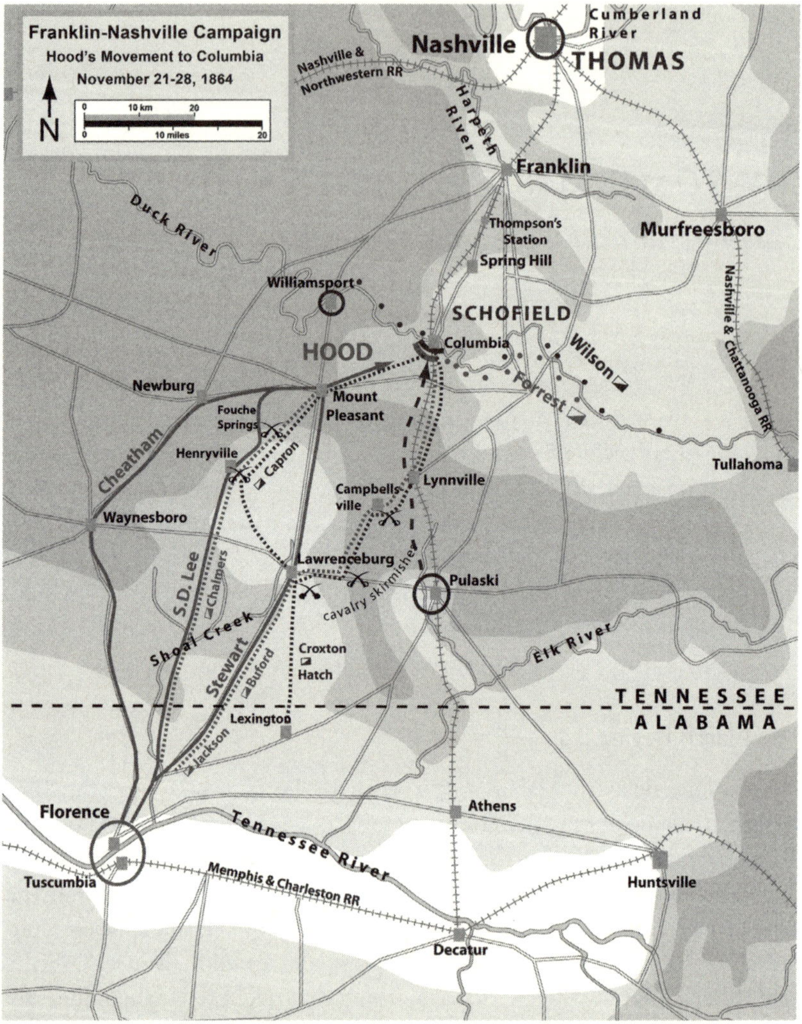

Map 5. Hood's campaign from Florence to Columbia. Map by Hal Jespersen, www.cwmaps.com.

Tennessee Cavalry continued their work well in advance of the rest of the army. Operating in small bands, they gathered intelligence and disrupted Union operations. Shortly behind the advanced scouts, the rest of Forrest's troopers screened the rebel artillery and infantrymen from the prying eyes of Union scouts. Forrest sent his three divisions along two lines of advance. To the west, General James Chalmers's Division advanced along a line that would take it through West Point, Kelly's Forge, Henryville, and Mount Pleasant. To the east, General Abraham Bufford's and General William Jackson's Divisions took the road towards Lawrenceburg. From there, they would advance on Pulaski from the southeast. The rebel horsemen advanced rapidly, enjoying "running fights" and "driving Yankees." The rebel wagons, artillery, and infantry trailed far behind the quick-moving cavalry. Cheatham's Corps trudged along the Waynesboro Road to the west, followed by Lee's Corps, which took the nearby Chisem Road. Stewarts's Corps traveled along the Lawrenceburg Road to the east.[3]

The Federals had been busy while the rebels waited near Florence, but their work remained unfinished. Hood had a well-deserved reputation as an unpredictable and aggressive opponent. Nobody knew what he might do next or what random location he might select as he objective, so preparing to defeat him was no easy task. The Federal defenders had large numbers of men, but most of the units defending Tennessee were of questionable quality. Sherman took the best units with him on his march across Georgia, leaving Thomas with an eclectic assortment of newly raised units, isolated garrisons, dismounted cavalrymen waiting for horses, convalescents who had just rejoined the army, and, as Captain John K. Shellenberger described them, "negro regiments never yet tested in battle." The troops were spread across the region from eastern Tennessee to central Missouri, and concentrating them into a cohesive and well-trained fighting force was difficult. While Federal commanders were understandably worried, they knew that time was on their side and felt confident that they would emerge victorious if they could force a fight on favorable terms. The prospect of an inevitable victory meant little to men like W. H. Avery of the 14th Colored Infantry, who predicted that, before the campaign ended, "somebody will certainly get pretty badly hurt."[4]

Union Camp at Stevenson, Alabama, March 4, 1864. Black ink and red ink drawing on white paper by G. H. Blakeslee. Library of Congress.

In response to Hood's renewed offensive, General Thomas, the overall commander of Union forces in Tennessee, ordered General Granger to withdraw his men from Decatur, Athens, and Huntsville, Alabama, and take them to northward to Stevenson, Alabama, and Murfreesboro, Tennessee, where they could guard the Nashville and Chattanooga Railroad. More Federal troops flowed towards Nashville from Pulaski, Tennessee, to the south. Thomas sent his inspector general, Colonel Von Schrader, to help with the organization of Federal troops at Chattanooga and instructed General Smith at Paducah, Kentucky, to bring his forces south as rapidly as possible. Hoping to give his men every advantage, Thomas ordered his engineers to improve fortifications at several locations, most notably Nashville, Tennessee.[5]

The Confederate Army of Tennessee Enters Tennessee

After marching for roughly fifteen miles beyond the banks of the Tennessee, the Confederate Army of Tennessee crossed into the state from which they took their name. H. K. Nelson of the 41st Tennessee Infantry recalled, "we heard cheering in front of us; and when we got to the State line, we found suspended from one tree to another across the road a canvas with the inscription 'Tennessee a Grave or a Free Home.'" Tennessee soldier E. H. Rennolds remembered that the men responded to the sign with "hearty cheers" and that "we Tennesseans stepped more briskly on our native soil." Joseph Boyce of the 1st Missouri Infantry recalled that the people greeted the rebel army with "enthusiasm and kindness."[6]

Many Tennesseans along the road supported the Union and opposed the Confederate advance. E. H. Rennolds described the "bushwhackers" as "numerous and bold." Tennesseans who remained loyal to the Union kept up a sporadic long-range rifle fire on the rebels, picking off men in gray and disappearing as quickly as they appeared. At other times, Tennessee's loyal sons terrorized the Confederate soldiers by killing stragglers. They also engaged in psychological warfare by cutting the ears and noses off rebels before sending them back to the Confederate ranks to spread fear amongst their comrades. Alabamian Joel Murphree told his wife that the area was "filled with Tories and deserters from both armies who bushwhack our men." A rebel patrol, seeking to eliminate the guerillas, captured four criminals of indeterminate origin, two Confederate deserters, and another man discharged from the Union army. Mississippian Jesse Henderson reported that the rebels captured and hung a man who had once served as a sharpshooter in his regiment.[7]

Despite their high hopes that Tennessee would be a land of plenty, the

Confederates found little to sustain them along the road. By the fall of 1864, Tennessee carried the scars of three years of warfare, and there was little left for the local civilians, much less armies. Risenar Etter noted that "the Yankees have torn up this country very much and most all of the people have gone away from home." Thomas Key visited old friends on their plantation near the line of march and discovered that "the abolition thieves had nearly broken them up by their thefts." Key noted that Middle Tennessee had once been "a rich farming country" but that the area's farms lay idle because "all of the laborers had been kidnapped by the unprincipled Yankees."[8] Although Key did not mention it, many of these laborers were undoubtedly slaves who decided that freedom was more appealing than bondage.

The rebels were forced to go without food for days, and the limited rations that were eventually provided left men very hungry. Hood ordered individual men not to forage but authorized the army's quartermasters to confiscate grain from local farmers. Every evening, men felled trees, cut holes in the trunks, filled the cavities with shelled corn, and pounded it into meal. Daily rations of roughly one biscuit per man failed to satisfy the men's hunger. Many men were frustrated at being "in the land of plenty" but being "half starved" by officers who ordered the men to ignore what little food they passed on the road. Although cavalrymen often had access to better supplies than their comrades in the infantry, James Anthony of the

A Rebel guerrilla raid in a western town, 1862. Wood engraving by Thomas Nast. Library of Congress.

28th Tennessee Cavalry "ate hundreds of meals of just bread and nothing else." Maryland artillery officer William Ritter recalled that men and draft animals starved in the cold as they marched north.[9]

Unsurprisingly, troops ignored official orders, stealing food whenever they could find it. In desperation, men even stole hardtack and pork from their beloved General Frank "Marse Frank" Cheatham. Two members of the 41st Tennessee Infantry tried to get around the prohibition on theft by claiming that they killed a hog in self-defense when it tried to bite them. The officer who caught them was not amused and forced them to carry the hog suspended on a fence rail. Robert Jarman laughed at men forced to wear the rotting hides of the animals they killed. Jarman bragged that he and his friends foraged carefully, ate well, and never got caught.[10]

Many of the rebels who marched north were addicted to nicotine and suffered when they were unable to obtain tobacco. Dr. Sheppard marched with the 18th Alabama Infantry and "was drinking just enough to be witty and cursing the government because it gave it gave such mean tobacco," when foragers from the regiment brought back some high-quality tobacco, which they happily shared with the rest of the regiment. In an oddly unappreciative twist, Dr. Sheppard denounced the foragers as "d—d suspicious characters" who "must have stolen it."[11]

The Confederate high command hoped to fill their ranks with eager recruits from the volunteer state, but they appear to have lost more men than they obtained. Aware that Tennesseans might be understandably hesitant to volunteer for service, the army's commanders took steps to enforce Confederate conscription laws. On November 25, General Stephen D. Lee distributed orders instructing every member of his corps to help "with enforcing the conscript act" and ensuring that every able-bodied man between eighteen and forty-five years of age was in the Confederate ranks. Jim Whittler had obtained an exemption due to his role as an overseer on a large plantation. When a passing detachment of rebels attempted to force Whittler into the army, he refused to serve, pointing out that the conscription law "allows every man who has twenty Negroes to stay at home." A Confederate officer was not impressed, stating, "law or no law—you fall into line, take this gun and cartridge-box, and march!" Peter Hotze of the 6th Arkansas Infantry had brought his slave with him to war to serve as a noncombatant laborer, but the slave slipped away from the army along the march and "was never seen thereafter." William McMurray of the 20th Tennessee Infantry claimed that several thousand troops from Tennessee left the army without permission and that many never returned.[12]

Chalmers's Division of cavalry initially brushed aside Federal opposition in advance of Lee's Corps. At Henryville, roughly eighty miles south of

Sergeant John E. Barlow of Co. M, 1st Mississippi Cavalry Regiment with sword and revolver. Library of Congress.

Nashville, the horsemen encountered Union soldiers who wanted to stand and fight. While Rucker's Brigade kept up a steady fire on the Union soldiers from the front, Forrest took his personal escorts on a looping route into the enemy rear. When the Yankees found themselves under assault from both the front and rear, they ran for their lives. Fifty Union soldiers were unable to escape and became prisoners.[13]

To the east of Lee's Corps, General Jackson's and Buford's divisions of cavalry screened the advance of Stewart's Corps. On November 22, Union cavalrymen tried to block the rebel's path near Lawrenceburg, Tennessee, roughly a hundred miles southwest of Nashville. Captain Young's battery opened fire on the Federals, and they retreated east, towards Pulaski, about nightfall. Early the next morning, General Ross led an advance towards Pulaski in search of the retreating Union cavalry. About twelve miles beyond Lawrenceburg, the Texans encountered their prey. The 3rd Texas Cavalry dismounted and, with help from two squadrons of the 27th Texas Cavalry, spent the day driving their opponents from a series of positions. On November 24, the Texans wheeled to the west and encountered General Edward Hatch's Division of Union troopers from Iowa, Illinois, and Tennessee in position near Campbellsville. Once again, Young's Battery fired the opening salvo. When Hatch's Union horsemen seemed to be preparing to withdraw, Ross ordered his cavalrymen to advance. The 9th Texas Cavalry and the 1st Texas Legion "rushed forward at a gallop and passing through the village fell upon the enemy's moving squadrons with such irresistible force as to scatter them in every direction." At the perfect moment, a portion of Armstrong's Brigade of Mississippi cavalry came into view, hitting the retreating Federals in the flank and destroying any possibility of a counterattack. As blue-coated survivors fled north, the rebels enjoyed the spoils of victory, including eighty-four prisoners along with their horses, weapons, equipment, four stands of colors, and sixty-five beef cattle.[14]

Rebel infantrymen expressed admiration for the cavalry's work. Joel Murphree of the 57th Alabama Infantry claimed that most of the Union troops evacuated in the face of the rebel advance and that Forrest's cavalrymen brushed aside the scattered bands who attempted to delay the Confederates. Tennessee infantryman James Cooper described the trail of horses and dead Yankees that Forrest's troopers left in their wake as a trail of breadcrumbs, showing infantrymen the path into Middle Tennessee. R. M. Collins of the 15th Texas Cavalry (dismounted) reported that Forrest's men were destroying every Yankee unit in their path and leaving the foot soldiers with "nothing to do" except march through the shattered debris.[15]

Many rebels were excited by their rapid advance. Tennessee cavalryman Charles Joy claimed that Union forces resisted but could not slow the Confederate advance and that "we moved on, fighting every day." He explained that Forrest's troopers were so successful because "our officers were our friends and comrades." General Ross counted only 686 men in his brigade of Texas cavalry, but he proclaimed the men "strong in heart and resolved to make up in zeal and courage what was wanting in numbers." Missourian Ephraim Anderson explained that, in spite of the cold, the men "advanced cheerfully without a murmur or complaint." R. M. Collins claimed that "the boys were all as gay as larks" and "rejoiced at the idea that a decisive blow was going to be struck." According to T. J. Walker of the 9th Tennessee Infantry "although the army was greatly reduced in size, yet the idea of again entering on Tennessee soil made us feel (at least us Tennesseans) buoyant and happy." John Copley described his regiment as a collection of starving men who wore rags and marched on bare feet but somehow were "buoyant and hopeful."[16]

Hate strengthened the resolve of some men. When Thomas Key received word that his wife and children were suffering because of Union raids on his home in Arkansas, he proclaimed that the Army of Tennessee was a sword of vengeance against "the hateful abolitionists and their negro associates." Georgian Walter Clark was angered by the behavior of northern troops. Clark quoted General Patrick Cleburne as saying, "I am not fighting for right, I am fighting for vengeance."[17]

Hopes of victory buoyed rebel spirits, but the cold brought many men back down to earth. James Lanning walked across sheets of ice one inch thick. H. K. Nelson nearly froze to death as he picked his way through a mix of ice, snow, and half-frozen mud. One night Risenar Etter was forced to sleep in the open, and he recalled, "my beard froze to my face." The rain "froze in a hard mass" on the mane of the horse that carried James Cooper, a mounted officer with the 20th Tennessee Infantry. Samuel Cooke of the 17th Texas Cavalry (dismounted) missed his long departed horse as he waded through freezing mud and water up to his waist. R. J. Black of the 7th Tennessee Cavalry noted in his diary that "I never suffered so much before with cold" as on the march into Tennessee. Perhaps adding insult to injury for many men, soldiers from Missouri cheered when it snowed. They told men from the lower South, "this is the kind of weather we want, regular old Missouri weather." They hated the "southern rains" and saw the cold as proof that they were on the way home. Captain John Dicks of the Fourth Louisiana Battalion claimed that no army in all of human history suffered "greater hardships than the little band of brave men who went from Florence, Ala."[18]

The men who marched north looked rough and must have smelled horrific. Edgar Jones recalled that all the men were filthy and suffered from body lice. He blamed the filth not on his comrades, who tried to keep clean, but on the nature of the campaign, which provided men with no time to bathe or wash their clothing. In desperation, men took off their clothing and held it over their evening campfires trying to find the ideal distance from the flames that would incinerate the lice that tormented them without scorching their precious garments. Despite their best efforts, Jones concluded that every rebel from the private to the general lost the war against dirt. Georgia soldier Walter Clark explained that most men gave up on bathing. Those who did try to keep clean poured water from a canteen onto their hands, which they then rubbed over whatever parts of their body they cared to clean. One woman who did laundry for Confederate soldiers claimed that she washed underwear for Forrest's cavalrymen that were "so stiffened with dirt that they were able to stand alone."[19]

The roads and draft animals were in terrible shape. With a teamster's eye for terrain, John Sparkman noted that the constant movement of armies and endless rains had destroyed the roads. He blamed the army's commissary department for the poor condition of the horses, which were "nearly broken down." In a desperate bid to keep the animals alive, some men with horses dismounted and walked their horses rather than ride them. The army was slowed to a crawl by the cannons and wagons that inched forward through the mud. Hood ordered entire regiments of infantrymen to push the artillery and supply wagons through the mud by hand. While pushing wagons was slow, it was the only way to keep the provisions moving. When a sergeant with the quartermaster's department became careless, two wagons slipped into a pond, drowning a mule and almost killing a "negro teamster."[20]

Barefoot men became desperate. Every morning shoeless men went to the pens where beef cattle were slaughtered and received bloody cowhides, which they crafted into crude moccasins. The moccasined troops began the day's trek happily enough, but their joy was often short lived. If the weather was cold and rainy, the moccasins sometimes protected the men's feet until they could return to the slaughter pens the next morning. However, if the sun came out, moccasins dried and shrank until the men were forced to cut the footwear off and resume the march with bare feet. Most afternoons the road was "literally strewn with pieces of cow skin that had been discarded by the men because it had drawn up, so it pinched their feet." Mississippi infantryman Robert Jarman was delighted when several of Forrest's cavalry troopers appeared fresh from capturing several Union transport ships on the Tennessee River. The horsemen all boasted extra shoes lashed to their saddles and handed them out to the barefoot infantrymen. When the cavalrymen ran out of extra shoes, barefoot infantrymen stole the shoes of sleeping troopers, reasoning that "it was no harm for a cavalryman to be barefooted" since "he had a horse to ride."[21]

The Confederate Army of Tennessee Arrives Near Columbia

While the infantry moved into position near Columbia, Tennessee, Forrest's cavalrymen skirmished with the Federals south of town. Lieutenant R. J. Black and the 7th Tennessee Cavalry drove "the enemy pell-mell before us" as they converged on Columbia. Federals twisted their lines around to cut off Rucker's Brigade from the rest of the command. Chalmers ordered a staff officer named Bleecker to ride out to warn Rucker of the danger. Bleecker rode through an orchard where "the enemy's shells were clipping off limbs and plowing up the ground." He delivered the message to Rucker and as he began his ride back to General Chalmers, "a grapeshot struck the pummel of his saddle and shattered it." Bleecker was unmoved by the fact that a bit of shrapnel passed within an inch of his body but was deeply troubled by the loss of his fine "Texas saddle."[22]

Union troops massed near Columbia, gathered from all over Tennessee. Units included the 4th Federal Corps with about 12,000 men, the 23rd Federal Corps consisting of about 10,000 men, and James H. Wilson's 7,700 cavalrymen. Large numbers of Union skirmishers occupied rifle pits that

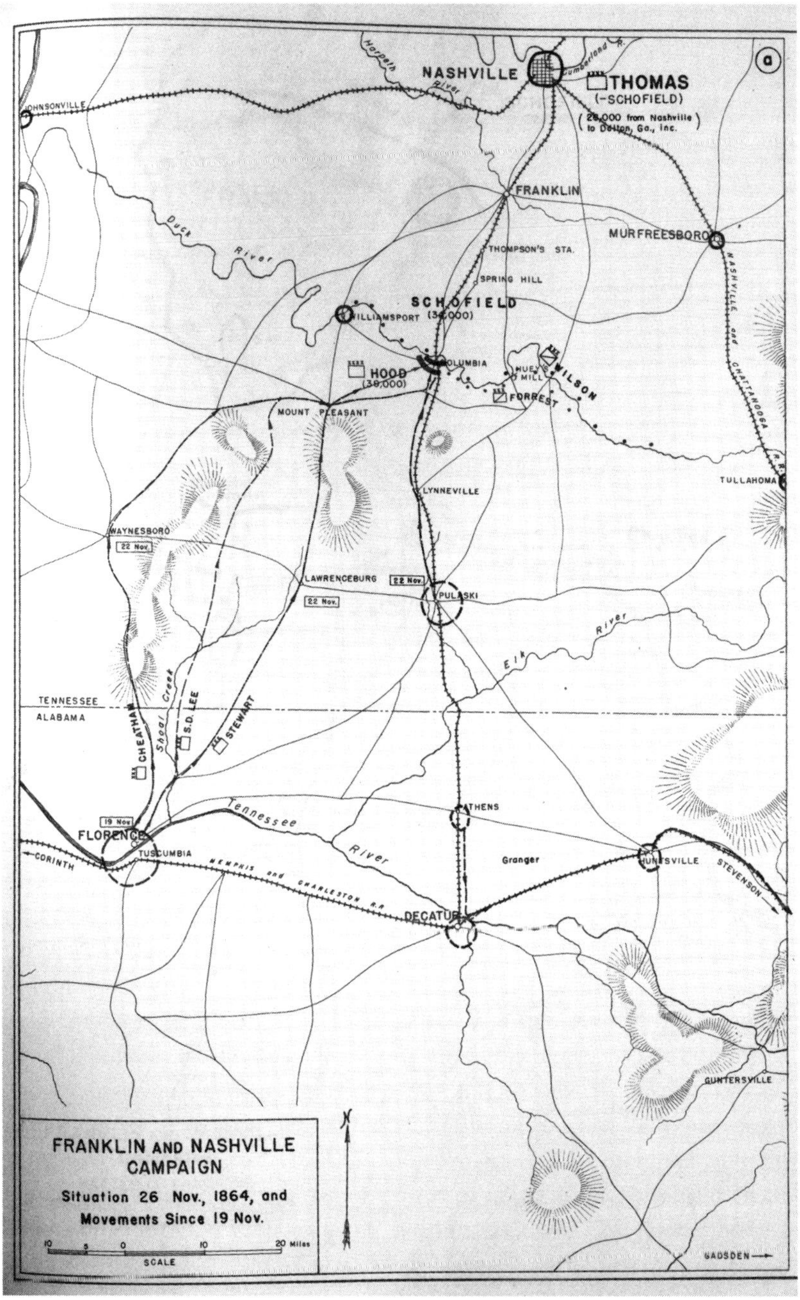

Map 6. Franklin and Nashville Campaign, November 26, 1864. United States Military Academy. Department of Military Art and Engineering, Vincent J. Esposito, and Matthew Forney Steele. *Civil War Atlas to accompany Steele's American Campaigns* (West Point, N.Y.: 1941). Library of Congress.

encompassed the town. Three lines of Union defenders waited in breastworks behind the skirmishers. The rebel cavalrymen tried to advance on the Federals, but the men in blue were secure within their rifle pits. Every time a rebel tried to move forward, "a volley would be poured forth." When General Forrest arrived on the scene, he demanded to know why the men were not advancing and rode forward. Union defenders responded to his advance with bullets that tore up the earth and killed the horse of one of his companions. The gunfire convinced Forrest that the enemy was well prepared to defend the town. He pulled back to wait for the infantry and artillery to arrive.[23]

The Confederate Army of Tennessee's infantry and artillery units began moving into positions near Columbia early on November 27. Lee's Corps rested its right flank on the Mount Pleasant Pike. Cheatham's Corps crossed over the Pulaski Pike and took a position with its right on the banks of the Duck River and its left on the Pulaski Pike. Roughly four miles south of Columbia, General Stewart ordered his corps into veer to the east, a track that took the troops on a meandering path through fields and woods before they encountered Union positions near the Pulaski Pike. Stewart's Corps continued its march down the Mount Pleasant and Columbia Pike and came to rest with its right on the Pulaski Pike and its left on the Mount Pleasant and Columbia Pikes. As the army came into line, staff officers and couriers came to life, galloping up and down the line. Veteran soldiers realized that the flurry of activity meant that the enemy was nearby.[24]

John Sparkman had enjoyed a brief furlough with his family in Middle Tennessee. It was the first time he had been home in nearly three years. He noted in his diary that "it is indeed very pleasant to be at home with relatives and friends and out of sight of the army." Everyone treated him "very kindly." He noted that his family had suffered as a result of the war, but that their condition was "not as bad as I expected." His happy homecoming stood in stark contrast to the miseries of army life. He confessed, "the more I soldier, the less I like it." Sparkman could have remained home like the many men who slipped away on the campaign, never to return. Sparkman's diary reveals an internal conflict. He wanted to remain home where he could help his family rebuild and enjoy "very pleasant" company, but he also felt an obligation to return to the army. Sparkman left home after only two days, "not because I like the army but there is my duty and I know I have to go."[25] He followed the Army of Tennessee's path of destruction across his home state and arrived just in time to help with the fight for Columbia.

Discovering that the enemy held strongly fortified positions on the south side of the Duck River, Hood ordered the army to perform a flanking movement and cut off the Federal route towards Nashville. Once again, Forrest's horsemen led the way. Hood sent the cavalrymen to cross the Duck River at several fords on the evening of November 27 to provide cover while the engineers threw a pontoon bridge across the river so the infantry and artillery could cross. Hood ordered Lee's Corps to spread out into line of battle as though he was preparing to make a frontal assault, in an effort to keep the Federals worried about an assault from the south. While Lee's Corps kept up the pressure, Cheatham's and Stewart's men prepared to slip across the Duck River and "play Sherman on them by a flank movement."[26]

General Schofield refused to sit still while Hood sprung his trap. General Thomas had ordered Schofield to hold the bridges at Columbia. When Scofield realized that the rebels were threatening to cut off his line of retreat, he made the tough decision to pull back to the north bank of the Duck River, destroy any supplies he could not take with him, and burn the bridges. Once on the northern bank, he hoped to find a stronger line on the road to Nashville. The men in blue completed their river crossing shortly before daybreak. Schofield regretted abandoning Columbia but believed he had no choice and sent word to General Thomas in Nashville that his forces were in a much stronger position on the northern bank, where "I can now stop Hood's advance."[27]

Early in the morning of November 28, Confederate forces advanced on Columbia and discovered that it was abandoned. Pleased that they did

Tennessee, Duck River bridge. Library of Congress.

not appear to be in danger but still feeling the cautious apprehension of veterans, men moved slowly towards the smoldering ruins of Union supply depots, taking possession of Columbia as the sun rose. Members of the 18th and 3rd Tennessee Infantry Regiments sought to secure the railroad bridge across the Duck River but the retreating Federals set it on fire before the rebels arrived. John Copley had hoped to fight a decisive battle against the Union forces at Columbia, but their unexpected disappearance delayed the showdown. W. E. Preston recalled that General Cleburne "gave us a talk to cheer us up." In his "richest Irish brogue," Cleburne told the men, "I will never surrender, I will die first."[28]

James Lanning took little comfort in rousing speeches from the generals. Lanning's diary revealed his conflicted feelings near Columbia. He was a homesick father and husband who wanted to "hasten to my dear ones at home there to live in peace." Lanning could have deserted—many other men did—but his diary reveals that he remained because he felt an obligation to stay with the army and could only return home in good conscience after the war was over. Interestingly, he said nothing about a Confederate victory in the diary entries from his period and offered a simple prayer that God "would close this cruel, unnatural war."[29] His emphasis on ending the war with no mention of who might win the conflict suggests that he may have wanted nothing more than peace, even if that peace came at the cost of a Confederate defeat.

Many residents of Columbia welcomed the rebel army. Joel Murphree claimed that the citizens of Columbia welcomed the Confederate soldiers with cheers and friendly greetings, which he offered as proof that "the citizens of this section are as loyal to the south as we are." He also noted that some residents had fled town, suggesting that some Tennesseans were not so happy to see the rebel army after all. J. P. Cannon and other members of "the younger portion of us" were soon "engaged in the more agreeable business of talking to the pretty young women."[30]

Firmly in possession of the town, the rebels gathered up all the supplies that the Yankees had failed to burn. When General Hood received reports that "Columbia had been wantonly and disgracefully plundered," he became outraged. In response, he issued General Orders No. 37, which prohibited "plundering by the army of both private and public property." The men ignored Hood's order, never pausing from their efforts to gather supplies. Joel Murphree described a free-for-all where merchants traded their goods for small sums of Confederate money, perhaps in an effort to support the cause or because soldiers were likely to steal things that they could not purchase for discount prices. Murphree had hoped to acquire a new hat and a pair of shoes, but by the time he got to town the shelves were bare. From the half burned bits of leather he found amongst the wreckage of an abandoned building, John Johnston of the 14th Tennessee Cavalry pieced together a new set of horse equipment to replace his worn out gear. Members of Stevenson's Division captured two siege howitzers and large quantities of ammunition. Several hundred Yankees prisoners marched to the rear "with hang dog countenances and ragged dirty clothes."[31]

The northerners were no longer in Columbia, but they menaced the men in gray from their positions north of the Duck River. Sporadic gunfire passed between the two armies. Newton Cannon and other members of the 11th Tennessee Cavalry had spent the last several weeks destroying railroads and telegraph lines. Facing relentless pursuit by reinforced Federal troops, the exhausted troopers split up, with each man trusted to make his way back to the rebel lines. Cannon explained, "the sound of the artillery was our principle way of finding out where Hood's army was."[32]

Early on the morning of November 29, the Confederate Army of Tennessee tried to intercept Schofield's withdrawing soldiers. General Lee remained in command on the south bank of the river. He supervised Clayton's Division, Stevenson's Division, and most of the army's artillery in their attempt to hold the enemy's attention. Union troops fired on the rebels from positions on the north bank of the river. The Confederate artillery responded by shelling the men in blue. Confederate gunners kept up a steady fire, and several artillerymen died in the duel. Robert Magill and the rest of the 39th Georgia Infantry took positions in an abandoned fort on the south bank of the river and traded gunshots their Union counterparts. The sporadic gunfire accomplished little. One bullet hit Magill's rifle and ricocheted into the head of another rebel, giving him a slight wound, but no other men in the fort were killed or wounded. Magill gave thanks to the sturdy fort for their relative safety.[33] While General Lee's men kept the Union defenders busy, General Hood ordered the rest of the army to cross Duck River.[34]

Forrest's troopers led the way. Cavalrymen forded the icy, swift-moving waters of the Duck River at several places. Chalmers's and Jackson's divisions of cavalry got across with minimal losses, but Buford's division faced a more daunting obstacle. Roughly twenty Union soldiers occupied a sturdy log fort that dominated the ford assigned to Buford's men. After analyzing the situation, Buford decided that a mounted crossing would be suicide, so he ordered his men to construct a log raft to take a small assault team of dismounted men across the river, upriver and out of sight of the fort, to sneak up on the Union defenders, attack the fort from the rear, and allow the rest of the division to cross in relative safety. Buford asked the 2nd Tennessee to provide twelve volunteers for the mission.

Colonel Clark Barteau, the twenty-nine-year-old raw-boned, heavily mustached veteran commander of the 2nd Tennessee Cavalry asked for volunteers, but nobody stepped forward. Barteau was born into a family of farmers in Ohio, where the evils of slavery were a topic of constant conversation. In 1855 he came south to see the peculiar institution for himself. After careful investigation, Barteau became an ardent defender of the south's racial hierarchy and published a pro-slavery newspaper. When war came in 1861, he bade a tearful farewell to his wife and enlisted as a private. By the fall of 1864, Barteau's wife was dead, his body carried the scars of wounds suffered on multiple battlefields, and he wore the gray frock coat of a full colonel.[35]

When nobody volunteered, Barteau boarded the raft and asked who would come with him. Impressed by his courage, many men rushed forward, providing far more volunteers than the plan required. The men piled onto the raft, which almost disintegrated in the icy, swiftly flowing water, but somehow the rebels made it across. Confederate soldiers who remained on the south bank near the ford kept up a steady fire on the Federals, ensuring that the men in blue did not notice the men who crossed on the raft and slowly slipped up behind them. With near perfect timing, the amphibious team assaulted the fort on foot, while mounted Confederates charged across the ford. Surprised and suddenly under attack from two directions, the Federals broke and fled. The Confederate cavalry pursued the fleeing Federals, but exhausted horses prevented the rebels from capturing their adversaries.[36]

With fords firmly in Southern hands, Confederate engineers set up pontoon bridges about three miles east of Columbia. Schofield continued withdrawing his troops, moving north along the Columbia Pike. Hood sent his men north along the rougher Rally Hill Pike and Old Settlers Road, which lay a few miles to the east of the Columbia Pike. Officers distributed orders to the men explaining that Hood's "intention was to beat them to Nashville and; that he expects us to march hard and not give up under any circumstances." Hood ordered artillerymen, including James Robert Maxwell of Lumsden's Alabama Battery, to leave their cannons, ammunition, and wagons behind with skeleton crews on the south bank of the Duck River and advance with the infantry of Reynold's Brigade. Hood hoped that his infantry would capture Union artillery. When that happened, the commanding general wanted to have gunners nearby who could make immediate use of the newly acquired ordnance. General Hood seemed to believe that, through sheer force of will, his starving and exhausted men could somehow outrun the Union soldiers, cut the road to Spring Hill, and destroy Schofield's outnumbered command before Schofield could rendezvous with Stanley's 5,500 Federal troops and the large quantities of supplies waiting at Spring Hill.[37]

Rebels rose to Hood's challenge and advanced at a "fox trot," with Cheatham's Corps in the lead. Unseasonably warm weather melted snow, turning roads into masses of mud where men "sank at every step." The roads were not wide enough for the entire army, so some men walked through fields and tripped over dense cornstalks. It was a difficult march "through cedar breaks and over read clay fields," but the men kept up a rapid pace since "the idea of our flanking the Yankees was such a good joke." Texas soldiers received encouragement when they passed by the house of a "good lady and her pretty daughters," who greeted the rebels with handshakes and cheerful greetings. R. M. Collins described the lady as the bearer of a "good rebel heart" because she proclaimed that wished she had a hand big enough to shake the entire Army of Tennessee at one time. John Copley and the rest of the 49th Tennessee Infantry recalled that the ground was a difficult trail "over rocks, hills, down steep hollows, over stone and rail fences, through thick underbrush." The men moved as quickly as they could, and "wherever the ground would permit, we went on a run." Sam Dunlap with the 1st Missouri Battery pushed his cannon forward until the rocks that cut his bare feet to shreds broke a wagon wheel. The artillerymen replaced it with a wheel stolen from a civilian wagon and pressed ahead. Bringing up the rear of the army, Robert Jarman and the rest of Johnson's Division in Lee's Corps guarded the wagons and artillery. Since the Yankees were fleeing, the Mississippians had little guarding to do and helped starving horses move wheels through the mud.[38]

While the infantry struggled forward, Forrest's cavalrymen skirmished with the Federals. John Young and the 7th Tennessee Cavalry made several mounted charges against Federal cavalrymen. Young watched as Private F. M. Nelson of his regiment traded saber blows with a Union horseman, who knocked the rebel from his horse. The bluecoat's victory was short lived because, an instant later, Nelson's comrade J. M. Tate rushed to defend Nelson, fired a pistol ball into the Federal trooper, and killed him instantly. In the face of determined resistance about two miles south of Spring Hill, Forrest ordered Frank Armstrong's Mississippi Brigade, some of the Kentuckians of Edward Crossland's Brigade, as well as the 14th Tennessee of Edmund Rucker's Brigade to form a line of battle and charge. The rebel horsemen pressed the attack with all their might, but the Union troopers stubbornly held their position at the crest of a hill and forced the rebels to retreat. Realizing that mounted assaults were doomed to failure, Forrest ordered his entire command to make a dismounted assault, which also failed. Forrest then took a position on a high hill, where he "discovered the enemy hurriedly moving his wagon train up the Franklin Pike." In an effort to close the road, Forrest launched more assaults, which all failed. At about that time, Hood sent orders for the cavalry to hold their positions and await the arrival of the infantry.[39]

When the Confederate infantry arrived near Spring Hill at around 3:00 p.m., the reinforced rebels prepared to renew their assaults. Cleburne's Division arrived first, followed soon after by Bate's and Brown's Divisions. Captain W. O. Dodd of Chalmers's Division of cavalry enjoyed the "beautiful day" as "the old rugged veterans of Cheatham's Corps" marched into view, their battle flags illuminated by afternoon sunlight. In the distance, he heard the rebel artillery playing "a lively music." Dodd believed that "the long-sought opportunity had at last arrived." In a few minutes the Confederates would close the road and win a great victory. General Hood was on the scene and personally ordered General Cheatham to "take possession of and hold that pike at or near Spring Hill," to "accept whatever comes," and to prevent the Federal withdrawal.[40]

Consistent with Hood's orders, General Cleburne of Cheatham's Corps ordered his division to prepare for an attack. Mark Lowery's Brigade of Alabamians and Mississippians formed on the right. Hiram Granbury's Texas brigade took a position on the left and slightly to the rear of Lowery's men. Patrick Cleburne himself rode with Daniel Govan's Arkansas brigade, which he kept in reserve behind Granbury's and Lowery's troops. Confederate cavalrymen dismounted and formed on the infantry's right. The men in gray set their sights on a steep, wooded hill southeast of Columbia, which was held by Federals who had repelled attacks by Confederate cavalry earlier in the day.[41]

Atop the hill, members of General Luther Bradley's Union 3rd Brigade watched and waited, secure behind a sturdy barricade of fence rails. The conglomeration of regiments from Illinois, Ohio, and Missouri were still catching their breath after a forced march from Pulaski, Tennessee, and a long day of sporadic skirmishes with the Confederate cavalry. When Cleburne's infantrymen approached the hill, the Federals responded with "a very destructive fire." For a few minutes an under-strength brigade held firm against an all-out assault by one of the finest divisions in the Confederate army. General Bradley believed that experienced troops could have repelled the attack, but "over one-half of the men of these regiments were recruits and drafted men who had never been under fire, neither had they been drilled." The Federals eventually retreated about a quarter of a mile, where they rallied with the rest of Wagner's Division.[42]

As Cleburne's infantrymen clashed with the Federals, dismounted cavalrymen wheeled around, catching fleeing Union soldiers in the flank.

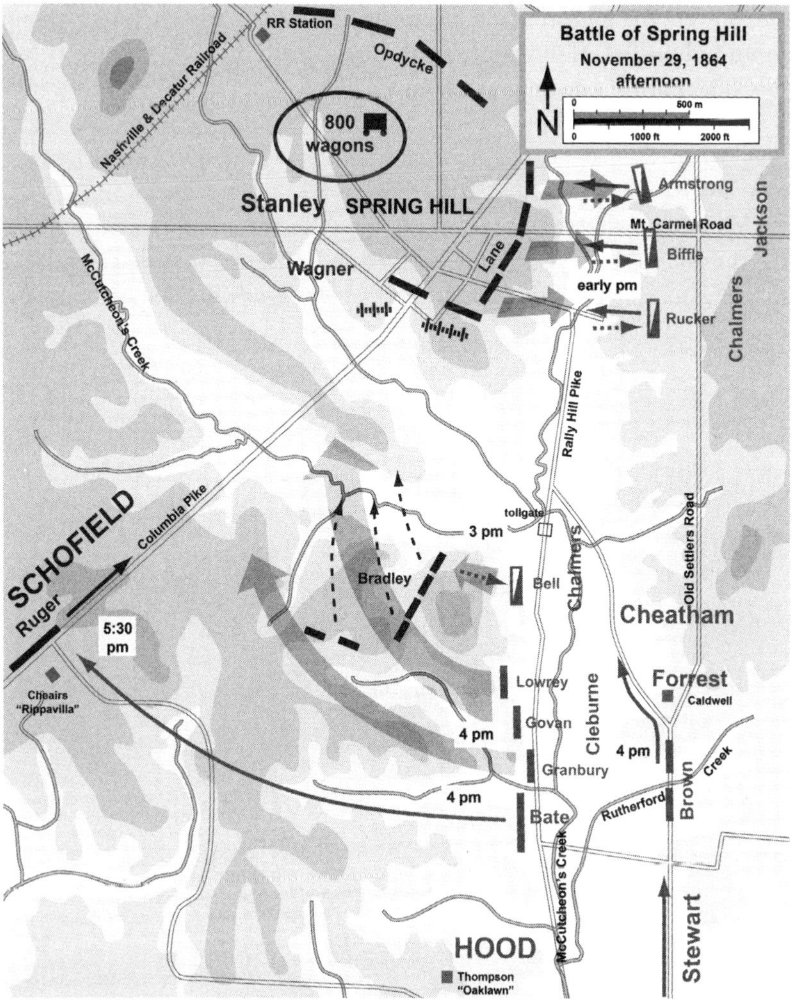

Map 7. Spring Hill, afternoon. Map by Hal Jespersen, www.cwmaps.com.

John Johnston of the 14th Tennessee Cavalry saw a Union soldier with a knapsack on his back run into the open with his back to the Confederate line. Before Johnston could react, one of his comrades took careful aim and fired. The blue-clad figure fell to the dirt and then almost instantly jumped back to his feet to continue his sprint for safety. Apparently, the bullet struck the knapsack, knocking the Federal off balance without seriously injuring him. General Forrest came up behind the Tennesseans, encouraging them to maintain a steady fire. The cavalry withdrew shortly thereafter with an understanding that the infantry would take their place and prevent the Federals from escaping. The exhausted cavalrymen set up camp and drifted off to sleep. Johnston explained, "I do not suppose that it was Gen. Forrest's intention that our small force should undertake to carry the enemy's position, but that his purposed was rather to menace and hold them where they were until our infantry could pass up and form across the road and intercept their march northward."[43]

More Confederate infantrymen arrived and attacked the Federals as the sun fell. In their haste, Union soldiers abandoned overloaded knapsacks weighing as much as fifty pounds. The rebels eagerly divided up the plun-

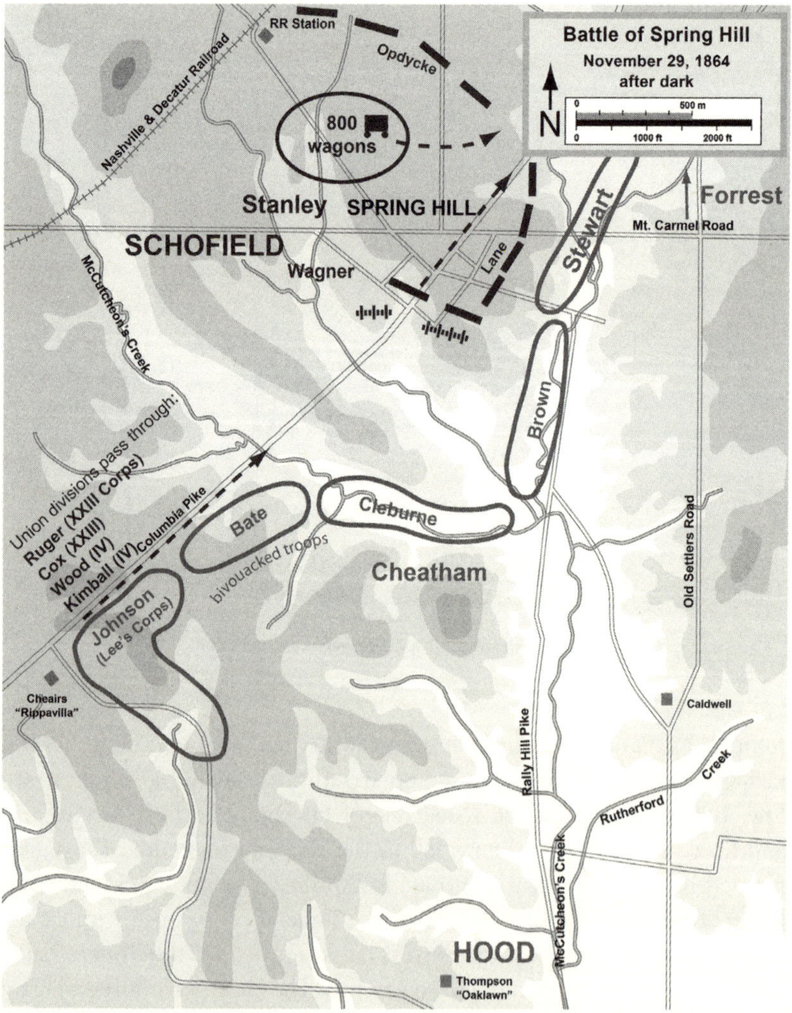

Map 8. Spring Hill, evening. Map by Hal Jespersen, www.cwmaps.com.

der, including new shoes. A group of Federals tried to cover their retreat by returning fire from behind a wooden hog trough. The boards provided little protection from the .54 caliber Austrian Lorenz Rifles carried by the 33rd Alabama Infantry. Lead slugs penetrated the thin planks and tore through northern bodies, which the rebels left lying on the ground. By this time, darkness was falling, and the exhausted rebels lay down in a small grove of trees without taking off any of their equipment except their blankets.[44]

The Federals continued their withdrawal in the darkness. R. M. Collins and the 15th Texas Infantry arrived near the Columbia Pike and were delighted to see a line of Union wagons hurrying north with only a thin line of skirmishers to protect them. Collins recalled, "the hearts of the boys beat high with joy at the prospect of getting to prowl all those wagons." Before the rebels could act, a battery of Union artillery located in Spring Hill, on their right flank, "poured the shot and shell into us." The Texans turned their attention to the Yankee gunners. Before they could silence the battery, darkness fell, and the rebels withdrew out of range for the evening. Edward Young McMorries and the 1st Alabama concluded their twenty-eight-mile march, "the greatest the regiment had ever performed," late that evening. After a brief dinner, the men spread their blankets and fell exhausted to the ground just a few yards from the Franklin Pike. The men of the 1st Alabama assumed that other units lay across the road, ensuring that the Federals would not escape that evening. As Tennessean John Copley and his comrades lay down to sleep that night, "we felt confident that the following day the whole army would be captured."[45]

General Hood listened intently for the sounds of battle from his headquarters near Spring Hill. When Hood heard the firing die down, he sent several couriers to urge Cheatham to close the road. Eventually, Hood concluded that Cheatham must have occupied a strong defensive position in Spring Hill or along the road and that the thwarted Federals had refused to attack. In fact, it was General Cheatham who refused to attack. When General Johnson begged Cheatham for permission to close the road with his division, which was temporarily attached to Cheatham, Cheatham refused on the basis that he "was opposed to night attacks." General Cleburne agreed, believing that "it was not best to bring on an engagement at night." Late in the evening, Hood met with Cheatham, who confessed that he had not attacked. Hood demanded to know why, and Cheatham explained that blocking the road would force him to spread his lines dangerously thin. Cheatham asked Hood to order General Stewart to bring his corps into alignment with Cheatham, so that Stewart's men could close the escape route. Hood agreed to send Stewart's Corps.[46]

About dusk, General Stewart found General Hood and asked for orders.

Hood introduced Stewart to a young man who lived in the neighborhood and would work as a guide and help Stewart move the right of his corps "across the pike beyond Spring Hill." Stewart was concerned because "this would have placed my line in rear of Cheatham's, except that my right would have extended beyond his." There was some confusion between the guide and the generals about exactly where everyone was supposed to be going and which road was the correct one. To further complicated matters, while Stewart was trying to find his way, an engineer officer from General Cheatham's Corps approached Stewart and gave him updated orders from Hood. The new orders required Stewart to take a position on the right of General Brown's Division, on the extreme right of Cheatham's Corps. Stewart believed that the orders were clearly a mistake. He also realized that it was late in the evening and that it would take all night to get to the new position. Therefore, Stewart ordered his men into camp for the evening and went in search of Hood for clarification.[47]

At about 9:30 p.m., Generals Forrest and Stewart met with Hood at the army's headquarters, located at Dr. Thompson's home, about two and half miles from Spring Hill. Isham Harris, the Confederate governor of Tennessee, listened but did not speak. According to Harris, Hood informed Stewart, "It is of great importance that a brigade should be put on the road tonight. Can you send one?" Stewart seemed reluctant, replying that his men were hungry and very tired. Hood then turned to Forrest and asked him if he could close the road. Forrest complained that his men were also exhausted and hungry, but he agreed to cut the pike. Convinced that the problem was solved, Hood and his staff went to bed.[48]

General Forrest ordered Ross's Brigade of Texas cavalry to block the road and prevent the Federals from escaping. The Texans successfully held a position astride the road for a short time, capturing numerous prisoners along the road, and thought that perhaps they had cut off the Federals. Before bedding down for the night, the Texans advanced up the pike for a final check. They bumped into a large unit of Federal cavalry. After half an hour of intense combat, the much larger body of Union troops forced the Texans to withdraw. Content that they had done everything they could, Ross's men withdrew and made camp. It is not clear if Ross reported his failure to close the road to Forrest, but it does not appear that anyone informed Hood that the road was open once more.[49]

Union soldiers made good use of the open path. Tennessee soldier L. M. Graham "could hear the tramp of the Yankees all night long." He and his comrades "wondered why Hood did not try to head them off." After a brief skirmish with the fleeing Federals, A. J. Batchelor and the 33rd Alabama Infantry made camp within eighty yards of the road. During the night the Alabamians heard Federals marching along the road. Several times during the evening, confused Union soldiers walked up to the Confederate campfires to warm themselves and inadvertently became prisoners. E. H. Rennolds explained that "by some misunderstanding among the generals no attack was made," even though "all through the early part of the night the Federals could be heard passing along the pike only a few hundred yards away." R. M. Collins remembered, "we were all astonished at our line not being thrown across the pike, capturing this whole train and completely cutting off Schofield's retreat." During the night, arguments broke out among the Texans of Granbury's Brigade as they heard troops moving nearby. Some men claimed that they were rebels and others were convinced that they were Union men. Captain Dick English, an officer on General Granbury's staff, finally exclaimed, "I'll be d-d if I don't intend to find out." English mounted his mule and disappeared into the darkness. The remaining Texans continued to argue about who was on the road. A little later, confused men in blue settled the disagreement when they wandered to the rebel campfires to light their pipes and became prisoners.[50]

General Lee's Corps trailed far behind the rest of the army. Delayed by their work pushing wheels through sticky mud, Robert Jarman and the rest of the 27th Mississippi Infantry were finally allowed to rest at two in the morning, still several miles from the road to Spring Hill. To get out of the mud, Jarman and his friends rested on a large limestone rock, preferring a hard bed to a wet one. They rested little as the temperature dropped and the stone became colder than ice. Their troubled sleep did not last long. At 2:30 a.m. on November 30, General Lee realized that the Federals had evacuated the area and ordered his men to begin a rapid pursuit northward up the Columbia Pike.[51]

The Union Forces Escape to Spring Hill

The sun rose at 6:59 a.m. on November 30, and the light revealed that the Federals had escaped. Chalmers's and Buford's cavalry divisions were out of ammunition. With their supplies lagging in Columbia, Forrest obtained ammunition from the infantry and ordered them to renew their attacks at daybreak. Chalmers reported that by the time he got his men into action, the Union infantry was already gone.[52] When the rebels realized that the men in blue had slipped away, powerful men began pointing fingers.

General Hood called a meeting of his key officers at Rippa Villa plantation in Spring Hill. The unhappy commanding general blamed Cheatham for the Federal escape. Hood argued that he gave Cheatham direct orders to block the Union retreat, that Cheatham verified that he understood the orders, and that Cheatham simply failed to obey. As a result, Hood believed the Confederacy lost their grandest opportunity "to utterly rout and destroy the Federal Army." In his official report, Hood even claimed, "Cheatham has frankly confessed of the great error of which he was guilty and attaches all blame to himself." Initially, Hood demanded Cheatham's removal from the army, but he relented after Cheatham apologized. Hood claimed, "had I dreamed one moment that Cheatham would have failed to give battle, or at least to take position across the pike, I would have ridden, myself, to the front and led the troops into action."[53]

Years later, Cheatham responded to Hood with a vigorous rebuttal and claims that he never confessed to any misconduct. Cheatham claimed that Hood initially ordered him to advance, but when he encountered stiff resistance from the Federals, Hood ordered Cheatham to report to army headquarters for new orders. When Cheatham arrived, he recalled, "the Commanding General there informed me that he had concluded to wait till morning, and directed me to hold my command in readiness to attack at daylight," a decision that "astonished" Cheatham, since "the road was still open" and the postponed attack meant that there would be "nothing to prevent the enemy from marching to Franklin." Later in the evening, when Hood discovered that Federal troops were traveling down the road unimpeded, the commanding general sent word for Cheatham to command "your picket line to fire into them." Cheatham ordered the men nearest the road to open fire, but General Johnson complained, pointing out that they were in Lee's Corps, and demanded to know why Cheatham did not order his own soldiers to open fire. When Johnson finally conceded, he scouted ahead and reported that there were no Federals on the road.[54]

Isham G. Harris, Confederate governor of Tennessee and a volunteer aid to General Hood on the campaign, told a very different story. Harris blamed a lowly staff officer and, to lesser degrees, General Forrest and General Stewart. Harris recalled that "Hood made some very harsh remarks about Cheatham's not having attacked in the night as ordered." Harris also claimed that Colonel Mason, a staff officer under General Hood, confessed to Harris that "General Cheatham is not to blame for that. I never sent him the order." Harris was shocked and demanded an explanation. Mason admitted that he fell asleep before writing the order. Harris concluded that Cheatham was blameless because he never received Hood's order to attack, that Stewart should have blocked the road as initially asked during the 9:30 p.m. conference, and that even Forrest deserved some blame because, while he did attempt to block the road, his men withdrew when they encountered resistance.[55]

While powerful men tried to assign the blame, ordinary soldiers were confused and worried. According to Tennessee infantryman John Copley, the men felt "chagrin and disappointment" when they discovered that the Federals had escaped "from such cause which I am unable to explain." General Forrest passed by, "pouring fourth volumes of wrath," and nobody dared to reply. Texan R. M. Collins noted that all of the important generals spent tremendous time and effort insisting that the blunder was somebody else fault, but he believed "the gods of battle were against us that day and injected confusion into the heads and tongues of our leaders." Maryland artillery officer William Ritter suggested that the darkness of the night might have played a role in the debacle. Thomas D. Duncan, a cavalryman from Mississippi, recalled that, while he was unsure what went wrong, he did know that "we plainly heard the artillery and wagons of the enemy's army marching out of Spring Hill and away from the sure defeat and capture, which would have been their fate had they kept their position until daylight of another day." Many years later, he wrote, "I never shall forget the gloom that settled over the ranks of our beaten troops." The Federal escape "seemed to smite the hearts of our men" because they knew the "deadly cost."[56]

The loss reminded T. J. Walker, a member of the 9th Tennessee Infantry, of Shakespeare:

> There is a tide in the affairs of men
> when taken at their flood leads on to fortune
> Omitted, all the rest of their lives
> Are bound in shadows and miseries.[57]

Hood's mood on the morning of November 29 was also the topic of heated debate. General Stephen Lee, present for the conference, described Hood as chagrinned and mortified but made no suggestion that Hood was angry. General French bumped into Hood a short time after the conference and reported that the army commander said, "we have missed the great opportunity of the war," which indicates Hood was unhappy but provides no evidence that he felt anger. The mistress of Rippa Villa, Susan Cheairs, overheard the meeting and reported that Hood's language "was not fit for women or children." The strongest evidence that Hood might have lost his temper comes from the testimony of Major Joseph Vaulx, who claimed Hood was "as wrathy as a rattlesnake" and spent the morning "striking at everything" with a determination to "charge the blame of it on somebody."[58] While Hood might have been angry, Vaulx was hardly an impartial observer. The Nashville store clerk turned soldier joined the 1st Tennessee Infantry in 1861, became General Cheatham's inspector general the next

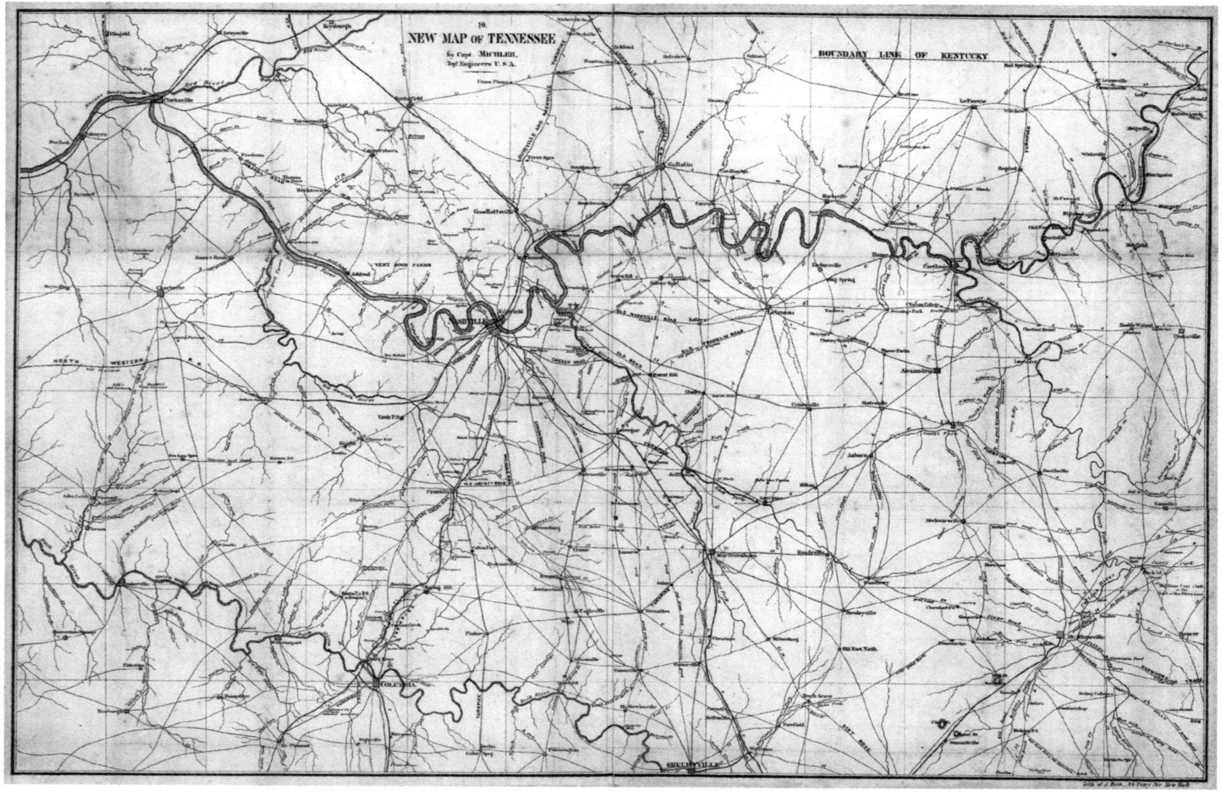

Map 9. A New Map of Tennessee. N. Michler, cartographer, 1860. Republished in Stephenson's Civil War maps, 1989. Library of Congress.

year, and served on Cheatham's staff until the end of the war. Vaulx may have found Hood's criticism of his longtime comrade in arms particularly stinging, a fact that could have colored his perception of Hood's mood.

Regardless of Hood's emotional state, the commanding general grossly exaggerated the loss when he suggested that he could have destroyed the Federal army. The Columbia Turnpike was not the only Union escape route, and, if the rebels had blocked it, the Federals could have traveled north by shifting a few miles to the west and using the road bed of the Alabama Railroad, the Carter Creek Turnpike, or a series of smaller roads. Even if the Confederate army had blocked the Columbia Turnpike and Schofield had failed to transition to other roads, there was no guarantee of overwhelming Confederate success. By the early evening of November 29, Schofield had concentrated his troops near Spring Hill and enjoyed numerical superiority near the potential battlefield, while Confederate forces were scattered across the countryside. Night attacks were rarely successful during the Civil War and widely regarded by commanders as "of little value," which is one reason why Cheatham and Cleburne were reluctant to attack in the dark. There is no reason to believe that General Schofield, a wily veteran who won a Medal of Honor for his valor at the Battle of Wilson's Creek, would have given up easily or that his men would have simply passed meekly into Confederate prison camps. Jacob Cox, commanding the Union 23rd Corps, reported that the Federals "easily checked" Confederate attacks and marched north with the "easy gait" of a well-disciplined and dangerous army withdrawing to more favorable ground. Other sources confirm that the Union forces near Spring Hill fought competently and killed at least 250 members of Cleburne's Division alone during the limited fighting on November 29.[59] Those same men in blue would once again prove themselves dangerous adversaries a few hours later, twelve miles north of Spring Hill, at the sleepy village of Franklin, Tennessee.

5
"VICTORY IS OURS BUT VERY DEARLY BOUGHT"
The Battle of Franklin

> We marched in line of battle for ¾ of a mile under one of the heaviest fires of small arms and artillery that was ever known, crossing their lines of breastworks and engaging them nearly all night; many noble braves fell to rise no more till God shall call them to judgement . . . The Federals crossed the river; leaving their dead and wounded in our hands and many articles of use to the army were captured. Deas Brigade held the works under a destructive cross fire such as was scarcely ever known before—the victory is ours but very dearly bought.[1]
>
> —James Lanning, 25th Alabama Infantry

On the morning of November 30, 1864, the Confederate Army of Tennessee renewed their pursuit. Forrest's cavalrymen moved out at daybreak and engaged the Union rear guard about two miles north of Spring Hill. Stewart's Corps came next, moving out at roughly the same early hour as the cavalry but at the slower pace of pedestrians. Cheatham's Corps followed close behind Stewart's men. Several miles to the south, Lee's infantrymen and most of the artillery trailed far behind the rest of the army. General Hood told the men that "it was only needed to press the enemy at this point and the campaign would be over."[2]

Like hungry wolves chasing a wounded rabbit, Confederate soldiers were excited by signs that the Federals were fleeing in disorder. J. P. Cannon was mortified that the Federals had "walked right out of the trap" but found encouragement among the burned Yankee wagons that proved the prey was still within reach. Colonel Ellison Capers of the 24th South Carolina Infantry reported that burned wagons and dead mules proved that their enemies were engaged in a "hasty retreat." Joseph Boyce of the

1st Missouri Infantry seemed to take pity on the poor mules on the side of the road, still in the harnesses that linked them to broken wagons. Their bodies were still warm, and steam rose from the bullet wounds their drivers had inflicted to their brains to prevent their capture by the pursuing Confederate army. In contrast, Boyce derived happiness from the civilians who lined the road cheering the rebels and calling out, "push on boys, you will capture all the Yanks soon they have just passed here on the dead run." The Missourians responded to the encouragement "with joyous cheers" and moved forward at the double quick.[3]

As the Confederate army drew closer to their enemies, excitement gave way to determined optimism. Edgar Jones recalled "an air of seriousness" since "trouble was brewing" and the men correctly deduced that "the men and officers who were so anxious to fight the night before were to be fully satisfied." Texas infantryman R. M. Collins felt pain with every step as sharp rocks in the road cut his bare feet into bloody masses, but he kept moving because he believed in the words of Hebrews 9:22, which stated, "there is no remission of sin without the shedding of blood." Collins did not reveal what "sins" he felt he or his army needed "remission" for, he simply quoted the scripture in his memoir without further explanation. Many years later, Louis Flatau, with Cowan's Mississippi Battery, explained that the rebels marching towards Franklin enjoyed grand delusions. They believed that their campaign across Georgia, Alabama, and into Tennessee was a huge success, that only luck had allowed the terrified Yankees to flee a step faster than they could pursue, and that the final moment of triumph was upon them. The veterans knew that victory could only come at an awful cost to what was left of their thinning band, but they raced forward anyway.[4]

At about 4:30 a.m., the Union 23rd Corps began arriving in Franklin. The city served as the county seat of Williamson County, resting about twelve miles north of Spring Hill and about twenty miles south of Nashville. The Harpeth River looped and meandered around the northern and eastern boundaries of the city. Founded in 1799 amidst some of the richest farmland in the region, by 1861 the city was a picturesque scene of carefully cultivated fields, whitewashed schools, beautiful homes, ornate churches, and a two-story courthouse reinforced with iron smelted at a nearby foundry. Fifteen hundred residents called the city home. Then the war came, bringing invading armies, ravenous soldiers, and constant threats of violence. The first Union soldiers arrived quietly in 1862 and soon began building lines of defensive works. On the east bank of the Harpeth River, the Union garrison built Fort Granger, towering two hundred feet above the nearby farmland, which cemented their control of the river as well as the Louisville and Nashville Railroad, which passed over a nearby bridge.

Aside from a few minor skirmishes, the fighting remained far away from Franklin for most of the war, but that was about to change. Finally within the confines of Franklin, exhausted Federals lay down to rest on the chilly ground and tried to get a few minutes of sleep in the predawn darkness.[5]

There was little time for the officers to rest, even as a few of their men napped. General Thomas in Nashville wanted Schofield to hold Hood in Franklin if possible, but Schofield believed that remaining south of the Harpeth River would only invite Hood's army to cut off and surround him. Therefore, he hatched a twofold plan to dig in and delay the rebels while his supply trains escaped to Nashville. Once the wagons were on the north bank, the rest of the army would follow. Schofield's plan was hampered by a pontoon bridge that had not yet arrived from Nashville, a ford that was almost impassable, and a burned-out wagon bridge. Only a single railroad bridge, which was difficult for wagons to cross, offered a viable path across the river.[6]

Time was vital. If Schofield could hold Franklin long enough to get across the river, his forces could join with Thomas's troops in Nashville and confront the rebels with an overwhelming superiority in men and materiel. They would also enjoy a secure position behind some of the most effective fortifications on the planet. If Hood could move quickly and cut the Federals off, he could make up for the mistakes at Spring Hill by defeating Schofield's forces. After that, the rebels might even have a chance of victory against Thomas's troops in Nashville.

As the Confederate army approached Franklin, Union soldiers rose from their brief rest and worked feverishly. The wagon bridge was burned, but only down to the water's edge, so the engineers were able to build a new bridge on the sturdy foundation of the old. They also built a wooden platform on top of the railroad tracks, which provided a smooth surface that the wagons could easily cross. Their efforts provided the Federals with two serviceable paths across the Harpeth and ensured that they could escape, if the rebels did not cut them off first. While engineers worked to get the army out of Franklin, most of the troops improved the town's fortifications to ensure that they could remain for as long as necessary.[7]

At about 11:00 a.m. Forrest's troopers bumped into Federals posted on the high ground at Winstead Hill, roughly three miles south of Franklin. At first the rebels thought it might be another ruse. Earlier in the day the Federal rear guard formed a line of battle across the road and appeared eager to make a stand, only to melt away as soon as the Confederate forces paused to transition into an attack formation. This time, the Federals were ready to fight. Infantrymen of George Wagner's Division partnered with John Croxton's Brigade of cavalry to make a stand. When Forrest's cavalrymen came within range, members of the 2nd Michigan let loose a hail of fire from their revolving rifles, and men of the 1st Tennessee Union Cavalry poured bullets from their breach-loading carbines. The rebel horsemen paid dearly for their aggression and retreated out of harm's way to await their infantry. At midday, Stewart's Corps arrived near Winstead Hill. Colonel Ellison Capers of the 24th South Carolina Infantry studied the men in blue, who waited "on a commanding ridge." The Federal rear guard had little hope against the might of Stewart's Corps, so they withdrew to the defensive lines around Franklin.[8]

General Hood arrived on the scene and ordered his army to form a line of battle in preparation for a direct assault. The news struck some men harshly. John Copley and the rest of the 49th Tennessee Infantry were filling their haversacks with beans from a neglected field and their minds with dreams of soup. Before they could complete their work, Billy Mumford, an aid to the brigade's commander General William Quarles, rode over to them and said, "boys you need not be gathering those beans." He explained that "we have to storm those breastworks over there" and pointed towards the Union lines. The once cheerful men suffered from another "cloud of disappointment" like the one they felt at Spring Hill. The wave of depression caused "our patriotic enthusiasm and most sanguine hopes to wane." The men lost all interest in soup, tossed the beans to the ground, and waited for official orders.[9]

The orders came quickly, and Confederate forces deployed for action. Lee's Corps and most of the army's artillery were still on the road. A more cautious commander might have waited to get his entire army into position, but Hood was aggressive, so he decided to make the attack with the units already on the scene. Stewart's Corps would form the right wing of the army on the eastern end of the valley. Cheatham's Crops would serve as the left wing to the west. The army's cavalry under General Forrest would split in two, screening both the extreme right and extreme left flanks of the army.[10]

Stewart lined up his divisions. Loring's Division was on the right flank, on the west bank of the Harpeth River. Walthall's Division formed on the left flank of Loring's men, and French's Division became the left flank of the corps, butting up against Cheatham's troops near the Nashville and Decatur Railroad. While the rest of the army was still getting into position, Loring's Division repelled a probe by Federal cavalry and drove them into a patch of trees to the north. The rebel cavalry added their weight to the attack but were unable to push the Union troops any farther. In an effort to move quickly, Hood had ordered most of the artillery to remain behind with General Lee's corps, bringing up the rear of the army. As a result, Stewart's entire corps had only a single battery, split up among the three divisions, to support the infantry. Artillerymen including James Robert Maxwell of Lumsden's Alabama Battery tagged along with Reynolds's Infantry Brigade of Walthall's Division. Hood had hoped to capture Union cannons on the road from Spring Hill that men like Maxwell could immediately turn on their former owners. The rebels failed to capture any cannons, leaving the unarmed gunners without any way to contribute to the attack. General Daniel Reynolds ordered the artillerymen to take refuge behind the hills south of Franklin and await further orders. Stewart's infantry moved through woods and fields until they found their positions roughly a mile and a quarter from Franklin.[11]

While Stewart's men moved into position on the right, Cheatham's Corps prepared for an assault on the left. The corps maneuvered behind Winstead's Hill. Cleburne's Division took a position on the right edge of Cheatham's line, butting up against French's Division of Stewart's Corps near the Nashville and Decatur Railroad. Brown's Division occupied Cheatham's center. Bate's Division took a place on the left flank of the corps. At about 3:00 p.m. General Cheatham ordered General Bate to move his division "by the left flank, pass a gap in the ridge to the left, circle around a mound which rose in the plain below and move toward the Carter Creek Pike."[12]

While Cheatham's and Stewart's Corps came into line, Lee's Corps hurried to join them. Infantrymen moved at the double quick, and teamsters pushed their animals to the breaking point. W. A. Callaway of Young's Georgia Battery trotted alongside his cannon as it bounced along the rocky road. After one particularly violent lurch, a pressure sensitive cap ignited a shell that blew up the entire trunk of forty explosive shells. The explosion shredded two artillerymen and almost killed Callaway. Nearby infantrymen dove for cover, convinced that they were under attack. Sadly, there was no time to mourn. The troops quickly regrouped and continued their rapid advance.[13]

Once General States Rights Gist brought his brigade of Georgians and South Carolinians into position as part of Brown's Division, he took a moment to make personal preparations for the attack. The thirty-three-year-old general was the son of Nathaniel Gist, prominent southern nationalist who gave his son an odd name to reflect his own politics. In 1861 States Rights Gist was a militia officer, lawyer, and military advisor to the governor of South Carolina. He joined the Confederate war effort and led troops into battle at Chickamauga, Chattanooga, and throughout the Atlanta campaign. Gist's slave Uncle Willy later recalled that as the veteran general surveyed the ground he was about to cross near Franklin, he devoured a hearty meal of pig's feet and biscuits. Gist believed that he might "git tripped up" before the day ended so he gave his watch, ring, and cash to

Uncle Willy with instructions to pass the items along to his wife if he did not survive the battle. The general's favorite horse was exhausted from the hard ride, so Gist ordered Uncle Willy to saddle his back up horse, Joe. Uncle Willy objected "you ain't got no business riding Joe, Joe ain't got no sense when de bullets come around." Gist replied that the horse would have to get used to the bullets. Uncle Willy wanted to argue, but he did not say another word because "when Marse States talked dat way, twarn't no use."[14]

Confederate soldiers lounged on the chilly ground and gazed at the terrain they were about to cross. The Federal lines curved across the plain to the south and west of Franklin in a broad semi-circle, with both flanks resting against the Harpeth River. R. M. Collins described the river as "clear, laughing, limpid waters." Joseph Boyce thought "the ground appeared as level to us as a floor." George Athey of the 22nd Alabama Infantry described the Federals as so numerous that they lay "as thick of hills of corn in the field."[15]

The first line of Union works lay six hundred yards in front of the rebels in a roughly semi-circle shape pierced in the middle by the Columbia Pike. A set of quickly improvised breastworks sat behind a ditch that was two and a half feet deep and provided some protection from a frontal assault, but both the left and right ends of the line floated in the air, making the line vulnerable to flanking attacks. Schofield ordered the 2nd Division of the 4th Corps, under the command of General George Wagner, to occupy the works and hold them until "seriously threatened by a superior force of infantry." Wagner ordered all three of his brigades to hold the position. While Colonel John Lane of the 2nd Brigade and Colonel Joseph Conrad of the 3rd Brigade complied, Colonel Emerson Opdycke refused to bring his 1st Brigade into line with the rest of the division. Opdycke argued that the advanced line was a death trap that would do nothing to protect the town. After an intense argument, General Wagner gave up, telling Opdycke, "fight when and where you damn please; we all know you'll fight." The colonel promptly marched his brigade back towards Franklin. Years later, John Schellenberger, who served in the 64th Ohio Infantry at the battle, claimed that Opdycke's refusal to occupy the army's front line "proved to be the salvation of our army."[16]

The second line of Federal defenses, several hundred yards north of the first line, was much stronger than the first line and garrisoned by most of the Union infantry and artillery. Masses of abatis, *cheval-de-frise*, and *bois d'arc* hedges, all of which functioned like wooden barbed wire to slow attackers, stood in front of the works. A ditch three and a half feet deep and four feet wide provided the defenders with additional protection. Behind the ditch, a wall of breastworks six feet thick was pierced with holes so that men could fire in relative safety. Other portions of the line were protected with head logs, which consisted of large beams suspended about four inches above the top of breastworks. The space between the walls and head logs was just large enough for a man to fire his rifle.[17]

Just behind the second line of Federal works, a collection of buildings belonging to Fountain Carter, a wealthy merchant and farmer, provided an additional bastion that bolstered a third and final line of Federal defenses. Fountain's twenty-four-year-old son Tod Carter was marching home with the Army of Tennessee in the 20th Tennessee Infantry. General Jacob Cox set up his headquarters for the 23rd Corps in the Carters' home, and army tents sprang up on the nearby grass. Kentuckians of James Reilly's 1st Brigade of the 3rd Division dug in just south of the Carter family's cotton gin. Opdycke's Brigade rested nearby, inadvertently providing a quick reaction force that could launch counterattacks against any rebels who broke through.[18]

With Franklin firmly within in the grasp of the infantry and artillery, General James Wilson took most of his cavalry across the Harpeth River to the east bank, where he could delay and hopefully defeat any Confederate units that used the numerous fords to cross the river and try to cut the roads leading north. Schofield believed that Forrest posed a very serious threat since "Wilson is entirely unable to cope with him." It is not clear if Wilson and his men were aware that their commander placed such little faith in them, but in spite of Schofield's doubts, Wilson believed he could match the infamous Forrest and drive him back across the river if the Confederate cavalry appeared.[19]

General Schofield placed his headquarters in Fort Granger, on the east bank of the Harpeth River. Rising two hundred feet above the water, the sturdy walls of Fort Granger offered clear fields of vision across the valley in every direction, allowing the army commander to keep a close eye on the entire battlefield and personally direct the defense of the two nearby bridges across the river. Gunners from Battery D of the 1st Ohio Light Artillery, under the command of Captain Cockerill, placed their 3-inch rifled ordnance cannon behind the fort's walls and prepared for action. The Ohioans' 3-inch guns could send ten pound projectiles out to an effective range of 2,800 yards, more than a mile and a half. Experienced gunners like the members of Battery D were capable of remarkably accurate fire even at extreme ranges, and the massed Confederate assault columns would provide easy targets.[20]

When Dr. G. C. Phillips, the senior surgeon for Featherston's Mississippi Brigade, arrived near Franklin, he ordered his staff to set up a field hospital a little south of town. While assistant surgeons and orderlies prepared to treat the inevitable wounded, he rode up a nearby hill to view the forming battle lines. Years later, he recalled that "the scene was beautiful." He thought "it seemed as if we were on the rim of a great bowl." The city of Franklin was "in the bottom, with a low semicircle of breastworks toward us some distance from the town, extending from the river above to another point below the town."[21]

The Federal defenses were so formidable that, for a moment, it looked like the Confederate army might not attack after all. General David Staley, commanding the Union 4th Corps, believed that "in view of the strong position we held . . . ," nothing appeared so improbable as that they would assault." There is some disagreement about exact numbers, but the Confederate Army of Tennessee probably had only about twenty-two thousand men on the field to confront twenty-eight thousand well-entrenched Federals. William McMurray of the 20th Tennessee Infantry claimed that so many men had deserted that no more than sixteen thousand men remained to make the charge. The Union troops also enjoyed an enormous advantage in artillery. Only a handful of cannons managed to keep up with Stewart's and Cheatham's Corps and were little match for the numerous cannons that studded Union lines around the town. General Cheatham pleaded with Hood to reconsider his plans for a frontal attack, explaining, "I do not like the looks of this fight," and pointing out that "the enemy has an excellent position and is well fortified." In response, Hood explained, "I prefer to fight them here where they have had only eighteen hours to fortify, than to strike them at Nashville where they have been strengthening themselves for three years." General Forrest also argued against a frontal assault, pointing out that the Harpeth River was fordable and asserting that his cavalry could cut off further Federal retreat, if they were supported by a column of infantry. Although the rebels had no way to know it at the time, Schofield's greatest fear was that Forrest would get across the Harpeth, lead a flank attack on the Federal line of retreat towards Nashville, and cut the Union army to pieces along the road.[22]

General Hood understood the objections of his subordinates but remained unmoved and repeated his orders for a frontal assault. He may have feared that an attempted flanking attack would fail, just as it failed at Spring Hill. Hood believed, "Franklin is the key to Nashville, and Nashville is the key to independence." Hood correctly identified the Union first line as a vulnerable position. He ordered the infantry to hold their fire as they approached the first line and force them out with the weight of numbers. When the Federals turned and ran, the Confederate infantry should "shoot them in the backs" as they ran to their second line, using the confusion to capture the Union second line. Hood may have been unaware that the Carter House concealed a third line of Union works, along with Opdycke's

The Carter House, HALS TN-7-B

Lotz House, HALS TN-7-C

Carnton Plantation, HALS TN-7-A

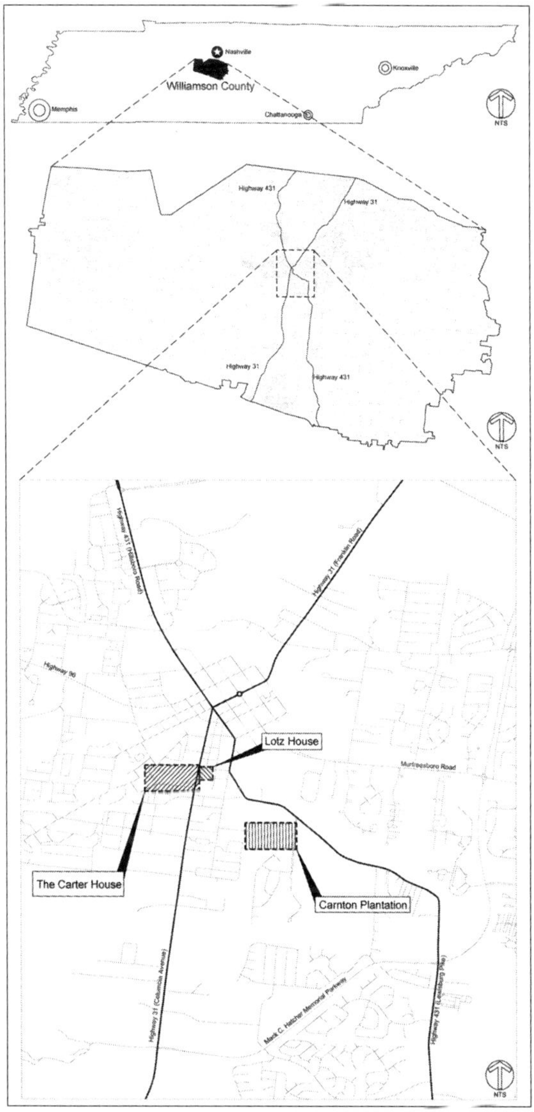

Map 10. The Landscapes of the Battlefield of Franklin, Tennessee. Historic American Landscapes Survey (HABS). Library of Congress.

Brigade, and may have believed that the Confederates would win the day if they could punch through the two clearly visible lines of Federal troops. Hood ordered General Cleburne's Division to occupy the place of honor in the center of the battlefield and ensure the breakthrough. Cleburne objected to the plan, but when Hood insisted, Cleburne replied, "I will take the works or fall in the effort."[23] Hood seemed to accept Cleburne's comment as a commitment to victory. In retrospect, it is easy to wonder if Cleburne might have conceded that he would die on that field.

Common soldiers knew that the assault would be difficult. Joseph Boyce was worried because "it was no boy's play to charge this western Federal infantry when well entrenched." The combat veteran did a grim equation of conventional thinking that said that one entrenched man was worth five in the open. He wasn't sure how many Union men were behind those breastworks, but he knew that the Confederate Army of Tennessee did not enjoy anything like a five to one advantage. Thomas Pulliam of the 22nd Mississippi Infantry believed the Union positions "seemed insurmountable." W. J. Worsham and C. W. Heiskell of the 19th Tennessee Infantry saw the Union positions as a "glittering belt of bayonet and cannon" just waiting to unleash its power on rebel flesh. Despite the danger, Hood repeated the order to attack "without the least faltering."[24]

East (front) elevation of Carter House, 1140 Columbia Avenue, Franklin, Tennessee. Historic American Buildings Survey, November 1971. Library of Congress.

When Edward McMorries wrote his personal story of the Civil War in 1904, he was a graying sixty-two-year-old history professor, but when he took the field at Franklin, he was a very different man. In 1861 the nineteen-year-old resident of Pike County, Alabama, abandoned his job of overseer on his father's plantation and his studies at the Perote Institute to join the 1st Alabama Infantry. By November 1864 the schoolboy was a veteran who had survived disease, battle, and even life in a prison camp, but nothing had prepared him for what he would face on that November day. The history

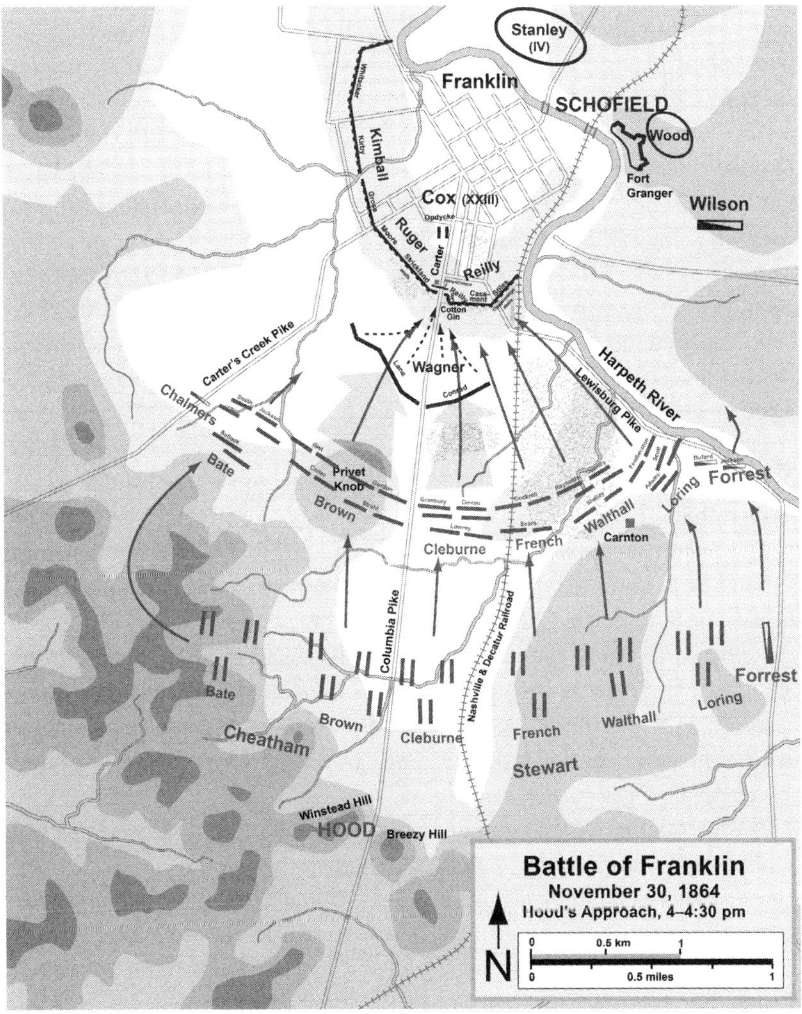

Map 11. Franklin, 4:00 p.m. Map by Hal Jespersen, www.cwmaps.com.

professor's mind drifted to the classics, comparing the "18,000 ragged and half-starved men with tattered banners" of the Army of Tennessee to "the shattered army of Hannibal" when it prepared to fight "the well-appointed legions of Scipio on the plains of the Ticinus."[25]

Mississippi captain R. N. Rea remembered it as "a clear, pleasant day." As the army formed for battle, "the men were in finer spirits than I had seen them for a long time." All the "generals in the army, their staffs, and every field officer sat upon their horses near us and in their proper places." Almost six decades later, the old veteran explained that "Such an inspiring scene was good to look upon."[26]

At 4:00 p.m., a staff officer from General Hood brought General Stewart orders to begin the assault, and Stewart immediately passed the order down to his subordinates.[27] After sending Chalmers's Division of cavalry to protect the army's left flank, Forrest personally led Buford's and Jackson's Divisions to the Confederate right flank on the Harpeth River. Edward McMorries watched as General Forrest "mounted on his black charger, hat in hand down by his side, his face radiant and dark eyes flashing, rode down our front." The men were "already eager for the fray" and "cheered him to the echo." The enthusiastic infantrymen "began advancing before the order was given." John Copley was a short distance from McMorries in the same brigade, but he remembered things very differently. In contrast to the cheers McMorries recalled, Copley claimed that "a profound silence pervaded the entire army." It reminded him of "one of those sickening lulls which precede a tremendous thunderstorm." As the men watched their officers hold a brief meeting, they "realized the depth of that yawning gulf of destruction which awaited them."[28]

W. J. Worsham and C. W. Heiskell noticed that the typically cheerful General Strahl seemed oddly quiet and standoffish in the moments before the assault. Later, they learned that Strahl told several other generals that he expected to die in the battle. Despite the enormous dread he felt, the Ohio-born lawyer of German descent was "true as steel" and "ready to be offered up." When the orders came to assemble, Strahl mounted his horse and told members of the 19th Tennessee Infantry, "boys, this will be short but desperate."[29]

As the infantry formed into line of battle on the "soft and beautiful November day," John Johnston watched General Strahl make a speech to "his ragged, dingy-looking men," urging them "to make a valiant fight for their state and country." The men cheered and waved their hats in response. Johnston thought, "it was a sad, forlorn sight." To Johnston's ears, "their cheers sounded like that which came from weary and cheerless hearts." Despite his doubts, Johnston concluded that "braver and truer soldiers never marched to battle." Another cavalryman told Johnston, "I'll bet they'll go right over them works." Johnston replied simply, "I hope so."[30]

R. M. Collins was near the center of the Confederate line. He heard the order to advance not as a rousing speech, but as a repeated murmur of "Gen. Hood says we must take those works." At that moment a Federal cannon sent a shell screaming towards the Confederate line. In response, the men tightened their belts and pulled their hats down low onto their heads, almost as though they were about to encounter a rain shower rather than the storm of steel and shot that awaited them.[31]

Joseph Boyce heard the order to advance as "the sun was going down behind a bank of dark clouds." He wondered if even the sun wanted to hide its eyes from the approaching massacre. The departing sun "threw a crimson light over the field," which Boyce considered "prophetic of our fate." Someone in Boyce's company pondered Nelson's famous order at Trafalgar and called out, "England expects every man to do his duty." Sergeant Denny Callahan responded, "it's a damned little duty England would get out of this Irish crowd." The Missourians, many of whom came from the Emerald Isle, laughed uproariously. General Cockrell shook the men from their laughter with gruff shouts of "Shoulder arms! Right shoulder shift arms! Brigade forward! Guide center! Music! Quick time! March!"[32]

Forty-eight years after the battle, Louis Flatau still remembered the scene with vivid detail. That day, he was a twenty-two-year-old corporal with Cowan's Mississippi Battery, not the broken-down, arthritic, half-blind seventy-year-old who told his story from a sick bed. He explained, "the men that composed our army at this fight were brawny-armed, sun-burned, and scar marked heroes every one of them." The cowards and weaklings were dead, back at home, or rotting in prison camps. All that remained in those ranks were veterans who looked across that valley at the closest thing mortal man has ever seen to hell and walked forward. The men knew that they might pay for that victory with their lives, but they had long ago determined that victory was more precious than life.[33]

The men of Stewart's and Cheatham's Corps moved forward simultaneously in an "unbroken phalanx." Captain Tod Carter was an assistant quartermaster on General Thomas Smith's staff. He did not have to enter combat—he was a staff officer, not a field commander—but the twenty-four-year-old lawyer turned soldier knew that his family and childhood home were just a few yards north. With a broad smile, Carter mounted his horse, drew his sword, and called out, "I am almost home! Come with me boys!"[34]

In contrast to other accounts of cloudy skies, D. W. Sanders, serving as a staff officer with General French, claimed that "not a cloud obscured the autumn sun, which shone upon the beautiful plain with its gentle slopes." The men looked forward to the slopes "they must pass to engage in mortal strife in the supreme effort to carry a strongly fortified line by a most reckless and daring assault."[35]

Lieutenant Mintz of the 5th Arkansas Infantry was in Govan's Brigade near the center of the action. He heard a bugler played the notes that indicated it was time to advance. The orders came down the line, "Right shoulder, Shift arms. Forward. Quick time. March." The men obeyed and pressed forward duitifully.[36]

Edwin Rennolds claimed that "the fearless General Cheatham" shed tears as the men advanced and proclaimed, "it is a mistake, and it is no comfort to me to say we are not responsible." As Cheatham allegedly cried, "the long lines of infantry moved steadily and grandly with the precision of trained soldiers on parade." The 5th Tennessee Infantry's band began playing "Dixie" and somewhere off to the east, one of the bands from Cleburne's Division played "The Bonnie Blue Flag." Rennolds remembered that assault as the one and only time "we went into battle cheered by the sound of martial music." It was "the grandest sight I ever beheld."[37]

T. J. Walker of the 9th Tennessee Infantry claimed that all the army's bands played "Dixie." He savored the line, "in Dixieland I'll take my stand to live or die in Dixie." It may be hard to believe, but Walker claimed that "we, as soldiers had never heard this particular song before played as we were marching into battle."[38]

Joseph Boyce enjoyed the sounds of "The Bonnie Blue Flag" and then "Dixie," a rare event since the "tooters" rarely kept playing while the "shooters" charged. He claimed that Cockrell's Missouri Brigade boasted one of the finest bands in the army. Every musician was also a veteran infantryman of two years or more hard service "and would have instantly exchanged their instruments for muskets if ordered to remain in the rear."[39]

Surgeon G. C. Phillips listened to the music. He heard "our bands played Dixie, Bonnie Blue Flag, and The Girl I Left Behind Me." Phillips recalled that "this was the first and only time I ever beard our bands playing upon a battlefield and at the beginning of a charge."[40]

Colonel Ellison Capers of the 24th South Carolina passed over a slight elevation "from which we beheld the magnificent spectacle the battlefield presented." Across the open field, "bands were playing, general and staff officer and gallant couriers were riding in front of and between the lines, 100 battle-flags were waving in the smoke of battle, and bursting shells were wreathing the air with great circles of smoke." As the Union fire intensified, "20,000 brave men were marching in perfect order towards the foe." Capers believed that "the sight inspired every man of the Twenty-fourth with the sentiment of duty."[41]

John Johnston of the 14th Tennessee Cavalry watched as Union shells began bursting in the sky, each leaving a "white wreath of smoke." As the rebels got closer to the Federal lines, the artillery fire intensified and was joined by whizzing rifle bullets. Soon the entire battlefield lay under a thick blanket of smoke.[42]

The Confederate army advanced towards Union forces, which enjoyed an enormous advantage in artillery. B. T. Roberts of the 24th Tennessee Infantry claimed that only a single battery, Bledsoe's Missourians, supported the assault. P. E. Hockersmith, a private with Douglas's Texas Battery, explained that his battery fired no shots during the battle because, by the time his unit arrived, the Union and Confederate lines were so entangled that they couldn't fire on the Federals without endangering their comrades. R. W. Banks of the 37th Mississippi Infantry believed that if all the Confederate artillery had opened fire, they could have defeated the Union forces. He claimed that they refused to fire because the Confederacy valued innocent lives more highly than victory. John Morton, an artilleryman with Forrest's cavalry, claimed that the rebel gunners avoiding firing on Franklin to protect civilians and directed their fire at Federal positions outside of town, mostly on Figuers Hill.[43] These accounts failed to mention either that most of the rebel artillery was absent because it could not keep up with the rapidly moving infantry or that Hood planned to blast Franklin with every cannon he had as soon as they arrived. If the reasoning was unclear, the deadly reality on the battlefield was apparent. Union artillery fired with horrific effect, and rebel gunners did little in response.[44]

The Start of Battle in the Center

Confederate soldiers advanced on the center of the Union line. W. E. Preston was in the 33rd Alabama Infantry, near the center of the battle. As rebels came within range of the advanced Federal line, "the minnie balls began singing by." Peter Hotze of the consolidated 6th/7th Arkansas Infantry suffered a severe wound to his leg as the firing began, and he fell to the ground. His comrades marched on without him and left him to fend for himself. Despite the heavy fire that began all up and down the line, the Confederates "advanced splendidly preserving a beautiful line." The intense fire did not deter the Confederate infantrymen, who continued their advance in "high spirits." Consistent with Hood's orders, many men resisted the temptation to return fire and pressed forward with loaded rifles. R. M. Collins of the 15th Texas Infantry saw General Cleburne ride his mare forward at a run, pointing to the Federal line with his hat in his right hand. Collins watched a bullet crash into Cleburne sending his lifeless

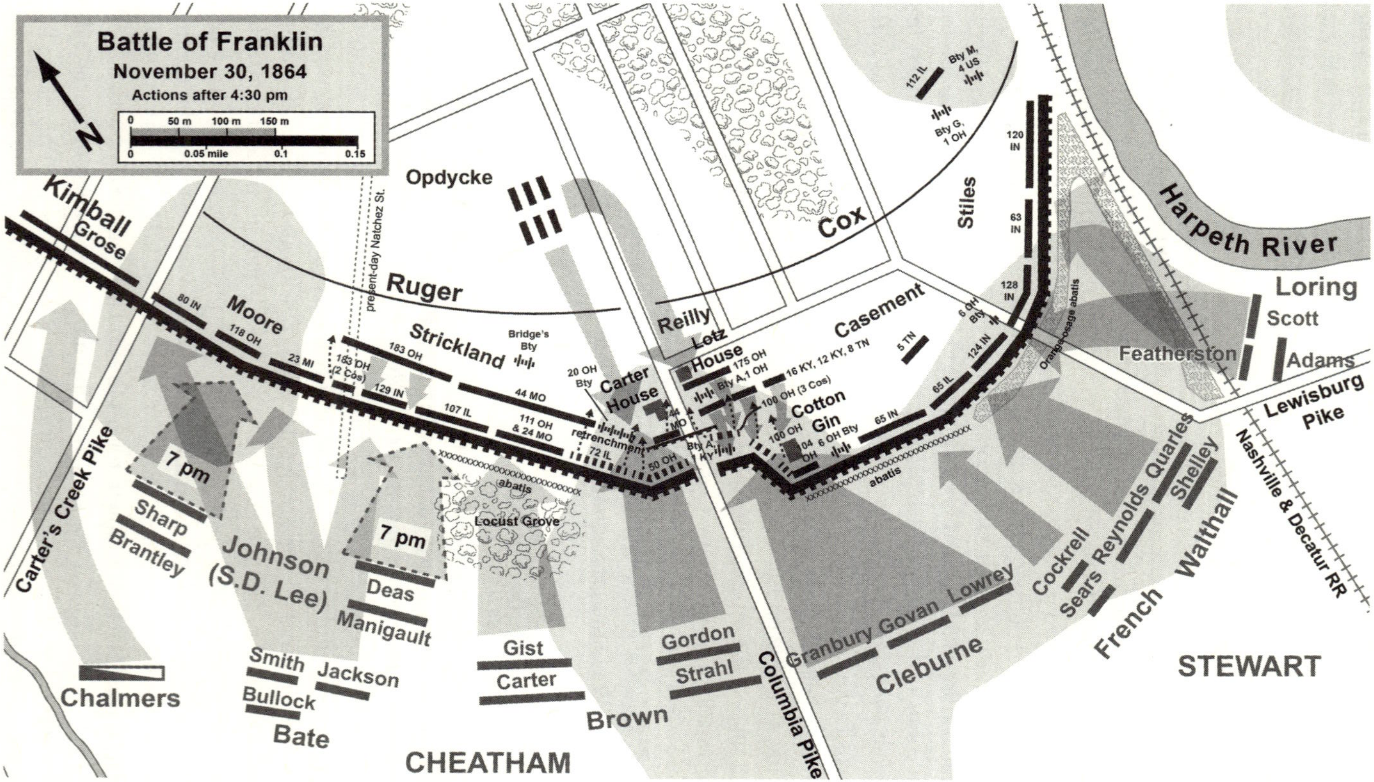

Map 12. Franklin, starting at 4:30 p.m. Map by Hal Jespersen, www.cwmaps.com.

Flag of Genl Cleburne's Division. Pencil and purple ink drawing on lined cream paper by Alfred R. Waud. Library of Congress.

body to the ground. Still, the men of Cleburne's Division charged forward, undeterred by the loss of their beloved general.[45]

At 4:30 p.m. the rebels crashed into the advanced line of Union works in the center. According to John Copley of the 49th Tennessee Infantry, the Federals "received us with a volley of musketry" in a desperate attempt to turn back the gray-jacketed onslaught, "but all opposition was inadequate to check our columns." The rebels carried the outer line, "annihilating nearly everything before us."[46]

General Walthall claimed that his men attacked the Federal line "so impetuously that the opposing force gave way without even retarding the advance and retired in disorder to the strong entrenchments in the rear. Capturing the outer works gave the rebel army "an electric shock" that filled the men with enthusiasm, and "the air resounded with loud shouts from the whole army" that "made the earth quake." The rebels raced towards the second line of Union works at even greater speed. Rebels were "yelling like fury and shooting at them at the same time." Joseph Boyce of the 1st Missouri Infantry "raised the glorious old yell." The rebels "rushed upon the main works a frantic, maddened body with overpowering impulse to reach the enemy and kill, murder, and destroy."[47]

Federals in the second line hesitated to fire towards their own men and temporarily lowered their volume of fire. The reduced fire saved both

Confederate and Union lives. Tangles of sharpened abatis stood in front of that second line, providing "a formidable and fearful obstacle." It protected the Union troops behind its shelter but slowed many of the retreating men in blue just enough to allow their Confederate pursuers to catch them before they got to their second line and send them to the rear as prisoners.[48]

The outer line of Union works was lightly defended, exposed on both flanks, and consisted of works that were hardly worthy of the name, but the second line was an entirely different beast. Rebels noticed that "every approach to the inner works was obstructed in every manner known to civil warfare." The fastest and luckiest Federals escaped capture, making it into their second line a few steps ahead of the rebels. Once most of the Union troops from the first line had become casualties or made it to the safety of the second line, the Federal line came to life once more, filling the air with a "hurricane of combustibles" that killed "countless numbers" of men. Entire platoons fell to the earth in perfect lines of battle, and the ground shook beneath the bare feet of the survivors. From across the river, Federal gunners continued to pour exploding shells into the rebel lines, catching the men in gray within the jaws of a horrific crossfire.[49]

B. T. Roberts of the 24th Tennessee Infantry watched the gunfire kill the horses pulling the guns of Bledsoe's Missouri Battery. The loss slowed but did not end the artillerymen's support of the infantry assault. The gunners "pushed their guns forward by hand."[50]

Lieutenant Smith Whitfield of Co. B, 24th Tennessee Infantry Regiment in uniform. Library of Congress.

According to Edward McMorries of the 1st Alabama, "owing to the stillness and rarity of the atmosphere, the smoke of musketry had settled in such a dense bank over the field in front, that friend could not be distinguished from foe at a distance of a few steps." The Federals in the second line "four lines deep behind strong entrenchments, were sweeping the old field between us with minnie balls and a battery of siege guns" across the Harpeth River "was tearing up the ground." Despite the hell that awaited them, the rebels pressed forward "through a tempest of iron, our officers still leading, and the rebel yell still ringing, the army in perfect order charged the inner line." W. E. Preston of the 33rd Alabama Infantry charged towards the second line of Union works until he was wounded. The painful injury earned him a ticket to the army hospital at Spring Hill and spared him the horrors that many others endured during the rest of the campaign. John Copley of the 49th Tennessee Infantry described the Union artillery and small arms fire as a "volcanic eruption" that "cast a deep shade of gloom" over the otherwise beautiful November afternoon. T. J. Walker of the 9th Tennessee Infantry was amazed "that the whole army wasn't killed or wounded" before they could get to the inner line of Union works since "we were in full range of shot and shell for one-half mile."[51]

According to Captain Irving Buck, a staff officer for General Cleburne, the men of Cleburne's Division and Brown's Division (Cheatham's old division) had long enjoyed a fearsome rivalry that motivated them to race towards the Federal inner line, taunting each other as each division vied for the honor being the first to capture a section of the inner works. John Morton, an artilleryman with Forrest's cavalry, watched the infantry assault from behind his cannon. He believed "never in the history of any war did troops, both officers and privates in the ranks, vie so gallantly with each other in the race for death as in this ill-starred battle." Edwin Rennolds of the 5th Tennessee was in the second line of the Confederate advance. The first line of rebel troops captured so many Federals that members of the rebel second line initially thought the prisoners were attacking them. Rennolds realized at the last moment that the men in blue were unarmed, and the rebels allowed them to pass to the rear without incident. Mumford Dixon of the 3rd Confederate Infantry was in front of the cotton gin where the rebels charged into the ditch but were unable to surmount the parapet and became stuck. The rebels trapped in the ditch were unable to advance or retreat, so they fought it out where they were, trading gunfire with Federals six feet away on the other side of the parapet.[52]

Yankee firepower pulverized the bodies of attackers, but gray-clad survivors somehow kept moving forward where "no organized force could go." What had begun as a grand battle just a few minutes ago disintegrated into hundreds of bloody fistfights between countless bands of hardened killers, all hell bent on murder. Thomas Head of the 16th Tennessee Infantry later admitted that he admired the Union soldiers who "held their ground with a tenacity unknown to former conflicts," somehow repulsing the men in gray, who repeatedly charged forward with "reckless daring and determination." Just to the left of the Columbia Turnpike, John Ward and the 11th Tennessee faltered after meeting stiff resistance. In desperation, General George Gordon dismounted his horse and urged the Tennesseans forward with, "Boys, Come On!" About a hundred men of the regiment followed Gordon, keeping their lines as organized as possible under the horrific gunfire from Union lines.[53]

Disorganized masses of rebels kept pushing forward. T. J. Walker and the 9th Tennessee Infantry captured a portion of the Federal inner line. Units to their left were unable to break through, and the 9th Tennessee was quickly under fire from both their front and left flank. As a result, "hundreds of our men were shot down in the trenches." Years later, Walker still mourned the loss of his friend John Sweet, who was shot through the head in that firefight and tumbled back onto Walker, knocking him into the ditch at the base of the earthwork. With Sweet gone, Walker lost "one of the best friends I ever had." Near of the center of the assault, Risenar Etter, a member of the 16th Tennessee Infantry, "fought hand to hand," but "the enemy was very stubborn" and "nocked our men down with their guns." An artillery shell ripped Missourian John Hickey's leg off as he approached the cotton gin. He fell to the ground, only to be wounded three more times as he lay in the open, unable to crawl to cover. E. H. Rennolds, who was with the second line of the assault, explained that "our lines had become broken" and the men rushed forward and "became solid masses." Every man raced against his comrades to reach the breastworks, where the men from the first wave were already engaged in a nasty hand-to-hand fight with the Union defenders. When the exhausted Federals saw that a second wave of Confederates were bearing down on them, they fled, leaving the rebels in possession of a short segment of their lines.[54]

Confederate soldiers tried to capitalize on their moment of success. South Carolinians and Georgians of Gist's Brigade as well as the Tennesseans of Gordon's Brigade in Brown's Division made it to the enemy's second line and overpowered the defenders from Ohio, Illinois, and Missouri. The rebels planted their colors on the parapet and forced the Federals to retreat a short distance. Samuel Foster with the 24th Texas Cavalry (dismounted) broke through the outer and inner lines of Federals works. Only the Union troops dug in around the cotton gin stood between the Texans and the rear of the Union army. Ensign Flowers of the 4th Tennessee Infantry climbed on top of the parapet and waved the regimental colors. A handful of the bravest clambered over the breastworks. On the other side of the barricade, they faced "a deadly hail of minnie balls," and the survivors scrambled back to the relative safety of the ditch in front of the breastworks, where they returned fire. Captain James Synnamon of the 6th Missouri Infantry recalled, "the air was all red and blue flames, with shells and bullets screeching and howling everywhere, over and through us." The "wounded and dying men lay all about in ghastly piles." A Union bullet struck Synnamon, and he was taken prisoner. Decades later, B. T. Roberts still took pride in the fact that his comrades "never once yielded," despite the overwhelming firepower that rained down upon them.[55]

Remnants of Cleburne's Division held the dearly bought breach of the second line of Federal works. For a few moments, the fate of the battle hung in the balance, and it was unclear if the men in gray or the men in blue would give way. The rebels had taken the center of the Federal line, but the Confederates "did not seem to know what to do with it." The Federals felt no such confusion. Before their officers could respond, the Union rank and file began piecemeal attacks on the rebels near the cotton gin.[56]

At about 4:45 p.m., Colonel Opdycke led his brigade—including his old regiment, the 125th Ohio Infantry, better known as Opdycke's Tigers—in a vicious counterattack against the rebel breakthrough. After a brief fight, the men in blue retook the position, killing, capturing, or routing every rebel in the vicinity. Opdycke's refusal to occupy the army's front line and his willingness to throw his men into the worst of the fighting at just the right moment might have saved the Union army.[57]

Men in the center of the Confederate line along the Columbia Pike were stuck in front of the cotton gin, surrounded by the dead and wounded. Men reached up to fire over the embankment. When they weren't shooting, they threw dirt clods and sticks. Mississippi soldier R. N. Rea was stuck in the ditch, unable to advance or retreat. Decades later, he explained, "If I ever prayed earnestly in my life, it was then."[58]

W. J. Worsham and C. W. Heiskell were confronted by works that were too high and steep for any man to climb alone, so men boosted their comrades to the top of the wall. Every climber was shot, so the Tennesseans gave up trying to get across and kept up a fight from the ditches in front of the parapet. Worsham and Heiskell claimed that they "had to fight Death, Hell and the Devil" for control of the Union breastworks and "fought with the desperation of mad tigers." In the ditch, the Tennesseans "went through the furnace" that burned "seven times hotter than ever before." Desperate survivors turned their dead friends into shields in hopes that dead flesh might absorb bullets intended for the living. E. H. Rennolds remembered, "in vain did the officers urge the men to cross the breastworks," but the men were exhausted, and "the fire was too deadly even for the bravest to face." Tennesseans of

Brown's Division kept up a steady rifle fire across the parapet. Men below loaded rifles and passed them to men on top of the wall, who fired them as best they could at combative Union defenders firing on anything in gray that dared reveal itself. The desperate struggle knew no rank. General Otho Strahl loaded rifles until a minnie ball crashed into his skull and ended his life. John Morton, an artilleryman with Forrest's cavalry, concluded, "war ever devours the bravest and best and here perished, unhappily and without profit some of the choicest officers in the Confederate service."[59]

The Tennesseans of Strahl's Brigade were still in the ditch as the sun fell. Many members of the brigade were dead, including General Strahl himself, and the fire of from Federal positions seemed endless, so the surviving members of the brigade began retreating singly or small groups. E. H. Rennolds of the 5th Tennessee Infantry decided to retreat as the darkness came. He ran to the rear while Union soldiers kept up a continuous "whir of minnies," which compelled the exhausted Tennessean to run ever faster until "my speed was increased to the highest possible limit." Rennolds returned to the Confederate lines unharmed and declared, "the god of battles only could direct the steps of anyone safely through such death-dealing missiles." Most men were not as fortunate. Rennolds was the only man of his company still fit for duty that night. John Ward and the 11th Tennessee Infantry fought it out in the ditch in front of Union positions. Unable to retreat or advance, they were stuck until darkness fell. Ward and a handful of survivors from his regiment slipped back towards their own lines shortly after midnight. Robert Mims, serving 45th Alabama Infantry, was still recovering from a bullet wound suffered months earlier when he took the place of a sick man in the ranks for the assault. Mims made his way back to camp unharmed after a long day of fighting and returned the sick man's rifle without comment. Peter Hotze of the consolidated 6th/7th Arkansas Infantry was trying to hobble away from the fighting on a badly wounded leg when he bumped into a lieutenant with a wounded arm. The men spotted an abandoned horse nearby and agreed to mount up together and ride away. Hotze helped the officer onto the horse, and the lieutenant tried to return the favor, but Hotze's leg was so badly damaged that he could not get up onto the horse, no matter how much his companion tried to pull him up. Hotze gave up, wished the lieutenant good luck, and crawled into a clump of bushes, where he passed out moments later.[60]

The Battle of Franklin on the Left

On the extreme left of the Confederate line, General Bate pressed his men forward without waiting for Chalmers's cavalrymen, who were supposed to

Battle of Franklin, November 30, 1864. Lithograph by Kurtz & Allison, 1891. Library of Congress.

help them. Bate extended his line to the left until it almost reached Carter's Creek Pike. Bate's men suffered from a heavy crossfire. Their right flank encountered the Union advance line, but the middle and left of the division received "a furious fire" from the much longer second line of Federal positions. The dismounted cavalrymen of Chalmers's Division failed to keep up with the infantry or protect the division's left flank. Bate ordered Finley's Brigade of Floridians to abandon their position in reserve and take up a new role protecting the division's left flank.[61]

Blue-coated gunners zeroed in on the South Carolinians and Georgians of Gist's Brigade, ripping holes in rebel flesh. Gist's horse was shot in the neck and began bucking violently. Somehow, Gist got off the dying beast without major injury. Now dismounted, he pushed forward on foot, waving his hat, cheering the men forward, and ordering them to charge. A bullet crashed into Gist's thigh but barely slowed him down. Colonel Ellison Capers of the 24th South Carolina watched Gist drift away into the smoke, "never more to be seen by the men he had commanded on so many fields." A short time later a bullet struck Gist in the chest, killing him instantly. Artillery shells filled the air "with a whizzing blare." Some shells ricocheted across the dirt until they burst into shrapnel or struck some unfortunate son of the South. Other shells struck the ground cleanly, burying themselves in the earth for an instant before exploding and tossing mounds of dirt and metal into the atmosphere.[62]

Bate's Division congealed into a single line without support and ran forward. The right of the division cleared the first line of Federal works and kept moving towards the second line, which was "strong and defiant, constructed on a slight elevation, with few obstructions in front for several hundred yards." William Yeatman, a junior captain in command of the 2nd Tennessee Infantry, led his men forward. The Tennesseans "fought hard, but to no effect." They were unable to break through, and the Federals greeted the regiment with "slaughter" The rebels "were mowed down like weeds."[63]

The Confederate attack was unable to make any major gains, and men in gray paid a horrific price. Bate's Division ran towards the second line of Union breastworks. The right half of the division made it into the second line. The left half of the division was driven back in disorder. Chalmers's Division of cavalry advanced on the Confederate left flank until they got within sixty yards of the Federal second line and were unable to advance any farther. Henry Reddick and the 1st Florida Infantry got stuck in the crossfire, unable to advance through the heavy brush obstacles or to retreat and face the deadly fire that swept the field. At about 5:00 p.m. Captain Tod Carter of the 20th Tennessee Infantry was wounded leading a charge on the left end of the Confederate line. He fell to the earth about five hundred feet southwest of his boyhood home in Franklin. The rebels kept pressing forward through the fire. They reached but were unable to capture or hold large sections of the inner line of Union breastworks.[64]

General Lee arrived with his corps near Franklin at around 7:00 p.m. He discovered that General Stewart and General Cheatham were already assaulting the Federal works, where the men in blue resisted stubbornly. Hood ordered Lee to send his two lead divisions, Johnson's and Clayton's, in position to support the assault and instructed him to coordinate his efforts with General Cheatham. When Lee found Cheatham at dark, Cheatham asked for immediate assistance. Lee ordered Johnson's Division to attack, but in the encroaching darkness and confusion, Johnson's men only struck the enemy about an hour after dark. They arrived on the Confederate left, occupied by the demolished soldiers of Bate's Division.[65]

C. Irvine Walker of the 10th South Carolina Infantry and the rest of Manigault's Brigade advanced rapidly but faltered when their commander, General Manigault, was badly wounded. Command passed to Colonel Shaw of the 19th South Carolina, but he was wounded a short time later. Next Colonel Newton Davis of the 24th Alabama took command of the brigade, but he too was soon wounded. The men suffered under horrific fire, and their shattered chain of command gave them little guidance. Eventually the men withdrew to the rear.[66]

Robert Jarman and the 27th Mississippi Infantry received orders to hold their fire until they made it to the ditch in front of the Federal works, where survivors from Bate's Division were reportedly waiting, out of ammunition. When the Mississippians got within four steps of the Federal lines, "we received a volley of musketry that made a considerable thinning in our lines." Jarman and his comrades responded to the deaths of their friends with "a shout and went at them." Within moments, they "carried the works by storm." While the rest of Johnson's Division fought well, Jarman condemned the men of Manigault's Brigade because "they ran and left us exposed on our right to a terrible cross fire," which inflicted heavy losses on the rest of the division.[67] He may not have known and probably would not have cared that Manigault's Brigade faltered in large measure because of the horrific losses to their leadership.

The second line of Union works to the southwest of Carter's Creek Pike was weak and might have fallen under better circumstances, but it contained a battery that kept up a steady fire all afternoon and into the evening. Robert Jarman and the 27th Mississippi Infantry kept up a steady fire on men in blue until late in the day. When the Mississippians ran low on ammunition, they managed to capture a member of the Federal ordnance service carrying a box filled with a thousand rifle cartridges, and "we used it well, to make a noise at least." Joseph Baumer of the 36th Alabama Infantry did not stumble across any Federal supplies and was forced to endure the evening without replying to the Federals, who kept up a sporadic fire.[68]

James Cooper of the 20th Tennessee was a veteran who first enlisted in 1861 and saw many of the war's most awful battles, but Franklin "was the most bloody." The ground near the Federal works was piled with dead in a scene that looked more like "a slaughter pen" than a battlefield. Men "were shot all to pieces," and one had forty-seven bullet holes through his body. The field was so grotesque that Cooper "felt sick at heart for days afterwards."[69]

The Battle of Franklin on the Right

The fighting was as hot on the right as in the center and left of the battle. John Copley of the 49th Tennessee Infantry on the Confederate right watched as Union cannons sent shells flying towards the men in gray and recalled that the Federal artillerymen "had a fine testing of their skill at long range." The Tennesseans moved slowly as they scrambled through the hedges that stood between them and the Federal lines. On the extreme end of the Confederate right, members of Loring's Division of infantry and Bufford's Division of cavalry encountered a screen of Federal cavalrymen, but the rebels quickly routed their adversaries. With the Federal cavalry in full retreat, Bufford's Division dismounted and advanced as a skirmish line between the Lewisburg Pike and the Harpeth River. Men on the Confederate right flank took fire not only from the Union soldiers in front of them, but also from the batteries on the hills across the river.[70]

The terrain broke up Confederate formations. General Walthall noted that an "impenetrable briar thicket" stood in front of Reynolds and ordered Reynolds to make his way around the thicket and rejoin the line on the other side. Reynolds encountered far worse terrain than anticipated and was unable to reform the line quickly. With no time to wait, Walthall ordered Cantey's Brigade to take the place of Reynolds's men. Edward McMorries of the 1st Alabama Infantry, fighting on the Confederate right, got within about a hundred yards of the first Union line and "received the first volley from the enemy." In response, the rebels charged, "cheers were changed to rebel yells," and "the rattle of musketry now drowned all commands of officers." No longer able to communicate verbally, the officers directed their men with waving swords and personal example as they led the way. When Alabamians got within rifle range of the Union right flank, "the infantry opened on us with terrible volleys."[71]

Rebel infantrymen pressed forward through the chaos. N. B. Nesbitt and the 55th Tennessee Infantry advanced up the Lewisburg Pike directly into the gun sights of infantrymen from Indiana and artillerymen from Ohio. General Quarles rode his "coal-black horse" twenty yards in front of his men and urged them forward by shouting encouragement over his shoulder. When the sounds of gunfire made it impossible to hear anything, the forty-year-old commander pulled off his cap, exposing his balding head, and waved his cap to urge the men forward. Nesbitt believed that Quarles was "brave to a fault" and did everything that "could be desired of a commander" until a bit of flying lead crashed into his arm, knocking him from his horse with a wound that almost killed him. Joseph Boyce and the 1st Missouri Infantry crossed open ground under heavy fire, where "our flag fell three times," as one man after the other carried it until death ripped it from his hands and another man picked up the banner. Ephraim Anderson, a corporal in the 2nd Missouri Infantry on the Confederate right walked into a particularly formidable wall of lead produced not by the single-shot muzzleloaders carried by most of the Federal infantry but by the far more advanced Spencer seven-shot repeaters carried by only the best-armed Union men.[72]

The cavalry tried to aid their brothers in the infantry. General Forrest noticed that Union troops were sending a flanking fire into the right end of the rebel line from a hill across the Harpeth and sent Jackson's Division across the water in an attempt to drive the Federals away from the position and protect the army's right flank. R. R. Hancock and the rest of the 2nd Tennessee Cavalry pushed the Union forces back towards Fort Granger on the banks of the Harpeth River. Both sides kept up a heavy fire, creating heaps of dead and wounded men from both armies.[73]

The infantry kept pressing forward against all odds. Thomas Pulliam of the 22nd Mississippi Infantry marched along the banks of the Harpeth River and right into murderous fire produced by men from Indiana, who fired rapidly, secure behind a deep ditch and a prickly hedge. The Mississippians "were in the veritable jaws of death and destruction." B. F. Weathers of the 17th Alabama Infantry kept moving forward even though "the fire of federal troops was so rapid that great clouds of smoke hung like a pall of universal darkness over the fatal field, completely obscured the movements of assaulting lines." As the rebels charged forward, flashes of gunfire lit up the scene, providing momentary glimpses of the disintegrating Confederate lines. W. W. McMillan "had forgotten the surrounding danger." He thought only about his plan to bayonet an adversary, when a musket ball struck him in the left thigh, "making a severe wound about 10 inches in length but not breaking the bone." The injury paralyzed his leg, sending him face first into the ground, where "I was past locomotion." While the blood flowed from his left leg, another bullet penetrated his right wrist and hand, "inflicting a very painful wound." Two more bullets grazed but did not penetrate his body. Other projectiles kicked up dirt all around him but did not strike him.[74]

J. P. Cannon and the 27th Alabama advanced on the right flank of the rebel line. The inner line of Union works along this portion of the line stood behind a dense hedge "almost impassable under any circumstances." The men took horrific losses as they tried to get through the hedge. Cannon thought, "it seemed as if not one of us could possibly escape the storm of grape, canister, and minnie-balls that were poured into us." With no leaders and precious few followers, the Alabamians decided that "it seemed like madness to attempt to go farther." As they began to retreat, "12 or 15 pieces of artillery" opened on them from across six hundred yards of level terrain. When Cannon discovered an abandoned Union rifle pit, he decided to take cover rather than retreat farther across the open, fire-swept plain.[75]

As the 4th Arkansas Infantry advanced into the Federal obstructions, a bullet struck George Bost in the head, badly wounding but not killing him. As he fell to the ground, a chunk of shrapnel tore through his back, possibly from the Federal artillery across the Harpeth River that was pouring a flanking fire into the rebel ranks. Almost instantly, another piece of shrapnel ripped through Bost's back, killing him.[76]

As Joseph Boyce penetrated the second line of Federal works, they "delivered one smashing volley" just as General Cockrell ordered his men over the parapet with empty rifles and fixed bayonets. Boyce charged across the Federal works and lunged towards a Union soldier, but the man in blue "was too quick for me," and Boyce fell to the ground, badly wounded. Looking up from the dirt, Boyce beamed with pride while his comrades wrestled the position away from the Federals. Years later, the old veteran boasted that the 1st Missouri Infantry "never failed to carry a line we were ordered to take" and "never did the enemy succeed in breaking our line."[77]

Edward McMorries of the 1st Alabama Infantry lamented that the "dead and wounded had fallen at every step of our advance, and our ranks were badly thinned." As the rebels reached the inner line of Union defenses, they realized that the odds were against them "but despising numbers or advantage of position they leaped down into the ditch, climbed up the embankment enveloped in a sheet of fire, and from the ramparts discharged their pieces in the face of the enemy." With no time to reload their single-shot, muzzle-loading Austrian and British rifles, the Alabamians ripped the flesh of men from Indiana and Illinois with their bare hands. Almost all their officers were dead, and their organization was obliterated, so the men from Alabama fought with "neither knowledge nor thought." The courageous Union defenders enjoyed more men, a better position, and far greater firepower than their gray-clad assailants, but as McMorries pointed out, "men have never been made so brave as to be wholly unmoved by such audacity as the Confederates exhibited." For thirty minutes it seemed the fight must go on forever, with the men on each side of that ditch preferring extinction to retreat. Finally, the Alabamians gave way and retreated in disorder.[78]

Rebels hurled themselves at the Union works with reckless abandon, but "in every instance the brave and heroic men were repulsed with loss of life too fearful to contemplate." Thomas Pulliam of the 22nd Mississippi Infantry lamented that, in the ditch in front of the Federal second line, "some of the most precious blood in the army was shed," as "thousands upon thousands of the bravest of the brave sons of the Southland went down to inevitable death under the galling fire of the enemy." John Copley came to rest in the ditch in front of the inner line of Federal works, and through the smoke he saw "the mangled and torn remains of many of our soldiers" who were "hanging on the long spikes" of the Union cheval-de-frise. Colonel Stephens of the 31st Mississippi Infantry was wounded in the right thigh and hip as he approached the Union breastworks, carrying the regiment's flag. As he fell, he passed the flag to Sergeant Hunter. Before Hunter could move, he was shot in the right arm and dropped the flag.[79]

John Copley caught his breath in the ditch surrounding the inner Union line and quickly realized that he was alone. Looking right and left, he could see no other Confederate survivors. He noted a dead Union soldier with two "large army pistols in his belt." Copley took the revolvers and fired them at the Federal soldiers just a few feet away on the other side of the parapet. Since he had no way to reload the pistols, Copley dropped the handguns and picked up his rifle, which he tried to shoot at nearby Union artillerymen who were firing their cannon with amazing rapidity from an embrasure in the breastworks. Copley got so close to the side of the cannon that the blast burned off his eyebrows, but he could not get a clear shot at the gunners, so he gave up and sought shelter in the bottom of the ditch.[80]

Federal infantry launched a determined counterattack. The rebels were unable to hold back the blue tide and retreated until they encountered gunners from Guibor's St. Louis Battery pushing two of their cannons forward by hand. As Joseph Boyce of the 1st Missouri Infantry limped to the rear on a leg wounded in the assault, he noticed that his comrades in the infantry rallied on the artillery and added their rifle bullets to the fire delivered by the cannoneers. A Union soldier took pity on the wounded Colonel Stephens. He cut off a chunk of the rebel's frock coat and bandaged Stephens's wound.[81]

The captured Union positions became the scenes of horror. John Copley crawled along the bottom of the ditch in front of the Federal inner line looking for survivors. Blood flowed across the ground, forming little streams and filling the bottom of the ditch "to the depth of the shoe soles." After climbing over countless corpses, he found a handful of unwounded men who "appeared to be undaunted" and shared "a look of stoic determination" on their "weather-beaten faces." They kept up a steady exchange of small arms fire with the Union soldiers a few feet away on the other side of the works. J. P. Cannon lay in an abandoned Union rifle pit on the extreme right of the rebel line while bullets and shells struck nearby. While he waited for an opportunity to escape, he feasted on hardtack Union soldiers had left behind and wrapped himself in a discarded Yankee overcoat. John Copley watched while several rebels sprang from the ditch and ran towards the Confederate rear. Copley prepared to move as well, determined to make his own retreat if the other men were successful. To his horror, a volley of rifle fire killed every single one of the men. Copley settled back down into the relative safety of the ditch while bullets and artillery shells struck nearby. Eventually he and a few other men concluded that escape was impossible, and they must decide between surrender and death. Captain

Williams of an Alabama regiment placed a piece of a white shirt on a ramrod and offered to surrender. A Federal officer ordered his men to cease fire and invited the Confederates across the parapet. As Copley crossed the lines, he took one final look at the heaps of dead bodies and "drew a sight of regret" for the men who lost their lives that day.[82]

W. W. McMillan lay in front of the inner line of Union works, suffering from the wounds that he received in the assault. He expected another bullet to end his life at any moment, but the fatal blow never came. McMillan thought about crawling back to his lines once the last of the light faded, but a Union defender noticed that McMillan was alive and ordered him to surrender. With no other option, McMillan complied and began crawling towards the Union lines as the firing slowed but did not stop. Just as he crossed the parapet, "a cowardly little scoundrel who was afraid to risk his head high enough to see what he was shooting at fired his piece in my face." The bullet missed McMillan, but the powder burned him badly. McMillan cursed the Union soldier for shooting a wounded man who had already surrendered, but the Union man denied firing the shot. Once behind the lines, two Irish soldiers picked up McMillan and carried him to a holding area for prisoners across the Harpeth River, where he waited with other men from the 17th Alabama.[83]

The horrific carnage slowly petered out. B. F. Weathers recalled that bodies lay thick on the battlefield, with privates, generals, and their colors all lying together "seven deep." Near the spot where the 29th Alabama Infantry planted their colors on the Federal works, rebel dead lay in a pile "like sheep." Weathers was luckier than many others. He became a prisoner. While he marched north to spend the rest of the war in a prison camp on Johnson's Island, in Ohio, he heard the "heart-rending," nearly insane "ravings" of the wounded. John Morton believed "the old soldiers all escaped but many of the conscripts, being afraid to run under fire, were captured."[84]

The Assaults on Franklin End

The main Confederate assaults on Franklin ended at around 9:00 p.m. General Clayton reported that "night mercifully interposed to save us from the terrible scourge which our brave companions had suffered." In the darkness, civilians sought to help the wounded. Members of the Carter family discovered Captain Tod Carter lying wounded a few hundred yards from his home. They brought him to the room where he was born, and he died early the next day.[85]

While the worst of the fighting was over by 9:00 p.m., the suffering and small-scale fighting continued. The Georgians of Stovall's Brigade were ahead of Clayton's Division, leading the way for Gibson's Louisianans and Holtzclaw's Alabamians. Stovall's men received orders to relieve spent troops occupying the first line of defenses held by the Federals at the start of the day. Sporadic firing continued throughout the evening, killing an officer and wounding two or three men of Stovall's Brigade. At 10:00 p.m., Lieutenant James Tillman led members of the 24th South Carolina in another assault and captured the colors of the 97th Ohio Infantry. After a long day of skirmishing with Federal forces across the Harpeth River, the men of Jackson's Division of cavalry returned to the main Confederate line after dark to replenish their ammunition. James Lanning reported that the fighting went on all night and "many noble braves fell to rise no more till God shall call them to the judgment." Edward McMorries recalled that the Federal defenders kept up a steady fire throughout the night, fearing a night assault. Most of the rebel troops were safely out of range to the south, so the fire fell primarily on the wounded of both armies, who were unable to move to safety. D. C. Marshall tried to retrieve the personal effects of his friend George Bost, who had died in the assault earlier that day, but was horrified to find that someone had robbed the corpse, stealing his cash and his prized pocket knife. Marshall was not sure if a Confederate or Federal had robbed his friend, but he cursed the thief regardless of his uniform. Robert Bevier could hardly stand the "cries and groans" of the thousands of wounded men caught between the lines and called the scene "a carnival of death."[86]

James Dinkins, a staff officer in Chalmers's Division, was mesmerized by the "sublimely and awfully grand" Federal shells that lit up the night. They "flashed and twittered like thousands of sky-rockets" until they burst and "all the sounds of hell could be heard." The sight and sound of those terrible shells still haunted him more than thirty years later when he wrote his memoirs and convinced him that "the devil had full possession of the earth" at the Battle of Franklin.[87]

Hood was still determined to break through the Union lines and ordered the remnants of the army to prepare for a morning assault. The bulk of the artillery finally caught up with the army that evening, and Hood planned for each fieldpiece to blast Union positions with one hundred rounds of ammunition beginning at 7:00 a.m. At 9:00 a.m., the entire army, or at least what was left of it, would surge forward in a mass charge.[88] The men in gray tried to sleep and dreaded the coming holocaust.

William Brown and Stanford's Mississippi Battery arrived near Franklin late that evening. They took up positions in the firing line and prepared to unleash hell from their guns at first light. Brown found it hard to focus on his work. The cries of the wounded were "very distressing." He wanted to help them, but "darkness and uncertainty of the whereabouts of the enemy prevents going to them."[89]

The Union army inadvertently saved their opponents from another bloodbath on December 1, slipping away while the Army of Tennessee slept. When General Cox received General Schofield's order to retreat, the 23rd Corps commander "made a manly protest against it." He told the staff officer who delivered the order that the Confederate army was in a "wrecked condition," that "retreat was wholly unnecessary," and that he would personally guarantee the security of the Union position at Franklin. Cox and many of his men did not want to retreat; they wanted to counterattack and destroy the shattered remnants of the Confederate forces before they could regroup. When Cox's staff officer delivered Cox's message, General Schofield agreed that "I have no doubt we could do as he suggests." In private, Schofield was more cantankerous, agreeing with Cox that "a fight to the finish then and there, might quite probably have given us the prize." Ultimately, he decided to withdraw primarily because he had already sent his reserve ammunition north and he feared running out of ordnance if he fought for a second day. Cox was unhappy with Schofield's decision but not unhappy enough to disobey a direct order. Reluctantly, he ordered his men to begin silently slipping away in the darkness.[90]

On the morning of December 1, 1864, the sun cast its rays over the blood-stained village along the Harpeth River and revealed that the contest for Franklin was over. Members of the 19th Tennessee Infantry agreed "the angel of death certainly held high carnival." Almost every member of the Federal army who could run, walk, or crawl away was gone. Confederate commanders were surprised, but some of the men were not. At about 3:00 a.m., Jesse Henderson and other members of the 41st Mississippi Infantry discovered that the Federals to their front were withdrawing. The Mississippians said nothing to their officers, preferring to allow the men in blue to retreat and enjoy the contents of abandoned knapsacks. When Hood learned that the Federals had escaped once again, he canceled his plan to take what was left of Franklin with a massive dawn assault. As the sun rose, the shattered remnants of the Army of Tennessee dealt with the aftermath. Charles Joy believed the battlefield "might well have been called the field of blood." In the words of E. H. Rennolds, "the slaughter of rebels has been great."[91]

In his official report, General Hood was remarkably optimistic, claiming that his forces only suffered a still sobering 4,500 total casualties of all causes. Hood lamented his losses but suggested that Federal losses were "equal or near our own." Hood's claims were incorrect, although it is not clear if he was intentionally dishonest or sincerely confused. The Federals inflicted far more damage than they absorbed. The Union army suffered 189 men killed, 1,033 wounded, and another 1,104 missing, for a total loss of 2,,326 men. The Confederates suffered far worse, although exact numbers are more difficult to ascertain. The Union army estimated that the rebels lost 1,750 dead, 3,800 badly wounded, 702 prisoners, and an unclear number of slightly wounded, for a minimum loss of 6,252.[92]

The actual Confederate casualties probably exceeded seven thousand total casualties, nearly a third of the Confederate troops who entered the battle that day. The losses were particularly heavy among Confederate officers. Sixty-five Confederate officers with the rank of captain or above were killed, wounded, captured, or simply disappeared at Franklin. Most notable among the deaths were Generals Patrick Cleburne, Hiram Granbury, States Rights Gist, Otto Strahl, and John Adams. In contrast to other battles like Gettysburg or Shiloh, which lasted several days, Franklin was a remarkably brief battle. The bulk of the fighting took place during a one hour and forty minute period, with most of the men on both sides falling within the forty minutes when the rebels made their most desperate bid to capture the second ring of Federal positions. Andrew Hill, a sergeant in the 16th Alabama Infantry, probably summed up the causes of the disparity in losses more succinctly that anyone else: "they cut us to pieces at Franklin as we fought through an open field and they behind breast works."[93]

Dead of Ewell's Corps, Spotsylvania, May 1864. Timothy H. O'Sullivan, photographer. Library of Congress.

Surprisingly, some Confederate soldiers claimed that Franklin was a victory. General Hood argued that, while the army suffered at Franklin, the battle also proved that the Army of Tennessee was unstoppable. Infantryman James Lanning was pleased to learn that the Union army had abandoned the field by the dead and wounded Union soldiers that littered the ground, by the many Union soldiers they captured, and by the large quantities of supplies that fell into Confederate hands. Lanning concluded, "victory is ours but very dearly bought." Maryland artillery officer William Ritter believed, "the charge was a brilliant one and was successful, as part of the enemy's line was captured," although he also admitted it came at a "fearful" cost. Missourian Joseph Boyce acknowledged that many men considered Franklin a victory for the Confederate army since it held the battlefield at the end of the fighting. However, the wounded soldier knew the pain of that supposed victory and concluded, "two such victories will wipe out any army."[94]

Other soldiers were even more grim. Arkansas soldier George Rozell described the battle as "the dreadful slaughter." Texas cannoneer P. E. Hockersmith described the battle as "a great blunder" that "could have been averted by a flank movement." Missouri artilleryman Sam Dunlap condemned "this needless butcher of Confederates." Texan Samuel Foster noted in his diary that "I have seen places where the blood run off in a stream," but Franklin was a place of "great destruction." Foster believed that "Gen. Hood has betrayed us," that "this is not the kind of fighting he promised us," and that it was not a "fight with equal numbers and choice of the ground." Foster believed that "the wails and cries of widows and orphans made at Franklin Tenn Nov 30th, 1864 will heat up the fires of the bottomless pit to burn the soul of Gen J B Hood." Edward Jones picked up a copy of *Don Quixote* he found lying on the ground as he entered Franklin. The Alabamian carried it throughout the remainder of the war and kept it as prized possession until the day he died.[95]

6

"FROZEN OUT"

The Siege of Nashville

> Ambition and even life itself, were almost frozen out of us. In the midst of all of this, we gazed defiantly at the enemy in his comfortable quarters, and the frowning cannon on forts Negley, Casino, and Morton, which were waiting like bloodhounds held in leash, eager to be turned loose upon us.[1]
>
> —W. J. Worsham and C. W. Heiskell, 19th Tennessee Infantry

As the sun rose on December 1, Forrest's troopers were already in the saddle, pursuing the fleeing Federals. Chalmers's Division of cavalry moved northwest along the Hillsboro-Nashville turnpike. Buford's and Jackson's Divisions moved northeast up the Franklin Highway under the direct command of General Forrest. The Harpeth River stood between the two wings of Forrest's command for the first phase of their advance. A few miles north of Franklin, gray-clad troopers caught up with retreating Federals. After a few blasts from one of Captain Morton's batteries, the men in blue attempted to flee. The lucky ones escaped, but others fell into rebel hands. Forrest's troopers kept up a running fight all the way to the outskirts of Nashville, punishing any Federal too slow, too tired, or too demoralized to stay one step ahead of the rebels. Hundreds of Union prisoners and horses fell into Confederate hands in a series of sharp skirmishes on the roads to Nashville.[2]

The horrendous losses in officers and men at the Battle of Franklin made an immediate pursuit by the Confederate infantry impossible. Roughly seven thousand Confederates, mostly infantrymen—including sixty-five officers with the rank of captain or above—were dead, wounded, captured, or simply missing. Many of the men still fit for duty were separated from their units. Tennessee cavalryman Charles Joy argued, "the best and most able generals and other officers were killed or wounded." John Ward of the 11th Tennessee Infantry reported that his regiment "had hardly a commissioned officer left." Samuel Foster reported that the army was "so badly cut up that we can't move . . . some officers have no men, and some companies have no officers." As a result, "we have to reorganize and consolidate."[3]

Bloodied rebels spent the early morning hours of December 1 reorganizing, burying their fallen comrades, and mourning their losses. During the battle, J. W. Kellum of the 3rd Florida Regiment carried his regiment's colors, but the next day he was given the horrific chore of helping to bury the dead. The field was covered in so many bodies that they resorted to the "uncivilized" practice of burying men in massive trenches. W. R. Bell was burying masses of the dead at Franklin when a Union soldier who initially appeared dead called out and begged Bell to shoot him. When Bell refused, the soldier assured Bell that it would be an act of mercy, not a sin. The wounded man offered to give Bell everything he had, but Bell still refused. Risenar Etter of the 16th Tennessee Infantry helped bury members of his regiment who fell in action that day and lamented the loss of men "torn to peaces by those missiles of death." He took some solace in the fact that "the ground was covered in blew coats." J. L. Boone, a veteran soldier who witnessed some of the war's most destructive battles, including Chickamauga and Murfreesboro, concluded that Franklin was "the greatest slaughter I ever saw." Many years after the battle, Richard Harris of the 6th Florida Infantry explained that the horrific image of so many dead men in such a small place was forever burned into his mind. Tennessee soldier James Cooper claimed that "men were so disheartened by gazing on the scene of slaughter that they had not the nerve for the work before them."[4]

General Hood was in a difficult position on the morning of December 1. One of the few things that prevented the wavering Army of Tennessee from collapsing was forward momentum. Many soldiers remained with the army, in large measure, because they believed that the offensive was working. It was true that the rebels were moving forward at a rapid pace, the Federals were retreating, and the Union high command was worried. However, it was also true that with every passing moment the Confederate forces grew weaker and the Federals grew stronger. Franklin was not a Confederate victory, but even if it was, it did not matter. The Union could survive more battles like Franklin, but the Confederacy could not. Hood claimed until his dying day that his army was triumphant at Franklin and that victory was within reach on December 1. Perhaps he simply lied because the truth would have meant admitting his own failures. It is also possible, and perhaps most likely, that he had little other choice. If he admitted failure on December 1, then the campaign was over. Many of his men, particularly those from Tennessee, would have deserted, and President Davis might have removed him from command. However, if Hood played the long odds and doubled down, then maybe, just maybe, it could work. Perhaps reinforcements would arrive from Texas, or the people of Tennessee would revolt against the Union army, or Federal commanders might make a serious mistake. On December 1, Hood made what was probably the greatest gamble of his life.

After deciding to press ahead, Hood issued General Field Orders #38 and ordered that it be read to each regiment. It congratulated the soldiers on their victory, which Hood claimed was the product of their "heroic and determined courage." The commanding general expressed grief at the loss of "gallant officers and brave men," but he tempered his grief with a claim that at Franklin the Army of Tennessee proved that "we can carry any position."[5]

Pushed forward by a commander who felt, or at least claimed to feel, that his men were victorious, the army moved north. The cavalry remained in the lead, moving forward at a rapid pace and skirmishing with Federal rear guards. The artillery and infantry trailed behind, strung out along the Franklin and Nashville Pike. Lee's Corps had arrived at Franklin last and missed the worst of the fighting, so Hood ordered them to take the lead. Stewart's Corps followed close behind. Cheatham's Corps brought up the rear.[6]

The army's objective was the city of Nashville, Tennessee, the most important piece of real estate in Tennessee and one of the most strategically significant locations on the continent. Founded in 1799, Nashville was the leading city in the state by outbreak of war in 1861, serving as the state's capital as well as the home of countless factories, stores, banks, schools, places of worship, and roughly seventeen thousand residents. Nashville stood at a great crossroads of turnpikes and railroad lines extending north towards Cincinnati, Ohio, and south to the Gulf Coast ports. Other roads passed through the city from the Unionist-dominated mountains of East Tennessee south towards the rail hub at Atlanta, Georgia, and west to Memphis, Tennessee, on the mighty Mississippi River. The Cumberland River, a tributary of the Mississippi, meandered along the northern edge of Nashville, making the city a center of river as well as road and rail traffic. Early in the war, Federal forces set their sights on Nashville, capturing the important city in February 1862. Nashville quickly became a center of the Union war effort. Federals transformed the peaceful city into the "fortress on the Cumberland."[7]

Along the road to Nashville, threadbare rebels gathered supplies left behind by Union troops more concerned with speed than frugality. When William Brown arrived in Franklin, he discovered "everybody out hunting Yankee plunder, which is very plentiful." James Lanning gathered up all the

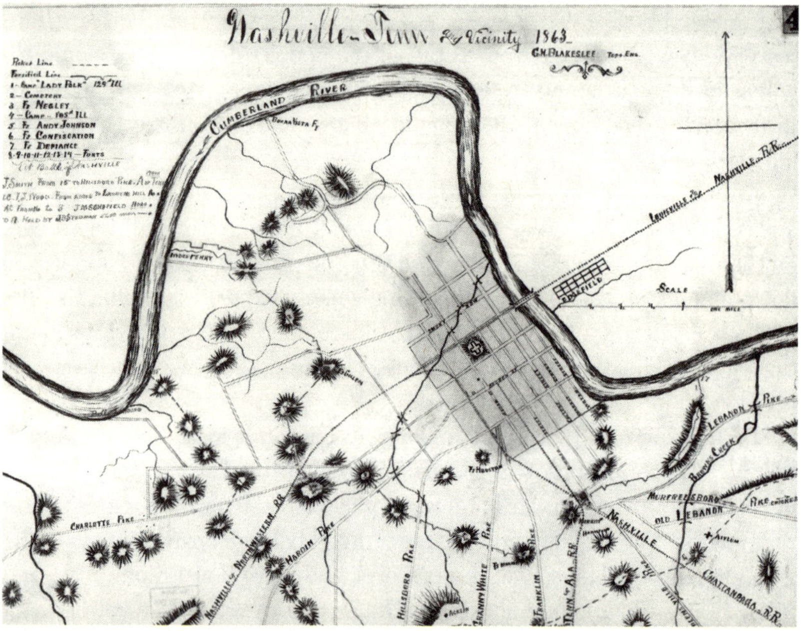

Map 13. Nashville, Tenn., and Vicinity, 1863. G. H. Blakeslee, cartographer. Library of Congress.

food, clothing, and trinkets he could carry along the road. Robert Maxwell noticed his slave Jim sitting by the road near a badly wounded Union soldier, waiting on the Yankee to die so Jim could take his shoes. Maxwell gave Jim permission to retrieve the shoes, but only if he allowed the man to die in peace first. Surviving accounts do not indicate if the dying soldier was awake. If the man in blue was aware of his surroundings, it must have made for an awkward departure from this world, knowing that a stranger sat quietly nearby waiting patiently for the moment he could acquire a new pair of shoes. Hours later Jim caught up with Maxwell and explained that the shoes did not fit him, so he sold them to a barefoot rebel. It is unclear if Jim was allowed to keep any of the money or delivered the entire sum to his master. Maxwell explained, "soldiers in rags and barefooted did not bury good shoes or any other clothing in the ground to rot. All such useful articles were utilized where most needed. It was only common sense."[8]

Despite their horrific losses, some rebels expressed happiness on the march northward. General Hood claimed that the men enjoyed higher morale after the Battle of Franklin because they had defeated the Union army. Edgar Jones believed that the Union forces at Franklin were "badly whipped" since "an army will not leave a fortified position in the night and retreat in haste unless he is whipped." Samuel Vann told his sweetheart that "we gained a complete victory." W. Jere Crook of the consolidated 154th and 13th Tennessee Infantry informed his cousin that "our campaign into Tenn thus far has been successful." Artillery officer Stouten Dent told his wife that the campaign "has been decidedly successful" and that the "Yankees are decidedly afraid of us." He hoped to be in Nashville soon. A. D. Rape, a drummer with the 46th Alabama Infantry, noticed dead Federals left unburied along the road, evidence of that Union soldiers were suffering as they fled north.[9]

Other Confederate soldiers felt differently as they moved northward. According to Charles Joy, "the spirit of the men was crushed." J. L. Boone of the 13th Mississippi Infantry recalled, "we went up to Nashville barefooted, worried, and disheartened." He claimed that it was possible to track the rebels by the bloody footprints their bare feet left in the road. Staff officer William Gale believed the army was "in mourning" as it moved towards Nashville. A Tennessee soldier reported that many men in the ranks felt that Hood was a fool to march on Nashville. James Arnold of the 30th Alabama Infantry believed that the attack on Franklin was "disastrous." Arkansan John Lavender condemned Hood for the frontal assaults on Franklin. He believed that a flank attack would have defeated the Federals "without losing a man." Staff officer James Dinkins claimed the men were unhappy because "our army was badly whipped" and "the flower of the army had fallen," which filled the men "with gloom and sorrow," ensuring that the army was never the same again. Joseph Jones of the 1st Arkansas Infantry bluntly claimed that the army was "perfectly demoralized."[10]

Roughly seven hundred Confederate soldiers moved north as prisoners of the Union army. Prisoners told Levi Scofield, an engineer officer with the Union 23rd Corps, that "the whole army was broken." According to Scofield, "all were ragged and dirty," most of the men wore "butternut homespun" topped with "black or gray slouch hats," many of which were pierced with bullet holes. Arkansas infantryman Peter Hotze had suffered a severe wound to his leg and crawled into a thicket of bushes, where he passed out until a Federal soldier revived him with a splash of water and the news that he was now a prisoner. A friendly Federal shared his crackers, pork, and water with Tennessee Confederate John Copley. It was a welcome gift to a man who had not eaten for several days. Copley recalled looking around at the "ghastly" rebel prisoners, their ragged clothing stained with blood, their faces blackened by gunpowder, and their hair singed off by gunfire. The Battle of Franklin demolished these men, convincing them that the Confederacy was doomed, that further resistance was folly, and that all their sacrifices had been meaningless. Copley wanted to lie down

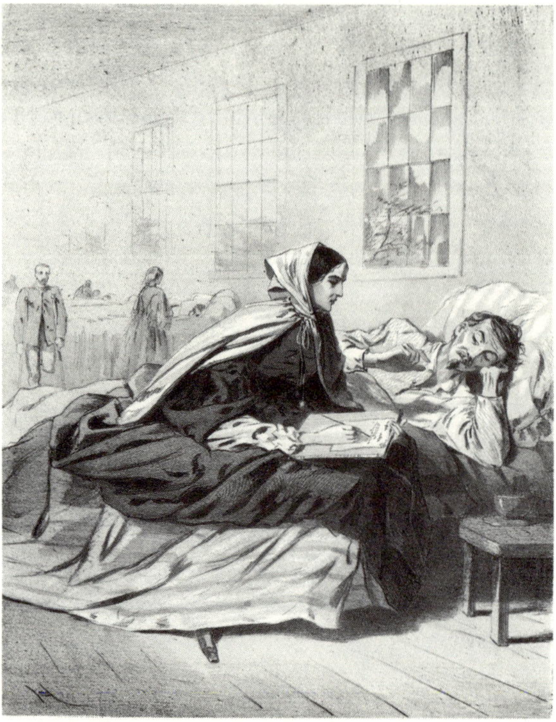

Campaign Sketches. The Letter for Home by Winslow Homer. A nurse writing a letter for a wounded Army of the Potomac soldier in a hospital bed. Lithograph published by L. Prang & Co., 1863. Library of Congress.

and sleep, but the men in blue ordered the rebels to rise and march north towards prison camps.[11]

Not every soldier moved north. Wounded rebels who were not captured remained near Franklin, some eventually succumbing to their wounds and others recovering. On December 1, Deering Roberts, a surgeon assigned to the 20th Tennessee Infantry, arrived in Franklin with eleven men, two wagons, and orders to care for the wounded of Bate's Division. Roberts selected an old carriage shop and nearby store for his hospital. He quickly put his men to work, cleaning out the buildings, gathering straw, and bringing in the wounded from the battlefield. The Confederate medical service worked tirelessly to help the wounded, most of whom suffered from injuries caused by the large, soft, lead Minnie balls fired by the rifles carried by most infantrymen. The Minnie balls did not typically punch through flesh like modern, steel-jacketed rifle bullets. Instead, they deformed and splintered on contact with the human body, turning flesh into bloody masses of meat, sinew, and bone. Roberts took great pride in the work he did in Franklin, boasting that only seven men died in his hospital; three from gunshots to the head, two from wounds to their abdomens, one from an amputated leg, and a final man who refused to submit to amputation. Many years later, the old doctor was proud to explain that "I never amputated a limb without consent of the wounded man."[12]

The people of Middle Tennessee helped the men who remained in Franklin after the armies moved on. Robert Bevier of the 5th Missouri Infantry expressed his gratitude to the people of Franklin, who approached the battlefield as soon as the fighting ended to care for the wounded. Civilians brought food to the hospitals and shared their homes with recuperating soldiers. Newton Davis suffered wounds to his upper thigh and abdomen during the Battle of Franklin but received excellent care at a private home in Franklin. Artillery officer Thomas Key passed through Franklin on an errand several days after the battle and took notice of the "beautiful ladies" who worked tirelessly to help wounded Confederates.[13]

Early on the morning of December 2, the Confederate Army of Tennessee resumed their march on Nashville. While the infantry and artillery plodded along, Forrest's fast-moving horsemen were already taking up positions within three miles of Nashville. Biffle's Brigade of Tennesseans formed to the west, across the Hillsboro and Harding Turnpikes to the southwest of town. General Forrest personally led Morton's Battery of artillery along with Buford's and Jackson's Brigade into positions across the Nolensville Pike southeast of town. Morton's gunners sent up near the junction of Wedgewood Avenue and the Nolensville Pike. The rebel horse artillery began firing on a detachment of Federals milling around a house and sent the men in blue running for cover.[14]

Some Confederate soldiers left the army, with or without permission, as it neared Nashville. Robert Battle noted in his diary that much of his regiment, the 9th Tennessee Cavalry, briefly abandoned the march on Nashville for visits to their homes. Tennessee infantrymen James Cooper and George Litton received permission to visit a friend who lived near the line of march and "enjoyed ourselves as only men can, who have not slept in a house for months, nor had enough to eat for years." According to Thomas Head of the 16th Tennessee Infantry, after the Battle of Franklin many of the army's best men, particularly from Tennessee, began leaving the army forever. They believed that, since the Confederacy was clearly doomed, they had a duty to leave the army and care for their families.[15] If Hood had admitted that the campaign was hopeless and ordered a retreat, many more men would have undoubtedly joined the deserters.

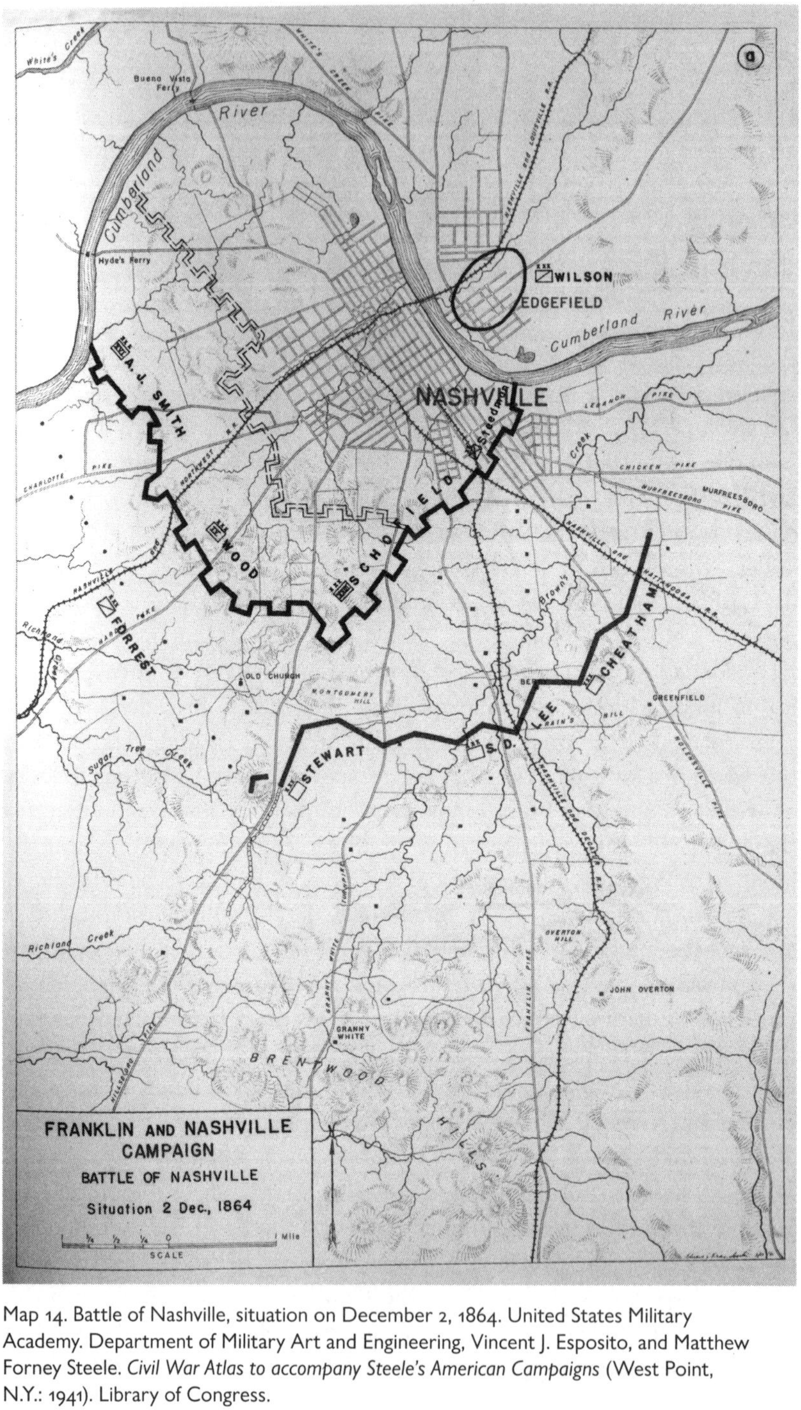

Map 14. Battle of Nashville, situation on December 2, 1864. United States Military Academy. Department of Military Art and Engineering, Vincent J. Esposito, and Matthew Forney Steele. *Civil War Atlas to accompany Steele's American Campaigns* (West Point, N.Y.: 1941). Library of Congress.

Lieutenant Hiram L. Hendley of Co. A, 9th Tennessee Cavalry Battalion with double-barrel shotgun and Bowie knife. Library of Congress.

By the middle of the day on December 2, Confederate infantry began relieving the cavalrymen outside Nashville, freeing the horsemen to resume their traditional roles of raiding and screening. General Abraham Buford split his division of cavalry, using most of Bell's Brigade of Tennesseans to protect the army's right flank and ordering Crossland's Kentuckians to assault Federal stockades guarding the Nashville and Chattanooga Railroad. The horsemen began by attacking blockhouse number one, five miles outside Nashville. The Union troops sheltered in a strong stockade, shaped like a crucifix and composed of unseasoned oak timber three feet thick, pierced with holes that allowed the defenders to fire without exposing themselves. Realizing that the Federals occupied a formidable position, Buford ordered Colonel Clark Barteau to bring his regiment, the consolidated 2nd/22nd Tennessee Cavalry, and support the Kentuckians. Rebel artillery opened fire on the Union position, but their shells did little damage to the thick wooden walls. Focused on taking the stockade, General Buford neglected to destroy the railroad tracks the blockhouse protected. Suddenly a train filled with "negro troops" arrived from Murfreesboro. Before the rebels could react, the Union reinforcements leapt from the train and joined their comrades in the blockhouse. At about the same time, General Forrest arrived, outraged that Buford had allowed the train to slip through. Forrest ordered Buford to capture the blockhouse immediately. An exasperated Buford asked Forrest how he was supposed to accomplish this feat. Without pausing, Forrest told him to block the firing slits with rails and burn the wooden blockhouse to the ground. The men who overheard Forrest's plan knew that it was a desperate tactic and felt relief when Buford ignored his chief's orders. Instead, Buford directed his cavalrymen to keep up a small arms fire while Morton's gunners unleashed their cannons on the position from closer range. Surrounded and under an intense fire, the Union defenders surrendered the next day. The Union blockhouse fell into rebel hands and went up in flames as eighty blue-clad defenders became prisoners of war.[16]

Late on the evening of December 2, additional Confederate infantrymen and artillerists arrived several miles south of Nashville and took up positions along the southern edge of the city. The Union artillery greeted the rebels with a "rapid and furious" bombardment of exploding shells. The heavy cannonading forced Confederate units back. John Holland of Corput's Georgia Battery claimed that "everyone" wanted to attack Nashville "immediately." Alabama infantryman Edgar Jones recalled that the entire army was drawn up in line battle, and for a brief time he believed that they were about to take the city in a single, glorious, charge. Years later, Jones still believed that the town was largely unguarded on December 2 and that the rebels could have taken the city if they had attacked immediately.[17] Jones was incorrect.

The Union forces in Nashville on December 2, 1864, faced challenges and were understandably worried by the Confederate advance, but they were perfectly capable of defending themselves. G. T. Cullens, serving in the 18th Alabama Infantry, recalled that the rebel army was "held at bay by an overwhelming force" that greeted them with a burst of fire. C. Irvine Walker of the 10th South Carolina Infantry examined the ring of sturdy forts surrounding Nashville and concluded that the defenses were "the strongest, perhaps, in this country." General Thomas commanded a force of more than 35,000 men in and around Nashville, and more were arriving daily. In contrast, Hood's depleted army consisted of 18,342 infantry, 2,405 artillery, and 2,306 cavalrymen, for a total of 23,053.[18]

Now that Hood had arrived at Nashville, he had to decide what to do there. Even the architect of the frontal assaults at Franklin knew that a direct attack on Nashville's large and well-prepared Union garrison would fail. The rebels could have attempted to cross over the Cumberland River, bypassing Nashville and threatening Federals in Kentucky and even Ohio, but Hood rejected this plan because it would have placed his small army in the midst of enemy territory, with Federal gunboats on the river that would

Nashville, Tennessee. Fortified bridge over the Cumberland River, 1864. George N. Barnard, photographer. Library of Congress.

cut off supplies and lines of retreat. Hood knew the local population was unlikely to support the Confederate army unless they decisively defeated the Union army first. With no other realistic option, Hood ordered his men to build defensive works.[19] Since the Confederates lacked the manpower needed to encircle Nashville, Hood ordered his men to form a broad, meandering, roughly convex, semi-circular arc around the southern edge of Nashville, with Stewart's Corps to the west providing the army's left flank near the Hillsboro Pike, Lee's Corps in the center straddling the Franklin Pike, and Cheatham's Corps forming the right flank on the east, extending towards the banks of the Cumberland River. Cavalry provided screens on each end of the line. The army's headquarters found a home in the residence of Mr. Overton, near the Franklin Pike, about five and half miles south of Nashville. Hood hoped that the Federals would launch an attack on his fortified lines, suffer a horrific defeat, and provide his forces with an opportunity for a counterattack.[20]

Hood's plan was unlikely to work, and many of his men knew it. Irving Buck, a staff officer in Cheatham's Corps, believed that Hood's plans were "beyond comprehension." Thomas's men in Nashville already outnumbered

Southwest view of Fort Negley. Library of Congress.

Hood's little army, and while every train brought Thomas more men, Hood was unlikely to get reinforcements. When Thomas got good and ready, he could leave Nashville and attack the rebels. If the Confederate army somehow repulsed the Federal onslaught, the men in blue could retire to their nearly impregnable works around Nashville and await additional reinforcements that would ensure the success of a subsequent assault. Missouri infantryman Robert Bevier condemned Hood's siege and argued that he should have continued his advance, crossed the Cumberland River, and cut Nashville off from the north. Bevier seemed unconcerned about the Federal gunboats that would have slaughtered any rebels foolish enough to attempt a mass river crossing. Napoleon Bonaparte reportedly suggested that "a passive defense is deferred suicide."[21] While that might be true, it is also clear that it could have been worse. Hood could have ordered another Franklin-style frontal assault, resulting in immediate suicide.

The Federal commander at Nashville, George H. Thomas, was perhaps the least likely general in either army to launch the ill-advised attack Hood hoped for. Born to a family of Virginia slave owners in 1816, by the outbreak of Civil War Thomas boasted a distinguished military career that began at West Point and included combat in both Florida and Mexico. When his home state left the Union, Thomas briefly contemplated resigning his commission before deciding that his oath to the army meant more than the accident of his birth. He demonstrated his devotion to the Union as he rose through the ranks, earning praise for his service on battlefields across West Virginia, Kentucky, and Tennessee. At the Battle of Chickamauga in 1863, he proved himself a master of defensive warfare. While the rest of the Federal army retreated in disorder, Thomas kept his corps together, covering the retreat and preventing a complete collapse of the Union line. In the process, the Virginian earned the name "the Rock of Chickamauga." Many of the men who knew Thomas best thought of him as more of a lion than a rock. He stood six feet four inches tall, with a thickly muscled body topped by a head of golden curls streaked with gray, which flowed into a thick crop of whiskers that looked more like a mane than a beard. Thomas rarely spoke, but when he did, he roared with a quiet but powerful voice that demanded obedience.[22] The Rock of Chickamauga would not move quickly, but when he did, he would crush everything that dared stand in his path.

The Union high command in Washington urged Thomas to attack quickly, but Thomas seemed immune to pressure. Secretary of War Edwin Stanton urged Thomas to attack. General Grant, in overall command of all Union armies, sent Thomas a blistering series of telegrams demanding an immediate assault. Grant was worried that the unpredictable Hood might somehow slip across the Cumberland River and move north to threaten Union forces in Kentucky or Ohio. In a more realistic vein, Grant also worried that the Confederate Army of Tennessee would dig in to provide a stubborn defense of their native soil. When Thomas still refused to attack, Grant threatened to remove Thomas from command if he did not launch an immediate assault. Despite the pressure, the rock would not be moved.[23]

Thomas understood the situation in Tennessee far better than Grant or Stanton. When Sherman began his march to the sea several weeks before, he took the best troops in the region, leaving Thomas to defend Tennessee with an eclectic collection of raw recruits, railroad guards, dismounted cavalrymen, and reorganized units of convalescents. General Thomas knew that even his imperfect assortment of infantry and artillery units was stronger than Hood's battered legions and that he could probably win a battle at virtually any time, but Thomas did not want to just win a battle. He wanted to win the war. Time was on his side, and he knew it. To achieve the decisive victory he craved, Thomas needed a cavalry force capable of defeating Forrest's famed troopers and pursuing a defeated enemy. Building up an excellent cavalry force would take time, but Thomas assured his superiors that "the moment I can get my cavalry I will march against Hood." Secretary of War Edwin Stanton lamented that by the time Thomas's cavalry got ready, "Gabriel will be blowing his last horn."[24]

While the Union high command was understandably unhappy that a Confederate army had parked itself on the doorstep of one of the most important cities in the nation and worried what the aggressive Hood might do, the Army of Tennessee posed little threat to the Union. A small portion of Thomas's command successfully defended themselves from the rebels at Franklin. Hood's army had neither the siege train nor the heavy artillery and ammunition needed to crush Nashville's forts. The Confederate forces lacked enough men to surround Nashville and starve it out. The Union forces controlled all the bridges across the Cumberland River with the aid of Federal gunboats that made a mass crossing of the river virtually impossible. Federal forces enjoyed strong logistical networks that brought a steady stream of reinforcements and supplies into Nashville. In contrast, the rebels had few supplies and no hope of significant reinforcements. While some northerners felt panic, others knew that as soon as Thomas assembled enough cavalry, he would attack Hood and win a great victory. The rebels were stuck. Unwilling to retreat and incapable of surviving a battle, the rebels might freeze to death while they waited for Union forces to kill them at their leisure.[25]

Confederate soldiers were aware of the difficult obstacles they faced. Sergeant John W. Sparkman rejoined his regiment near Nashville after a furlough on December 3 and noted in his diary that "I do not think we will take it soon if we do at all." Samuel Vann told his sweetheart that Nashville was filled with Yankees who kept up a steady fire against the rebels and wrote, "if we have to charge the place many more of us will fall." Richard Harris of Selden's Alabama Battery seemed despondent when he referred to the men near Nashville as "what was left of the Confederate Army under General Hood," suggesting that he saw the army as nothing more than a remnant of its former self.[26]

Settling in for the winter, rebels built a wide array of improvised shelters, including huts made of corn stalks and semi-underground shelters framed with wood and covered with dirt. Members of the 18th Alabama Infantry dug holes in the ground between two and three feet deep and wide enough for three men to lie down side by side. They covered the bottom of the holes with whatever brush, grass, and twigs they could find to insulate themselves from the ground. At night the men would lie down next to each other to share body heat and cover themselves with their blankets. The temperature within the simple shelters was far warmer than above the ground. R. B. Meadows of the 35th Alabama Infantry reported that many men made their sleeping pits long enough to build a fire at one end. It worked great until the wind inevitably shifted and blew blinding smoke into the men's eyes. While many men were grateful for the warmth, the shelters gave Alabama soldier Edgar Jones "a sort of graveyard feeling" since they bore an obvious resemblance to a soldier's grave.[27]

While the infantry tried to stay warm, the cavalry remained aggressive. On December 4, Confederate cavalrymen under the command of General James Chalmers captured two transports on the Cumberland River, seven miles from town, and acquired three hundred mules and horses. The Federals quickly recaptured their boats, but the Confederates took pride in the capture of precious horseflesh. A. C. McLeary of the 12th Tennessee Cavalry explained that the rebel horsemen captured unarmed Federal supply boats by threatening them with artillery and then wading out to loot the vessels. McLeary and his comrades ate better than most members of the Army of Tennessee because they gorged themselves on captured provisions.[28]

Some of Forrest's troopers rejoiced in the capture of boats, and others moved on to trains. General Forest personally led members of Buford's Division and an artillery detachment commanded by Captain Morton in an attack on Stockade No. 2, near Antioch, a short distance from Nashville. Morton's gunners sent a barrage of shells slamming into the blockhouse, killing ten men and wounding twenty. As the artillery fire raged, a train filled with "negro troops" approached the blockhouse with the intent to reinforce the Federal position. Before the train's engineer could react, rebel gunners shifted their cannons and fired shells that crippled the train's engine. The Federal troops on the train raced away from the burning wreckage and retreated into the woods on both sides of the tracks. Later the same day, Forrest's troopers captured Blockhouse No. 3 without firing a shot and burned it.[29]

Late on December 4, Hood ordered Forrest's troopers to advance on Murfreesboro, Tennessee, roughly forty miles to the southeast of Nashville. Forrest's men continued their string of successes as they moved southeast, capturing small Federal garrisons at Laverne, which was roughly twenty miles southeast of Nashville, and Smyrna, which was another five miles down the road. Along the march, men continued to come and go as they pleased. Although Captain Morton was a highly respected and dedicated artillery officer, even he felt the call of home and briefly left the army without permission to visit his mother, who lived nearby. F. E. Henderson, the fifteen-year-old daughter of a wealthy merchant living between Murfreesboro and Nashville, looked on with satisfaction while Federal troops pulled back towards Murfreesboro and were quickly followed by swarms of Confederate soldiers, who burned the abandoned blockhouses.[30]

In response to Forrest's successes on the road the Murfreesboro, Hood provided the cavalry commander with reinforcements. On December 5, Hood sent Sears's and Brown's infantry brigades, Bate's Division of infantry, and two batteries of artillery towards Murfreesboro with orders to report to General Forrest. William McLeod and the rest of the 7th Florida Infantry took delight in destroying railroad tracks as they moved towards a rendezvous with Forrest's cavalry. Late on December 5, Bate's Division of infantry caught up with Forrest's cavalrymen, and the unified command made plans to capture Murfreesboro.[31] It would not be an easy task.

The Federal forces around Murfreesboro consisted of roughly 8,000 men in a series of forts. In contrast, Forrest's command boasted only around 6,500 troops, even with the reinforcements of infantry and artillery. In spite of the difficult odds, Forrest was eager to take the town and skirmished with Federals, looking for weak spots in the Union defenses. Rebels got within four miles of Murfreesboro's center on December 6 before Union defenders pushed them back. While the troopers probed, they also teased the Federals, trying to get the men in blue to attack, but the Union troops refused to take the bait. Colonel Clark Barteau, commander of the consolidated 2nd/22nd Tennessee Cavalry, personally led a scouting expedition towards the Union lines as darkness fell. As his horse jumped a ditch, the animal "made one of those peculiar snorts that 'Old Selim' was noted for." In the same moment, a shot flew out from the nearby trees and slammed into Barteau's body, causing a painful wound that ended his service with the army.[32]

While Forrest's men tried to capture Murfreesboro, the Confederate artillery near Nashville used a few of their precious shells to remind the Federal garrison that they were still alive on December 6. John Copley and other Confederate prisoners in the city responded to the rebel gunfire with cheers and hopes that their comrades would soon rescue them. According to a journalist writing for the *Nashville Daily Union*, the people of Nashville were unimpressed with the rebel bombardment, noting that the rebels did little more than to deplete their undoubtedly meager supplies of ammunition. After the shelling subsided, Federal forces probed the Confederate lines of Cheatham's Corps. Federal gunboats supported the probe, launching heavy shells that echoed through the Confederate lines.[33]

December 7 witnessed additional fighting near Murfreesboro. The rebels occupied a crescent-shaped line. On the eastern end of the Confederate line, General Buford's Division of cavalry straddled the Woodbury Turnpike. Palmer's Brigade of infantry occupied a hill just south of the Wilkerson Turnpike, on the western end of the line. The Confederate forces noticed a large column of Federal infantry along the Salem Road. General Forrest repositioned his forces to meet the threat, ordering Sears's and Palmer's brigades of infantry to occupy the center with a brigade of Jackson's cavalry division on each flank. The Confederates began to give way under a sustained Federal assault. Ross's Brigade of Texas cavalry led a counterattack against the Union front, while Armstrong's Brigade of Mississippians hit the Federal flank. Surprised by the counterattack, General Robert Milroy began to withdraw his Federal troops into town. Confederate cavalrymen under the command of General Buford rushed into town with the aid of Captain Morton's artillerymen. They encountered little resistance, and soon Morton's gunners sent shells flying into the courthouse, where Union troops sought cover. The men in blue responded, focusing their fire on the precious horses of Morton's artillery. Dead and wounded horses fell to the ground. Realizing that the tables were turning, Morton ordered his men to use the remaining horses to pull their guns out of harm's way. When the surviving horses proved unequal to the task, dismounted cavalrymen and artillerymen put their shoulders into the work and helped move cannons to relative safety half a mile away. Once out of the line of fire, Morton noticed that his coat was pieced by eleven bullet holes and three more had punctured his hat.[34]

General Milroy led a Union counterattack on the fleeing rebels. The Tennesseans pulled back and built barricades to protect themselves from the advancing men in blue. Milroy refused to launch a head-on assault and briefly withdrew his men out of range. Sheltered behind the relative safety of earth and wood, Confederates remained in place until 3:00 p.m., when Federal troops came into view once more. Rather than throw his men against the strongpoint, Milroy led his men in a flanking maneuver through concealing woods. Without warning, Milroy's troops charged the Confederates along their unprotected flank. Forrest wheeled his troops to face the threat. His infantry and artillery stood in front, while his cavalry withdrew a short distance behind, prepared to counterattack.[35]

Forrest's plan to hold the line failed. Most of the Confederate infantry fled to the rear. General Forrest, General Bate, and other officers personally tried to rally the infantrymen and restore the line, but the panicked men refused to halt. The 20th Tennessee Infantry along with the rest of Tyler's Brigade began forming a new line across Wilkinson Pike, but before they were all in position, the Union troops came into view once more. Men from Tennessee and Georgia gave the Federals a warm reception and called up artillery support. The famed Washington Artillery of New Orleans added the weight of their shells to the fire produced by their brothers in the infantry. Unable to advance, the Union troops lay down in a cotton field and kept up a steady fire on the Confederate defenders. For some unclear reason, the Confederate right suddenly began to evaporate at just the moment when they appeared to have thwarted the Union advance. The disappearing Confederate right forced the entire rebel force to withdraw. The 20th Tennessee helped form a rear guard, allowing other Confederate troops to retreat in relative safety. The consolidated 2nd/22nd Tennessee Cavalry also supported the withdrawal, launching a mounted charge that retarded the Union advance. Gaus, Forrest's German bugler, sounded the charge as bullets perforated his bugle. Somehow, the rebels stopped the Federal advance. At about the same time, General Milroy received word from General Lovell Rousseau in Murfreesboro, who needed Milroy's support. Milroy withdrew rather than press the attack on Forrest's still wavering line outside town. James Cooper of the 20th Tennessee Infantry recalled with pride that

General Forrest arrived on the scene and complimented the regiment, while pointing out that "other troops acted shamefully." William Yeatman, with the 2nd Tennessee Infantry, provided a possible explanation for the poor performance of some units, claiming that they entered the fight with "a few rounds only."[36] Even the bravest men can do only so much when they run out of ammunition.

After the battle, Confederate morale fell. William Hardy, a staff officer in Cheatham's Corps, was distraught over the rebel failures at Murfreesboro and worried what it might indicate about the future. Homesick and frustrated with the lack of progress, R. R. Hancock and every other member except one of Company C of the 2nd Tennessee Cavalry decided to leave the army without permission and visit home. The lone member of the company who remained only did so because his remote home was too difficult to reach. After several days, Hancock and most (but not all) of his comrades returned. J. E. Hawkins was killed while he was gone, and J. W. Stevens became a prisoner.[37]

The Confederate forces outside Nashville did little better than their comrades at Murfreesboro. On December 7 the Union forces probed Cheatham's lines with an assault by "colored troops" led by white officers.

Spare Cartridges. Black ink drawing on cream paper by Alfred R. Waud. Probably drawn after war-time pencil sketch, for postwar illustrated publication. Library of Congress.

Artillery officer Thomas Key noted with seeming pleasure in his diary that "several of the misceginators were killed." On December 8 General Lee's Corps advanced towards the Federal positions near their left flank. Lee's men sent "the bluecoats running." The rebels took up new positions in the rifle pits abandoned by the Union troops. To get a better look at the fighting, rebel officers took a position on a high hill south of the Federal lines. The Union artillery did not appreciate the presence of men in gray on the high ground, loaded a 30-pounder Parrott rifle, and "sent one of those deadly missiles traveling over our heads at the rate of 800 miles per hour." The rebels got the hint and fled to less vulnerable positions.[38]

By December 9 General Hood had all but given up on capturing Murfreesboro. He ordered Bate's Division of infantry to return to the army near Nashville. The journey was difficult for men, like William McLeod of the 7th Florida Infantry, who lacked shoes. Unlike McLeod, James Cooper had shoes, but he found the suffering of his less fortunate comrades, who left bloody tracks in the snow, devastating. Cooper had heard stories from the American Revolution of patriots with bloody feet, but this was the first time he saw the sight, which was "eclipsing in suffering all that I had ever imagined." Thomas Head also thought of the American Revolution when he pondered the suffering of his comrades. Stories of Washington's brave men gave him hope and convinced him that, like the patriots of a previous century, the Army of Tennessee might emerge victorious.[39]

The rebels used up the few resources outside Nashville and withdrew a short distance in search of supplies. On December 10 Stewart's and Lee's Corps took up new positions where they had greater access to wood. The men were in desperate need of wood because the weather was "quite severe" and snow covered the ground. The precious fuel was "very scarce," and the shortage caused tremendous suffering. A. D. Rape, a drummer with the 46th Alabama Infantry, later claimed that "the wood was issued to us like rations," but this does not appear to have been a common practice. Robert Magill of the 39th Georgia Infantry was not pleased with the green elm he acquired since it burned poorly and created clouds of acrid smoke that burned his eyes. R. M. Collins acquired old fence rails for his fire but felt disappointment when the dried out wood disappeared in a rapid conflagration and bundle of ash, rather than the slow-burning blaze he wanted. George McWhirter of the 52nd Georgia Infantry reported that the men in the trenches closest to the Federals were forbidden from lighting any fires at all since they might reveal the Confederate positions.[40]

On December 10 Hood ordered his corps commanders to begin constructing "self-supporting detached works." Hood instructed Stewart, on the army's left, to find good locations for these works in the rear of his left

Federal Camp in Nashville, Tennessee, September 10, 1863. Black, green, and red ink drawing on tan paper by G. H. Blakeslee. Library of Congress.

flank; Cheatham, occupying the army's right, to find good places in the rear of his right flank; and Lee, in the center of the army's line, to find strong positions for works on both his right and left flanks. Alabamian Edward McMorries helped construct a redoubt on the army's left. After constructing the position and occupying it for several days, McMorries and his comrades withdrew a quarter of a mile into the valley and handed the redoubt on the extreme left (Redoubt No. 5) over to unidentified "barefooted men."[41]

The fortifications meant little to the men in blue who were spoiling for a fight. Levi Scofield, an engineer officer in the 23rd Corps, believed that his corps could have counterattacked on December 1 and destroyed the Confederate Army of Tennessee before it took a single step north of Franklin. According to Scofield, the Federal soldiers in Nashville chafed under the orders that prevented them from attacking the Confederate army as soon as it dared approach Nashville. John Miller of the 123rd Indiana Infantry spent much of November 1864 on the run from the rebels, but after a short period of recuperation at Nashville, he felt stronger than ever and was eager to punish the Confederacy. In preparation for an attack, reequipped Federal cavalry forces began concentrating at Edgefield, just north of the Cumberland River, on the east end of Nashville. Union scouting parties conducted reconnaissance missions and captured Confederate soldiers who strayed too far in search of provisions. Henry Maley of the 84th Illinois Infantry told his parents that Hood seemed confident that he would capture Nashville, but men from Illinois would soon show him the error of his ways.[42]

The increasingly cold weather tormented the Confederates. Georgian Walter Clark reported that the temperature fell to nine degrees. George McWhirter of the 52nd Georgia Infantry shivered under snow and sleet that was up to eight inches deep. Cavalryman Charles Joy froze in weather that was "very severe, raining and snowing every day." Alabama infantryman Robert Mims described the army as "almost naked." W. Jere Crook of the consolidated 154th and 13th Tennessee Infantry told his cousin that "I am anxious for winter quarters the weather is now cold and covered with snow." Floridian William McLeod noted in his diary that December 11, 1864, "was the coldest day I ever saw." Icy winds constantly blew in his face and his bare feet froze as they walked across ground covered with ice two or three inches thick. Edmund Pettus, commanding a brigade in Stevenson's Division, informed his wife that snow covered the ground and that the wind was so cold that it was possible to throw water into the air and watch it freeze before it hit the ground. W. J. Worsham and C. W. Heiskell of the 19th Tennessee Infantry recalled that "ambition and even life itself, were almost frozen out of us." T. H. Knight of the 55th Alabama Infantry was surprised that so many men remained, but "it is strange how much privation people will endure, for what they think is right."[43]

The rebels suffered from hunger. Risenar Etter reported that he received no more than half rations and savored a small portion of beef feet and head. Robert Mims remembered the army provided little food, no more than "a quarter pound of graham bread" made from non-sifted whole wheat flour, or two ears of corn, and a little beef per day. William Thompson of the 6th Mississippi Infantry reported that men in his regiment lived for days at a time on nothing more than a single ear of corn, still in the husk. Members of the 27th Mississippi Infantry raided their own army's supply wagons, stealing meat and bread in the middle of the night. Alabama artilleryman Robert Maxwell resorted to eating bits of grain the horses did not want. James Harmon of the 35th Alabama Infantry summarized that "the army was in a fix." Since "the troops being in this awful condition caused them to weaken very much."[44]

Many Confederate soldiers lacked shoes, and more became barefoot with each passing day. Edward McMorries claimed that one-third of Confederate soldiers were barefooted. The fortunate men with shoes "were poorly shod," and the rest wrapped their feet in rags as a poor substitute for leather. Texan R. M. Collins explained that many of the men who obtained shoes were unable to fit them on their frozen, swollen, and bleeding feet. Fredrick Moose of the 52nd Georgia Infantry borrowed shoes from a friend when he was on picket duty.[45]

As the farcical siege wore on, Hood redoubled his efforts to obtain supplies and reinforcements for his destitute men. The commanding general begged for troops from Texas or for a diversionary attack into Kentucky from West Virginia. When it became clear that infantrymen were unlikely to arrive, Hood requested that "all available cavalry to be sent to this army as soon as Sherman completed his raid." He sent a stream of telegrams to General Beauregard, commander of the Department of the West, and General Dabney Maury, commander of the Department of Alabama, Mississippi, and East Louisiana, asking them to repair the Memphis and Charleston Railroad to Decatur, Alabama. Hood hoped that he could repair the Tennessee and Alabama Railroad from his position in Tennessee south to Decatur and provide his army with an unbroken rail line to their supply bases.[46] In spite of the commander's hopes, the railroad remained in disarray. Even if the iron rails had extended to the Army of Tennessee, the southern heartland had little to send.

When the Confederate government proved unwilling or unable to provide subsistence, the rebels tried and mostly failed to obtain supplies from nearby civilians. While Middle Tennessee had been a land of plenty before the war, it had little to spare after three years of bloodshed. Many Tennesseans fled in panic from the Confederate soldiers, who took everything of value they encountered. Teamster John Porcher led a team of men with three wagons down the Lebanon Pike in search of leather. Along the road, a woman informed Porcher that the rebels would find no supplies since the area was populated by Union supporters who would not surrender their supplies to the Confederates. Other rebel foragers found that the locals showed little sympathy for suffering rebels and tried to hide everything of value. In desperation, Confederate soldiers took supplies at gunpoint. William Hardy, a staff officer in Cheatham's Corps, believed that many residents of Tennessee hated the Union but kept the rebels at arm's length and resisted their demands for provisions since they "have no confidence in our ability to remain here."[47]

Few reinforcements joined the Army of Tennessee while it waited outside Nashville. Brigade commander Edmund Pettus informed his wife that, while a trickle of volunteers joined the rebel army, they were far fewer than he had expected. He praised the local women as "true patriots" but claimed that many men had taken the Union oath of allegiance to protect their property. Staff officer William Hardy believed that, while Tennesseans "hate the Yankees and Yankee oppression, they dread the service in the Confederate army more." Hood sent Colonel B. J. Hill and the 48th Tennessee Infantry into Bedford, Giles, and Marshall counties with orders to "break up and destroy the home guards" and "to conscribe men liable to military duty." In desperation, General Hood also sent a note through the lines, asking General Thomas to help him fill out his ranks with an exchange of prisoners. Thomas replied that an exchange of prisoners was impossible since he had already sent all Confederate prisoners north, beyond his area of control.[48]

While they may have been the exception to the rule, some of Tennessee's civilians helped the rebel army. E. H. Rennolds received a furlough and returned home to Henry Country, Tennessee, where he found his home largely deserted and "almost destroyed by the war." He took joy in the fact that the few residents he encountered were happy and eager to help the Confederacy. Tennessee cavalryman Robert Battle claimed that the Tennesseans he encountered were "delighted" by the return of the rebel army and that "the Tennesseans are flocking to Hood in large numbers." F. E. Henderson, the fifteen-year-old daughter of a wealthy merchant living between Murfreesboro and Nashville, noted in her diary that her family sheltered Confederate soldiers and reported with seeming pride that, when General Forrest spent the night in their house, "I had the honor of mending his pants." James Lanning enjoyed plenty of "hog & Beef & Cabbage & Turnip & Some bread" eagerly provided by supportive Tennesseans. Staff officer James Dinkins recalled that a farmer living near Franklin presented a horse to a dismounted Confederate officer. The officer eagerly accepted and rode away on the newest cavalry horse in the Army of Tennessee.[49]

As conventional methods failed to produce enough quantities of supplies, the Army of Tennessee sought supplies from less typical sources. Hood pressured Forrest's troopers to conduct raids to capture supplies while simultaneously protecting the army's flanks. The army handed out furloughs to men who lived in the area in hopes that civilians would supply their family members, even as they hid materiel from soldiers they did not know. This process might have worked better if soldiers could have offered payment to sympathetic civilians in exchange for supplies, but the Confederate paymasters had little cash, and most men went unpaid. Men scavenged for wild game, eagerly devouring any animals that fell into their hands. Officers even turned a blind eye to the forbidden practice of trading with the enemy.[50] All of these methods provided materiel, but the trickle of goods was not nearly enough to maintain an army in the field.

The ever-growing Union army taunted the rebels with their strength. On December 11 Federal forces advanced on the Cheatham's Corps, drove the rebels back, stole firewood, and returned to their lines. It was unclear if the Federals wanted the fuel or simply stole it to prove that they could take anything they wanted from the rebels at any moment of their choosing.

Nashville Railroad yard and depot with locomotives, the capitol in distance. Gen. John B. Hood brought his reduced army before the defenses of Nashville, where it was overthrown by Gen. George H. Thomas on December 15–16, in the most complete victory of the war. If the date borne on this photograph is correct, it was taken in the course of the battle. George N. Barnard, photographer. Library of Congress.

W. J. Worsham and C. W. Heiskell believed Nashville's Union garrison rested in forts bristling with cannons and "comfortable quarters," waiting "like bloodhounds held in leash, eager to be turned loose on us." Alabama artilleryman Richard Harris believed the train whistles he heard "every hour day and night" signaled the arrival of more men preparing to drive the Confederates out of Tennessee. James Arnold claimed that he heard trains arrive in Nashville "every ten minutes" that he knew must be "loaded with soldiers." Arnold angrily noted that "Gen. Hood never received a single recruit but the yank were reinforced by thousands." Richard Harris heard "trains every hour day & night." Harris knew that each train brought more men eager to kill him.[51]

Federals probed the Confederate lines as the weather turned colder. Texan Samuel Foster explained that "negroes" engaged rebel pickets, who killed the Federals a short distance from the Confederate line. Dead men froze hard as wood in the winter weather. At about 1:00 p.m. on December 13, while Foster was on picket duty, a Federal skirmish line advanced on the rebel lines. About three hours into the skirmish, a bullet tore into the front of Foster's right leg, about six inches above his knee, and exited the back of his leg without hitting any bones. Foster hobbled back to the rear in search of a doctor. The physician took Foster to a house, where he ripped open the rebel's trousers and examined the wound by sticking a finger of one hand into the front of the wound and the finger of his other hand into the rear of the wound. Foster's account does not reveal if the doctor's fingers met in the middle. The lady of the house nearly fainted as the doctor withdrew his fingers and dressed the wound. An ambulance conveyed Foster to the brigade hospital, where he received a dose of morphine and fell asleep on "the hardest floor imaginable," which he shared with numerous other soldiers. The next morning, Foster took an excruciatingly painful wagon ride to the hospital at Franklin, Tennessee.[52]

By the middle of December, many Confederate soldiers were no longer interested in fighting. John Coleman of the 3rd Texas Cavalry informed his sweetheart back in Texas that he wanted to leave the army, marry her, and rescue her from her abusive father. James Lanning noted in his diary that his wife gave birth to a daughter and that he longed to go home and hold the little girl in his arms. Edmund Pettus informed his wife that he was sick of the war and ready to go home. J. L. Boone of the 13th Mississippi Infantry received orders to go on sentry duty. Boone believed that walking through the snow on bare feet meant certain death, so for the first time in his three-year military career, Boone refused to obey an order. Insubordination had become so common that the officers ignored his refusal, and he suffered no consequences for his misconduct. Tennessean James Cooper wanted to return home but was unable to obtain the furlough to make it legal and was unwilling to violate his soldier's oath to follow orders. He explained, "very tantalizing indeed it was to be in sight of home and not allowed to go there."[53]

Many men gave into temptation and left the army without permission. A trickle of Confederate deserters had wandered into the Federal camps around Nashville since the Confederate evacuation in 1862, and their numbers increased in the winter of 1864. Only 72 rebel deserters, including 1 officer and 3 noncommissioned officers, joined the Union forces in November 1864, but in December, 8 officers, 28 noncommissioned officers, and 281 privates joined the Union army at Nashville. These numbers do not include prisoners, who were listed separately, only men who voluntarily left the Confederate army and turned themselves into the Federals in Nashville. Slaves working for the Confederate army slipped away and joined the Federals.[54] Unclear numbers of other men disappeared into the countryside, never to return to the Confederate army.

The Confederate Army of Tennessee's flesh was in no condition to fight, even if the spirit had been willing. According to staff officer William Hardy, the ground was covered in ice so thick that "we can't move a wheel." Artillery officer Thomas Key noted that his cannons were coated with half an inch of ice and their carriages were frozen to the ground. With a sense of impending doom, Key stated that he did not "want to fight in such weather as this." Robert Bevier of the 5th Missouri Infantry described his comrades as "supremely miserable." Risenar Etter claimed that he would feel pity for an animal left out in the extreme cold that he somehow endured. William Yeatman of the 2nd Tennessee Infantry had long believed that if he could just get to Nashville, "then home and pride would surely incite me to do my best." The freezing weather proved stronger than homesickness and forced him into a sick bed.[55]

By December 13 Hood knew that an attack was imminent and increased his efforts to gather intelligence. The Army of Tennessee was down to only 20,753 men effective and present for duty. If his army was going to have any chance at all at repelling the Federal assault, he needed know exactly when and where his enemy would strike. Captain S. A. Hayden of the 16th Louisiana Infantry was commanding his company on the picket line in the center of

From Fort Negley in Nashville, looking northeast, March 1864. George N. Barnard, photographer. Library of Congress.

the Confederate line, not far from Fort Negley, when a staff officer brought him a five-dollar bill and ordered him to buy a newspaper from the Federals. Many rebels purchased newspapers from Union soldiers, so Hayden assumed that it would be a simple chore. He approached the Union lines and announced his desire to purchase a paper. Several men in blue stepped forward with papers in hand, offering to make the exchange. Before Hayden could complete the transaction, a Federal officer galloped up to Hayden and made him a prisoner. Thomas was now as eager to ensure secrecy as Hood was to acquire information. Hayden pleaded for his release, and the Union soldiers who offered to sell him the paper echoed his cries, but the Union officer was resolute, noting that the rebel captain had acquired an excellent view of Fort Negley, and sent Hayden away as a prisoner of war.[56]

On December 14 the weather turned slightly warmer, thawing the snow and turning the ground into mud. Maxwell Cameron of the 18th Alabama Infantry wrote his sister on December 14 that the wind whipped through the lines and made the men "white with shivers." Risenar Etter peered at the Union lines but could see little through the thick fog. Alabamian J. P. Cannon enjoyed lying in the sun, but the Union artillery kept up a sporadic fire and gave them little rest.[57]

That evening, the Federals wheeled right in preparation for an attack. Federal gunners carefully positioned their cannons with plans to send every shell directly into Confederate ranks. Captain John Lavender, commanding the picket line for the 4th Arkansas Infantry, heard Federal troops shifting to his left and correctly deduced that the Union army would launch a flank attack the next morning. Sergeant Baker agreed, suggesting, "they will give us the Devil when morning comes." Lavender sent an urgent warning to General Daniel Reynolds, in command of the brigade, but Reynolds did not reply or make any obvious efforts to prepare for the impending attack.[58]

7
"PUT AN END TO THEM"
The Battle of Nashville

> From the noise I heard I knew they were coming again. Some of the boys said let's put an end to them this time. Sure enough here they came pell mell as before and as before we waited our opportunity and a volley sent them in wild confusion backward.[1]
>
> —Edgar W. Jones, 18th Alabama Infantry

Preparing for Battle

Everybody knew the fight was coming, but nobody was quite sure when. The Federal high command back east grew more impatient with every passing instant. General Grant, in overall command of all Union forces, had urged Thomas to attack ever since Hood arrived in Middle Tennessee several weeks before and threatened to remove Thomas if he did not advance. Thomas assured Grant that he would attack as soon as he reequipped his cavalry and the weather improved. By December 15 Grant was done with excuses. He wrote orders that removed Thomas from command and named Schofield the new commander in Middle Tennessee. With papers in hand, he boarded a train in Virginia en route to Tennessee, with plans to deliver the orders personally and supervise the offensive.[2]

As Grant rode towards Nashville, the Rock of Chickamauga was ready to roll. Patches of snow and ice remained in the shady spots, but they were rapidly melting under the sun's warming rays, turning frozen earth into mud. Thomas would send roughly fifty-five thousand troops into the fray, leaving another fifteen thousand behind to protect Nashville. General James Steedman's detachment from the District of the Etowah would begin the battle with a feint towards the Confederate right flank to the east, in an effort to pin down the rebels and distract Hood. Once Thomas was convinced that the Confederate forces were focused on their right flank, Thomas would send General Andrew Smith's detachment of infantry from the Army of Tennessee against the Confederate left to the west. Wilson's cavalrymen, finally equipped and eager to face the enemy, would form on the right flank of Smith's infantry and try to whip around the Confederate left flank. Many of Wilson's troopers carried Spencer carbines.[3] These formidable seven-shot repeaters fired their .56 caliber rimfire cartridges ten times faster than the muzzle-loading weapons carried by the Confederate infantry. If Wilson's troopers could get into the Confederate rear, the heavily armed Federals could wreak havoc.

At 4:00 a.m. on December 15, bugles sounded in the Union camps. Everybody knew that the music meant battle. Fog obscured the stars, and men got lost in their own camps as they made final preparations for the fight, filling cartridge boxes and pockets with ammunition, strapping down blankets to their knapsacks, and topping off canteens with water. The Federals were unusually cheerful; laughter rang through the camps, and officers who typically demanded curt salutes exchanged broad smiles and handshakes with their men. A Union chaplain believed that many men concealed fear of death behind boisterous masks.[4]

Battle Begins on December 15

At about 9:00 a.m. the Union army formed lines of battle and began groping through dense gray fog towards the waiting rebels. As the mist gradually dissipated, they became more visible, skirmishers leading the way, with lines of battle not far behind. Men picked their way forward in nearly perfect silence. A shot rang out as the Federals approached, but the battle had not yet begun. A single Union soldier accidently shot himself with his own rifle.[5]

As the men in blue advanced towards the Confederate right, waiting rebels prepared for action. D. W. Sanders, a Confederate staff officer, looked through his field glasses and estimated that twenty-thousand Federals were massed for an assault. Moments later, the battle began as Union artillery opened up and opposing skirmishers began firing on each other, their shots sounding like the popping of champagne corks punctuated by the "deep solemn jubilant roar" of artillery. Robert Battle of the 9th Tennessee Cavalry was in Nolensville, about twenty miles south of Nashville, rounding up recruits for the Confederate army when he heard "cannonading as heavy as I have ever heard" coming from the direction of Nashville. Battle mounted up and rushed towards the sound of the guns. John Johnston of the 14th Tennessee Cavalry was stationed near Murfreesboro. He had just enjoyed a hearty breakfast of boiled beef when he heard sounds of gunfire in the distance towards Nashville. He and his comrades mounted their horses and rode towards Nashville. S. A. Hayden of the 16th Louisiana Infantry, taken prisoner shortly before the battle began, listened to "the first burst of the storm of death" from his prison cell in Nashville. Hayden could not see the battle, but the veteran "saw in imagination, my brave comrades meet the foe." He recognized the sounds of rifle fire and knew that the air must be filled with smoke. He hoped that the sounds of battle might inch closer to him, indicating a victory for the Confederacy and liberation for himself.[6]

On the Confederate right, former slaves from Tennessee advanced towards former masters from Tennessee in a battle for the fate of their shared home state. Confederate defenders watched "a division of negro troops" moving "boldly in the charge." William McMurray, a twenty-one-year-old member of the 20th Tennessee whose father owned seven slaves and a farm near Franklin, Tennessee, held his fire until last possible moment. The rebels "did not give them any quarter, neither asked any." The artillery added their weight to the defense, blasting away once the men in blue stepped within two hundred yards. Unable to break though the rebel lines, the "negro troops" retreated, only to encounter a second line of Federals, who greeted them with fixed bayonets. Stuck between a rock and a sharp place, the survivors regrouped and charged again, only to be repulsed once more. So many dead Federals fell into a small pond at the base of the Confederate position that they turned it black with their corpses.[7]

A slightly different scene played out along the Chattanooga Railroad. Charles Martin of the 1st Georgia Volunteer Infantry watched as "negro troops" approached the north end of the tracks, which cut deep into the earth and wound behind the Confederate lines. Sensing a grand opportunity, the Georgians laid a trap, allowing the Union infantrymen to enter the railroad cut and move towards the rear of the Confederate position. At the very moment when the Federals were about to burst out of the cut, the Confederates appeared and snapped the trap shut, catching the Union infantry in a horrific crossfire. The Georgians "took no prisoners."[8]

Hood sent portions of Manigault's, Deas's, and Brantley's Brigades from the center and the left to stiffen the wavering right flank. Robert Jarman of the 27th Mississippi Infantry moved forward at a run to reinforce the threatened section of line. Federals fired on the men from Mississippi and blew off the hammer of Jarman's trusty old rifle. He was able to replace it with a "Tower Rifle" that he found nearby, probably left behind by a dead or wounded soldier who no longer needed it. The new weapon worked well enough, but Jarman was unhappy that the new rifle was longer and heavier than his previous rifle, although both were in the same caliber, which allowed him to keep using his old ammunition and equipment.[9]

From his perch on Lawrence Hill, within the Federal outer works, General Thomas watched the battle. The men in gray were holding their ground against the attack on their right, but it meant little. Steedman's assault was merely a diversion. Thomas ordered Generals Smith and Wilson to begin their attack against the Confederate left. Steedman's men kept up the pressure against the Confederate right, while Smith's infantry and Wilson's cavalry took the Hardin Pike southwest out of Nashville until they were roughly parallel with the Confederate left flank along the Hillsboro Pike.[10]

William Gale, a staff officer with General Stewart, received word that Federals were advancing in force towards the Hillsboro Pike on the Confederate left. General Stewart immediately traveled to the front to investigate in person. Gale remained in the corps' headquarters, where he sent a flurry of dispatches to Generals Hood, Cheatham, and Lee informing them of the assault.[11]

At about the same time, just as the fighting began, General Chalmers and his staff arrived on the Confederate left flank near Davidson's Landing and found Rucker's Brigade of cavalry trying to hold off a much larger force of Federal cavalry. Chalmers called up a battery of smoothbore artillery, which got into position just as a reinforced column of Federal cavalry renewed their assault. As the men in blue advanced, "grape shot were used with fearful effect," repulsing the charge and sending Federals fleeing from the scene. General Rucker grabbed a flag, waved it over his head, and ordered a charge. Many Confederates horsemen fell in the charge, but the survivors pushed the Federals all the way back to their breastworks. The rebels then withdrew rather than face the fire of Federal gunboats in the Cumberland River.[12]

The 14th Tennessee Cavalry dismounted on the Confederate left and took a position behind fence rails, where they were soon under fire from Federal skirmishers. Bullets tore through gaps in the rails, making the rebels wonder if their barricade offered any protection at all. A bullet whacked Ed Dickerson in the chest knocking him to the ground. Dickerson ripped open his shirt and found a large pink welt where a spent ball had struck him but not penetrated his flesh. The whole line laughed uproariously at Dickerson's near-death experience and a comrade yelled, "you are all right!"[13]

J. T. Tunnell of the 14th Texas Infantry, stationed near the Hardin Pike on the Confederate left, watched Federal cavalry advance on their position until "our thin line in rifle pits gave them a warm reception." When the Union line "got uncomfortably near, we hastily fell back."[14]

Robert Maxwell and the rest of Lumsden's Artillery Battery occupied the still unfinished Redoubt No. 4, west of the Hillsboro Pike on the Confederate left flank. A screen of rebel infantry and cavalrymen initially shielded the gunners from Union assaults, but as the Federals launched increasingly determined attacks, the cavalry and infantry gave way. Maxwell looked on as

Captain Lumsden, commanding the battery, urged the infantry and cavalry troops to stand and fight since the redoubt "must be held to the last limit." An unnamed Confederate colonel refused to stop, explaining that the Federals vastly outnumbered his troops. Union gunners concentrated the fire of twenty-four three inch rifled guns on Lumsden's Battery. Shells impacted the redoubt from batteries stationed six hundred to eight hundred yards in front of the rebel position and from nine hundred to a thousand yards away on the right. With few guns and little time, the Alabamians ignored the Union batteries on their right and responded only to the bombardment to their front. Soon, Union rifle bullets began to slip through the embrasures, adding their sting to the exploding shells that showered rebels with shrapnel.[15]

The Union assault against the Confederate left was making good progress, but General Thomas was not satisfied. He ordered General Schofield and his 23rd Corps, which had been resting in reserve, to take up a position on the right flank of General Smith's infantry, which allowed Wilson's cavalrymen to cut loose from the main Union line and move in a wider looping sweep against the Confederate rear.[16]

Even with reinforcements, Union cavalry and infantrymen could not break through. At about 2:00 p.m., Thomas ordered his men to pull back a little and give the big guns a chance. Federal artillery increased their rate of fire, bombarding the entire Confederate line. Sailors on the gunboats added the weight of waterborne artillery to the fray and "jarred the earth with their volcanic belchings of nitre." So many Union cannons fired from ship and shore that "it resembled one continual roar."[17]

Once Thomas was convinced that the artillery had softened the rebels, he sent the infantry and cavalry forth once more. John Johnston and the rest of the 14th Tennessee Cavalry watched as a mass of Federals began their assault on the Confederate left. Johnston later explained, "we stood and looked on with a feeling of helplessness. The hill and field were black with them. There was in our front an entire division of Federal infantry." At first the rebel cavalrymen were uncertain of how to respond to the masses of men coming to kill them, but then they noticed a Union officer riding on a horse thirty feet in front of the main line, waving his sword and urging his men to attack. Someone near Johnston called out, "shoot at that fellow," as though killing this single leader might deter the raging blue hoard. In response to a flurry of bullets, the Union officer turned and ran away. Unsurprisingly, the retreat of one man did little to deter the massive blue host. The rebels kept up a steady fire until the Federal lines got uncomfortably close and then withdrew three hundred yards away to reform and try to slow the Union troops again.[18]

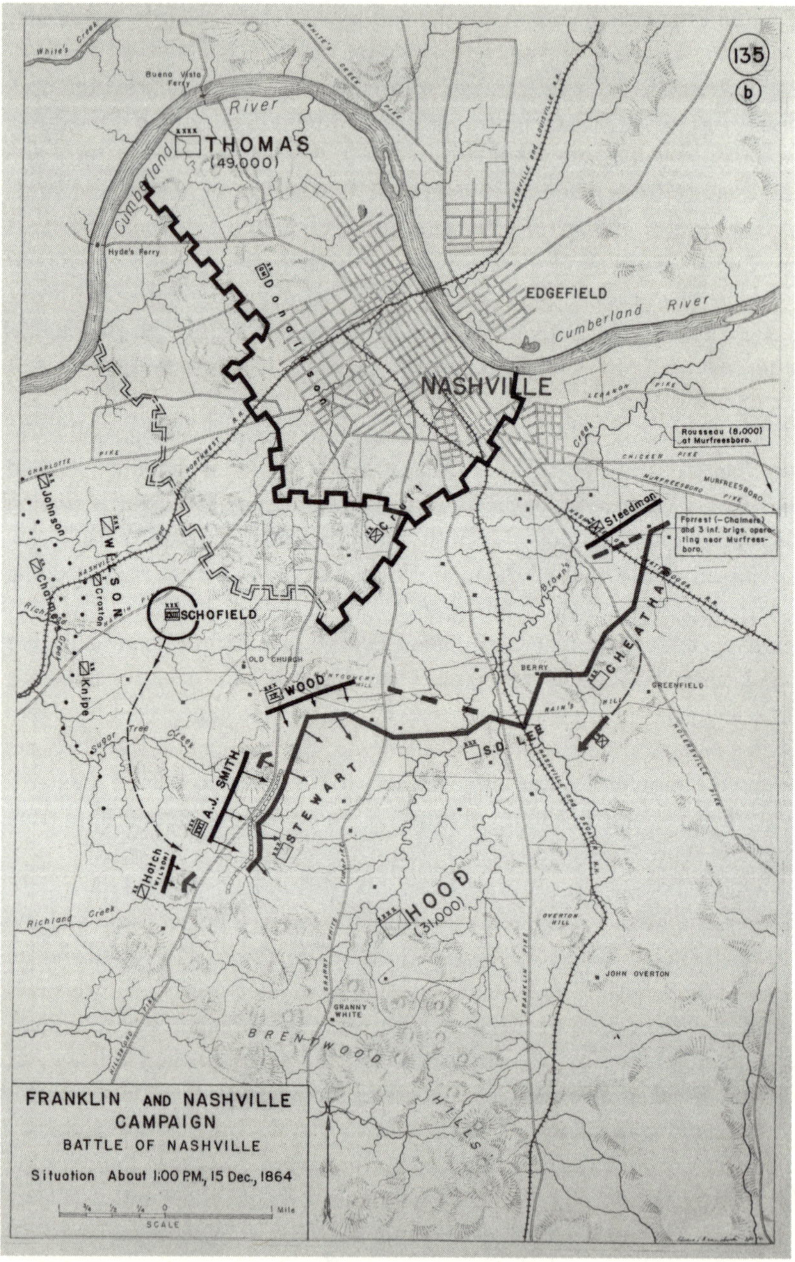

Map. 15. Battle of Nashville, situation around 1:00, December 15, 1864. United States Military Academy. Department of Military Art and Engineering, Vincent J. Esposito, and Matthew Forney Steele. *Civil War Atlas to accompany Steele's American Campaigns* (West Point, N.Y.: 1941). Library of Congress.

Sergeant John W. James and the rest of the 39th Alabama Infantry took a position behind a stone fence on the Confederate right. The field "was black with Yankees forming for assault." Colonel Clifton called, "I want us to whip them or go north." Sergeant James replied, "Colonel, we will go north." Clifton looked at James without replying. Moments later, the Confederate line broke, and James fled for his life.[19]

Jesse Henderson and the rest of the 41st Mississippi Infantry reinforced the collapsing Confederate left. Before the Mississippians could catch their breath from a rapid two-mile march through the mud, a Federal attack pierced Brantley's Brigade nearby. Members of the 41st Mississippi stood their ground until Union soldiers turned their left flank, forcing Henderson and his comrades to retreat to a more secure position on a hill about half a mile in the rear.[20]

Robert Dacus and the rest of the 1st Arkansas Mounted Rifles (dismounted) moved into line on the Confederate left. The Alabamians of Cantey's Brigade were supposed to form on their left. When the Alabamians came to a stone fence, they refused to leave the relative safety of the position. General Reynolds moved his men to the vacant position to the left, but before the men from Arkansas could get into place, the Federals were "subjecting us to one of the most deadly fires any troops ever tried to form under." Federal bullets struck Confederate flesh, dropping men to the ground. Eventually, the men from Arkansas gave up on occupying the newly assigned position and withdrew. Of the fourteen men from Company H of the 1st Arkansas Mounted Rifles (dismounted) who entered the fight a few minutes before, only five remained.[21]

The 11th Missouri Union Infantry surged towards Redoubt No. 4 west of the Hillsboro Pike on the Confederate left flank. The gunners of Lumsden's Alabama Battery greeted them with canister rounds that took an awful toll on the attackers but failed to stop the assault. As the blue tidal wave poured through the embrasures, Captain Lumsden, the battery's commander, ordered the men to "take care of yourselves boys." Some men fell to the earth in surrender, while others, including Robert Maxwell, ran "with all the speed my legs could put on."[22]

Manigault's Brigade of Alabamians and South Carolinians moved towards Hillsboro Pike on the Confederate left to reinforce the collapsing line. The brigade became disorganized in the woods, and when they emerged into the pike, they walked right into a Federal assault. C. Irvine Walker of the 10th South Carolina Infantry recalled that, even though the men were disorganized and outnumbered, "we butt ourselves against them," his phrase reminiscent of rams battering their horns against an enemy. The men from South Carolina tried to stand fast, but they were an under-strength brigade attacking a corps in an open field, and "the necessary consequences followed."[23]

Redoubt No. 5 on the extreme Confederate left flank gave way, allowing the Federals to continue their encirclement of the Confederate left. Rebel reinforcements arrived near the redoubt to counterattack but proved too little and too late to turn the tide. The Federal attack to the west drove a wedge between the Confederate left flank and the Cumberland River, breaking the rebel lines and forcing the southerners to withdraw.[24]

Selden's Alabama Battery on the Confederate left retreated at about 4:00 p.m. as the entire Confederate line gave way. Selden's Battery lost "5 or 6 men—pieces of artillery & a great many horses." As soon as the Union troops reached the abandoned cannons, they turned the guns around, pouring shells into the fleeing Alabamians from their own weapons.[25]

From high ground far to the east, Thomas Key watched the "sublime sight" of the Federal assault. His vision was obscured by clouds of smoke from the guns. When Key realized that the Union forces had penetrated the rebel lines, "my heart ached."[26]

As the Confederate left under Stewart fell apart, Hood sent portions of Cheatham's Corps west, providing a new line of resistance behind the retreating units of Stewart's Corps. Rebels formed a new line of battle. They briefly stopped the Federal advance.[27]

Sergeant James Bishop White of Co. B, 60th Tennessee Infantry Regiment, with a smoothbore musket and British accoutrements. Library of Congress.

James Cooper of the 20th Tennessee Infantry fled across the Franklin Pike. Everywhere he looked, the able-bodied men fled and the wounded tried to keep up. Artillerymen rode their horses, the cut leather harnesses indicating the gunners had abandoned their irreplaceable cannons.[28]

Edward McMorries watched Confederate soldiers run towards the rear. As he explained years later, "it would have been laughable, had it not been so serious," and yet, "we did laugh, notwithstanding Yankee bullets." The barefooted men who ran "in every direction" did so "not only with the agility of well shod men, but of men with springs in their shoes."[29]

A Union cavalryman chased Cole Hargrove as he fled from Redoubt No. 4. The horseman fired every round from his pistols, drew his saber, got in front of Hargrove, and demanded the rebel's surrender. Hargrove decided to bring a stick to a sword fight. He defiantly picked up a branch and glared at his assailant. The Union soldier showed no mercy, taking a mighty swing towards the rebel head. Hargrove parried with his stick, the blade split the branch and hit Hargrove in the head, which "hurt like everything." The blade was mercifully dull and did not cut. At that moment, Confederate bullets grazed the Federal's horse, driving the animal wild and carrying the blue-coated rider off into the distance.[30]

Robert Magill of the 39th Georgia Infantry remained in camp during the fighting on December 15, since he was horribly ill, but at nightfall he was forced to either retreat or get captured. Somehow the sick Georgian kept one step ahead of the Federals and avoided becoming a prisoner that evening.[31]

Major G. W. Garrett and the rest of the 23rd Mississippi Infantry received orders to cover the retreat. Garrett bluntly told his men that they "were to be sacrificed for the good of our army and our country." He told the men, "we must accept the fate."[32]

John Johnston and the rest of the 14th Tennessee Cavalry stumbled across McDonald's Battalion of the 3rd Tennessee Cavalry in the retreat. The two units joined forces and withdrew until they crossed the Charlotte Pike on the extreme westward end of the battlefield, where they encountered General Chalmers, commanding a division of cavalry. Chalmers ordered them to charge a Federal position on a nearby hill. The rebel horsemen obeyed and drove the Union soldiers off the high ground.[33]

S. A. Hayden, taken prisoner shortly before the battle began, spent December 15 listening to the sounds of a battle he could only see in his imagination. The firing stopped, and Hayden knew that the day's fighting was over. He hoped that his comrades had somehow repulsed the Union advance but feared that the rebels were withdrawing to the south.[34]

As darkness fell on December 15, the Confederate army was battered and bloodied but remained intact, making a mostly orderly withdrawal and preparing to fight again. General Chalmers realized that every other Confederate unit had slipped away, leaving his cavalrymen about three miles outside the new Confederate lines. With little other option, he led a fighting withdrawal to the new Confederate line.[35]

Artilleryman Robert Maxwell eventually regrouped with other men from his unit at a "red brick farmhouse" roughly two hundred yards east of the Hillsboro Pike. While officers reported to General Stewart, Maxwell found an infantryman's rifle and was looking for a cartridge box when Captain Lumsden asked Maxwell what he was doing. Maxwell explained that since the battery's cannons were gone, he planned to join the infantry. Lumsden ordered Maxwell to drop the weapon and remain with the rest of the battery. Maxwell reluctantly complied.[36]

John Johnston and the rest of the 14th Tennessee Cavalry occupied high ground near the Charlotte Pike, on the extreme left end of the rebel line. Union cavalrymen assaulted their position, but the outnumbered rebels held their ground for a while because "we put on a bold front." After several failed assaults, Union cavalrymen advanced again, this time pushing the men in gray off the hill. As Johnston withdrew, a bullet struck his horse in the face. Without pausing, Johnston removed his saddle and bridle from the animal, who wandered off to die. After Johnston dragged the saddle a short distance, another man from his unit approached with a captured Federal horse. Johnston replaced the Union McClellan saddle with his and rejoined his mounted comrades, as shells from Union gunboats in the Cumberland River landed nearby. They "burst with a sound that seemed to make the earth quiver." Johnston remembered the sound as "about the most awful noise that I heard during the war."[37]

Staff officer William Gale, with General Stewart in the Confederate center, gathered up the corps' staff and withdrew moments before Union soldiers arrived. While Gale tried to reorganize the corps' staff, Mary Bradford, a Confederate supporter, pleaded with the fleeing infantrymen to stand and fight. They ignored her and continued to retreat. The men "seemed utterly lethargic and without interest in battle."[38]

While most of the Confederate army fled south to fight another day, some rebels fell into Union hands, joining prisoners taken at Franklin. G. W. Garrett and a few survivors of the 23rd Mississippi Infantry obeyed their orders to protect the Confederate retreat and became prisoners only after Garrett was convinced that his men had inflicted far more casualties than they suffered. John Lord of the 72nd Illinois felt sympathy for the rebels who surrendered. He later recalled, "why shouldn't they want to quit?" He pointed out that "not one of them had enough clothes to wad a single-barreled shotgun and many of them had nothing on their feet but any old rags they could find." Consistent with Confederate sources, Lord claimed, "many of them left blood in their tracks." Elijah Edwards, a chaplain with the 7th Minnesota Infantry, greeted southern prisoners as they moved towards captivity in Nashville. Edwards noted that most had neither shoes nor hats. He believed that most of them were happy to become prisoners since they claimed to be unwilling conscripts and joked with their captors about the weather. The fighting was over for the day, but Edwards knew that, just a few miles away, thousands of Confederate soldiers were still out there. The man of God prayed that the rebels might "fold up their tents like the Arabs and as silently steal away."[39]

Battle Ends on December 15

Many rebels believed they were victorious on December 15 and were not ready to abandon Middle Tennessee. General Hood claimed that the Federals "were repulsed at all points of the general line with heavy loss." Captain Irving Buck, a staff officer with General Smith, echoed Hood's comments, arguing that the Army of Tennessee repulsed almost every Federal attack and suffered minimal losses. John Holland, a member of Corput's Georgia Battery, believed that the Confederate forces did quite well on December 15, repulsing repeated Union advances and only pulling back late in the evening when a small portion of their lines suffered a minor break. Tennessee cavalryman Stephen Jordan took apparent pride the day's fighting, which he summarized as a "general engagement killing 900 negroes."[40]

General Thomas disagreed with optimistic Confederate accounts, pointing out the capture of sixteen cannons, 1,200 Rebel soldiers, several hundred small arms, and forty wagons. Even more importantly, Federal troops forced the Confederates back at every point, inflicting losses on the men in gray while suffering surprisingly few casualties of their own. Thomas attributed the victory to the excellent battle plan, which his troops carried out with unprecedented steadiness. As darkness fell, Federal soldiers camped out in line of battle and prepared to renew their attacks in the morning.[41] At first light, the Union artillery would pound Confederate positions. The infantry and cavalry would launch diversionary attacks against the Confederate right before unleashing their primary blow against the rebel left flank.

Before settling down for a well-deserved rest, Thomas informed his superiors of the day's victory. At about 11:00 p.m. he sent President Lincoln and Secretary of War Stanton a telegram informing them of the Federal success and providing them with one less worry that evening. About thirty minutes later, Thomas sent a similar telegram to General Grant. The master of unconditional surrender replied that, while he had been on his way to Nashville, he no longer felt the need. Grant congratulated Thomas but cautioned him that "much is now expected."[42] The threat was very real, if only implicit. Grant was happy to leave Thomas in command if he won battles, but Grant would not hesitate to remove Thomas if he became lethargic.

The Confederate Army of Tennessee withdrew a short distance that evening, taking up new positions roughly six miles south of the state capitol building. Cheatham's Corps, which had successfully defended the army's right flank during the day, moved west. Lee's Corps now formed the army's right flank. Lee's line stretched across the Franklin Pike and curled around Overton Hill, which dominated the Franklin Pike as well as the Nashville and Decatur Railroad. Stewart's Corps occupied the army's center, between the Franklin Pike to the east and the Granny White Pike to the west. After a rapid march, Cheatham's Corps formed the left flank of the army's new line. The east end of their line rested against Stewart's Corps near the Granny White Pike. To the west, Cheatham's line crossed the Granny White Pike and anchored on the thickly wooded Brentwood Hills to the southwest. As a precaution, Hood did send the army's wagons to Franklin, a move that William Gale, a staff officer, believed convinced the men that Hood had already given up and sapped the army's morale, making them less inclined to hold the line. Hood ordered his army to entrench along the new line and prepare to defend themselves.[43] Hood ordered the men to build defensive works, an order easier given than followed.

The new Confederate line was not perfect, but it was better than the line they initially occupied on December 15. The line was shorter, and both flanks rested on steep hills that protected avenues of retreat to the south. On the left flank, the 19th Tennessee Infantry perched on top of Compton's Hill, later renamed Shy's Hill. The ground was frozen, and the men had no tools, but they somehow scratched breastworks out of the icy earth with their fingertips. The 20th Tennessee Infantry tried to dig in nearby, but they had no entrenching tools, so they rolled fallen trees into a crude breastwork that offered limited protection from small arms and virtually no shelter from artillery fire. Edward McMorries and the rest of the 1st Alabama Infantry, positioned near the Confederate center, occupied trenches behind a stone fence facing a cornfield studded with old stalks and rendered into sticky mud by melting snow, which would make any attack both slow and difficult. When the Alabamians looked east, they enjoyed the comforting sight of Bate's Division atop a hill, protecting their flank with help from two cannons. Exhausted members of the 10th South Carolina Infantry decided that trenches were more valuable than sleep and stayed up all night preparing their defenses on the Confederate right flank. T. J. Walker of the 9th Tennessee Infantry believed his regiment enjoyed a strong position on a steep hill on the army's left flank. A battery of Napoleons captured at the Battle of Perryville (October 8, 1862) supported the infantrymen. The 3rd Maryland Artillery constructed breastworks that were large enough to protect their cannons and gunners, but they did not have time to produce the much larger works that could have protected their horses as well. As a result, several artillerymen removed the horses to safety behind a hill. This meant that the artillerymen would have less manpower to work the guns and that it would be difficult for them to quickly move the guns if things went badly. Things were, of course, about to go very badly. While the rebels worked through the night, they listened to the campfire conversations of a mighty host determined to kill them at first light. Occasionally the Federals fired a round into the Confederate positions as a preview of the carnage to come. While the Confederate positions of December 16 were better than the lines occupied the day before, the situation was still grim. The rebels had barely fifteen thousand troops and few cannons to defend a line three miles long from nearly fifty-five thousand well-equipped adversaries and more artillery than they could cram into their line of battle.[44]

Battle Resumes on December 16

The Federals opened the second day of battle with a massive artillery barrage. James Cooper of the 20th Tennessee Infantry awoke to an "infernal racket" caused by Union cannons, which "crowded every hill" and attempted to "blow us out of creation." According to James Harmon of the 35th Alabama Infantry, Federal gunners fired "with all the vengeance possible." W. J. Worsham and C. W. Heiskell believed that the Federals were trying to destroy the Confederates with artillery fire alone. Ed Smith and the rest of Douglas's Texas Battery on the Confederate right tried to find shelter in improvised earthworks as they suffered from an intense bombardment for two hours. Robert Jarman of the 27th Mississippi Infantry, on the army's right, believed that the Federals were "shooting crooked cannons" since "they could throw their shells right in our midst." The "crooked cannon" fire that fell on the Mississippians was highly effective, striking men and horses until a small creek nearby "ran red with blood." Samuel Kelley and the rest of the 30th Alabama Infantry had stayed up all night and were still digging into the Tennessee soil as shells began to fall on their position near the Confederate right flank. In spite of the deadly projectiles, the men kept working to complete their defensive works and eventually, "we were ready." The men of Finley's Florida Brigade on the Confederate left were not ready for the shells that destroyed their meager fortifications, leaving them with no protection from the inevitable onslaught. With no breastworks to protect him, William McLeod in Finley's Florida Brigade clung to the ground. He watched as a shell "shot off our adjutants head." Despite the carnage, McLeod and most of his comrades initially refused to retreat. Selden's Alabama Battery lost three cannons on December 15, but they returned fire with their one remaining field piece. As shells blew holes in the Confederate lines, a handful of Federal skirmishers crawled to within rifle range of the rebels and began peppering the men in gray with rifle bullets. Occasionally a Federal shell fell short or exploded prematurely, killing or wounding Union soldiers.[45]

After the Federal artillery did everything they could to soften up the rebels, General Thomas sent Wood's 4th Corps south down the Franklin Pike to launch a diversionary attack against the Confederate right. Alabama soldier James Harmon said the Federal infantry "emerged all at once in three lines of battle." Thomas Head watched the Federals move forward "with spirit and determination." The Union infantry brushed aside a handful of Confederate skirmishers, who provided little resistance. Ed Smith of Douglas's Texas Battery recalled that the Federals advanced "in splendid order." For a moment the Texans enjoyed the display of Federal parade ground precision before opening fire with their big guns. As the men in blue came within range of the infantry, rebel riflemen greeted their adversaries "warmly." The Confederate artillery waited so long to open fire that Fredrick Moose of the 52nd Georgia Infantry wondered if their guns were all disabled. Eventually the cannon roared to life, proving that the gunners were patient, not impotent. The first wave of Union attackers suffered horribly from the intense Confederate fire. They wavered, reformed, and resumed their assault. Confederate troops held their ground, driving the Federals "back with slaughter," which made the men in gray "cheerful."[46]

As on the day before, the Union attack on the Confederate right failed to break through. It meant little more than it had on the first day of battle. While the Confederate army dug in their heels on the right, Thomas ordered a general assault all along the line. Wood's 4th Corps would once again push south down the Franklin Pike towards Lee's Corps on the Confederate right. Smith's detachment from the Army of Tennessee would attack Stewart's Corps in the center of the Confederate line, between the Granny White and Franklin Pikes. While both Wood's and Smith's men had an important role to play, the Federals focused the bulk of their power against the Confederate left. The infantry of Schofield's 23rd Corps would launch a direct assault on the Confederate left flank, held by Cheatham's Corps. Meanwhile, Wilson's cavalrymen would slip around the Confederates, who would be busy defending themselves from Schofield's troops, and try to hit them in the rear. Thomas hoped that Wilson's men would roll up the Confederate left flank and cut off their line of retreat to the south. William Gale watched the Federals move forward from his position in Stewart's headquarters on high ground, near the center of the Confederate line. In the distance, he saw the Tennessee state capitol building. The Federals advanced in three lines with supporting artillery in a scene Gale found "magnificent."[47]

Union batteries opened a heavy covering fire against the Confederate line as the infantry and cavalry advanced. James Cooper claimed that the fire was so loud that "all the fiends in pandemonium could not have created a more incessant or more devilish noise." He believed that "a mouse could scarcely have lived on that hill," and he considered it "almost a miracle that anyone escaped." Cooper almost died on that hill when "five or six" bits of shrapnel penetrated a nearby log, but the Tennessean escaped harm. Rebel fire peppered the Union lines, and men fell to the ground, but the mass of men kept "pressing as a whole solidly onwards."[48]

Edgar Jones, on the Confederate right, saw Union troops approach through the woods to his front, "making a great noise" as the officers urged their men forward with curses and threats. The Alabamians braced for the assault and discovered that "to our disgust they were negroes." When the rebels realized the race of their attackers, the "discovery removed all doubt as to what the result would be." The Alabamians fired a volley, and men in blue "fell like wheat before a mowing machine," convincing the surviving Federals to flee in confusion. Jones took pride in the fact that "the ground was literally blue and black with dead and wounded niggers." Surviving Union soldiers withdrew, reformed, and marched forward for "another dose of lead pills and blue whistlers." Jones claimed that the "black braves" were driven forward by "white skinned though black hearted officers." The Alabamians repulsed this second assault as easily as the first, but the men in blue reformed for a third charge. The Union soldiers advanced, and the men in gray poured lead into their ranks. After the volley, a rebel leapt over the stone fence and sprinted forward to pick up a precious trophy, a Federal flag. Jones saw that the flag bore the words "Presented by the ladies of Murfreesboro" and became outraged at the idea that "white women had done what seemed to me to be an outrageously low-down thing." Then Jones saw that the full inscription read "Presented by the Colored ladies of Murfreesboro," and "my indignation turned to wrath at the idea of Negro wenches being called ladies." The Federals retreated, leaving their dead and wounded behind.[49]

The rebels in the center also held firm. G. T. Cullens and the 18th Alabama Infantry enjoyed a strong position behind a stone wall. The Federals charged the wall, but the men from Alabama kept up a steady fire that repulsed the men in blue. Richard Harris and the rest of Selden's Alabama Battery poured fire into the Union attack formations. Edward McMorries explained that "though the enemy was much superior in position and number, every charge was promptly met and repulsed in front of our regiment." J. P. Cannon of the 27th Alabama Infantry felt cocky after repelling repeated Union assaults and taunted the Federals to try again. Robert Battle claimed that the fighting was "very heavy, surpassed anything I have heard during the war." Despite the overwhelming force thrown at the Confederate lines, Battle believed the men "behaved with great gallantry" and "repulsed eight or ten charges."[50]

At about 4:00 p.m., the Federals crashed into Cheatham's men posted on the Confederate left. The infantry of Schofield's 23rd Corps hit the rebels head on, while Wilson's cavalrymen moved in a wide looping arc towards the Confederate rear. Initially rebels like Samuel Conley of the 65th Georgia held firm, repulsed the Federal onslaught, and optimistically believed that they might win the battle. The Federals did not give up easily. While the blue-clad infantry kept the Confederates busy, Wilson's cavalry troopers systematically used their superior manpower to keep wrapping around the Confederate flank. E. H. Rennolds and the 5th Tennessee Infantry were able to hold their position, but Rennolds could tell from the sounds of firing that the Union troops "were gradually getting into our rear." As the Union lines wrapped around the rebels, the Federals unleashed a devastating crossfire on their adversaries. Fredrick Moose of the 52nd Georgia Infantry watched several of his friends die. He later recalled, "for the first and only time during the whole war I cried like a child." Moose "felt like I had lost every friend on earth."[51]

Confederate Lines Collapsed on December 16

The Confederate defenders could do little to stop the inevitable. The ragged men in gray were too few and too tired to repel the mighty host bent on killing them. Finley's Brigade of Floridians collapsed under the intense pressure. Artillery officer Thomas Key believed that the Floridians "shamefully broke and fled before the Yankees were within 200 yards of them." Missouri artilleryman Sam Dunlap spoke highly of cannoneers like himself and Forrest's cavalrymen but blamed the defeat on infantrymen guilty of "giving way." John Holland of Corput's Georgia Battery claimed that Bate's Division (including Finley's Florida Brigade) "without any apparent cause broke and fled in the wildest confusion." Many of the troops to the left and right of the breakthrough held their ground until they received orders to

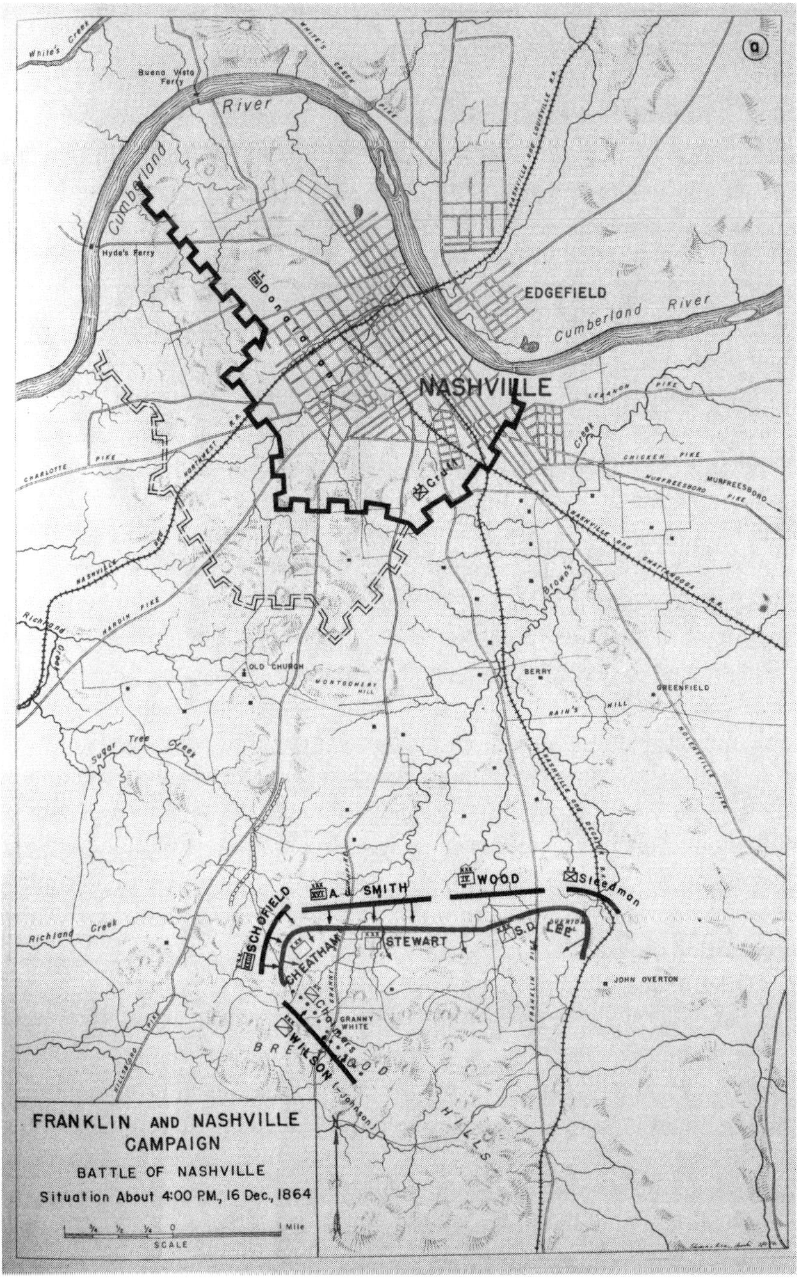

Map 16. Battle of Nashville, situation about 4:00, December 16, 1864. United States Military Academy. Department of Military Art and Engineering, Vincent J. Esposito, and Matthew Forney Steele. *Civil War Atlas to accompany Steele's American Campaigns* (West Point, N.Y.: 1941). Library of Congress.

withdraw, at which point they panicked, convinced that they would only get the order to withdraw if something had gone horribly wrong. J. W. Kellum of the 3rd Florida Regiment in Finley's Brigade defended his unit's honor. He claimed the Floridians were surrounded and forced to surrender. The color bearer used his last moments of freedom to tear his regiment's flag into strings and prevent its capture.[52]

As the line collapsed, Colonel William Shy, commander the 20th Tennessee Infantry, tried to rally his men to hold their position on the high ground. For a moment it looked like it might work, that perhaps a single, beloved, cheering, sword-waving son of Tennessee could push back a blue tidal wave, but just when the implausible might have been possible, the grim realities of battle intervened. A Federal soldier pressed his rifle between Shy's eyes and pulled the trigger, sending a .58-inch, one-ounce chunk of soft lead hurdling through the colonel's skull, killing him instantly and burning his skin around the wound. After the battle, the Compton family renamed the hill Shy's Hill in honor of the departed officer.[53]

Confederate positions began to fall like a line of dominos, beginning with the punctured left flank and sweeping down the line. From his post at Stewart's headquarters near the Confederate center, staff officer William Gale watched the collapse, which quickly sent the entire army fleeing south. When Samuel Conley saw Federals pouring through the lines, he retreated without waiting for orders. R. M. Collins and the 15th Texas Infantry tried to reinforce the failing Confederate left, but Federals set up a two-gun artillery battery on "the pike" (probably the Granny White Pike) and "sent a shell about every two seconds down just to the left." The artillery shells were "screaming like the damned in purgatory, plowing up the earth and splattering us with mud." The fearful scene "put our boys on the run for the first time during the war."[54]

Richard Harris of Selden's Alabama Battery, near the Confederate center, was feeling pretty good about his battery's work repelling Union assaults on their position when he suddenly realized that the left end of the Confederate line was falling back. Major Trueheart, commanding all the artillery for Walthall's Division, ordered the Alabamians to spike their cannon and retreat. The day before, Federal troops turned captured cannons on the rebels, and Trueheart would not let it happen again.[55]

Edward McMorries of the 1st Alabama Infantry, near the Confederate center, looked on in horror as his regiment's left flank suddenly became exposed, subjecting them to a devastating crossfire at the same moment that another detachment of Union troops began to assault their front. For a moment the Alabamians stood their ground, hoping that Hood would send reinforcements, but no help came. The Army of Tennessee was stretched to the breaking point; every available man was already in the line. Realizing that they were alone, the Alabamians fled through their own trenches to the right. As they retreated, they kept up a steady fire, but their bullets did nothing to slow the Federals who ran towards them. When the Union forces were almost on top of the Alabamians, every man suddenly realized that he had a choice. Some men surrendered, but others threw down everything, abandoned the minimal safety of the trench, and made a mad dash across the open ground. Bullets crashed into fleeing bodies, sending men to the ground, but others kept running and eventually made it back to the rear of their army.[56]

R. B. Meadows of the 35th Alabama Infantry saw that the Confederate line was broken. He turned to an officer and yelled, "why don't they send somebody to protect our flank?" The officer looked at the charging Federals in silence. There was nobody left to send. Years later, Meadows realized that "he knew our fate was sealed."[57]

As the Confederate line gave way, General Walthall ordered General Reynolds to hold the high ground near the Franklin Pike, so Cheatham's Corps could retreat down the road. Men from Arkansas held the ground for a few precious minutes but withdrew as soon as the last of Cheatham's men arrived, just moments ahead of the Federals.[58]

For a few moments after the Federals broke through, Thomas Head and other members of the 16th Tennessee Infantry tried to hold their position on the Confederate right, believing that "the war was to be decided in this battle" and hoping for reinforcements to plug the gap. No reinforcements came. The Confederate lines "were taxed to their utmost" and "wholly unable to withstand so powerful an onslaught." The Tennesseans withdrew.[59]

Ed Smith and other gunners on the rapidly disintegrating Confederate right poured double cannister into the attacking columns. Decades later, Smith remembered that "the demons of war were reveling in the high carnival of battle." When the Texans saw that they were outflanked, they realized "the only resource left was flight." Retreating but refusing to panic, the Texans limbered all but two of their guns and withdrew in good order.[60]

Edgar Jones and the 18th Alabama Infantry enjoyed a rest after successfully defending themselves against repeated Union assaults and watched a Confederate battery on high ground to their left pour fire into the Federals across the field. Satisfaction turned to terror when Jones realized that the cannons had turned and were now firing at Confederate, rather than Federal, positions. Minutes later, Union forces attacked the Alabamians in the left flank, and Jones heard the order to retreat.[61]

When the Federals broke through the Confederate lines, Thomas Fowler, a sixteen-year-old Tennessean who joined the army just days before, heard a Confederate officer order the retreat. As Fowler turned to run, "I looked back and saw a whole world of Yankees." The men in blue proved quicker than the young rebel, and Fowler became a prisoner moments later.[62]

Near the Confederate center, Alabamian R. B. Meadows and his comrades began to flee for their lives. They looked over their shoulders as members of the Pointe Coupee Artillery of Louisiana stood their ground. Later, he recalled "those noble men . . . held their fire until the Yankees were within about fifteen or twenty feet of their guns, then turned the four guns loose." The devastating fire "gave us a little show to get away."[63]

Samuel Kelley and the 30th Alabama Infantry had repulsed the only attacks aimed at them, but suddenly "to our surprise and dismay we saw men a half mile to our left running to the rear." Union troops were a few steps behind the rebels. Kelley heard one call out "surrender you d—d rebels." The Alabamians were in no mood to comply and ran away.[64]

According to Arkansas soldier George Rozell, "the army was fleeing." This was not an orderly withdrawal by men in search of a better defensive position. The men were "panic stricken." The Confederate Army of Tennessee was dissolving into chaos.[65]

As George Brewer of the 46th Alabama Infantry retreated, cavalrymen of Chalmers's Division passed through the mass of infantry and taunted the foot soldiers, saying, "boys don't be uneasy, we are going back to show you how to fight Yankees." The Confederate cavalry "could not be distinguished by dress." Forrest's men had recently captured "blue overcoats and the Confederates were clad in them." The Union and Confederate horsemen looked alike, but their similarities were little more than overcoat deep. The Confederate cavalrymen boasted in vain. They were unable to stop the Federal advance.[66]

As Alabama drummer A. D. Rape fled, he heard a voice from a Federal just a few yards away call out, "stop you little devil with that drum!" Rape jumped behind a tree. Moments later, he looked up to see the Union solider going in another direction. Hiding proved a momentary solution to a very large problem.[67]

Confederate staff officer James Ratchford tried to grab retreating soldiers and force them to fight. When he grabbed one soldier's gun, the man happily abandoned it to keep up the retreat. When he then grabbed another man by the coat, the soldier slithered out of it, preferring frostbite to delay. Ratchford was shocked that the men even threw away their rations to flee faster.[68]

C. Irvine Walker of the 10th South Carolina Infantry, on the Confederate right, spent most of December 16 absorbing artillery shells from the Federal gunners and refusing to give ground. At about 5:00 p.m., they noticed that the entire rebel army was collapsing all around them. Unwilling to face the Federal army alone, the South Carolinians retreated. Spared from the worst of the day's fighting, Walker and his comrades did not realize the true scope of the disaster until they made their way to the Franklin Pike, where the road was littered with "wagons, guns, officers, men, ambulances, everything running in the wildest confusion to the rear." At that moment, "the true magnitude of the disaster strikes us."[69]

The Retreat Became a Rout

Many years after the battle, Edward McMorries defended the Confederate soldiers who fought at Nashville. He took pride in the fact that "we killed and wounded many times more Federals at Nashville than they did of Confederates." McMorries argued that the men who eventually fled from the field never panicked. They were simply veteran soldiers who wisely withdrew to fight again another day when they faced an overwhelming onslaught.[70]

McMorries's claim of an orderly withdrawal stands in stark contrast to the testimony of many other men who participated in the retreat. Robert Magill reported that, by 5:00 p.m., the entire army was in full retreat. The Georgian had "been in good many retreats, but this was the wildest I have ever seen." There was "no semblance of order" as the men ran away "in wild confusion." At least one woman ran into Confederate positions as soldiers fled. B. L. Ridley, a soldier from Tennessee, reported that "the heroine" Mary Bradford "rushed out in the thickest of the storm cloud and begged the soldiers to stop and fight." She pleaded in vain, as soldiers continued their retreat.[71]

Edwin Rennolds paused for a moment as he mounted the breastworks and reported that "as far as I could see our troops were in retreat." The army's retreat became a "stampede" unlike anything Rennolds had ever seen before. The rebels were now in "a race for liberty between the enclosing wings of the Federals." The ground was a morass of "sticky mud" and "crabgrass" that "adhered to our shoes and soon loaded us with weights," which slowed the fleeing rebels in their race with the men determined to kill them. A few Confederates, feeling particularly bold, occasionally paused to fire a round at their pursuers before resuming their retreat, but the feeble fire did nothing to slow the Federal advance.[72]

James Cooper and the rest of the 20th Tennessee Infantry engaged in one of the "liveliest chases of the war." The Tennesseans ran across a ploughed field of knee-deep mud, and right behind them the Union troops were "shooting as fast as the Devil would let them, and he seemed to have very little objection to their shooting as fast as possible." The Federals "turned our own cannon on us and were using it better than we could ever do."[73]

Alabamian R. B. Meadows began the retreat with his brother and Lieutenant Kellogg. As they ran, Kellogg "was shot through and fell." The officer "looked at me as pitiful as a child ever looked at its mother." Meadows's brother stopped to help, but Meadows refused, leaving his brother and the wounded officer behind.[74]

Alabama infantryman J. P. Cannon ran for his life. The sticky mud slowed his progress as bullets and shells struck within inches. One projectile scraped his thigh, but Cannon kept running until he found a Confederate artillery battery with their cannon stuck in the mud. The gunners gave up on rescuing the artillery and cut their horses loose so they could escape on horseback. Cannon asked the battery commander if he could take one of the horses, and the officer told him he was welcome to anything he wanted. As the officer galloped away, Cannon picked out a fine black horse and began to cut him loose from the artillery harness, when a large Irishman told Cannon that he would take the horse. Cannon argued but conceded when he figured that the Irishman was perfectly willing and able to kill Cannon. Horseless, Cannon fled on foot.[75]

T. J. Walker of the 9th Tennessee Infantry was on the right end of the Confederate line. He looked on in horror as Federals broke through the Confederate lines to the right and left of his regiment's position. With no time to remove the cannon they were supposed to protect, the Tennesseans spiked the guns and began to race to the rear. As the Tennesseans ran, General Cheatham raced by, telling the men, "Take care of yourselves, boys, the best you can. I am going to make it through the ridge or die in the attempt." As their general fled into the distance, Walker concluded that "the army was lost beyond all help."[76]

Lieutenant Colonel Finley of the Florida brigade tried to reform the men along a gap in one of the ridges south of town. Finley ordered the men to stop. In desperation, he even threatened them with his revolver, but the Federal army seemed far more dangerous than a single Floridian with a pistol, so almost every man kept retreating. After a few minutes, Finley and the handful of men who had stopped realized that that their position was hopeless and joined the fleeing throng.[77]

As R. M. Collins and other members of the 15th Texas Cavalry (dismounted) retreated, a wounded mule came crashing through the Texans. They grabbed the animal, crowded onto his back, and rode the mule, which ran "like a Texas jack rabbit getting out of the way of the hounds." The mule and its riders careened between horses and wagons and barreled right through masses of men on foot, "swiping them down platoons at a time." Several times, Collins and his comrades heard infantrymen call out for someone to "shoot that blasted feller on the mule." The Texans were not concerned by the threat since "we much preferred being shot by our own men to going to a northern prison." Collins and his friends had all been prisoners of war earlier in the conflict, and they were not going back.[78]

Florida infantryman Henry Reddick described it as "a prefect stampede." There was no order to the chaos, in which some men were "surrendering, some falling dead, others trying to get up the hill to make their escape." The officers were "dashing across the hills trying to rally the men with pistols and swords drawn over their retreating men." Officers "would get thirty or forty men rallied in a squad and dash off to rally another squad," but "the first rallied would break ranks and run for life."[79]

As Arkansas soldier James Tanner retreated, he heard a young rebel call out, "I surrender," from behind a tree. Tanner assured the youngster that they could both escape with ease. The young man refused to believe that he could get out alive. Tanner eventually coaxed the young soldier to run with him to a nearby tree, and then to another, and then another after that. Eventually the young man realized that he was safe. The young soldier thanked Tanner for helping him but refused to reveal his name since he was ashamed of how he had acted and feared what his family might think. Years later, Tanner wrote to *Confederate Veteran* magazine in hopes that the soldier might contact him.[80]

Alabama soldier Edgar Jones approached a stone fence and pondered how he could best clear the obstacle without slowing down. At that moment, a cannon ball raced past him and knocked a fifteen-foot-wide hole in the fence. Never one to question providence, Jones raced through the gap, ignoring the Federals who ordered him to halt. Jones passed by an exhausted comrade, who exclaimed, "I am going to stop." Without a moment's hesitation, Jones replied, "I am not," and kept running as bullets crashed all around him.[81]

Fleeing Confederate soldiers gathered on the high ground near the Lee family's farm. The men had no interest in fighting, only in escaping. They had abandoned their weapons and equipment, and some had even lost their hats in the wild dash for safety. The Federals had cut the Granny White and Franklin Pikes, eliminating the only obvious paths away from Nashville and filling the milling rebels with fear that they would soon become prisoners. Unlike most of the men, Henry Hogan of the 23rd Tennessee Infantry was from Nashville and had spent his childhood chasing wild game through the scruffy woods south of the city. Hogan approached Colonel Tillman, the highest-ranking officer he could see, and asked the colonel, "how are you going to get us out of this trap?" Tillman confessed, "I don't know." This was the private's moment to shine. With a broad smile, Hogan said, "I will take you out. Follow me; I will get you to Brentwood." Fifty-eight years later, the old rebel smiled when he told a reporter, "I was their Moses."[82]

Alabama soldier James Arnold saw General Lee sitting on his horse, his ankle broken by a Minnie ball, begging the fleeing men to stand their ground. Nearby, ladies echoed Lee's urgent pleas, imploring the men to stop and fight. General Pettus eventually put together an infantry rear guard, who stood their ground for a few minutes. Gunners from Douglas's Texas Battery unlimbered their guns and joined the infantry, firing a few shells that slowed the Federal advance. Drummer A. D. Rape later recalled that, as he was about to pass General Lee, Lee ordered Rape "to beat the long roll." Rape complied and for a moment the Federals slowed their advance. Years later, Rape speculated that the Union forces paused because they thought that the sound of the drum meant that reinforcements were gathering for a counterattack.[83]

James Dinkins, a staff officer to General Chalmers, listened when Hood ordered Chalmers to form a line across the Franklin Pike and force every retreating soldier to return to the fight. Chalmers convinced about five hundred men to make a stand, but then a wave of thoroughly demoralized soldiers tried to push through the line. For a moment all was confusion, but then General Hood, "greatly distressed," countermanded his previous order and "let them go." The line of resistance faded away, and the retreat continued. Dinkins observed that any soldier could take joy in the attack, but "it takes a man to smile on a retreat."[84]

The Battle of Nashville found William Yeatman of the 2nd Tennessee Infantry so sick that he was unable to participate in the fighting. When the Confederate lines broke, he tried to scurry south, but after he stumbled for about two miles, Federal cavalry captured him. When he saw the men in blue appear, he felt "mortification" at the sudden realization that "my soldier life had ended."[85]

W. J. Worsham and C. W. Heiskell fled east through a cornfield. The "bare-footed, half frozen Confederates, and well-shod, stall fed Federals" raced through slippery mud and stunted corn stalks. Worsham and Heiskell asked the readers of their memoir, "Did you ever have in your sleep a night mare? when something was after you and you could not run fast enough? Well ours was a veritable, wide awake, night mare."[86]

James Cooper joined the retreat down the Franklin Pike, where "all was confusion and dismay." Walking in darkness as part of the "completely demoralized" mob that had once been the proud Army of Tennessee, Cooper concluded that "the Confederacy was indeed gone up, that we were a ruined people."[87]

In a desperate bid to prevent the capture of what remained of his army, General Hood begged General Chalmers, "for God's sake, drive the Yankee cavalry from our left and rear or all is lost." Chalmers's Division of horsemen mounted up and rode forward in a bid to push back the blue tide. Captain W. A. Polk of the 7th Tennessee Cavalry heard the call and led all the men he could find into action. The battle became a brawl as Federal and Confederate troopers got mixed up in a confused knot of men and horses that destroyed all sense of organization but somehow bought time for the fleeing Confederates. Perhaps nobody summarized the Battle of Nashville better than A. J. Meadows of the 4th Tennessee Infantry, who stated, "we got licked."[88]

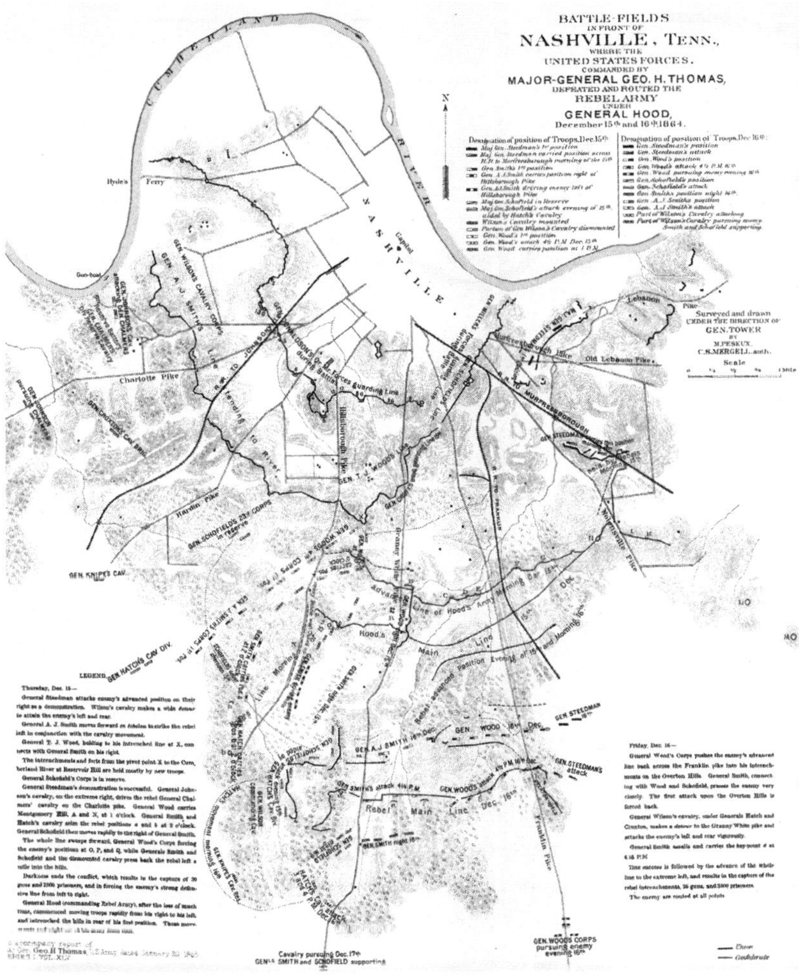

Map 17. Battle of Nashville, December 15–16, 1864. United States, War Department. *Atlas to Accompany the Official Records of the Union and Confederate Armies*. Washington, D.C.: Government Printing Office, 1891 (2 vols.). Library of Congress.

Confederate Losses in Men and Materiel at Nashville

The Army of Tennessee retreated from Nashville, but many of the men remained. The Confederates suffered 5,962 casualties during the battle. Roughly 1,500 of those men were killed or wounded. The Federal army captured the remaining 4,462. Newspapers reported that the area around Nashville was filled with rebels who were tired of suffering and choose to desertion over retreat or capture. As previously noted, official reports from the Union army show that 8 officers, 28 noncommissioned officers, and 281 privates joined the Union army at Nashville in December 1864. From January 1–20, 1865 (for some unclear reason, the report only covers the first twenty days of January), even more rebels deserted to the Federals at Nashville, with 20 officers, 61 non-commissioned officers, and 660 privates joining the Federals.[89] As before, these numbers include only men who voluntarily left the Confederate army and turned themselves in to the Federals in Nashville. Prisoners were listed separately.

John Crittenden of the 34th Alabama Infantry had written a steady stream of letters back to his wife and parents in Tallapoosa, Alabama, but on November 13, they abruptly stopped. On December 13, 1865, over a year after the last surviving letter from John Crittenden, his father finally received word regarding his son's fate. The message from the army hospital at Nashville explained that "there can be no doubt of the fact that your son was killed during the battle and was interred on the battle ground." While the letter acknowledged the tragedy and offered sympathy, it also pointed out that "many a gallant young man has met a similar fate." John Crittenden's wife, who he called "dear Bettie," never remarried and lived the rest of her life with her extended family, including her son John, the child who was born shortly after his father disappeared.[90]

The Army of Tennessee suffered irreparable damage to its artillery at the Battle of Nashville. The rebels crossed over the Tennessee River with 124 pieces of artillery. When the Confederates took stock of their remaining cannons several days after the Battle of Nashville, they had only 59 guns. The Federal army captured 55 cannons at the Battle of Nashville. Others may have included the 4 guns the Union forces captured at Murfreesboro, Pulaski, and Columbia, Tennessee, between October 1, 1864, and January 20, 1865. Most of the artillery that fell into Union hands was quite good. Of the 55 cannons the Federals captured, 49 were excellent, light, 12-pounder guns, prized by both the Union and Confederate armies for their versatility and close-range firepower; 6 were rifled cannons, renowned for their long range; and only 9 were obsolete 6-pounder smoothbores and 12-pounder howitzers.[91] The Army of Tennessee never recovered from the loss of this precious artillery.

Table 1.
Artillery Equipment Captured by the Union Department of the Cumberland, October 1, 1864–January 20, 1865

Artillery Type	No.
Light 12-pounder guns, rebel model	37
Light 12-pounder guns, US model	7
Light 12-pounder howitzers, US model	7
3-inch rifles, rebel model	3
10-pounder Parrotts, caliber 2.9-inch, US model	1
Field carriages and limbers complete	50
Field carriages and limbers without wheels	2
Field carriages, no limbers	2
Field caissons and limbers	16
Field caissons, no limbers[92]	4

Source: "Report of Ordnance Material Captured," *OR*, ser. 1, vol. 45, pt. 1, p. 49.

Table 2.
Infantry Equipment Captured by the Union Department of the Cumberland, October 1, 1864–January 20, 1865

Munition Type	No.
Infantry small-arms of different models, no bayonets	3,079
Bayonets of different models	262
Cartridge-boxes, infantry	1,208
Cartridge-box plates	238
Cartridge-box belts	234
Cartridge-box belt-plates	141
Waist belts	178
Waist-belt plates	181
Bayonet scabbards	166
Cap pouches	364
Gun slings	231

Source: "Report of Ordnance Material Captured," *OR*, ser. 1, vol. 45, pt. 1, p. 49.

The Confederate Army of Tennessee's infantry left behind vital materiel at Nashville but did not suffer materiel losses nearly as badly as the artillery. Union reports provide unique insights into the items carried by Confederate soldiers in Army of Tennessee. The Federals captured 3,079 infantry small arms without bayonets but only 262 bayonets and 231 gun slings, indicating that the vast majority of Confederate infantrymen at Nashville used neither bayonets nor slings. The Union army also captured 1,208 infantry cartridge boxes, but only 238 cartridge box plates, which indicates that many Confederate infantrymen either used southern-manufactured cartridge boxes, which omitted the largely ornamental cartridge box plates to reduce the cost of construction, or had removed the plates from captured Union boxes.[92]

Numerous Confederate soldiers reported that men threw down their weapons as they retreated, but studies of the available numbers suggest that those stories were exaggerated. Roughly 19,053 enlisted infantrymen were present for the Battle of Nashville. The 3,079 captured infantry weapons represented roughly 16 percent of the weapons used by the 19,053 enlisted infantrymen. The Federals recovered many of these weapons from the 5,962 Confederates who were killed, wounded, or captured during the battle.[93] Further complicating the numbers, many of the casualties were officers, artillerymen, or cavalry troopers, who would not have carried infantry weapons. Undoubtedly, some infantrymen did throw down their weapons as they fled south, but the numbers indicate that they were a very small minority. The exaggerated stories of discarded Confederate small arms suggest that the men believed the army to be disintegrating, even more than it was.

8

"RAGAMUFFINS FLEEING IN DISGRACE"

The Retreat from Nashville

> Christmas day dawned bright and beautiful but upon what a scene did that morning's sun arise. A poor half starved, half clad band of ragamuffins fleeing in disgrace from their last chance for freedom and independence. Poor devils, they little knew what would be the results of that retreat.[1]
>
> —James Cooper, 20th Tennessee Infantry

The Battlefield Near Nashville

The Battle of Nashville ended in the darkness of December 16, but for many men the suffering was just beginning. The thunderous cannonading ceased, leaving only the cheering of victorious Union soldiers and the cries of wounded men. Henry Maley of the 84th Illinois Infantry was wounded at Nashville and described the hospitals as unpleasant places, where "once in a while they take a mans leg or pull a lot of boans out of a mans arm."[2]

Evening of December 16, Near Brentwood

Survivors from the Army of Tennessee bivouacked in relative safety south of town, near Brentwood, on December 16. As men trudged into the impromptu camp along the road, they heard men calling out directions, sending men towards their units as the army sought to regain some measure of organization. J. P. Cannon of the 27th Alabama Infantry was disappointed that only 17 men of his regiment made it to safety. In his company, which numbered 110 men in 1861, he was one of only 3 survivors. Edgar Jones arrived near Brentwood in the "inky black" of night as rain fell. Confused and disoriented, he "knew nothing that was going on except in my immediate presence." Jones recalled that, during that night, "my surroundings indicated anything other than cheerfulness and optimism." According to Charles Joy, "they looked like an army of tramps."[3]

Near Brentwood, R. M. Collins paused to dismount from the wounded mule that took him several miles south of the battlefield. As he walked alongside the animal, he saw Generals Hood, Forrest, Ross, and others try to rally the men. Soldiers walked past the officers "just as if they had been common mortals." One of Forrest's staff officers, "with a bright, shining, ivory-handled pistol in hand," ordered Collins to explain "what in mischief are you doing here?" Collins pointed to the flood of Confederate soldiers all around him who were moving south and explained that he was just like them, "whipped and tempestuously demoralized, and trying to get away." The staff officer conceded and stood aside. In his memoir, Collins admitted that this story might seem odd, but "the reader must bear in in mind that we are not telling all we know." Whatever the exact details might have been, Collins was certainly headed south, and he had plenty of company.[4]

Tennessee cavalryman P. T. Martin and several of his comrades got cut off from the rest of the army somewhere south of Nashville. The troopers needed rest but had to keep moving, so they took turns sleeping in the saddle. One man would sleep, slumping in the saddle, while a comrade led his horse and kept a look out for Federals. After a while, they would trade roles. This unique method allowed men to keep moving south without having to pause for rest.[5]

General Stephen D. Lee took command of the men gathering near Brentwood and attempted to organize a rear guard. Edgar Jones, a corporal in the 18th Alabama Infantry, led one of the army's few intact squads. Jones and his comrades tried to cover the retreat by holding the high ground overlooking the Little Harpeth River. The Alabamians kept up a steady fire on Federals who seemed indifferent to the bullets and advanced until the rebels were forced to flee. Jones watched as a mounted Federal cavalryman tried to capture Alex Dees, a "long legged and gangling" man "not considered a first-class soldier." Dees refused to surrender and somehow outran the Union soldier, even though Dees was on foot and the Federal was on horseback. The man in blue swung his saber, but somehow Dees dodged every blow. When Dees came to the bank of the Little Harpeth River, he dove in headfirst and quickly swam away, carrying his gun and equipment with him. While Dees escaped, another Union cavalryman ordered Lieutenant Hardwick to surrender. Hardwick pulled his pistol, shot the horseman, and ran for the river one step ahead of a crowd of Federal cavalrymen bent on revenge. Hardwick swam across the river at about the same time and place as Dees.[6]

Many Confederates were understandably unhappy. Thomas D. Duncan, a cavalryman from Mississippi, claimed, "no one who participated in it can forget the suffering and hopeless anguish of that weary, running march." Walter Clark of the 1st Georgia Infantry claimed, "the morale of the army was shattered if not destroyed." Clark overheard a soldier from Tennessee say, "Ain't we in a — of a fix, one-eyed president, a one-legged general and a one-horse Confederacy." Robert Battle recalled years later that he "never in my life felt so awful" as on that retreat. Forty-four years after the fateful Battle of Nashville, R. W. Banks of the 37th Mississippi Infantry recalled, "it was at the time when Thomas was aggressively endangering Hood's escape after the calamitous disasters, December 15 and 16, 1864, which shattered the Army of Tennessee and practically destroyed its organization; crushed the ambitions of its ill-starred leader; dissipated every dream of success for the cause it upheld; drove hope from the hearts of its private soldiers, and filled the souls of its officers with despair."[7]

A few men remained dedicated to the cause. A member of the 66th Georgia Infantry, who was simply referred to as Clinton in the sources, proclaimed that he wanted "to fight to the last." Risenar Etter was pleased that most of his comrades made it to the relative safety of the Brentwood rally point, even though the Union army shattered their division, cut off their line of retreat, and forced every man to cut his own path through the Federal lines. Robert Maxwell recalled that his commanding officer, Captain Lumsden, told Maxwell, "you have lost all hope in our cause," and confessed, "few of us have any hope left." Lumsden argued that the army must remain together "to get the best terms possible." For Lumsden, it was no longer a matter of victory, only of softening the inevitable blow of defeat. Years later, Maxwell still protested, adamant that he believed in victory even after the Battle of Nashville.[8]

When difficult roads and insufficient horses made it impossible for Fenner's Louisiana Battery to keep all their cannons moving south, they dismantled three guns and buried them rather than allow them to fall into Federal hands. Battery captain Charles Dreux bragged that "these were the only guns we ever lost."[9]

The Confederate Army of Tennessee Begins to Scatter

Many rebels left the army as it headed south. Texas soldier R. M. Collins recalled that the men were walking like they "were bound for home," and many were. Company C of the 27th Alabama Infantry consisted of only three men. All three agreed to abandon the army and travel to their homes in Lauderdale County, Alabama. Stephen Jordan of the 19th Tennessee Cavalry decided that for him the war was over and slipped away from his regiment, never to return. Tennessee cavalryman Robert Battle left the army after the Battle of Nashville and visited family in southern Tennessee. Everyone was "anxious to hear the news of the battle." The rebel horseman was conflicted. He wanted to be honest, but he knew that honesty would upset his family. Torn between a desire to say something encouraging and a conflicting need to be honest, Battle said as little as possible since he was "indisposed to give it by detail hoping to hear something encouraging." The rebel horseman eventually rejoined his regiment for a brief time in the final days of the war, but the remainder of his diary indicates that he never again heard "something encouraging" about the Confederacy. Agatha Woodson, a woman living near Tazewell, Tennessee, in the eastern portion of the state, roughly two hundred miles from Nashville, encountered an unnamed Confederate soldier of Bate's Division several days after the battle. The exhausted man sat down near Woodson and admitted that he had thrown away his gun and accouterments but claimed that "I am whipped, badly whipped and somewhat demoralized but no man can say I am scattered."[10]

December 17, Franklin

The army traveled through the battlefield at Franklin on December 17. Tennessee cavalryman John Johnston recalled that "the Yankees must have been very late and slow in starting out that morning, for we were not disturbed until late in the morning." Sometime before noon, the men in blue appeared, advancing through drizzling rain mixed with snow, and began pushing the rebels south. The hills echoed with the sounds of sporadic rifle fire.[11]

Somewhere near Franklin, Captain W. A. Polk and a few dozen members of the 7th Tennessee Cavalry made a stand. Confident that their numbers would win they day, a mass of Union cavalry didn't bother to form a line of battle. They simply drew sabers and attacked while still in a road column. The men from Tennessee fired on their adversaries, but they were outmatched and outgunned. Rebel artillerymen sent shells flying over their heads into the Union ranks. After firing their last bullets, the Confederate troopers retreated. As Polk fled, he saw Colonel William F. Taylor of the 7th Tennessee refuse to give ground. Taylor covered the retreat, fighting on alone with Confederate artillery shells flying all around him, until he died in action. Forty-one years after the guns fell silent, Polk still remembered how one brave man died to save his friends somewhere near Franklin.[12]

As the Confederate cavalrymen retreated, infantrymen of Pettus's Alabama Brigade and Cumming's Brigade of Georgians formed a rear guard, with one brigade on either side of the pike. Artillery formed in the center on the muddy road. Cavalrymen formed on their flanks. A large force

Unidentified Confederate soldier with an Enfield rifle. Library of Congress.

of Union cavalry assaulted the rebel rear guard, charging "with a bravery not surpassed in the war." Soon the blue-clad horsemen were tangled in hand-to-hand combat with the men in gray. The Confederate cavalry fled, exposing the infantry's flanks. For a moment it looked like the line might collapse, but Captain Brewer of the 46th Alabama Infantry pleaded with the soldiers of his regiment to stand their ground, and the men responded with "a steady determination to fight to the death." The men who ran away the day before would run no more. Their courage was infectious and soon the entire rear guard stood firm and repulsed the Federals. Georgia infantryman George McWhirter claimed that the rear guard was undaunted and fought bravely to the last. Many years later, George Brewer still felt pride in the performance of his regiment that day. The men had been constantly on the move with little sleep and less food for days, but on muddy ground drenched in freezing rain, with the memories of a demoralizing defeat fresh in their minds, "the regiment and its commanders had covered themselves in glory."[13]

After temporarily repelling the Union advance, the rear guard formed into two bodies. While one put up resistance, the second group formed a bit farther south on the road. When the first group could resist no longer, they broke and retreated, forming a new line south of the other group. This leapfrogging arrangement kept the Federals at a respectful distance as the army worked its way south.[14]

Infantryman Edgar Jones did not enjoy fighting a second battle near Franklin. The area was "a gruesome sight," where "I saw more than one hand or foot exposed," sticking out of shallow graves, and "I distinctly felt my foot rest on a dead body as it sunk into the mud." Jones was grateful for the handful of artillerymen who remained with the rear guard, operating two cannons that the infantryman confessed "did as much in keeping back the enemy, or more than the infantry."[15]

Captain F. G. Terry and the 8th Kentucky Cavalry had been away from the main body of the army during the Battle of Nashville. Near Franklin, the Kentuckians rejoined the Army of Tennessee. The fresh troopers threw themselves into action, helping the exhausted rear guard keep the men in blue at bay.[16] Confederate reinforcements were a very rare sight on that retreat.

The rebels repelled Federal advances, but the men were miserable. Sam Dunlap began the retreat wearing an old pair of boots, but they quickly fell apart, and his bare feet soon left a visible trail in the snow. Sharp rocks lacerated the bare feet of Fredrick Moose, who "left blood in every track of my bare feet." Thomas Key noted in his diary that the men had received no food for two days; they shivered in the freezing rain and wanted nothing more than for "this cruel war" to end. He believed that "everybody is despondent." R. R. Hancock described the weather as so cold, the roads so muddy, and the men so hungry that "despondency was now stamped upon the somber features of the hardiest." Samuel King Vann became ill. He thought about finding a house where he might rest, but he knew that if he stopped, he risked capture, so he decided to keep moving even if he had to crawl back to his home in Alabama. Robert Dacus claimed that what had once been an army was nothing more than a rambling "herd of wild Texas cattle" that only followed Hood "because that was their only chance to obtain subsistence." Some men sought food from other sources. John Sparkman of the 48th Tennessee believed that generous civilians inadvertently helped the Federals. He claimed that once soldiers "found out that the citizens would freely give them the best they had; they strolled over the country from place to place and were not with their command at all."[17]

As the army left Franklin, it presented troops in the local hospitals with a choice. They could flee south or become prisoners to the advancing Federals. Newton Davis of the 24th Alabama Infantry had been badly wounded at the Battle of Franklin and was still recuperating in a private home as the Army of Tennessee retreated south. Unable to march, Davis became one of many Confederate prisoners who fell into Federal hands when the men in blue occupied Franklin. Captain Samuel Brown of the 33rd Mississippi Infantry had received a terrible wound to his right arm at the Battle of

Franklin. The Confederate retreat found him nursing his wounds in a hospital in town. Although still in great pain, he refused to become a prisoner and joined the army on its retreat south.[18]

December 18–19, Columbia and Spring Hill

On the morning of December 18, the disorganized mob that had once been the Army of Tennessee continued reorganizing themselves and resumed their march southwards. Men at every level began to wonder where they would stop. James McNeilly, a Tennessee chaplain, heard men repeatedly ask, "where will me make the stand?" General Forrest told General Hood that, unless the army quickly retreated south of the Tennessee River, the army would be destroyed. Samuel Conley noted in his diary on December 18 that "we are bound for the Tennessee River." Thomas Key noted that "the weather adds to our gloomy feelings" and that "the thought of having to evacuate Tennessee after having possessed it but two weeks was extremely depressing."[19]

Hood asked Forrest to take command of the rear guard and buy time for the rest of the army to escape. Forrest hand selected eight infantry brigades to help his cavalrymen. He excused about 400 men of those brigades who lacked shoes and formed the remaining 1,600 infantrymen into an improvised rear guard. Forrest wanted Mississippi general Edward Walthall to command the rear guard's infantrymen. The request was a great compliment to Walthall, but it also would place the Mississippian in a very dangerous position. As a result, Hood refused to order Walthall to take the post and instead asked him to consider the assignment. Georgia infantryman George McWhirter listened as Walthall accepted the post, noting, "he had never sought a hard place for glory nor a soft one for comfort but took his chances as they came." Forrest responded to Walthall's decision with, "now we will keep them back."[20]

Members of the rear guard fired at advancing Federal cavalrymen, who charged towards the rebel artillery. The gunners realized the danger and began hitching up the cannon to the limber to withdraw it. The Federals surrounded them, cutting the cannon loose from the horses and striking the rebels down with their sabers. Remnants of the 18th Alabama Infantry formed a hollow square to defend themselves from Federal cavalrymen, who charged moments later. This was the only time many men ever saw a square in battle. The Alabamians held their fire until their muzzles almost touched Federal horseflesh, unleashing a volley at the last possible instant. The Union cavalry somehow captured a rebel soldier before they retreated, dragging the man behind their horses and releasing him a few minutes later for some unknown reason. E. H. Rennolds described the rear guard as a "heroic band" who stood "as a stone wall between the remnant of Hood's army and their victorious pursuers." Texan R. M. Collins recalled that, at Columbia, the rebels proved that even an "armed mob" could still put up a fight. Charles Joy of the 14th Tennessee Cavalry claimed the rear guard led by Walthall "saved the army from destruction." Alabama drummer A. D. Rape took clothing, a horse, and rations from a Federal soldier gunned down just a few feet from him. Sixty-three years later, Rape thought about that Union soldier, writing, "I hope he was prepared to die and is in heaven now."[21]

Federal sources provide a far less dramatic version of the fights near Spring Hill and Columbia. Henry Campbell, an officer with the 101st Colored Infantry, suggested that the fleeing rebels offered no meaningful resistance and that the Union army would have taken far more prisoners but was "too tired to follow the Rebels far." General Thomas blamed the "impassable roads" for the Union failure to destroy the last scattered bits of what had once been the Confederate Army of Tennessee.[22]

The rebels crossed a pontoon bridge spanning the Duck River late on December 18 at Columbia. R. M. Collins listened nearby while Generals Cheatham and Forrest "passed some hot, unladylike words about whose corps should cross first." According to Collins, "Cheatham gave way." James Cooper appears to have witnessed the same argument between Cheatham and Forrest. Cooper recalled that "tall cursing ensued but no one was hurt." He also suggested a possible motive for the heightened tensions: "it was bitter cold, and we were all wet, and I don't think I ever saw men suffer so much."[23]

W. J. Worsham, C. W. Heiskell, and other members of the 19th Tennessee Infantry told a very different story about the encounter that revealed important conflicts within the retreating army. According to Worsham and Heiskell, Cheatham should have already crossed, but his men were engaged in defending the rear of the army and were delayed. It was then time for Forrest's men to cross, and this led to an argument between the two commanders. The argument became so heated that members of the 19th Tennessee Infantry cocked their rifles and whispered to each other, "if he touch old Mars Frank we will shoot him and his command into eternity." Tempers cooled a moment later, the men uncocked their rifles, and the rebels did not murder each other.[24]

John Johnston and the rest of the 14th Tennessee Cavalry waited nearby while Forrest and Cheatham cursed at each other. Unlike the infantry, the troopers do not appear to have have prepared to shoot a Confederate general. Perhaps the cavalrymen had long ago grown accustomed to Forrest's legendary temper. To pass the time, Johnston entertained his friends by singing the song "Do They Miss Me at Home?" At about the same time, Johnston noticed that many men from his regiment had disappeared, perhaps to seek the answer to the song's title. When the 14th Tennessee Cavalry finally crossed the water, barely fifty men remained with the regiment.[25]

The weather turned colder as the men crossed over the river. Risenar Etter noted in his diary that, on December 19, "it rained as hard as it can" and "the wind is very cold." Barefooted men left bloody footprints in the snow. Exhausted men paused for one day in Columbia but got little rest because "it rained very hard." Some of the men slept in chicken coops to avoid the rain and hopefully ambush unwary fowl, but the shelters leaked, and the birds remained one step ahead of starving men. Charles Joy claimed, "the suffering and hardships endured by the soldiers on that retreat cannot be described."[26]

J. W. Preston of the 33rd Alabama Infantry was wounded at the Battle of Franklin and lay in a hospital near Columbia, Tennessee. As the army withdrew through the town, all the men who could walk, including Preston, received "two or three pounds of flour and a pound or two of meat and [were] told to get south." The men who limped out of the hospital were "a lame crowd," including "some with one hand, many with their arms in a sling, some with broad crutches, some wounded in the body, and others with their heads bandaged." Some of the men moved forward well, and others barely moved at all.[27]

Somewhere near Columbia, Tennessee, Captain John Dicks of the Fourth Louisiana Battalion took command of guards escorting Union prisoners south towards the Tennessee River. The weather paid no attention to the color of uniforms and unleashed misery on every man on that muddy road. Three decades later, Dicks still shuddered when he remembered the suffering of the guards and their prisoners as they made their way south together.[28]

December 20–23, Near Pulaski

Near Pulaski, rebels once again formed an improvised rear guard and punished Federals who pursued them too eagerly. Edgar Jones was still in the rear guard, "wet, tired, and hungry." The Alabamians fought on "until overcome by weariness, fatigue, and hunger, we lay down in the mud and dampness and fell asleep." James Cooper recalled that, after the Confederate rear guard defeated the Federals near Pulaski, "we were not molested by them" again.[29]

The remnants of the army continued to suffer. Barefooted artilleryman Sam Dunlap stole a pair of shoes from a sleeping soldier he did not know. Dunlap made good use of the shoes, but decades later he wondered how much suffering his theft might have caused some poor soldier, probably little different than himself. Thomas Key was "so cold that my clothes froze on me" on December 20. The long-serving veteran lamented that "the suffering we endured was so intense that we shall never forget this bitter cold night." The lack of food and warmth also took a horrible toll on the horses, which became so weak that the rebels abandoned them along the road. Key loathed "the want of foresight and confusion that now prevails in this army has never been witnessed in it before!"[30]

Morale plummeted, and the men began fighting each other. A soldier from Tennessee reported that barefoot men quarreled and nearly came to blows as they sought to obtain the few available raw cowhides to be cut into crude moccasins. Edward Jones recalled that "the morale of the army was not good by any means." The men "felt that we were beaten and unable to rally or make a stand." A few men claimed that history would prove that Hood was a great general, but most believed that "Hood was a failure." Disagreements between Hood's supporters and detractors became violent. R. M. Collins watched as a supply wagon got stuck in the icy mud and General Cheatham got down off his horse to help push it free. While some men helped the general, others kept walking and even refused to help. The insubordination enraged Cheatham, who picked up a camp kettle to lash out at the first disobedient soldier within reach. He "struck the fellow flat between the shoulders with it," making a sound that "could have been heard half a mile."[31]

Men continued to drift away from what was left of the army, often with official endorsement. General Hood granted numerous furloughs, particularly to men from Tennessee. Risenar Etter of the 16th Tennessee Infantry joined the army in 1861, but somewhere on the road south of Nashville, he decided that he was done. He got a pass to visit his family and never returned to the army. J. P. Cannon and other members of the 27th Alabama Infantry received permission to leave the army with orders to return to the "army where it may be found" when their leave expired. Cannon worried that "our prospects look gloomy" and "it looks as though our cause is lost." He took one final look at "our shattered columns" and began "the saddest march I had made since I left home three years before." Cannon made it home on Christmas Eve and never returned to the army.[32]

The remaining rebels wanted to get on the south side of the Tennessee River but worried that they might not make it. John Johnston heard a rumor that ten thousand Federal cavalrymen had looped around the Confederates and cut off the line of retreat. A short time later, he was relieved to learn that the road south remained clear. As rebels moved west, they crossed Wayne County, Tennessee, known for its fearsome "bushwhackers," who hated the Confederacy. Fear brought the remnants of the army closer together as they marched only "in the middle of the road." Edgar Jones remembered that "it was remarkable how anxious the men were to get back to the south side of the Tennessee." They felt that if they would be safe if only they could cross the river. He explained, "as I remember it, it was al most a craze." Men heard rumors that the water had risen to a point where Federal gunboats could cross the typically shallow waters of Muscle Shoals, Alabama, cutting off the Confederate retreat. Jones described the worry as a "contagious" fear that filled the men with gloom. E. H. Rennolds noted that "wagons are abandoned, and ammunition destroyed."[33]

The Army of Tennessee needed pontoons to cross the Tennessee River but lacked the wagons and animals needed to transport them, so they burned the precious pontoons. William Gale, a staff officer with General Stewart, noticed that every man counted the abandoned pontoons with increasing worry. None of them knew how many pontoons they needed or how many the army had, but they did know that every pontoon turned to ashes on the side of the road made it just a little more likely that they would never again cross the Tennessee.[34]

December 23: The Army Leaves Pulaski, Tennessee, for Bainbridge, Alabama

On Christmas Eve, the rebels began crossing Shoal Creek near the Tennessee River. Robert Jarman noted that, although four inches of snow covered the ground, several men rolled up their pants and began to cross. The instant "icy waters touched their naked legs they came out of it," and they adamantly refused to try again. Meanwhile, General William Brantley, commander of the brigade, was crossing on horseback until his mount slipped on a rock, throwing Brantley into the frigid water. The Mississippians laughed uproariously and crossed the creek without further complaint. Artillerymen had a tougher time crossing Shoal Creek than most units. The deep water and rocky bottom were nearly impassable for wheels. Precious "mules and horses were drowned by the dozens." In the distance, the gunners heard the "roar of the enemy's gunboats."[35]

December 25–27: The Rebels Cross the Tennessee River at Muscle Shoals

According to James Cooper, "Christmas day dawned bright and beautiful." While the weather was beautiful, the men were "a poor half starved, half-clad band of ragamuffins" who were "fleeing in disgrace from their last chance for freedom and independence." As bad as it was, the men "little knew what would be the results of that retreat." The undisciplined mass that had once been an army fired off precious ammunition in Christmas salutes. Other men were even less upbeat than Cooper. Georgia soldier Robert Magill was sick when he paused on the banks of Shoal Creek. Magill noted in his diary that he did not care for his only Christmas present, an order to wade across the frigid waters. Walter Clark of the 1st Georgia Infantry was exhausted, hungry, and cold. Thirty-six years later, he remembered "of all the Christmas days that have come to me in my life, only this stands out in gloomy prominence as utterly wanting in every element of the season's cheer and gladness."[36]

When staff officer William Gale arrived at the Tennessee River, he discovered that the army no longer had enough pontoons to cross the river. For a moment it looked like the last remnants of the Army of Tennessee might die with their backs to the chilly waters, but then a flotilla of pontoons came into view. According to Gale, cavalrymen under General Phillip Roddy had captured Federal pontoons at Decatur, Alabama, and briefly abandoned their horses for boats, floating their little armada down the river to Muscle Shoals. The men lashed several pontoons together and used them to ferry several cannons and horses across the water to protect the crossing from prowling Union gunboats.[37]

Arkansas soldier H. N. Pharr told a slightly different tale about the arrival of the pontoons. According to Pharr, engineer officer R. L. Cobb "saved the Army of Tennessee." Realizing that the army lacked enough pontoons, Captain Cobb gathered a group of teamsters and mounted them on some of the last mules in the army. Their objective was a collection of pontoons that Cobb hoped were still near Decatur, Alabama. The army approached the banks of the Tennessee just as Cobb's detachment returned, resulting in cries of "Cobb has come!" from the soldiers on the bank. It might be that both Cobb's and Roddy's men played a role in obtaining the pontoons that saved the retreating rebels.[38]

The Federal army was miles away, but brown water gunboats adorned with the stars and stripes attempted to cut off the rebel's retreat. The pontoon bridge across the Tennessee River was not yet complete when James Cooper arrived on the banks, so he and his comrades waited while Union gunboats threw shells into their camp, which scared the men to death but did not cause any physical harm. E. R. Boaz of the 30th Alabama Infantry watched two Federal gunboats bombard the pontoon bridge near Muscle Shoals and worried that he was about to die. Four rebel batteries assembled on the south bank of the Tennessee River to protect the slender thread of canvas that stretched across the river. When a Federal gunboat approached the crossing, rebel gunners opened fire, sending a shot through the boat's boiler and forcing it to withdraw. Florida infantryman Henry Reddick was grateful for "all the sharpshooters we had left" because they used "their long-range one-thousand-yard guns, along the bank of the river and whipped the gunboats back down the river."[39]

The bridge earned mixed reviews from exhausted rebels. R. M. Collins was amazed that the engineers could build a bridge across the churning waters that bucked "like a Texas mustang." As he walked across the shifting pontoon bridge, he said, "well this knocks the socks from Caesar's bridge across the Rhine." He predicted that school boys would long learn about the incredible construction of the bridge, even after the Confederacy was forgotten. Charles Joy described it as "a frail-looking affair." Edgar Jones was far less impressed. Moments after Jones stepped onto the bridge, a portion of it collapsed, sending Alabamians into the cold water. It was a terrible day for a swim, but the rebels were not turning around, so they pressed ahead. The uneven, rocky shoals provided an unpredictable path. One step brought Jones almost entirely out of the water, and the next plunged him in over his head. Years later, Jones recalled the mass of cursing, freezing, stumbling, and nearly drowning rebels as the "most laughable" scene he ever witnessed.[40]

Roland Gooch of the 42nd Tennessee Infantry recalled that the rear guard did their work until the last moment. They stood their ground until the rest of the army had made it safely to the southern bank. Only then did the rear guard follow their brothers to the relative safety of that southern shore. More than thirty years later, Gooch still remembered the men who protected the rest of the army. He published his thanks to "do justice to as noble a set of men as there was in any brigade of the Confederate army."[41]

Tennessee cavalryman P. T. Martin and several of his comrades were cut off from the rest of the army and unable to locate the bridges south. Desperate to get to the south bank, they crossed the river in improvised boats made from old horse troughs.[42]

The Army of Tennessee Regroups on the South Bank of the Tennessee River

Once across the Tennessee River, the Confederate Army of Tennessee pushed towards Corinth and, eventually, Tupelo, Mississippi. Alabama soldier Robert Maxwell described the men who crossed the river as "a forlorn looking set." Maxwell wore a jacket with holes in the elbows, the seat of his trousers lay open, his hair stuck through a hole in his hat, his socks were long gone, and only a pair of boots held together with string protected his feet. Despite his rough condition, he wrote, "I was about as well off as anyone

Company B of the 9th Mississippi in a Confederate camp, Warrington Navy Yard, Pensacola, Florida. J. D. (Jay Dearborn) Edwards, photographer. Library of Congress.

else." J. W. Preston reported that most men were nearly naked, wearing crude moccasins or nothing at all on their feet. John Morton, an artilleryman with Forrest's cavalry, believed that the retreat had been "almost as disastrous as the battle itself."[43]

To make up for dwindling manpower, the army tried to make more effective use of slaves and former slaves under their control. Elbridge Littlejohn informed his wife that, in camps on the south side of the Tennessee River, men heard reports of the Confederate government's plans regarding "arming and putting negroes in the field." Some men supported the measure, but most loathed the suggestion since it would be wrong "to adopt a principle which they have been fighting against." Samuel Kelley of the 30th Alabama Infantry visited "the negro prisoners" and found a slave he had once owned named Sam among them. Kelley informed his wife that Sam was dirty, tired, and eager for Kelley to take him back. The rebel planned to file the proper papers and make Sam his personal camp servant once more but also stated, "if there is reason for the slightest suspicion of him I shall have him shot or hanged." In a letter written a day later, Kelley described Sam's behavior as "very poor," "seeming dejected" and consequently "of little service." Kelly did not reveal if he ever carried out his threats to murder the man.[44]

Many soldiers did little to prepare for action and seemed to be waiting for permission to leave the army. The army's paymaster handed out wages, but most men spent their money on tobacco or other luxuries rather than on the equipment that might sustain them on future campaigns. Georgia infantryman Robert Magill believed the Army of Tennessee was the "worst demoralized army it is possible to see." He pointed out that roughly a quarter of the men were barefoot. When the men heard a rumor that President Davis was dead, many men were "glad to hear it," men refused to drill, and "two-thirds of them declare that they are going home." James Cooper reported that the men were filled with uncertainty and that "almost everyone thought the war was about over, in fact that we were a subjected people." John Holland of Corput's Georgia Battery heard rumors that his battery would soon return home to Georgia and stated, "we are very glad." Alex Hall of the 3rd Alabama Cavalry believed that two-thirds of the men were demoralized and completely worthless. Hall believed that "all would lay down their arms upon any reasonable proposition of Lincoln."[45]

General Hood's popularity continued to fall as soldiers analyzed the failed campaign. Alabamian George Brewer reported that "the movement of Hood seemed to me a miserable military blunder," a "failure that nearly destroyed a gallant army." Robert Dacus believed that no more than twelve thousand of the forty thousand men Hood once commanded remained with the army and that no more than five thousand of those men would have followed Hood into another battle. Joel Murphree of the 57th Alabama Infantry believed that Hood "was a good fighter when executing the orders of superior officers, but could not direct an army himself." Murphree explained that, after the Battle of Nashville, the men realized that Hood was an incompetent who had wasted their lives recklessly: "their spirits were broken and confidence in the success of our cause gone on our return through Tennessee." Staff officer William Gale plaintively asked his wife, "what next?"[46]

The Confederate Army of Tennessee Scattered

Confederate soldiers were torn by conflicts that convinced many men to drift away from the camps south of the Tennessee River. Robert Magill and some of his friends wavered about what to do next. They debated the difference between the moral duty of a soldier and the sinful crimes of a murderer. Eventually, they concluded that "to fight and kill men under the present conditions would simply be murder, and that we would have no further part in it and determined to go home." Magill's service in the Confederate army, which began in April 1862, ended as he began the long walk home. Southern men were also caught between their conflicting identities as the protectors of their families and defenders of their nation. Many soldiers left the army after "realizing the Confederate cause was lost." Of these men, "many went home to care for their families." The motives of most deserters will remain forever unknown, but there was no doubt that, as Joel Murphree explained, "a great many men quit the ranks."[47]

General Hood continued sending men home on furloughs, with priority given to men with homes west of the Mississippi River or in the state of Tennessee. According to Edwin Rennolds, almost every man from west Tennessee received permission to go home for thirty days. Most of the men never fought another battle, and "some thought the fate of the Confederacy already sealed and remained at home." Rennolds was one of only a handful of men from his regiment who eventually rejoined the Army of Tennessee in North Carolina. Mississippi soldier R. N. Rea received a pass to visit his home, along with several of his comrades. He rode back to Marion, Mississippi, on the top of an old boxcar and returned just in time to surrender at Mobile, Alabama. Samuel Cooke and the rest of the 17th Texas Cavalry (dismounted) threw dice to determine which of the regiment's men would receive furloughs. Cooke won his toss, joined forces with other men headed west, and returned to his home in Elysian Fields, Texas. Several months later, he attempted to return to the army, but before he could cross the Mississippi River, he received word that the war was over and returned home for the final time. James Cooper was "completely disgusted" with the army. He obtained a furlough but returned to the army for the last few days of the war. Mississippi soldier Robert Jarman received permission to leave the army and visit relatives who lived nearby. Unlike many men, he returned quickly and surrendered with the last remnants of the Army of Tennessee in North Carolina in April 1865. Larry Johnson remained with the army, determined to be "loyal to the end." He surrendered with the fragments of the Army of Tennessee in North Carolina on April 26, 1865.[48]

The Confederate high command scattered what was left of the Army of Tennessee. Hood accepted responsibility for the campaign, resigned his post as the army's commander, and received a new assignment in Texas. James Arnold of the 30th Alabama Infantry was still with the Army of Tennessee when his regiment received orders to go to North Carolina. Arnold decided that the planned journey seemed "quite a lengthy trip," and as a result "the furlough fever struck me." Much to his own surprise he obtained permission to leave the army for a brief time. He rejoined the army in North Carolina just in time to surrender. Elbridge Littlejohn of the 10th Texas Cavalry (dismounted) and the rest of his regiment were split from the Army of Tennessee and traveled south to aid in the unsuccessful defense of Mobile, Alabama. Stouten Dent and the rest of Dent's Alabama Battery also traveled to Mobile, Alabama, to help defend the city. W. P. Chambers of the 46th Mississippi Infantry spent most of the Tennessee campaign at home in Mississippi, recovering from a shoulder wound he suffered at the Battle of Allatoona on October 5, 1864, but by January 1865 he had recovered enough to rejoin his regiment just about the time it shipped out to Fort Blakely, near Mobile. In his memoir, Robert Bevier of the 5th Missouri Infantry detailed the long and difficult history of his army before concluding that, on the banks of the Tennessee River, "the Army of Tennessee ceased to exist."[49]

CONCLUSION

Scattered remnants of units that had once served in the Confederate Army of Tennessee gathered for a final stand culminating in the Battle of Bentonville, North Carolina (March 19–21, 1865). The last fragments of an organization known as the Confederate Army of Tennessee surrendered a few weeks later. Several scholars have written excellent histories of these final weeks. Readers in search of a good, brief overview of this campaign and other final campaigns of the Civil War might consider reading *The Civil War Ends, 1865*, by Mark L. Bradley, one of the wonderful campaign studies produced by the Center of Military History. Nathaniel Cheairs Hughes's *Bentonville: The Final Battle of Sherman and Johnston* provides a good study focused on the Battle of Bentonville. For a social history focus, readers should consider reading *The Confederate Surrender at Greensboro: The Final Days of the Army of Tennessee, April 1865*, by Robert M. Dunkerly.

This work ends on the banks of the Tennessee River for several reasons. It was the end of a campaign. More importantly, this story ends there because, while there was some fighting in 1865, in the words of Confederate soldier Robert Bevier, the Confederate Army of Tennessee "ceased to exist" after the retreat from Nashville.[1] It was the Army of Tennessee, not the Army of North Carolina. The army grew out of a desire to protect the state from Union forces and, even after it was pushed out of the state, the army continued to rally around hopes of a counteroffensive that would retake Tennessee. As late as the Battle of Nashville, some men in the army held out hope, if unrealistically, that they could return Tennessee to the rebel fold. Men in blue forever extinguished that hope when they broke Confederate lines outside of Nashville on December 16, 1864, and sent the army fleeing south, never to return. When Joseph Johnston took command of the forces that had once been the Army of Tennessee several months later, he had no hopes of recapturing Tennessee or any intention to try. He took to the field once more only in hopes of earning "fair terms of peace."[2] This does not denigrate the men who participated in the final stand, but it does emphasize the fact that there was a fundamental change after the Battle of Nashville.

For most of the men who were once in the Confederate Army of Tennessee, the suffering of war ended shortly after the Battle of Nashville.

Reconstruction was a difficult period for many Americans, but it paled in comparison to the Civil War, the deadliest conflict in American history. This work bears the title *Suffering in the Army of Tennessee* because suffering was the most common theme in primary sources about this campaign, particularly in those produced by Confederate soldiers. The life of a Confederate soldier during this campaign was difficult in ways that the people of the present will probably never fully appreciate.

Confederate soldiers struggled with difficult internal conflicts on this campaign. Officers were torn by a desire to protect their men and an obligation to send those men to their deaths in an effort to achieve victory. Soldiers realized that their presence inflicted pain on southern civilians, while they also tried to protect them from the Union army. Combat veterans loathed the sight of young boys and old men in the ranks, even as they lamented the army's dwindling numbers. Soldiers struggled with their desire to go home and their duty to remain in the army.[3] Many Confederate soldiers became deserters, not because they were cowards, but because they decided that their greater duty was to protect their families rather than their nation.[4] The appearance of a conflicted southern masculinity stuck between competing identities provides additional support for Ted Ownby's excellent work, *Subduing Satan: Religion, Recreation, and Manhood in the Rural South*.[5]

This work complicates the traditional perception of the ragged rebel. The Confederate soldiers who took part in this campaign were not barefoot scarecrows carrying squirrel rifles, nor were they as well supplied as their Union counterparts. Inspection reports and other primary sources indicate that most Confederate soldiers on this campaign lacked the clothing, camp equipment, and food they needed. However, those same primary sources also suggest that the men were remarkably well armed with most of the weapons, accouterments, and ammunition needed by a mid-nineteenth-century army. They had little of what they needed to live but almost everything they needed to fight. In the words of one observer commenting on another rebel army, Confederate soldiers were "a lean and hungry set of wolves."[6]

While the campaign might look like the failed adventure of a dying army with no hope of success to modern readers, primary sources provide a very different perspective. Surviving sources indicate that the men who remained on the campaign did not think their army was dying. The men who thought the army was dying joined the ranks of the deserters who went home and played no role in this campaign. The constant forward momentum the rebels enjoyed on much of the campaign gave men reason to believe that victory was just one good fight away. A shocking number of

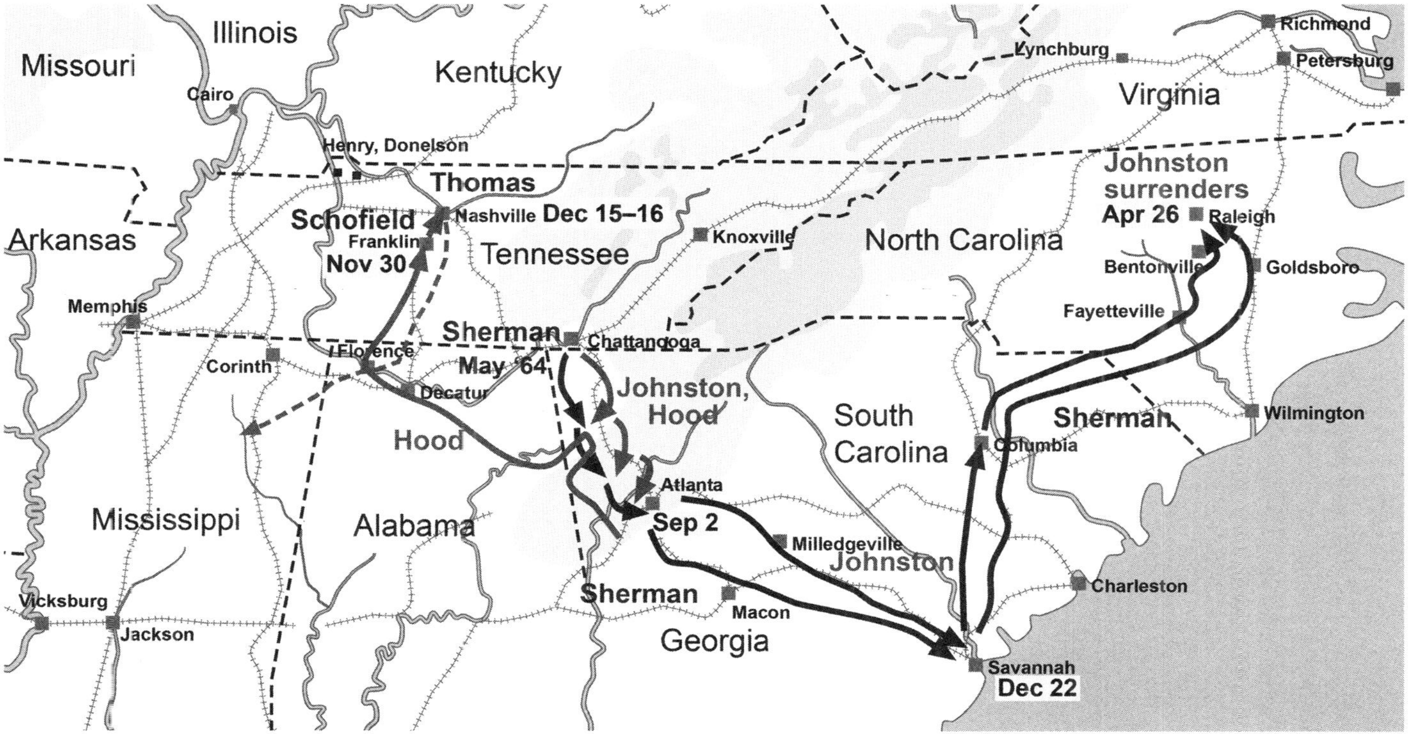

Map 18. Western Theater, Chattanooga to the Carolinas. Map by Hal Jespersen, www.cwmaps.com.

southern soldiers preferred the danger of headlong assaults to the boredom of trenches. Many contemporary accounts indicate that morale climbed on the offensive and plummeted on the defensive. Even the horrific Battle of Franklin, which many scholars have argued destroyed the army, increased many men's morale. Suffering in the relative safety of freezing trenches outside of Nashville and on the long retreat south did more to destroy the army than the slaughter of Franklin. The Confederate Army of Tennessee died "not with a bang, but a whimper."

> This is the way the world ends
> This is the way the world ends
> This is the way the world ends
> Not with a bang but a whimper.
> —T. S. Eliot[7]

APPENDIX
Inspection Reports for the Confederate Army of Tennessee

The sky is bathed in hellish ochre hues of a burning Atlanta. A shattered army clothed in dirty rags retreats down a meandering country road. Starving scarecrows, adorned with bloodstained bandages carry little more than rifles and the bodies of their comrades who can walk no farther. A wagon of refugees led by Rhett Butler and Scarlet O'Hara pauses to survey the dejected remnant of a dying South. At the turn to Tara, a smirking Rhett explains that he is leaving Scarlet behind to join the army. In response to Scarlet's passionate protests that the soldiers are retreating, Rhett assures the raven-haired belle, "they'll turn and make a last stand if I know anything about them." A later comment in the film reveals that Butler was subsequently decorated for valor at the Battle of Franklin (November 30, 1864), a horrific slaughter where the Army of Tennessee made a defiant bid for glory. The image of ragged rebels slowly fleeing the fall of Atlanta is one of the many iconic scenes in the unforgettable film *Gone with the Wind.* Few observers can doubt the emotional impact of the scene, but many have cast aspersions on its authenticity.

Virtually every great scholar of the conflict has weighed in, at least obliquely, on the image of starving men in dirty gray defending their homeland from an unstoppable blue juggernaut. The debate, particularly as regards the Army of Tennessee, is heated, with some scholars such as Thomas Connelly and Wiley Sword emphasizing the Confederate government's inability to provide their army with the most essential equipment.[1] A rival assortment of experts, including Leslie Jensen and Harold Wilson, claim that the Confederate army was often well supplied. Wilson even argued that the men who invaded Tennessee a few weeks after the fall of Atlanta were "dashingly outfitted."[2] All of these scholars share an emphasis on anecdotal accounts with little or no information drawn from the inspection reports produced by the armies.

Methodology

This article provides new insights into the question of the ragged rebel by focusing on the inspection reports produced by the Army of Tennessee in the brief interval between the time it abandoned Atlanta on September 2, 1864, and before it pushed into Tennessee roughly two weeks later for the campaign that included the battles of Spring Hill, Franklin, and Nashville. In an effort be concise, this project focuses primarily on brigade-level inspections of the army's infantry units. By focusing on one branch of one army at one time and place, with an unprecedented statistical analysis of the extensive records produced by the army, this article will introduce a degree of mathematical insight into the question of the ragged rebel and provide a greater understanding of that moving image of a battered army wandering down a dusty Georgia road on a winding path to annihilation.[3]

With the ruins of Atlanta smoldering in the distance, the Army of Tennessee took stock of itself. General Hood ordered his officers to conduct a thorough inspection of the army in September 1864. This order was consistent with the regulations for the Confederacy, which required periodic inspections of the nation's soldiers.[4] The preprinted forms used by the army's inspectors provided entries for copious amounts of information on almost every aspect of the army, including detailed accounting of the men, their discipline, and, most importantly to any understanding of their raggedness, their personal clothing, arms, and equipment. These records are rich but imperfect sources of information that include inconstancies, blank entries, and illegible notes, while still providing a rare snapshot of an army on the precipice of its last bid for glory.

The monumental task of compiling these inspection reports fell to thirty-one mostly well-qualified junior officers.[5] Most of the inspectors were experienced soldiers, with roughly two-thirds having enlisted no later than 1862. Many of them had worked their way up the ranks; eight joined the army as enlisted men, and eleven initially received commissions as junior officers with the line regiments before earning promotions to the brigade staffs. Many were experienced infantrymen as well as veteran soldiers; twenty-three of the thirty-one inspecting officers had served in the same infantry units that they inspected in September 1864. Most of these men had probably experienced combat, five suffered wounds on one or more occasions, four had been prisoners of war, and two had horses shot out from under them. Promotion to the brigade staff was no guarantee of safety; five became casualties at the Battle of Franklin on November 30, 1864.

Although a single example, the letter of recommendation written by General Edmund Pettus that propelled Captain John McKee Gould into the job of inspector provides insights into the characteristics of inspectors. Pettus explained that Gould was an ideal inspector since his prewar occupation of planter made him an experienced manager. His long and courageous service in the army (beginning on September 9, 1861) proved that he was devoted to the Confederacy, and his brief time on temporary duty with the general's staff convinced Pettus on a personal level that Gould was a man of the highest quality. While some men like Gould climbed the ranks, others fell, such as William Ramsey, who was court martialed and removed from the service in April 1864. The presence of well-qualified experienced soldiers on the brigade staffs is consistent with the argument of Herman Hattaway and Archer Jones in *How the North Won* that the Army of Tennessee displayed unprecedented professionalism and flexibility during its final months.[6]

While the inspectors might have been tempted to exaggerate the needs of the troops, particularly their comrades in their old regiments, to obtain more supplies or higher praise for their friends, there is no evidence to indicate that they succumbed to this desire to any significant degree. An examination of the reports does not reveal any obvious preferential treatment towards the officers' former regiments, the most likely beneficiaries of any fraud they might have been tempted to commit. Inspectors never singled out their old regiments for special praise, and in many cases inspectors reported that their old regiments were neither the best nor the worst equipped units in any category of analysis.[7] As further evidence of their refusal to show favoritism, inspectors often made singular comments on the quality of brigades as a whole, such as when Henry Tupper reported that the rifles of every regiment in Brantley's Brigade, which included his old regiment, the 24th Mississippi, were clean but that the coats of every regiment were in poor condition.[8] In a rare example of something that might be considered favoritism, Joseph Flanagan argued in his inspection of Cockrell's Missouri Brigade that these men were in more urgent need of resupply from the Confederate government than other troops. He supported his claim with the observation that Missourians were cut off from their homes by Union forces and were therefore unable to obtain items from home, unlike the soldiers from areas closer to the army's camps.[9]

Any desire the inspectors might have felt to inflate the needs of the troops was probably tempered by a competing need to defend themselves and their men from claims of mismanagement. In March 1863 ordnance officer Lieutenant Colonel H. Oladowski observed that, after the Battle of Murfreesboro (December 31, 1862–January 2, 1863), many of the men "carelessly wasted" their weapons, equipment, and ammunition. He blamed the officers as well as the men for this problem. Quartermaster General

Lawton was quick to argue in 1864 that many officers and men in the Army of Tennessee suffered because they sold or threw away their clothing and equipment. The inspectors were probably aware of these accusations. Captain Joseph Flanagan seemed to address them directly, arguing that the men he inspected in September 1864 were in desperate need of numerous items "through no negligence or carelessness on their part."[10]

Weapons

The Army of Tennessee was well armed as it prepared for the 1864–1865 campaign into Tennessee. Roughly 91 percent of the army's 28,857 available infantrymen had a weapon.[11] Even these deficiencies might have been more transitory than systemic. The inspection of Cantey's Brigade of Alabamians and Mississippians noted optimistically, "the ordnance officers have not been able to arm all the men yet," suggesting that the inspector expected more weapons to arrive.[12] Most of the army's weapons were in good working order, with only 509 listed as unserviceable; therefore, roughly 89 percent of the army's infantry carried a fully functional rifle or musket. The Atlanta arsenal had repaired five hundred weapons every week, but the fall of the city left the Army of Tennessee with little of hope of repairing their weapons at that facility and resulted in the destruction of at least five thousand Enfield rifles that could not be evacuated before the city fell.[13] Facilities and material lost in the fall of Atlanta also indicated, in contrast to the optimism expressed in the inspection of Cantey's Brigade, that the army might have a hard time acquiring new weapons or repairing damaged ones as the campaign unfolded.[14] The army's weapons were typically clean, even if the men themselves were not. Inspectors reported that roughly 70 percent of the army's regiments carried clean weapons and about 15 percent were dirty, and the inspectors of the remaining 15 percent of regiments either did not comment or provided illegible notes.[15] Clean weapons were, and remain, one of the hallmarks of excellent soldiers.[16] The fact that the vast majority of infantrymen in the Army of Tennessee carried clean weapons provides additional evidence that these men were competent soldiers.

The Army of Tennessee infantry was better armed than ever before in September 1864. In early 1862 Confederate forces in Tennessee were so desperate for weapons that the army acquired broken civilian weapons and hired gunsmiths to repair them, in an attempt to give the men anything that would shoot. After the Battle of Shiloh (April 6–7, 1862), more than half of the men in A. P. Stewart's Division carried a mix of smoothbore percussion muskets and assorted flintlocks. As late as March 1863, the Army of Tennessee reported that 11,869, or roughly 37 percent, of its infantrymen carried antiquated smoothbore muskets.[17] While the September 1864 inspections do not provide a comprehensive number of total weapons, the army appears to have largely rectified the problem of antiquated weapons. No more than 15 percent of the army's regiments used smoothbore muskets. No regiment reported making exclusive use smoothbore muskets, and only 3 percent are listed as using a mixture of smoothbore and rifled weap ons. If the 12 percent of regiments with missing information were armed like the majority of the rest of the army, the number of regiments using rifles could have been as high as 97 percent.[18] Captain John F. Tate, who had been with the Confederate armies in the west since the fall of 1861, noted in his inspection of Cantey's Brigade that the men of the brigade were better armed than at any point in the past.[19]

The Army of Tennessee's weapons were good, but they were far from uniform. Of the inspected regiments or consolidated regiments, 29 percent were armed entirely with Enfields, the excellent British-made weapons prized by both Union and Confederate soldiers, and 19 percent carried a mix of British Enfield and American-made Springfield rifles.[20] Many of the Springfield rifles were undoubtedly captured from the Union army.[21] Roughly 17 percent of regiments were simply listed as carrying rifles with no model clearly specified. The inspections of a little over 12 percent provide no indication of which weapons were used. Another 6 percent of regiments made exclusive use of Austrian rifles. Approximately 11 percent of regiments used various combinations of rifles. One regiment, the consolidated 8th and 32nd Mississippi, carried Confederate-made Fayetteville rifles. Men of the consolidated 1st and 3rd Missouri dismounted cavalry regiment, serving as infantry, carried two Henry rifles along with the Enfields that armed the rest of the regiment. Based on these numbers, it is safe to conclude that, in September 1864, the Army of Tennessee's infantry units were reasonably well armed.[22] However, the situation was still far from ideal. While John F. Tate, the inspector for Cantey's Brigade, noted that the brigade's inventory of Austrian, Enfield, and Mississippi rifles was an improvement over the weapons that the men had carried in the past, he also lamented the odd mix of rifle calibers and models.[23]

Ammunition

The army carried larger quantities and better-quality ammunition than at any time in its past. Confederate chief of ordnance Josiah Gorgas later recalled that, at the start of the war, "there was little ammunition of any kind, or powder, at the arsenals of the south," and hardly any small arms ammunition had been manufactured in the South for fifty years. The surrender of

Fort Donelson to Union forces in February 1862 was due, at least in small measure, to the depletion of Confederate ammunition. An April 1863 report from Colonel Oladowski, the Army of Tennessee's chief of ordnance, explained that much of the army's ammunition was of inferior quality and did not function properly. The same report noted that officers at the arsenals were aware of the problem and had plans to improve production.[24]

Infantrymen in the Army of Tennessee carried a sufficient quantity of high-quality ammunition. The inspection form did not specify if ammunition should be counted as total rounds or as rounds per man, and it failed to indicate if the totals should only include the amount of ammunition actually with the troops or rounds with the men and in their regimental baggage. The inspecting officers were therefore unsurprisingly inconsistent, providing a wide array of responses and little indication of their methodology. In some cases, the inspectors declined to provide any information at all on the amount or quality of ammunition carried by the troops. Inspectors recorded ammunition inventories in terms of rounds per man for 126 regiments. These reports reveal an average of roughly 43 rounds per man. In 26 regiments, ammunition was reported as grand totals, which makes it more difficult to determine how well equipped each soldier was, but dividing the number of reported rounds for these units by the average number of men inspected per regiment yields a rough estimate of 109 rounds per man.[25] If the inspectors who recorded rounds per man counted only the ammunition in each soldier's possession, and inspectors who supplied grand totals for each regiment counted rounds in both the hands of soldiers and their regimental reserve, then the Army of Tennessee was carrying something in the vicinity of the standard recommended load of 40 rounds per man, with another 60 rounds held in reserve.[26] Obviously, if some or all of the inspectors utilized an alternative method, the conclusions could be very different. Despite the omissions and lack of clarity, the reports do clearly indicate that 125 regiments carried good quality ammunition, as opposed to the bad ammunition carried by 5 units. Entries for the remaining 31 regiments are either blank or illegible.[27] The available information on ammunition quality is far from perfect, but most the army's infantry regiments carried a reasonable amount of good quality ammunition.

Ammunition supplies were undoubtedly complicated by the wide array of calibers used by the army's infantry weapons. Inspectors reported that roughly 28 percent of the regiments possessed only .57 caliber ammunition, which was typically used with Enfields; around 5 percent of the regiments had only .54 caliber ammunition, often used with Austrian and Mississippi rifles; and about 10 percent of regiments reported the exclusive use of the .58 caliber round most typically associated with Springfield rifles. The remaining 57 percent of regiments carried a bewildering array of .54, .57, .58, .69, and Henry (presumably .44 caliber rimfire) ammunition. Further complicating any attempt to understand the army's supply system are the confusing combinations of weapons and calibers. For example, the inspector for Govan's Brigade reported that the entire brigade used "Enfield Rifles and Rifle Muskets" and records every regiment except one using the .57 caliber ammunition consistent with the weapon. In the same brigade, the inspector listed the consolidated 5th Arkansas/13th Arkansas/3rd Confederate regiment as making exclusive use of .58 caliber ammunition that would have been too large for the Enfields supposedly carried by the entire brigade and specifically listed as the only weapon carried by that particular regiment.[28] The numerous irregularities like this paint a complicated picture that serves to emphasize the administrative problems faced by the army.

Accouterments

The Army of Tennessee was reasonably well accoutered. Numbers of missing accouterments were remarkably consistent in every category but one. More soldiers were more deficient in bayonet scabbards than in any other item, with 5,487 needed to fully equip the troops. This shortage should come as no surprise since the men knew that bayonet wounds were rare and many soldiers were perfectly willing to throw away the archaic weapons they saw as a useless encumbrance. Other men twisted their bayonets into pothooks, which would not have fit into their scabbards, and rendered the accouterment useless.[29] In contrast, inspectors reported that the army needed only 3,234 cartridge boxes, 3,240 cap boxes, 3,573 shoulder belts, and 3,683 waist belts. The army's infantry therefore had enough accouterments, except for bayonet scabbards, to fully outfit roughly 87 percent of the troops, a number consistent with the 91 percent of infantrymen who carried a functional firearm. Undoubtedly, some men were able to serve effectively without all the required items, even if it was a less than ideal situation. Shoulder belts were useful for supporting the cartridge box, but most boxes were equipped with belt loops that allowed men to carry the box on their hip rather than suspended from their shoulder. So many men carried their cartridge boxes on their waist belts that it created an epidemic of hernias and motivated military doctors to urge the men to begin carrying their cartridge boxes on shoulder belts, if available.[30] Alternatively, an enterprising soldier could make do without any of the other items by shuffling his ammunition among his pockets, haversack, and whatever accouterments he did have. The accouterments were mostly of good quality, but there were exceptions. Lieutenant Jones noted that some of the men in Tyler's Brigade of Georgians and Tennesseans were carrying oilcloth cartridge boxes from Crown and Co. that were poorly made and should be deemed a failed experiment. The inspectors concluded that the accouterments of 120 regiments were in good condition, while the accouterments of 5 were in bad condition, and left the entries blank for the remaining 36 regiments.[31]

Despite constant improvement, the Army of Tennessee was not as well armed or as well accoutered as the Army of Northern Virginia. Paddy Griffith argued that the Army of Northern Virginia was fully equipped with modern rifles by the Battle of Gettysburg, but that the Army of Tennessee lagged behind its eastern counterpart and was "far from ideally armed" in 1864. Arthur Fremantle, a British military observer, reported that, on June 20, 1 863, he witnessed "an enormous pile of excellent rifles" captured by the Army of Northern Virginia at Chancellorsville "rotting in the open air." He explained that the rebels ignored these weapons because they were so well supplied with modern rifles that they had no need for additional weapons. It seems impossible to imagine that the Army of Tennessee would have treated modern weapons so apathetically since, at roughly the same time, almost twelve thousand infantrymen, more than one out of three of their foot soldiers, carried old smoothbore muskets.[32] Fremantle's comment also provides some insight into one reason why the Army of Northern Virginia was better armed and equipped that the Army of Tennessee. Both armies used captured weapons, but the Army of Northern Virginia controlled the field after far more battles and was therefore more often able to capture Union material than the Army of Tennessee. In 1862 alone, the Army of Northern Virginia captured more than 75,000 weapons and sets of accouterments, in contrast to the 27,500 captured by the Army of Tennessee in the same year.[33]

Camp and Personal Equipment

Men do not live by arms or accouterments alone, and the inspectors also inventoried the men's camp and personal equipment. Inspectors reported serious deficiencies in the items needed to live in the field. The inspectors did not reveal what basis they used for determining how much camp equipment the men needed. According to the official regulations for the Confederate army, which were based on regulations for the United States Army, every fifteen infantrymen were suposed to have one tent, two spades, two axes, two pickaxes, two hatchets, two camp kettles, and five mess pans. Additional tents, axes, and hatchets were allocated to officers.[34] Illegible and missing information in the reports makes it impossible to provide exact numbers of officers and their ranks, and therefore an exact accounting of equipment is probably impossible. However, a rough estimate can be obtained by ignoring the additional items allocated to officers and making calculations based on the ratios mandated for enlisted men. According to the regulations, the army's 28,857 infantrymen should have possessed at least 1,924 tents, but inspectors reported that they needed 1,645 tents. Assuming that the inspectors were using the official regulations as the guide, the men may have had as few as 279 tents, or about 16 percent of the tents they should have had, a serious deficit. The men also suffered from serious shortages of all other camp items, needing 647 axes, 482 spades, 1,065 camp kettles, and 1,384 mess pans. These figures clearly indicate that soldiers in the Army of Tennessee lived in rustic camps that lacked even the most essential comforts, and they undoubtedly suffered as a result.

While the official regulations do not provide detailed lists of how many items of personal equipment troops were supposed to recieve, the inspectors did report serious shortages. The men needed 4,669 haversacks, 4,091 knapsacks, and 4,016 canteens. Perhaps most troubling, the army also needed 16,101 bankets, a figure that indicates that roughly 56 percent of the infantrymen in the army did not even have a blanket to protect them from the harsh winter weather of 1864.[35] This shortage of blankets might seem difficult to believe, but it corresponds to accounts in other primary sources. A Union soldier reported that many of the Confederates captured after the fall of Atlanta lacked blankets. One Confederate soldier, writing home, claimed that less than 25 percent of men in the army had a blanket, which he called "that great treasure." A Union prisoner of war noted that many of the Confederates he encountered suffered terribly in the cold because they had no blankets.[36]

Clothing

Inspectors reported that men were in desperate need of shirts and underclothing. In a three-year enlistment, soldiers should have recieved seven flannel shirts and nine pairs of underwear each.[37] This was probably a reasonable quanity of these items in theory, but a combination of hard service, inferior quality, and the quartermaster department's failure to provide the mandated quantities conspired to ensure that many men were left with little or nothing between their skin and rough wool or wool-blend uniforms. The inspectors noted that the infantrymen needed 16,756 shirts and 15,115 pairs of underwear. Since the army's infantry branch consisted of roughly 28,857 men, this meant that nearly 58 percent of the men needed a shirt and 52 percent needed a pair of underwear. Even when Confederate Quartermaster General Lawton defended his work, he admitted that his department had been unable to supply every soldier with a shirt. Most of the inspectors said little about the men's shirts and underwear, but Lieutenant Tupper reported that the men of Brantley's Mississippi Brigade had particularly good underclothing, although he provided no indication of why they might have had exceptionally nice underpants or what made their underwear so good that it deserved a note in the official records.[38]

More than half of the army's 28,850 infantrymen went without coats, pants, or both, inspections noted that 15,549 coats and 17,913 pairs of trousers were needed to fully equip the army's infantry. Official regulations mandated the issue of four coats during a three-year enlistment. According to the official regulations, these coats were supposed to be long and double breasted, with a cadet gray body, and faced in the branch of service color. Men should have also received seven pairs of loose fitting sky blue trousers over the course of a three-year enlistment.[39] While these uniforms would have looked delightful on parade, there is no evidence that any of the men inspected in 1864 were wearing them. Arthur Fremantle, a British observer, reported that the Army of Tennessee's clothing was anything but uniform, consisting of a wide assortment of colors and styles. The army's shortage of clothing was exacerbated by the poor quality of the items they did have. Lieutenant Tupper reported that the men of Brantley's Mississippi Brigade suffered from poor quality pants and coats. Captain Flanagan noted that the men of Cockrell's Missouri Brigade wore lightweight cotton pants that were "too thin for the fall season" and left men "quite chilly." Just a few weeks before the September inspection, Texas soldier Sebron Sneed wrote a letter to his wife explaining that, in the Army of Tennessee, "one hole in the seat of the britches indicates a captain, two holes a lieutanant, and the seat of the pants all out indicates that the individual is a private." The inspector of Cantey's Brigade noted that, while the men were in good spirits, the lack of jackets, shoes, and blankets was becoming increasingly problematic because the weather was turning colder with each passing day.[40]

The army's infantrymen were in desperate need of overcoats in September 1864. According to Confederate regulations, every infantrymen sould have recieved a cadet gray, double-breasted overcoat.[41] The reality was far different. Inspectors reported that the men needed 14,307 overcoats.[42] These were vital items for men on the verge of a winter campaign, but roughly half of the army's infantrymen did not have one. Even when Quartermaster General Lawton defended his work supplying the Army of Tennessee during the campaign, he freely acknowledged that he had been unable to provide sufficient overcoats.[43]

Although the preprinted inspection forms did not include a listing for headgear, several inspectors wrote it in. The lack of a heading for headware is a curious omission since the official regulations stated that every soldier should receive four caps during a three-year enlistment.[44] Caps and hats were also essential items in the opinion of at least some inspectors. In the fifty-two regiments where inspectors noted a need, the army's infantrymen needed a total of 4,520 hats and caps. In contrast to the French-inspired kepis and linen and oilcloth covers that were mandated by the army's official regulations, most men preferred to wear civilian-style broad-brimmed hats like the ones they wore before joining the army.[45]

Shoes

The inspection reports did include a listing for shoes, and the numbers revealed a serious problem. The September 1864 inspections reported that the army's 28,857 infantrymen needed 13,010 pairs of shoes, or roughly one new pair of shoes for every 2.2 infantrymen.[46] Lieutenant McGee of the 2nd Arkansas Dismounted Cavalry claimed that the lack of shoes was the primary cause of disability in the regiment. The press reported that many of the Confederate soldiers taken prisoner after the fall of Atlanta were barefoot. A Union prisoner claimed that barefoot Confederate soldiers suffered horribly in the cold. An editorial in the *Daily Chattanooga Rebel* claimed that the "noble defenders" of the nation "want clothing and shoes."[47] Shoes, important as they were, did little more than blister men without socks. The army reported that it needed 25,016 pairs of socks to fully supply its infantrymen in September 1864, which means that roughly 87 percent of the army's infantrymen needed socks.[48]

The problem of barefoot troops plagued the Army of Tennessee almost from the begining, but the situation was probably better in September 1864 than it had been in the past.[49] As early as November 1862, the shortage of shoes was so severe that the army issued special orders that men without shoes should camp near the railroads until rail cars to transport them became available. An April 1863 report claimed that the troops were in desperate need of shoes but noted optimistically that the Atlanta depot was producing 150 pairs of shoes per day.[50] Obviously, this resource evaported with the fall of Atlanta to Union troops shortly before the Septmeber 1864 inspections. In February 1864, the Army of Tennessee's infantrymen needed roughly one pair of shoes for every 2.8 men, which was a little more than the roughly one pair needed for every 2.2 infantrymen needed in September 1864.[51]

Every Confederate army suffered shortages in 1864, but members of the Army of Northern Virginia probably suffered less than men in the Army of Tennessee in late 1864. An August 1864 inspection of Pickett's Division explained that the men benefited from "quite liberal" issues of clothing and large quantities of shoes. In his book *Welcome the Hour of Conflict: William Cowan McClellan and the 9th Alabama,* William McClellan concluded that, while Confederate forces in Virginia suffered due to a lack of food in late 1864, "most men had shoes." An Alabama soldier serving with the Army of Nothern Virginia in 1864 had enough extra clothing to send his wife shirts and underwear. He explained that he obtained the items not because he needed them or had any desire to wear them but so that she could rework the material into clothing for their children. A November 1864 report from the Army of Northern Virginia noted the presence of "large quantities" of shoes at the Richmond depot.[52] The continuous operation of the Richmond depot and the port at Willmington, North Carolina, in comparison to the collapse of vital depots and ports of the Deep South, may be one reason for the disparity of supplies between the two major armies. However, without an exhaustive comparison of inspection reports, which is outside the scope of this article, it is impossible to make a conclusive comparison of the relative needs for shoes and clothing in the Army of Tennessee and the Army of Nothern Virginia.

Quality of Camp Equipment, Personal Equipment, and Clothing

The September 1864 inspections combined camp equipment, personal equipment, and clothing into a single section and asked inspectors to comment on the condition of these items as a whole. Inspection forms included openings to categorize these items as good, poor, or bad. In contrast to the generally high quality of arms and ammunition, the men suffered from very poor quality of these other items. The inspectors of eighty-two regiments either did not comment or left ambiguous comments that did not fit cleanly into any of the three categories. While the lack of information on over half of the regiments is frustrating, a clear picture emerges from the inspectors who supplied a complete report. In the seventy-nine regiments where inspectors commented on the quality of these items, only ten regiments, or around 12 percent, possessed good quality items; fifty-five, or roughly 70 percent, tried to make do with poor quality goods; and fourteen, or about 18 percent, suffered from bad quality materials.[53] A cynic might suggest that the numbers are worse than they appear at first glance and argue that many inspectors may have left the quality statement blank if they felt that everything was of good quality. The biggest problem with that assertion is that most of the same inspectors who declined to comment on the quality of clothing and personal equipment did give regiments high marks for carrying clean weapons and good quality ammunition, so they were clearly not inclined to remain silent in the presence of high-quality goods[54]

Supplies of Weapons Versus Clothing

Infantrymen in the Army of Tennessee were mostly well armed but poorly clothed as a result of both the physical characteristics of these items and the nature of the Confederate logistics system. Small arms are remarkably durable if they are carefully maintained, and the men of the time were well aware of this fact.[55] Once a soldier received a firearm and accouterments, they were likely to survive the rest of the war, barring mismanagement or accident. Even ammunition could last extended periods of time, as long as it was not fired and was kept safe from the elements in the leather accouterments used by most of the army's infantrymen. In contrast, clothing and shoes do not last very long and were not expected to. The Confederate army's regulations for the replacement of clothing tiems were based on the Union regulations and are pictured in this article. The regulations indicated that shoes were expected to last roughly three months, shirts were expected to last four months, and even blankets were expected to wear out.[56] Therefore, to keep a soldier supplied in the field, the Confederacy only needed to send him a single firearm and set of accouterments, as well as enough ammunition to supply him when he was actively engaged in combat, but that same soldier needed a steady stream of clothing even during extended lulls in the fighting.

The Confederate government was well aware of this fact, but they often devoted more production capacity and gave higher logistical priority to weapons and ammunition than to clothing and shoes. President Jefferson Davis told Josiah Gorgas, the Confederate chief of ordnance, that the government must provide men with food, weapons, and ammunition above all else since "if they are fed and have arms and ammunition they can fight." Early in the war, the Confederacy attempted to provide volunteers with arms and ammunition but ordered each man to "furnish their own uniform." The general idea appears to have been that, while almost every household was capable of producing clothing, modern weapons and ammunition were far rarer commodities in the typical home. In early 1862 an editor for the Milledgeville, Georgia, *Southern Recorder* pridefully claimed that "there was never an army in the world, except the 350,000 soldiers now in the service of the Confederate states, whose clothing was furnished by direct private contributions." The policy failed by late 1862, and the Confederacy began issuing large numbers of uniforms, but issues of clothing from the Confederate government, unlike its supplies of weapons and ammunition, never kept up with the Army of Tennessee's needs, forcing men to rely on clothing from home, captured material, and items taken from civilians near their areas of operation.[57]

Conclusion

The Army of Tennessee in September 1864 was probably in the best logistical shape of its life, but it never matched the condition of the Army of Northern Virginia, and it quickly deteriorated during the campaign into Tennessee. By early 1862 the Confederate government was aware that its transportation networks, particularly its railroads, were incapable of supporting a centralized system of wartime production and turned instead to a decentralized set of depots spread across the Confederacy, with each army drawing from the closest depots.[58] This was probably the best possible solution, and it worked particularly well for the Army of Northern Virginia, which drew most of its material from the Richmond depot. This depot remained safely behind Confederate lines until the last few days of the war in Virginia. The system did not work as well for the Army of Tennessee, which lost a series of crucial depots to advancing Union armies, including depots in Nashville in March 1862, New Orleans the following month, and finally Atlanta in September 1864, losing large quantities of precious material with each evacuation. With the fall of Atlanta, the Army of Tennessee began to draw material from the depot at Selma, Alabama. While Selma was important, it did not produce anywhere near the volume of material that came from the Atlanta and Richmond depots. It also lacked a direct railroad connection to the Army of Tennessee during the fall 1864 campaign, which put a strain on the army's supply trains at a time when they could little afford to wear out their horses and wagons.[59] A detailed inspection of the Army of Tennessee during the campaign into Tennessee would provide priceless insights, but it appears that the army did not produce any such inspection, for obvious reasons. Many items that were not produced in the depots came through the increasingly effective Union blockade, which also caused more problems for the Army of Tennessee than the Army of Northern Virginia. The Confederacy lost all of the major ports that primarily supported the Army of Tennessee, including New Orleans in April 1862 and Mobile, Alabama, in August 1864, before the fall 1864 campaign began, but the Army of Northern Virginia continued to draw supplies from Wilmington, North Carolina, until the final weeks of the war in 1865.[60] When the Confederate authorities tried to ship material from the Richmond depot or the port of Wilmington to the Army of Tennessee, the material had to make a nearly impossible journey over thinly stretched rail lines and roads that Union forces cut into ever-smaller pieces.[61] The fact that the Army of Northern Virginia operated within a fairly limited theater of operations less than a hundred miles across in the fall of 1864 also made for an easier logistical task than that facing the Army of Tennessee, which took a roundabout four-hundred-mile trek across Georgia, Alabama, and Tennessee in the fall of 1864. General Hood, for all his faults, was aware of precarious logistical state of his army in September 1864, noting immediately after the fall of Atlanta that "Sherman is weaker now than he will be in future, and I as strong as I can expect to be."[62]

After the Tennessee campaign was over, Quartermaster General Lawton responded to a congressional inquiry into the shortages faced by the army after the fall of Atlanta. Lawton was eager to dispute the notion his office was to blame for the Army of Tennessee's hardships. He admitted that his office had not provided the men with enough overcoats but blamed the deficiency on wool shortages, which were beyond his control. The quartermaster general also acknowledged that his office had only partially filled requests for shirts, although he did not provide a reason for that shortage. While he admitted some problems, Lawton adamantly argued that, overall, his department had supplied generous quantities of clothing to the troops. In addition to clothing issued by the Confederate government, he also pointed out that the states, particularly Georgia and North Carolina, provided large quantities of clothing to the Army of Tennessee. Lawton also claimed that he had over one hundred thousand pairs of socks and twenty-five thousand pairs of underwear available on request. Lawton responded to the numerous reports that Confederate soldiers were suffering for the lack of clothing by blaming the men for abandoning or selling their clothes.[63]

Some scholars, most notably Harold Wilson, have accepted Lawton's claims uncritically and used Lawton's report as proof that the Army of Tennessee was "dashingly outfitted" during the fall and winter of 1864–1865, but this claim does not survive careful scrutiny.[64] A quick glance at the army's inspection reports definitively refutes the notion of a well-clothed Confederate Army of Tennessee in the fall of 1864. Even Lawton did not claim that the army was well outfitted with everything it needed. He acknowledged the limited supplies of overcoats and shirts while freely admitting that many soldiers were suffering. A careful reading of Lawton's letter makes it clear that he did not argue that the army was well prepared for a winter campaign, only that his department was not to blame for shortages. Even Lawton's lesser claims of shortages caused by the mismanagement of individual soldiers are highly questionable. While it is true that men would occasionally discard items they deemed nonessential, such as bayonets, there is little evidence to support his assertion that large numbers of men decided to march barefoot through the snow.[65] Captain Joseph Flanagan adamantly refuted Lawton's claims with his observation that Cockrell's Missourians were in desperate need of resupply and had lost items "through no negligence or carelessness on their part." On at least one occasion, a soldier willed his clothing and blanket to his comrades, indicating that these items were carefully guarded, not carelessly discarded.[66]

Lawton's suggestion of numerous soldiers in the Army of Tennessee selling off their clothing stands in stark contrast to accounts in numerous other sources, which indicate that needy soldiers and their families worked tirelessly to supplement their government-issued supplies with clothing from other sources. Many men received clothing from their families, who could be quite creative in supplying their loved ones. Numerous civilians in Union-occupied Tennessee purchased clothing directly from Union army suppliers and surreptitiously shipped items south to their men in Confederate service. The practice became so common that the Union army's high command took steps to stem the flow.[67] Confederate authorities encouraged women to ship clothing to their men in the army and even purchased items directly from civilians. Confederate troops frequently depended on their friends and family to supply them with the winter clothing the government could not provide. The inspector for Cockrell's Brigade urged an immediate issue of clothing for men who were unable to obtain items from home, thus indicating that many men were wearing clothing provided by their families rather than their government.[68]

Many of the items that appear on the September inspection reports were probably captured from the Union army. Confederates frequently clothed and equipped themselves with items taken from Union soldiers. On at least one occasion, Confederate soldiers ordered Union prisoners to hand over their overcoats. In response, the captured men insisted that leaving them without overcoats to protect them against the cold was illegal and inhumane, but the rebels were clearly more concerned about their own shortages than the comfort of their captives and took them anyway. According to one report, as many as three-fifths of the men in the Army of Tennessee wore hats and overcoats captured from the Federals at one time. A Tennessee newspaper reported that so many Confederate soldiers wore captured Union shoes that the phrase "all a Yankee is worth is his shoes" became a common joke among the troops, and men supposedly became so adapt at scavenging enemy casualties that they could strip every dead Yankee they passed without ever coming to a halt. The Confederate practice of taking clothes from dead and captured Federal troops was so common that Union soldiers learned to expect it and even felt sympathy for the half-naked rebels who robbed corpses rather than freeze to death.[69]

Despite the serious deficiencies in clothing and equipment, inspectors reported that the vast majority of infantrymen in the Army of Tennessee were excellent soldiers who were well disciplined, projected a soldierly bearing, and maintained a military appearance. Of these three categories, the inspectors identified discipline as the most serious problem, while still praising most of the men. In the inspected regiments, 136, or roughly 84 percent, were classified as having good discipline. Inspectors identified 21, about 13 percent of regiments, as possessing lax discipline.[70] The entry for the remaining 4 regiments is odd. In his inspection of Cantey's Brigade of Alabamians and Mississippians, John Tate ignored the preprinted options of good or lax and instead wrote in the phrase "moderate in all" for all 4 regiments. The rest of the inspection provides no definitive clue into why he used that phrase.[71] Inspectors gave the men very high marks for their demeanor, reporting that 160 regiments maintained a "soldierly bearing." Only a single regiment, the 31st Alabama serving in Pettus's Brigade, received a rating of "unsoldierly." As with the mysterious raking of moderate discipline in Cantey's Brigade, the inspector's comments provide no clear reason for this rating. While the men suffered because of deficiencies in the most basic items, they somehow managed to look like soldiers. Inspecting officers reported that 155 regiments maintained a "military appearance" and that only 6 regiments were of an indifferent appearance. Several inspectors lamented the lack of soap, none more emphatically than Captain Pickens in his inspection of Holtzclaw's Brigade, who stated, "soap should be issued in abundance."[72] Many of the men reportedly washed at every opportunity, but their opportunities were rare. The inspectors' conclusion that many of the troops maintained a military appearance might be as much a testament to lowered expectations as to the ingenuities of the men. Lieutenant Jones claimed that the clothing of Tyler's Brigade of Georgians and Tennesseans was quite good, considering the scarcity of soap. The inspector of Quarles's Tennessee Brigade was even blunter, summarizing that the men appeared "good as can be expected."[73] The men in the Army of Tennessee who were "good as can be expected" became weaker, not stronger, as the late 1864 campaign unfolded, largely as result of collapsing Confederate logistics systems in the western theatre.

Captain Simms probably surmised the overall tone of the inspection reports better than anyone in his report on Tucker's Brigade of Mississippians, in which he observed that "both men and officers greatly need shoes and clothing" but that "the men work well, march well, and fight well."[74] These reports indicate that time and combat had transformed the Army of Tennessee from an enthusiastic early war "mob" into a highly professional organization by the fall of 1864.[75]

Gone with the Wind presents the Army of Tennessee retreating from Atlanta as dirty, tired, and ragged but still heavily armed and capable of making a heroic last stand. The September 1864 inspections of the Army of Tennessee and other primary sources are consistent with the movie's image of a ragged army that was dirty and defeated but not yet broken. Most of the men were well armed with modern weapons and carried the accouterments they needed to operate those weapons effectively. They had everything they needed to fight but precious little of what they needed to live. In a diary entry from September 1864, Lucy Virginia French described men from the Army of Tennessee who came to her farm in the fall of 1864 as "ragged, dirty, and devil may carish," and she concluded that they were "ragged rebels sure enough."[76] That last phrase emphasizes the duality of the Army of Tennessee in its final months. They were ragged, but they were also rebels, and their rebellion was far from over.

NOTES

Introduction

1. For examples of officers conflicted about protecting their men and sending them into combat, see James Cooper Nisbet, *Four Years on the Firing Line*, 307; and Edwin Hansford Rennolds, *A History of the Henry County Commands*, 104. For examples of soldiers realizing the pain they inflicted on civilians while trying to protect them, see Watson Landingham to his mother, July 14, 1864, Irenus Watson Landingham Collection, AUA; Hiram Smith Williams, Lewis Nicholas Wynne, and Robert A. Taylor, *This War So Horrible*, 106; and Samuel T. Foster and Norman D. Brown, *One of Cleburne's Command*, 143. For examples of veterans' discomfort with old and young soldiers and dwindling numbers, see Benjamin Rountree, "Letters from a Confederate Soldier," *Georgia Review* 18, no. 3 (Fall 1964): 285; and James Robert Maxwell, *Autobiography of James Robert Maxwell*, 244. For examples of soldiers conflicted about their duty to the army and their duty to family, see Hugh Black to his wife, July 20, 1864, Hugh Black Papers, FSUA; John W. Sparkman, *The Diary of Sergt. John W. Sparkman*, 78; Larry Johnson, "16th Regiment Tennessee Infantry, CSA," SRNBP; Hosea Garret to his uncle, August 1, 1864, Hosea Garrett Jr. Civil War Letters, KRC, AHC; and James Lanning Diary, entry dated November 28, 1864, ADAH.
2. Ted Ownby, *Subduing Satan: Religion, Recreation, and Manhood in the Rural South, 1865–1920* (Chapel Hill: Univ. of North Carolina Press, 2014).
3. For Confederate inspection reports, see the appendix in this work, "Inspection Reports for the Confederate Army of Tennessee"; For the quote "lean and hungry set of wolves see Shelby Foote, *The Civil War: A Narrative, Fort Sumter to Perryville*, 663.
4. For examples of soldiers believing victory was close, see Edgar W. Jones, "History of the 18th Alabama Infantry," ADAH; John S. Holland to his friend Dr. William Farell, January 1, 1865, John S. Holland Civil War Letters, KRC, AHC. For examples of soldier morale increased by the Battle of Franklin, see James Lanning Diary, entry dated November 30, 1864, ADAH; Samuel King Vann and Nancy Elizabeth Neel Vann, *"Most Lovely Lizzie,"* 63; and W. Jere Crook to his cousin Hattie Crook, December 10,

1864, W. Jere Crook Letters, TSLA. For examples of soldiers demoralized by the siege at Nashville, see W. J. Worsham and C. W. Heiskell, *Old Nineteenth Tennessee Regiment*, 152; William McLeod Diary, entry dated December 12, 1864, FSA; and Charles Gore Joy, "The Stampede at La Fayette, Ga.," *Confederate Veteran* 20, no. 10 (October 1912): 476.

1. "We Hav [*sic*] Took Our Stand Here"

1. Angus Benjamin Rountree, "Letters from a Confederate Soldier," 288.
2. On Confederate troop strength at the beginning of the campaign: William L. Barney, *The Oxford Encyclopedia of the Civil War*, 20; Maxwell: James Robert Maxwell, *Autobiography of James Robert Maxwell*, 248.
3. On Union troop strength at the beginning of the campaign: William L. Barney, *The Oxford Encyclopedia of the Civil War*, 20; Jackman: John Jackman and William C. Davis, *Diary of a Confederate Soldier: John S. Jackman of the Orphan Brigade*, 118; Sherman: W. T. Sherman, Major General, "HD-QRS. Military Division of the Mississippi, June 23, 1864," *OR*, ser. 1, vol. 38, pt. 4, pp. 572–73; Confederate soldiers: Larry Johnson, "16th Regiment Tennessee Infantry, CSA" SRNBP; Porcher: John Porcher, dictated to his daughter Elinor Porcher, "Father's War Story," in *United Daughters of the Confederacy. Recollections and Reminiscences, 1861–1865 Through World War I. [S.C.]: South Carolina Division, United Daughters of the Confederacy, 1990*, 383 Southern History Collection, BPL.
4. Confederate forces' desperate stands: Spencer Tucker, James R. Arnold, Roberta Wiener, Paul G. Pierpaoli, and David Coffey, *American Civil War: The Definitive Encyclopedia and Document Collection*, 103; Jackman: John Jackman and William C. Davis, *Diary of a Confederate Soldier*, 127; Battle of Kennesaw Mountain: Thomas Leonard Livermore, *Numbers and Losses in the Civil War in America, 1861–1865* (Boston: Houghton, Mifflin, 1901), 121; Hagan: Bell Irvin Wiley, "The Confederate Letters of John W. Hagan," *Georgia Historical Quarterly* 38, no. 3 (September 1954): 273; blue steamroller: Spencer Tucker et al., *American Civil War*, 1066; Sherman: W. T. Sherman, *OR*, ser. 1, vol. 38, pt. 4, p. 573.
5. Sherman: W. T. Sherman, *OR*, ser. 1, vol. 38, pt. 4, p. 385; summer rains: W. T. Sherman, *OR*, ser. 1, vol. 38, pt. 4, p. 401; Bennitt: John Bennitt Diary, entry dated June 1, 1864, GVSUA.
6. Harris: Dick Harris to his father, May 18, 1864, in Civil War Letters, vol. 2, East Tennessee, Southern History Collection, BPL.
7. Brown's letter: Allen D. Candler, *The Confederate Records of the State of Georgia*, vol. 3 (Atlanta, GA: C. P. Byrd, state printer, 1909), 582; Davis's response: Candler, *Confederate Records of the State of Georgia*, 583; Brown's response: Candler, *Confederate Records of the State of Georgia*, 587.

8. Austin: J. P. Austin, *The Blue and the Gray; Sketches of a Portion of the Unwritten History of the Great American Civil War*, 128; Chambers: W. P. Chambers, *Chamber's [sic] Confederate Journal*, 87; Hardman: C. T. Hardman to his wife, May 25, 1864, Hardman Family Letters, Southern History Collection, BPL; Neal: Andrew Neal, diary entries dated May 15 and May 20, 1864, Andrew Jackson Neal Papers, EU; Reddick: H. W. Reddick, *Seventy-Seven Years in Dixie: The Boys in Gray of 61–65* (Santa Rosa, FL: H. W. Reddick, 1910), 48 .
9. Wyatt: J. N. Wyatt, "Dalton – Atlanta Campaign," *Confederate Veteran* 5, no. 10 (October 1897): 519; Hardin: Thomas Hardin to his wife, May 6, 1864, Thomas Hardin Letters, ASA; Murphree: Joel Dyer Murphree, "Autobiography and Civil War Letters of Joel Murphree of Troy, Alabama, 1864–1865," *Alabama Historical Quarterly* 19 (Spring 1957): 172; Banks: R. W. Banks, *The Battle of Franklin, November 30, 1864, The Bloodiest Engagement of the War Between the States* (New York: Neale Publishing Company, 1908), 18.
10. Large number of Confederate desertions: John Bennitt Diary, entry dated July 4, 1864, GVSUA; May and June Confederate desertions: Richard M. McMurry, "Confederate Morale in the Atlanta Campaign of 1864," *Georgia Historical Quarterly* 54, no. 2 (Summer 1970): 229; former Confederates as civilian workers for the Union: A. G. G., "A Rebel," E. Merton Coulter Manuscript Collection, UG.
11. Diminished Confederate morale due to desertions: Hugh Black to his wife, July 20, 1864, Hugh Black Papers, FSUA; and Samuel R. Watkins, *"Co. Aytch": Maury Grays, First Tennessee Regiment, or, a Side Show of the Big Show* (Chattanooga, TN: Times Print. Co., 1900), 151; Helms: Russell S. Bonds, *War Like the Thunderbolt: The Battle and Burning of Atlanta* (Yardley, PA: Westholme, 2009), 49; Bragg: Junius Newport Bragg and Helen Bragg Gaughan, *Letters of a Confederate Surgeon 1861–65* (Camden, AR: Alexander Street Press, 1960), 210; Black: Hugh Black to his wife, July 20, 1864, Hugh Black Papers, FSUA.
12. Sparkman: John W. Sparkman, *The Diary of Sergt. John W. Sparkman, Sr., of the Quartermaster's Department: 48th Tennessee Regiment, C.S.A., 1881–1865* (Birmingham, AL: Library, 1940), 70; Jarman: Robert Jarman, "The History of Company K, 27th Mississippi Infantry and its First and Last Muster Rolls," MDAH; Austin: J. P. Austin, *The Blue and the Gray*, 128; Murphree: Joel Dyer Murphree, "Autobiography and Civil War Letters of Joel Murphree of Troy, Alabama, 1864–1865," 182.
13. Southern civilians distressed by approaching armies: Jefferson Davis, *The Rise and Fall of the Confederate Government*, vol. 2 (New York: D. Appleton and Co., 1881), 556; Landingham: Watson Landingham to his mother, July 14, 1864, Irenus Watson Landingham Collection, AUA; Williams:

Hiram Smith Williams, Lewis Nicholas Wynne, and Robert A. Taylor, *This War So Horrible: The Civil War Diary of Hiram Smith Williams, 40th Alabama Confederate Pioneer*, 106; Crittenden: John Crittenden to his wife, Bettie, June 10, 1864, AUA; Patrick: Robert Patrick, *Reluctant Rebel*, ed. F. Jay Taylor, 168.

14. McDermid: Benjamin Rountree, "Letters from a Confederate Soldier," 288, 285; Littlejohn: Elbridge Littlejohn, "The Civil War Letters of Elbridge Littlejohn," pt. 2, ed. Vicki Betts, *Chronicles of Smith County, Texas* 18 (Summer 1979): 27; Ruffin: Jeff Toalson, *No Soap, No Pay, Diarrhea, Dysentery & Desertion*, 187; Coleman: John Coleman to his sweetheart Virginia Adkins, July 10, 1864, John and Virginia Adkins Coleman Paper, Texas Collection, BUL, Waco, Texas. True to his word, John returned home after the war, married Virginia, worked as a successful merchant, and fathered six children with his wife before his death in 1880. Black: Hugh Black to his wife, July 20, 1864, Hugh Black Papers, FSUA; Hunter: Benjamin Hunter to his wife, May 1, 1864, Benjamin T. Hunter Papers, KRC, AHC; Hardin: Thomas Hardin to his wife, May 6, 1864, ASA.
15. Wyatt: J. N. Wyatt, "Dalton—Atlanta Campaign," 519; blackberries and religious services: J. P. Cannon, *Inside of Rebeldom*, 236; Roberts: Charles Roberts to his wife, July 18, 1864, Charles Roberts Collection, Civil War Archive, UM; 4th Louisiana Infantry jollification: Patrick, *Reluctant Rebel*, ed. F. Jay Taylor, 173; apples: Jesse Henderson Diary, entry dated July 18, 1864, UM; McDermid: Benjamin Rountree, "Letters from a Confederate Soldier," 289.
16. Trade across the lines, newspapers: E. H. Rennolds Diary, entries dated July 14–16, 1864, UTK; tobacco for coffee: Charles Roberts to his wife, July 18, 1864, Charles Roberts Collection, UM; Crittenden on Federal claims and exorbitant southern pricing: John Crittenden to his wife, Bettie, July 15, 1864, AUA; Cox: Mamie Yeary, *Reminiscences of the Boys in Gray*, 158. Officially no members of the United States Colored Troops participated in the battles for Atlanta. Sherman was an unrepentant racist who wanted nothing to do with men of African ancestry. However, at least one photograph of what appears to be a corporal of African descent in Atlanta does exist, and the Union army hired former slaves to work as civilian laborers in Atlanta. Matthew J. Gallman and Gary W. Gallagher, *Lens of War: Exploring Iconic Photographs of the Civil War* (Athens: Univ. of Georgia Press, 2015), 216. It is also possible that Cox was confused and saw the "Negroes" at some later battle where large numbers of those men served. Johnson: Larry Johnson, "16th Regiment Tennessee Infantry, CSA," SRNBP.
17. Rennolds: E. H. Rennolds Diary, July 15, 1864, UTK; Hood execution penalty: "Gen. Hood," *Western Democrat* (Charlotte, NC), September 13, 1864;

informal truces to provide Union uniforms: Richard M. McMurry, "Confederate Morale in the Atlanta Campaign of 1864," 230.

18. Sharpshooting: J. P. Cannon, *Inside of Rebeldom*, 236; Etter: Diary of Risenar Etter, SRNBP; Smith: Hiram Smith Williams, Lewis Nicholas Wynne, and Robert A. Taylor, *This War So Horrible*, 105.
19. Confederate supply regulations: Confederate States of America, *Army Regulations, Adopted for the Use of the Army of the Confederate States, in Accordance with Late Acts of Congress* (New Orleans: Bloomfield and Steel, 1861), 106; Maxwell: James Robert Maxwell, *Autobiography of James Robert Maxwell*, 247; Nisbet: James Cooper Nisbet, *Four Years on the Firing Line*, 306; Austin: J. P. Austin, *The Blue and the Gray*, 128.
20. Dunlop: Colin Dunlop to his sister, August 13 and August 17, 1864, Colin Dunlop Civil War Letters, KRC, AHC; Sloan: William Sloan Diary, entry dated July 28, 1864, TSLA; Henderson: Jesse Henderson Diary, entry dated July 18, 1864, UM.
21. Johnston supporters and opponents: Larry J. Daniel, *Soldiering in the Army of Tennessee*, 143; Jefferson Davis's hesitation and military support for Johnston's removal: Jefferson Davis, *The Papers of Jefferson Davis: October 1863–August 1864*, ed. Lynda Lasswell Crist, 543; civilian calls for Johnston's removal: Jefferson Davis, *The Rise and Fall of the Confederate Government*, vol. 2, p. 556; Davis's telegram and Johnston's inadequate response: Scott Walker, *Hell's Broke Loose in Georgia: Survival in a Civil War Regiment*, 147; Johnston relieved and Hood appointed: Thomas Lawrence Connelly, *Autumn of Glory: The Army of Tennessee, 1862–1865*, 421.
22. Chesnut: Mary Boykin Chesnut, Isabella D. Martin, and Myrta Lockett Avary, *A Diary from Dixie: The Civil War's Most Celebrated Journal, Written 1860–1865 by the Wife of James Chesnut, Jr., an Aide to President Jefferson Davis and a Brigadier-General in the Confederate Army* (New York: Portland House, 1997), 230; careers of Hood and Johnston: William L. Barney, *The Oxford Encyclopedia of the Civil War*, 182, 164; and George C. Rable, *The Confederate Republic: A Revolution against Politics*, 264.
23. Johnston as master of defensive tactics: Neil Kagan and Stephen G. Hyslop, *Eyewitness to the Civil War: The Complete History from Secession to Reconstruction* (Washington, DC: National Geographic, 2006), 316; Johnston as timid: Stephen Davis *Atlanta Will Fall*, 17; Hood as aggressive commander: Grady McWhiney and Perry D. Jamieson, *Attack and Die*, 72; the "Gallant Hood": G. Moxley Sorrel, *Recollections of a Confederate Staff Officer*, 169; Hood as bully with bloodlust: John Watson Morton, *The Artillery of Nathan Bedford Forrest's Cavalry*, 14; Lee praises Hood: Stephen Davis, *Atlanta Will Fall*, 109; Hood as "all lion": James M. McPherson, *Battle Cry of Freedom: The Civil War Era*, 753.

24. Army outraged by Johnston's replacement: Larry J. Daniel, *Soldiering in the Army of Tennessee*, 143; Young: Lot D. Young, *Reminiscences of a Soldier of the Orphan Brigade*, 90; Rozell: George Rozell, "General Joseph E. Johnston," *Confederate Veteran* 4, no. 12 (December 1896): 429; Watkins: Samuel R. Watkins, *"Co. Aytch,"* 151; Cleburne's response to Hood's promotion: Peter Hotze, "Memoir," Hotze Family Papers, ASA; Shotwell: R. H. Shotwell, "Hood's Campaign Through North Georgia," *Confederate Veteran* 1, no. 10 (October 1893): 311; Hadaway: Claude Lee Hadaway, "With Loyalty and Honor as a Patriot: Recollections of a Confederate Soldier," ed. Royce Shingleton, *Alabama Historical Quarterly* 33 (Fall/Winter 1971): 256.
25. Littlejohn: Elbridge Littlejohn, "The Civil War Letters of Elbridge Littlejohn," pt. 2, p. 27; Livingston: Archie Livingston to his brother-in-law, July 19, 1864, in John Coski, ed., "I am In for Anything for Success: The Letters of Sergeant Archie Livingston, 3rd Florida Infantry," *North and South* 6, no. 3 (April 2003): 77; Hagan: Bell Irvin Wiley, "The Confederate Letters of John W. Hagan," 286; Roberts: Charles Roberts to his wife, July 18, 1864, Charles Roberts Collection, Civil War Archive, UM; Etter: Diary of Risenar Etter, SRNBP.
26. Edwin Hansford Rennolds, *A History of the Henry County Commands*, 87; E. H. Rennolds Diary, entry dated July 18, 1864, UTK.
27. Lambert: R. A. Lambert, "In the Georgia Campaign," *Confederate Veteran* 38, no. 1 (January 1930): 21; Dacus: Robert H. Dacus, *Reminiscences of Company "H,"* 14; Buck: Irving A. Buck, *Cleburne and His Command*, 266; Guild: George B. Guild, *A Brief Narrative of the Fourth Tennessee Cavalry*, 66; Hadaway: Claude Lee Hadaway, "With Loyalty and Honor as a Patriot: Recollections of a Confederate Soldier," 256.
28. Anderson: Frank Anderson, "A Courier at the Battle of Resaca," *Confederate Veteran* 5, no. 6 (June 1897): 297; McMorries: Edward Young McMorries, "History of the First Alabama Volunteer Infantry CSA," ADAH, 87; "Chapter at Galveston Texas," *Confederate Veteran* 6, no. 10 (October 1898): 461.
29. Hardin: Thomas Hardin to his wife, May 6, 1864, ASA; Johnston's postwar claims: Bradley T. Johnston, *A Memoir of the Life and Public Service of Joseph E. Johnston*, 117; Battle of Kennesaw Mountain: Spencer Tucker et al., *American Civil War*, 1066; Johnston's standing: Thomas Lawrence Connelly, *Autumn of Glory*, 287; Sherman dismisses Johnston's trap: Willis Fletcher Johnston and O. O. Howard, *Life of Wm. Tecumseh Sherman*, 581; Sherman on losses: William T. Sherman, Brooks D. Simpson, and Jean V. Berlin, *Sherman's Civil War: Selected Correspondence of William T. Sherman, 1860–1865*, p. 660; Sherman letter to Grant supporting aggressive tactics: United States Congress Joint Committee on the Conduct of the War, B. F. Wade, and Daniel Wheelwright Gooch, *Report of the Joint*

Committee on the Conduct of the War at the Second Session, Thirty-Eighth Congress, vol. 1 (Washington, DC: GPO, 1865), 161.

30. Edgar W. Jones, "History of the 18th Alabama Infantry," ADAH.
31. Schofield's describes Hood as "bold": William T. Sherman, *Memoirs of General William T. Sherman*, vol. 2, p. 72; Schofield warns Sherman about Hood: David R. Kaufman, *Peachtree Creek: A Natural and Unnatural History of Atlanta's Watershed*, 134; Sherman urges caution: William T. Sherman, *Memoirs of General William T. Sherman*, vol. 2, p. 72.
32. John Bell Hood, *Advance and Retreat*, 165.
33. Thomas Lawrence Connelly, *Autumn of Glory*, 168.
34. John Bell Hood, *Advance and Retreat*, 168; Andrew Haughton, *Training, Tactics, and Leadership in the Confederate Army of Tennessee: Seeds of Failure* (London: Frank Cass, 2000), 166.
35. J. P. Cannon, *Inside of Rebeldom*, 237.
36. James Cooper Nisbet, *Four Years on the Firing Line*, 307.
37. Robert H. Dacus, *Reminiscences of Company "H,"* 15.
38. Edwin Hansford Rennolds, *A History of the Henry County Commands*, 88.
39. R. M. Collins, *Chapters from the Unwritten History of the War between the States*, 228.
40. James Cooper Nisbet, *Four Years on the Firing Line*, 307.
41. Mamie Yeary, *Reminiscences of the Boys in Gray*, 52.
42. J. P. Cannon, *Inside of Rebeldom*, 238.
43. T. J. Walker, "Reminiscences of the Civil War," ed. Russell B. Bailey, *Confederate Chronicles of Tennessee* 1 (June 1986): 65.
44. James Cooper Nisbet, *Four Years on the Firing Line*, 308.
45. J. P. Cannon, *Inside of Rebeldom*, 238.
46. James Cooper Nisbet, *Four Years on the Firing Line*, 308.
47. R. M. Collins, *Chapters from the Unwritten History of the War between the States*, 229, 231.
48. Robert H. Dacus, *Reminiscences of Company "H,"* 15.
49. T. L. Flynt, "Report of Lieut. Thomas Flynt, Sixth Texas Infantry," July 29, 1864, *OR*, ser. 1, vol. 38, pt. 3, p. 748.
50. Confederate withdrawal at night: Edwin Hansford Rennolds, *A History of the Henry County Commands*, 89; Bost: George Bost to his father, August 2, 1864, BCAS.
51. J. P. Cannon, *Inside of Rebeldom*, 238.
52. Union and Confederate figures for the Battle of Peachtree Creek: Thomas Leonard Livermore, *Numbers and Losses in the Civil War in America, 1861–1865* (Boston: Houghton, Mifflin, 1901), 122; Patrick: Robert Patrick, *Reluctant Rebel*, ed. F. Jay Taylor, 199; Young: Lot D. Young, *Reminiscences of a Soldier of the Orphan Brigade*, 90.

53. James Cooper Nisbet, *Four Years on the Firing Line*, 309, 310; John Bell Hood, *Advance and Retreat: Personal Experiences in the United States and Confederate States Armies* (New Orleans: Published for the Hood Orphan Memorial Fund by G. T. Beauregard, 1880), 253.
54. McPherson's vulnerable left flank, Stewart's Corps in Atlanta, and Hood's attempt to replicate Jackson's victories: John Bell Hood, *Advance and Retreat*, 173–75; attack plan for Hardee's Corps and McPherson's trap: William Royal Oake and Stacy D. Allen, *On the Skirmish Line Behind a Friendly Tree*, 233; Federal supply wagons: Robert Scott Davis, *Civil War Atlanta* (Charleston, SC: History Press, 2011), 67.
55. Robert Jarman, "The History of Company K, 27th Mississippi Infantry," MDAH.
56. Flynt: T. L. Flynt, "Report of Lieut. Thomas Flynt, Sixth Texas Infantry," July 29, 1864, *OR*, ser. 1, vol. 38, pt. 3, p. 748; Nisbet: James Cooper Nisbet, *Four Years on the Firing Line*, 310.
57. Richard Beard, "To the Editor," *Military Essays and Recollections: Papers Read Before the Commandery of the State of Illinois, Military Order of the Loyal Legion of the United States*, vol. 1 (Chicago: A. C. McClurg and Company, 1891), 336.
58. William Ritter, "Sketch of the Third Battery of Maryland Artillery," *Southern Historical Society Papers* 31 (1883): 192.
59. Walker: T. J. Walker, "Reminiscences of the Civil War," 65; Reddick: H. W. Reddick, *Seventy-Seven Years in Dixie*, 48; Flynt: T. L. Flynt, "Report of Lieut. Thomas Flynt, Sixth Texas Infantry," 748.
60. John W. Sparkman, *The Diary of Sergt. John W. Sparkman*, 71.
61. Mims: Wilbur F. Mims, "War History of the Prattville Dragoons," SRNBP; teamsters retreat with wagons: Werina Goborin, *The Atlanta Campaign* (New York: AnVi Open Source Knowledge Trust, 2015), 130.
62. Richard Beard, "To the Editor," *Military Essays and Recollections*, 336, 337.
63. Lot D. Young, *Reminiscences of a Soldier of the Orphan Brigade*, 91.
64. W. E. Preston, "Unit History—33rd Alabama Infantry," ADAH.
65. T. L. Flynt, "Report of Lieut. Thomas Flynt, Sixth Texas Infantry," July 29, 1864, *OR*, ser. 1, vol. 38, pt. 3, p. 749.
66. James Cooper Nisbet, *Four Years on the Firing Line*, 312.
67. W. E. Preston, "Unit History 33rd Alabama Infantry," ADAH.
68. 9th Tennessee Infantry: T. J. Walker, "Reminiscences of the Civil War," 65; Spence: Mark Christ, *Getting Used to Being Shot At*, 98.
69. James Cooper Nisbet, *Four Years on the Firing Line*, 313.
70. Edwin Hansford Rennolds, *A History of the Henry County Commands*, 91.
71. T. J. Walker, "Reminiscences of the Civil War," 66.

72. W. E. Preston, "Unit History—33rd Alabama Infantry," ADAH.
73. James Robert Maxwell, *Autobiography of James Robert Maxwell*, 244.
74. 5th Tennessee Infantry: Edwin Hansford Rennolds, *A History of the Henry County Commands*, 91; cluster of men reaching and retreating from last Federal line: Edwin Hansford Rennolds, *A History of the Henry County Commands*, 92.
75. Benjamin Rountree, "Letters from a Confederate Soldier," 290.
76. Hosea Garret to his uncle, August 1, 1864, Hosea Garrett Jr. Civil War Letters, KRC, AHC.
77. W. E. Preston, "Unit History—33rd Alabama Infantry," ADAH.
78. Wirt Armistead Cate, *Two Soldiers*, 98, 99.
79. Union and Confederate figures for the Battle of Atlanta: Thomas Leonard Livermore, *Numbers and Losses in the Civil War in America*, 123; Young: Lot D. Young, *Reminiscences of a Soldier of the Orphan Brigade*, 91.
80. W. J. Worsham and C. W. Heiskell, *Old Nineteenth Tennessee Regiment*, 129.
81. Union sharpshooters: "How We Fight in Atlanta," *Harper's New Monthly Magazine* 29 (October 1864): 666; Walker: T. J. Walker, "Reminiscences of the Civil War," 67.
82. Fighting on the Sabbath: Wirt Armistead Cate, *Two Soldiers*, 99; Sparkman: John W. Sparkman, *The Diary of Sergt. John W. Sparkman*, 72; Hood's orders: E. H. Rennolds Diary, entry dated July 28, 1864, Special Collections Library, Univ. of Tennessee, Knoxville.
83. James Robert Maxwell, *Autobiography of James Robert Maxwell*, 247.
84. W. E. Preston, "Unit History—33rd Alabama Infantry," ADAH.
85. Stanley F. Horn, *The Army of Tennessee*, 360; Stephen Davis, *Atlanta Will Fall*, 153.
86. Edward McMorries, "History of the First Regiment Alabama Volunteer Infantry," ADAH, 76–77.
87. Stanley F. Horn, *The Army of Tennessee*, 360; Stephen Davis, *Atlanta Will Fall*, 153; Starke Oliver, "Report of Capt. Starke H. Oliver, Twenty-fourth Alabama Infantry, of operations July 28," August 2, 1864, *OR*, ser. 1, vol. 38, pt. 3, p. 783.
88. Robert Jarman, "The History of Company K, 27th Mississippi Infantry," MDAH.
89. Wirt Armistead Cate, *Two Soldiers*, 108.
90. Smith: Austin W. Smith, "Service with the 4th Louisiana Battalion," *Confederate Veteran* 19, no. 11 (November 1911): 542; Oliver: Starke Oliver, "Report of Capt. Starke H. Oliver, Twenty-fourth Alabama Infantry, of operations July 28," August 2, 1864, *OR*, ser. 1, vol. 38, pt. 3, p. 783.
91. Edward McMorries, "History of the First Regiment Alabama Volunteer Infantry," ADAH, 78.

92. Edward McMorries, "History of the First Regiment Alabama Volunteer Infantry," ADAH, 79.
93. Sherman: William T. Sherman, *Memoirs of General William T. Sherman*, vol. 2, p. 91; Hood: John Bell Hood, *Advance and Retreat*, 195; Union and Confederate figures for Battle of Ezra Church: Thomas Leonard Livermore, *Numbers and Losses in the Civil War in America*, 124; Patrick: Robert Patrick, *Reluctant Rebel*, ed. F. Jay Taylor, 200.
94. Confederates saw battles as victories: Larry J. Daniel, *Soldiering in the Army of Tennessee*, 144; Hardee report: W. J. Hardee, "Report of the Operations of My Corps About Atlanta," April 5, 1865, *OR*, ser. 1, vol. 38, pt. 3, p. 699; Banks: R. W. Banks, *The Battle of Franklin, November 30, 1864*, p. 18; Sparkman: John W. Sparkman, *The Diary of Sergt. John W. Sparkman*, 72; Neal: Andrew Neal, diary entry dated August 4, 1864, Andrew Jackson Neal Papers, EU; Jarman: Robert Jarman, "The History of Company K, 27th Mississippi Infantry," MDAH; Crittenden: John Crittenden to his wife, Bettie, July 24, 1864, AUA; Spence: Mark Christ, *Getting Used to Being Shot At*, 98; Confederate preference for aggressive attacks: Grady McWhiney and Perry D. Jamieson, *Attack and Die*, 191.
95. Dismounting of Roddy's Cavalry Brigade: J. P. Cannon, *Inside of Rebeldom*, 242, 243; 3rd Alabama Cavalry: Wilbur F. Mims "War History of the Prattville Dragoons," SRNBP; Hood's musket orders: Kate Cumming, *A Journal of Hospital Life in the Confederate Army of Tennessee*, 148.
96. Warrick: Thomas Warrick to his wife, Martha, August 10, 1864, Thomas Warrick Papers, ADAH; wounding of 30th Tennessee Infantry soldiers: Diary of L. Jackson Sanders, entry dated October 26, 1864, SRNBP; Littlejohn: Elbridge Littlejohn, "The Civil War Letters of Elbridge Littlejohn," pt. 2, p. 27; Alabama soldier "J": Kate Cumming, *A Journal of Hospital Life in the Confederate Army of Tennessee*, 148.
97. Jordan: Stephen Jordan Diary, entry dated August 7, 1864, TSLA; Mims: Wilbur F. Mims, "War History of the Prattville Dragoons," SRNBP; Littlejohn: Elbridge Littlejohn, "The Civil War Letters of Elbridge Littlejohn," pt. 2, p. 28; Baker: T. G. Baker, "Sketch of T. G. Baker," *Recollections and Reminiscences*, 135, Southern History Collection, BPL.
98. Davis description: Compiled Service Record of Newton Davis, 24th Alabama Infantry, National Archives; Davis letter: Newton Davis to his wife, Bettie, August 9, 1864, Newton N. Davis Papers, ADAH.
99. King: Edward King to his aunt Elizabeth Barkley, July 29, 1864, Barkley and King Family Civil War Correspondence, KRC, AHC; McDermid: Benjamin Rountree, "Letters from a Confederate Soldier," 291, 292; Chambers: W. P. Chambers, *Chamber's Confederate Journal*, 89; Williams: Hiram Smith Williams, Lewis Nicholas Wynne, and Robert A. Taylor, *This War So*

Horrible, 107; Vann: Samuel King Vann and Nancy Elizabeth Neel Vann, *"Most Lovely Lizzie,"* 41; Wharton: Richard Wharton, diary entry dated August 3, 1864, Richard Wharton Papers, Southern Historical Collection, Manuscripts Department, Wilson Library, UNCSHC; Young: Lot D. Young, *Reminiscences of a Soldier of the Orphan Brigade*, 94.

100. James Cooper Nisbet, *Four Years on the Firing Line*, 315.
101. Confederate conscription law: Confederate States of America, *Laws of Congress in Regard to Taxes, Currency and Conscription, Passed February 1864* (Richmond: James E. Goode, 1864), 29; Confederate versus Union conscription: James R. Arnold and Roberta Wiener, *American Civil War: The Essential Reference Guide* (Santa Barbara, CA: ABC-CLIO, 2011), 60; Union conscriptions ending at inopportune times: Chris Perello, *The Quest for Annihilation: The Role and Mechanics of Battle in the American Civil War* (Bakersfield, CA: Strategy and Tactics Press, 2009), 54; Millican: Frank Millican to his sweetheart Sarah Delosier, August 9, 1864, in Frank Millican Letters, Civil War Letters of East Tennessee, vol. 2, Southern History Collection, BPL.
102. Richard M. McMurry, "Confederate Morale in the Atlanta Campaign of 1864," 229.
103. Porcher: John Porcher, dictated to his daughter Elinor Porcher, "Father's War Story," John Porcher Papers, *Recollections and Reminiscences*, 383, Southern History Collection, BPL; Key diary and civilians burrowing for safety: Wirt Armistead Cate, *Two Soldiers*, 108; Spence: Mark Christ, *Getting Used to Being Shot At*, 100.
104. Start of August 20 engagement: James Robert Maxwell, *Autobiography of James Robert Maxwell*, 249; Little: George Little, *A History of Lumsden's Battery*, 49; end of engagement: James Robert Maxwell, *Autobiography of James Robert Maxwell*, 249.
105. J. P. Cannon, *Inside of Rebeldom*, 247.
106. Hiram Smith Williams, *This War So Horrible*, 108, 109.
107. Jones: Edgar W. Jones, "History of the 18th Alabama Infantry," ADAH; Wharton: Richard Wharton, diary entry dated August 7, 1864, Richard Wharton Papers, Southern Historical Collection, Manuscripts Department, Wilson Library, UNCSHC.
108. Union penetration of South created dilemma for Confederate soldiers: Mark A. Weitz, *More Damning Than Slaughter*, 122; Key: Wirt Armistead Cate, *Two Soldiers*, 120; Miller: George Knox Miller, *An Uncompromising Secessionist*, 247; Garrett: Hosea Garrett to his uncle, August 1, 1864, Hosea Garrett Jr. Civil War Letters, KRC, AHC; interrupted communication lines: Charles Roberts to his wife, July 18, 1864, Charles Roberts Collection, Civil War Archive, UM; Higgins: George Washington Higgins to his wife, August

2, 1864, Corinth National Park; Confederates deserting to protect families: Weitz, *More Damning Than Slaughter*, 30.

109. Key: Wirt Armistead Cate, *Two Soldiers*, 120; Athey: George Athey to his father, September 5, 1864, George Athey Letters, SRNBP; Williams: Hiram Smith Williams, *This War So Horrible*, 110; Sparkman: John W. Sparkman, *The Diary of Sergt. John W. Sparkman*, 73; Watson: William. J. Watson Diary, entry dated August 27, 1864, TSLA.
110. Russell S. Bonds, *War Like the Thunderbolt*, 253.
111. W. E. Preston, "Unit History—33rd Alabama Infantry," ADAH.
112. Edgar W. Jones, "History of the 18th Alabama Infantry," ADAH.
113. Cooper: James Cooper, "Memoir of James Cooper, 20th Tennessee Infantry," NTPL; weapon details: James Jones, Inspection of Smith's (also known as Tyler's) Brigade, September 18, 1864.
114. E. H. Rennolds Diary, entry dated August 31, 1864, UTK.
115. Robert M. Magill, *Personal Reminiscences of a Confederate Soldier*, 62.
116. W. E. Preston, "Unit History—33rd Alabama Infantry," ADAH.
117. Hiram Smith Williams, *This War So Horrible*, 110.
118. William McMurray, *History of the Twentieth Tennessee Regiment Volunteer Infantry*, 419.
119. W. J. Worsham and C. W. Heiskell, *Old Nineteenth Tennessee Regiment*, 132.
120. George C. Bittle, "Fighting Men View the Western War, 1862–1864," *Florida Historical Quarterly* 47, no. 1 (July 1968): 32.
121. A. D. Kirwan, *Johnny Green of the Orphan Brigade*, 157.
122. Preston: W. E. Preston, "Unit History—33rd Alabama Infantry," ADAH; Green: A. D. Kirwan, *Johnny Green of the Orphan Brigade*, 158; Spence: Mark Christ, *Getting Used to Being Shot At*, 103.
123. Thomas Leonard Livermore, *Numbers and Losses in the Civil War in America*, 125.
124. Hood: John Bell Hood, *Advance and Retreat*, 215; Green: A. D. Kirwan, *Johnny Green of the Orphan*, 157; Neal: Andrew Neal Diary, entry dated July 13, 1864, Andrew Jackson Neal Papers, EU.
125. Chambers: W. P. Chambers, *Chamber's Confederate Journal*, 87; Scott: John Thomas Scott to his sweetheart Miss Philo, August 1, 1864, and September 5, 1864, AUA; Matthews: W. E. Matthews Memoir, ADAH; Adair: Robert Adamson, "Gov. Harris at the Close of the War," *Confederate Veteran* 5, no. 8 (August 1897): 402; Rea: R. N. Rea, "Mississippi Soldier of the Confederacy," *Confederate Veteran* 30, no. 8 (August 1922): 287.
126. W. P. Chambers, *Chamber's Confederate Journal*, 91–92.
127. Ellen McCord, "Cared for a Sick Soldier Boy," *Confederate Veteran* 3, no. 1 (January 1895): 9.
128. Strong: Russell S. Bonds, *War Like the Thunderbolt*, xxi; Brown: Allen D.

Candler, *The Confederate Records of the State of Georgia*, vol. 2 (Atlanta, GA: C. P. Byrd, state printer, 1909), 735; Lincoln's improved reelection chances, Atlanta as Confederate supply hub, and goods destroyed: Thomas Lawrence Connelly, *Autumn of Glory*, 468; Hood: John Bell Hood, *Advance and Retreat*, 253.

129. Number of fighting men remaining in Army of Tennessee: John Bell Hood and Stephen M. Hood, *The Lost Papers of Confederate General John Bell Hood*, 100; remaining artillery equipment and ammunition: Larry J. Daniel, *Cannoneers in Gray: The Field Artillery of the Army of Tennessee, 1861–1865*, 176, 179; Confederate cavalry: Dabney H. Maury, Major General Commanding, "Headquarters District of the Gulf," August 9, 1864, *OR*, ser. 1, vol. 39, pt. 1, p. 427; and Spencer Tucker et al., *American Civil War*, 2120.
130. William T. Sherman, *Memoirs of General William T. Sherman*, vol. 2, p. 130.

2. "Such Men Will Not Be Conquered"

1. Thomas Deavenport Journal, entry dated September 23, 1864, TSLA.
2. Army of Tennessee in retreat: James L. McDonough and Thomas Lawrence Connelly, *Five Tragic Hours: The Battle of Franklin*, 5; Lanning: James Lanning Diary, entry dated September 26, 1864, ADAH; regrouping at Lovejoy's Station: Newton Davis to his wife, Bettie, September 4, 1864, Newton N. Davis Papers, ADAH.
3. Spence: Mark Christ, *Getting Used to Being Shot At*, 103; Green: A. D. Kirwan, *Johnny Green of the Orphan Brigade*, 157; Cannon: J. P. Cannon, Noel Crowson, and John V. Brogden, *Bloody Banners and Barefoot Boys*, 59; Chambers: W. P. Chambers, *Chamber's Confederate Journal*, 93; Adair: Robert Adamson, "Gov. Harris at the Close of the War," 402; Whetstone: Adam Henry Whetstone, *History of the Fifty-Third Alabama Volunteer Infantry Mounted*, 74; Roberts: Charles Roberts to his wife, September 6, 1864, Charles Roberts Collection, Civil War Archive, UM.
4. Etter: Diary of Risenar Etter, entry dated September 15, 1864, SRNBP; Scott: John Thomas Scott to his sweetheart Miss Philo, September 24, 1864, and November 4, 1864, AUA; Johnson: Larry Johnson, "16th Regiment Tennessee Infantry, CSA," SRNBP; Athey: George Athey to his father, September 5, 1864, George Athey Letters, SRNBP; Douglas: Jeff Toalson, *No Soap, No Pay, Diarrhea, Dysentery & Desertion*, 216; Confederates and the oath of allegiance: John Bennitt Diary, entry dated September 6, 1864, GVSUA.
5. Jarman: Robert Jarman, "The History of Company K, 27th Mississippi Infantry," MDAH; Patrick: Robert Patrick, *Reluctant Rebel*, ed. F. Jay Taylor, 230.
6. Cumming: Kate Cumming, *A Journal of Hospital Life in the Confederate Army of Tennessee*, 148; *Chattanooga Rebel*: "Yankee Exultation," *Chattanooga Rebel* (Griffin, GA), September 8, 1864; *Wilmington Journal*: "The

Facts," *Wilmington (NC) Journal*, September 15, 1864; *Yorkville Enquirer*: "From Georgia," *Yorkville (SC) Enquirer*, September 21, 1864; *Daily Dispatch*: "From Georgia," *Daily Dispatch* (Richmond, VA), September 28, 1864; surplus houses: Alva Sinks to his father, George Sinks, September 20, 1864, Alva Sinks Letters, GHS, Savannah, GA.

7. Warrick: Thomas Warrick to his wife, Martha, September 5 and 8, 1864, Thomas Warrick Papers, ADAH; Roberts: Charles Roberts to his wife, September 6, 1864, Charles Roberts Collection, Civil War Archive, UM; choice between duty to nation and duty to family: Mark A. Weitz, *More Damning Than Slaughter*, 30.
8. Lanning: James Lanning Diary, entry dated September 29, 1864, ADAH; Vann: Samuel King Vann and Nancy Elizabeth Neel Vann, *"Most Lovely Lizzie,"* 51; Dent: Stouten Hubert Dent to his wife, Anna, September 13, 1864, S. H. Dent Papers, AUA; slow and inaccurate casualty reports: Drew Gilpin Faust, *This Republic of Suffering*, 104.
9. Crane: Daniel Cone, *Last to Join the Fight: The 66TH Georgia Infantry*, 147; Higgins: George Washington Higgins to his wife, September 14, 1864, Corinth National Park; Cannon: J. P. Cannon, Noel Crowson, and John V. Brogden, *Bloody Banners and Barefoot Boys*, 59; Maxwell: James Robert Maxwell, *Autobiography of James Robert Maxwell*, 254.
10. Henderson: W. H. Henderson to his father and mother, September 9, 1864, William Henry Henderson Papers, PMNC; Deavenport: Thomas Deavenport Journal, entry dated September 23, 1864, TSLA.
11. Memoir of W. E. Preston, ADAH.
12. Robert Jarman, "The History of Company K, 27th Mississippi Infantry," MDAH.
13. Soldiers aware of McClellan as Democratic presidential nominee: J. P. Cannon, Noel Crowson, and John V. Brogden, *Bloody Banners and Barefoot Boys*, 59; Hardman: C. T. Hardman to his wife, September 2, 1864, BPL; Dent: Stouten Dent to his wife, Anna, September 10, 1864, S. H. Dent Papers, AUA.
14. Higgins: George Washington Higgins to his wife, September 14, 1864, Corinth National Park; Henderson: Jesse Henderson Diary, entry dated September 11, 1864, UM; Dent: Stouten Dent to his wife, Anna, September 10, 1864, S. H. Dent Papers, AUA; Cannon: J. P. Cannon, Noel Crowson, and John V. Brogden, *Bloody Banners and Barefoot Boys*, 60; Bibles delivered to Confederate army: "Bible from the North For Hood's Army," *Daily Dispatch* (Richmond, VA), September 29, 1864.
15. Robert Patrick, *Reluctant Rebel*, ed. F. Jay Taylor, 238.
16. Wirt Armistead Cate, *Two Soldiers*, 135–36.
17. Hood's claims: John Bell Hood, *Advance and Retreat*, 218; historians'

figures: James L. McDonough and Thomas Lawrence Connelly, *Five Tragic Hours,* 5; and John Bell Hood and Stephen M. Hood, *The Lost Papers of Confederate General John Bell Hood,* 100; departure of Georgia militia: Robert M. Magill and Brenda D. Phillips, *Personal Reminiscences of a Confederate Soldier Boy,* 63; Davis: Newton Davis to his wife, Bettie, September 8, 1864, Newton N. Davis Papers, ADAH; Hood's order on teamsters: *OR*, ser. 1, vol. 39, pt. 1, p. 804; Cumming: Kate Cumming, *A Journal of Hospital Life in the Confederate Army of Tennessee,* 149.

18. Warrick: Thomas Warrick to his wife, Martha, September 25, 1864, Thomas Warrick Papers, ADAH; Hardman: C. T. Hardman to his wife, September 2, 1864, BPL; Davis: Newton Davis to his wife, Bettie, September 8, 1864, Newton N. Davis Papers, ADAH; Roberts: Charles Roberts to his wife, September 6, 1864, UM; Dent: Stouten Dent to his wife, Anna, September 13, 1864, S. H. Dent Papers, AUA; 1st Alabama obtaining supplies: Daniel P. Smith and Jim D. Moody, *Company K First Alabama Regiment,* 108.
19. Hood requested pay for army: Francis Shoup, "Journal of Francis A. Shoup, C.S. Army, Chief of Staff," *OR*, ser. 1, vol. 39, pt. 1, p. 804; McLeod: William McLeod Diary, entry dated September 26, 1864, FSA.
20. Davis: Newton Davis to his wife, Bettie, September 13, 1864, ADAH; Dent: Stouten Dent to his wife, Anna, September 13, 1864, AUA; Cannon: J. P. Cannon, Noel Crowson, and John V. Brogden, *Bloody Banners and Barefoot Boys,* 60.
21. Etter: Diary of Risenar Etter, entry dated September 12, 1864, SRNBP; Roberts: Charles Roberts to his wife, September 20, 1864, UM; Confederate soldier 1864 pay: W. Buck Yearns, *The Confederate Congress,* 113; food prices: Newton Davis to his wife, Bettie, September 25, 1864, Newton N. Davis Papers, ADAH; Maxwell: James Robert Maxwell, *Autobiography of James Robert Maxwell,* 248.
22. Sparkman: John W. Sparkman, *The Diary of Sergt. John W. Sparkman,* 73; theft in Quarles's Brigade: Robert Patrick, *Reluctant Rebel,* ed. F. Jay Taylor, 230; Chambers: W. P. Chambers, *Chamber's Confederate Journal,* 93; Jarman: Robert Jarman, "The History of Company K, 27th Mississippi Infantry," MDAH.
23. Sherman's order to leave Atlanta: William Tecumseh Sherman, *Memoirs of General William T. Sherman,* vol. 2, p. 118; Davis: Newton Davis to his wife, Bettie, September 8, 1864, ADAH; Hood's response to Sherman's order: John Bell Hood, *Advance and Retreat,* 230.
24. Deavenport: Thomas Deavenport Journal, entry dated September 23, 1864, TSLA; Roberts: Charles Roberts to his wife, September 6, 1864, UM; Key: Wirt Armistead Cate, *Two Soldiers,* 139.
25. Rumor the Army of Tennessee would go to Virginia: Newton Davis to his

wife, Bettie, September 16, 1864, ADAH; Scott: John Thomas Scott to his sweetheart Miss Philo, September 24, 1864, AUA; Eggleston: Edward Noyes, "Excerpts from the Civil War Diary of E. T. Eggleston," *Tennessee Historical Quarterly* 17 (December 1958): 350.

26. Hood leading his forces north: John Bell Hood, *Advance and Retreat*, 247; Hood's claims of unanimous support from generals: John Bell Hood to the historian Sarah Dorsey, March 30, 1867, published in John Bell Hood and Stephen M. Hood, *The Lost Papers of Confederate General John Bell Hood*, 106; Hood urging men to endure difficult campaign: John W. Sparkman, *The Diary of Sergt. John W. Sparkman*, 73.
27. Sanders: D. W. Sanders, "Hood's Tennessee Campaign," *Southern Bivouac* 3 (1884–1885): 100; Stewart: Alexander Stewart, "Report of Lieut. Gen. Alexander P. Stewart, C. S. Army, Commanding a Corps," *OR*, ser. 1, vol. 39, pt. 1, p. 812; Lee: Stephen D. Lee, "Report of Lieut. Gen. Stephen D. Lee, C. S. Army, Commanding a Corps," *OR*, ser. 1, vol. 39, pt. 1, p. 810; Bates: James C. Bates and Richard G. Lowe, *A Texas Cavalry Officer's Civil War*, 324; Walker: C. Irvine Walker, "Sketch of the Career of the 10th and 19th South Carolina," *Recollections and Reminiscences*, 366, Southern History Collection, BPL; Clayton: Henry Clayton to his wife, September 21, 1864, UA; Hager: George Hager, "Second Tennessee Cavalry," in *The Military Annals of Tennessee. First Series: Embracing a Review of Military Operations, with Regimental Histories and Memorial Rolls*, ed. John Berrien Lindsley, (Nashville: J. M. Lindsley and Co., 1886), 619.
28. "From the Georgia Front," *Edgefield (SC) Advertiser*, September 7, 1864; "Highly Important from the Georgia Front," *Wilmington (NC) Journal*, September 22, 1864; "From Richmond," *Wilmington (NC) Journal*, September 29, 1864; "From Georgia," *Daily Dispatch* (Richmond, VA), September 22, 1864; "Gen. Hood's Army," *Western Democrat* (Charlotte, NC), October 4, 1864.
29. Sherman: William T. Sherman, *Memoirs of General William T. Sherman*, vol. 2, p. 144; Lincoln: Anne J. Bailey, *The Chessboard of War*, xiv; Grant: John Russell Young, *Around the World with General Grant*, vol. 2, pp. 294–95.
30. Davis's speech: Jefferson Davis, "Speech at Macon, Georgia," September 23, 1864, Jefferson Davis Papers, RU; Davis endorsing Hood's plan: D. W. Sanders, "Hood's Tennessee Campaign," 103, Southern History Collection, BPL; Grant's response: James M. McPherson, *Battle Cry of Freedom*, 808.
31. Hood: John Bell Hood, *Advance and Retreat*, 253; Bevier: R. S. Bevier, *History of the First and Second Missouri Confederate Brigades*, 243; Worsham and Heiskell: W. J. Worsham and C. W. Heiskell, *Old Nineteenth Tennessee Regiment*, 134; Porcher and General Manigault quotation: John Porcher, dictated to his daughter Elinor Porcher, "Father's War Story," *Recollections*

and Reminiscences, 385, Southern History Collection, BPL; Foster: Samuel T. Foster and Norman D. Brown, *One of Cleburne's Command*, 135.

32. Daily training: J. P. Cannon, Noel Crowson, and John V. Brogden, *Bloody Banners and Barefoot Boys*, 59; Henderson: Jesse Henderson Diary, entry dated September 11, 1864, UM; officer inspections: William McLeod Diary, entries dated September 13, 17, FSA; Patrick: Robert Patrick, *Reluctant Rebel*, ed. F. Jay Taylor, 228; Porcher: John Porcher, dictated to his daughter Elinor Porcher, "Father's War Story," *Recollections and Reminiscences*, 383, Southern History Collection, BPL.
33. Orphan Brigade sent south to recuperate: John Jackman and William C. Davis, *Diary of a Confederate Soldier*, 127; consolidated Tennessee regiment: E. H. Rennolds Diary, entry dated July 13, 1864, UTK; Johnson: Larry Johnson, "16th Regiment Tennessee Infantry, CSA," SRNBP; Yeatman: William Yeatman, "My Military Life," SRNBP; Lavender: John W. Lavender and Ted R. Worley, *The War Memoirs of Captain John W. Lavender*, 117; Hardee ordered to leave: Francis Shoup, "Journal of Francis A. Shoup, C.S. Army, Chief of Staff," *OR*, ser. 1, vol. 39, pt. 1, p. 805.
34. Barron: S. B. Barron, "Wade's Supernumary Scouts," *Confederate Veteran* 11, no. 3 (March 1902): 115; assault on Dalton, GA, supply depot: "Dispatch from Gen. Hood," *Alexandria Gazette* (Alexandria, DC) September 5, 1864; action near Athens, AL: William Chester, "Notes and Documents: The Diary of Captain Elisha Tompkin Hollis," *West Tennessee Historical Papers* 39 (1985): 110; capture of Sulfur Creek trestle bridge: George Hager, "Second Tennessee Cavalry," in *Military Annals of Tennessee. First Series*, 620.
35. McCleary: A. C. McLeary, "Humorous Incidents of the Civil War," UNCSHC, 10; Sloan: William Sloan Diary, entry dated September 28, 1864, TSLA; Joy: Charles Gore Joy, "The Stampede at La Fayette, Ga.," 473.
36. Adam Henry Whetstone, *History of the Fifty-Third Alabama Volunteer Infantry Mounted* (Montgomery, AL: Confederate Publishing Company, 1985), 58.
37. Rumors of Forrest's exploits: Newton Davis to his wife, Bettie, September 25, 1864, Newton N. Davis Papers, ADAH; Lanning: James Lanning Diary, entry dated October 1, 1864, ADAH; Kelley: Samuel Kelley letter home, September 8, 1864, ADAH; Georgia newspaper correspondent: "Gen. Hood's Army," *Western Democrat* (Charlotte, NC), October 4, 1864.
38. Three days' worth of rations: E. H. Rennolds Diary, entry dated September 28, 1864, UTK; Foster: Samuel T. Foster and Norman D. Brown, *One of Cleburne's Command*, 138; Higgins: George Washington Higgins to his wife, September 28, 1864, Corinth National Park.
39. Nelson: H. K. Nelson, "Tennessee, A Grave or a Free Home," *Confederate Veteran* 15, no. 11 (March 1916): 508; crossing the Chattahoochee River:

John Bell Hood, *Advance and Retreat*, 256; Etter: Diary of Risenar Etter, entry dated October 1, 1864, SRNBP; Rennolds: E. H. Rennolds Diary, entries dated September 29, 30, October 6, 1864, UTK; Smith: Robert Davis Smith, *Confederate Diary of Robert D. Smith*, 75; Harvie: *OR*, ser. 1, vol. 39, pt. 3, p. 781.

40. "Latest News," *North Carolina Standard* (Raleigh, NC), September 30, 1864; "Cheering," *Daily Dispatch* (Richmond, VA), October 12, 1864; "The Macon Papers," *Daily Dispatch* (Richmond, VA), October 19, 1864.
41. McNeill: J. H. McNeill, "Humors of Soldier Life," *Confederate Veteran* 1, no. 10 (October 1893): 309; Nelson: H. K. Nelson, "Tennessee, A Grave or a Free Home," 508.
42. Edgar W. Jones, "History of the 18th Alabama Infantry," ADAH.
43. Rennolds: E. H. Rennolds Diary, October 4, 1864, UTK; Williams: Hiram Smith Williams, Lewis Nicholas Wynne, and Robert A. Taylor, *This War So Horrible*, 115; Lanning: James Lanning Diary, entry dated October 4, 1864, ADAH.
44. Chambers: W. P. Chambers, *Chamber's Confederate Journal*, 94; John Battle to his wife, September 28, 1864, John Battle Letters, GSA.
45. Assault at Big Shanty, GA: *OR*, ser. 1, vol. 39, pt. 1, p. 806; Smith: Robert Davis Smith, *Confederate Diary of Robert D. Smith*, 75; Confederate victory and prisoners captured: John Bell Hood, *Advance and Retreat*, 256; Murphree: Joel Dyer Murphree, "Autobiography and Civil War Letters of Joel Murphree of Troy, Alabama, 1864–1865," 196.
46. Smith: Robert Davis Smith, *Confederate Diary of Robert D. Smith*, 75; Sparkman: John W. Sparkman, *The Diary of Sergt. Sparkman*, 75.
47. Destruction of fifteen miles of railroad: Robert Davis Smith, *Confederate Diary of Robert D. Smith*, 75; Foster: Samuel T. Foster and Norman D. Brown, *One of Cleburne's Command*, 140; Sparkman: John W. Sparkman, *The Diary of Sergt. John W. Sparkman*, 76.
48. Sherman's troops pursuing Army of Tennessee: William T. Sherman, *Memoirs of General William T. Sherman*, vol. 2, p. 146; northern press coverage: "A Puzzle," *Daily Ohio Statesman* (Columbus, OH), October 20, 1864; Patrick: Robert Patrick, *Reluctant Rebel*, ed. F. Jay Taylor, 232; rumor of Union retreat: Samuel T. Foster and Norman D. Brown, *One of Cleburne's Command*, 135; Davis's speech: Jefferson Davis, "Speech at Columbia," October 4, 1864, printed in Aaron Charles Sheehan-Dean, *The Civil War: The Final Year Told by Those Who Lived It* (New York: Library of America, 2014), 409.
49. Breakdown of Union and Confederate troops at Allatoona: Richard Todhunter, "Ector's Texas Brigade at the Battle of Allatoona," *Confederate Veteran* 26, no. 8 (August 1918): 340; a million rations at Union supply depot: Edwin Hansford Rennolds, *A History of the Henry County Commands*, 101.

50. Anderson: Ephraim Anderson, *Memoirs: Historical and Personal*, 392; Shotwell: R. H. Shotwell, "Hood's Campaign Through North Georgia," 311; Chambers: W. P. Chambers, *Chamber's Confederate Journal*, 95; Bevier: R. S. Bevier, *History of the First and Second Missouri Confederate Brigades*, 243.
51. Start of battle and demand for Federal surrender: Edward Noyes, "Excerpts from the Civil War Diary of E. T. Eggleston," 351; return of courier: R. S. Bevier, *History of the First and Second Missouri Confederate Brigades*, 243.
52. Position of Confederate troops: William Ludlow, *The Battle of Allatoona*, 14; position of artillery: Edward Noyes, "Excerpts from the Civil War Diary of E. T. Eggleston," 351.
53. W. P. Chambers, *Chamber's Confederate Journal*, 96.
54. Richard Todhunter, "Ector's Texas Brigade at the Battle of Allatoona," 341.
55. R. S. Bevier, *History of the First and Second Missouri Confederate Brigades*, 244.
56. R. N. Rea, "Mississippi Soldier of the Confederacy," 287.
57. 46th Mississippi Infantry charge: W. P. Chambers, *Chamber's Confederate Journal*, 95; Eggleston: Edward Noyes, "Excerpts from the Civil War Diary of E. T. Eggleston," 351.
58. Coleman: David Coleman, "Report of Col. David Coleman, Thirty-ninth North Carolina Infantry," *OR*, ser. 1, vol. 39, pt. 1, p. 821; Hampton: Ezekiel H. Hampton, "Report of Maj. Ezekiel H. Hampton, Twenty-ninth North Carolina Infantry, Ector's Brigade," *OR*, ser. 1, vol. 39, pt. 1, p. 821.
59. W. P. Chambers, *Chamber's Confederate Journal*, 95.
60. David Coleman, "Report of Col. David Coleman, Thirty-ninth North Carolina Infantry," *OR*, ser. 1, vol. 39, pt. 1, p. 822.
61. Ezekiel H. Hampton, "Report of Maj. Ezekiel H. Hampton, Twenty-ninth North Carolina Infantry, Ector's Brigade," *OR*, ser. 1, vol. 39, pt. 1, p. 821.
62. R. S. Bevier, *History of the First and Second Missouri Confederate Brigades*, 244.
63. Ezekiel H. Hampton, "Report of Maj. Ezekiel H. Hampton, Twenty-ninth North Carolina Infantry, Ector's Brigade," *OR*, ser. 1, vol. 39, pt. 1, p. 821.
64. Chambers: W. P. Chambers, *Chamber's Confederate Journal*, 96; Shotwell: R. H. Shotwell, "Hood's Campaign Through North Georgia," 311.
65. R. S. Bevier, *History of the First and Second Missouri Confederate Brigades*, 245.
66. Ezekiel H. Hampton, "Report of Maj. Ezekiel H. Hampton, Twenty-ninth North Carolina Infantry, Ector's Brigade," *OR*, ser. 1, vol. 39, pt. 1, p. 821.
67. W. P. Chambers, *Chamber's Confederate Journal*, 96, 97.
68. Bevier: R. S. Bevier, *History of the First and Second Missouri Confederate Brigades*, 245; Anderson: Ephraim Anderson, *Memoirs*, 393.

69. 29th North Carolina Infantry: Ezekiel H. Hampton, "Report of Maj. Ezekiel H. Hampton, Twenty-ninth North Carolina Infantry, Ector's Brigade," *OR*, ser. 1, vol. 39, pt. 1, p. 821; Coleman: David Coleman, "Report of Col. David Coleman, Thirty-ninth North Carolina Infantry," *OR*, ser. 1, vol. 39, pt. 1, p. 822.
70. Union recaptured supplies: John Bell Hood, *Advance and Retreat*, 260; French: Samuel G. French, "Reports of Maj. Gen. Samuel G. French, C. S. Army, Commanding a Division," *OR*, ser. 1, vol. 39, pt. 1, p. 813.
71. Bevier: R. S. Bevier, *History of the First and Second Missouri Confederate Brigades*, 243; erroneous report of large Union advance on French: *OR*, ser. 1, vol. 39, pt. 1, p. 802; northern press coverage: "Great Importance of Altoona," *Dayton (OH) Daily Empire*, October 20, 1864.
72. Confederate casualties at Allatoona: Richard Todhunter, "Ector's Texas Brigade at the Battle of Allatoona," 341; Eggleston: Edward Noyes, "Excerpts from the Civil War Diary of E. T. Eggleston," 351; Shotwell: R. H. Shotwell, "Hood's Campaign Through North Georgia," 311; Chambers: W. P. Chambers, *Chamber's Confederate Journal*, 95, 101.
73. French's Division targeting Dalton, GA, garrison: Edwin Hansford Rennolds, *A History of the Henry County Commands*, 101; destroying rail lines en route: J. P. Cannon, *Inside of Rebeldom*, 256; Rennolds: E. H. Rennolds Diary, entries dated October 10 and October 12, 1864, UTK; Howell: Wilson Howell Manuscript, Department of Archives and Manuscripts, BPL.
74. Samuel T. Foster and Norman D. Brown, *One of Cleburne's Command*, 138.
75. Sparkman: John W. Sparkman, *The Diary of Sergt. John W. Sparkman*, 75; Eggleston: Edward Noyes, "Excerpts from the Civil War Diary of E. T. Eggleston," 352; Smith: Robert Davis Smith, *Confederate Diary of Robert D. Smith*, 76; Cannon: J. P. Cannon, *Inside of Rebeldom*, 256.
76. Eggleston: Edward Noyes, "Excerpts from the Civil War Diary of E. T. Eggleston," 352; Lanning: James Lanning Diary, entry dated October 9, 1864, ADAH; Boyce: Joseph Boyce, "Missourians in the Battle of Franklin," *Confederate Veteran* 24, no. 3 (March 1916): 101.
77. Richard Harris, "Historical Sketch of Selden – Lovelace Battery," ADAH.
78. Harris: "Historical Sketch of Selden – Lovelace Battery," ADAH; Union cavalrymen unsuccessfully attacking the departing Confederates: Samuel T. Foster and Norman D. Brown, *One of Cleburne's Command*, 138.
79. Hood's demand for surrender: John Bell Hood, *Advance and Retreat*, 262; Hood's promise of parole for white soldiers and threat of no prisoners taken in assault: Lewis Johnson, "Reports of Col. Lewis Johnson," *OR*, ser. 1, vol. 39, pt. 1, p. 718; McLeod: William McLeod Diary, entry dated October, n.d., FSA.
80. Conflict between Johnson and Hood: Lewis Johnson, "Reports of Col.

Lewis Johnson," *OR*, ser. 1, vol. 39, pt. 1, p. 720; larger conflict between Union and Confederacy over treatment of prisoners: Paul J. Springer and Glenn Robins, *Transforming Civil War Prisons*, 14.

81. Confederate reports of captured men and material: *OR*, ser. 1, vol. 39, pt. 1, p. 809; little initial resistance by Union soldiers: Lewis Johnson, "Reports of Col. Lewis Johnson," *OR*, ser. 1, vol. 39, pt. 1, p. 718.
82. Watkins: Samuel R. Watkins, *"Company Aytch,"* 307.
83. Johnson: Lewis Johnson, "Reports of Col. Lewis Johnson," *OR*, ser. 1, vol. 39, pt. 1, pp. 720, 721.
84. Jones: Edgar W. Jones, "History of the 18th Alabama Infantry," ADAH; Rennolds: E. H. Rennolds Diary, October 13, 1864, UTK; Cannon: Newton Cannon and Campbell H. Brown, *The Reminiscences of Sergeant Newton Cannon*, 57; Nelson: H. K. Nelson, "Tennessee, A Grave or a Free Home," 508; Livingston: Archie Livingston to his brother, October 15, 1864, in Coski, ed., "I am In for Anything for Success," 77; Lanning: James Lanning Diary, entry dated October 15, 1864, ADAH.
85. H. W. Reddick, *Seventy-Seven Years in Dixie*, 48.
86. Federal units in pursuit: Edwin Hansford Rennolds, *A History of the Henry County Commands*, 102; 27th Mississippi crossing: Robert Jarman, "The History of Company K, 27th Mississippi Infantry," MDAH; broken bridge: E. H. Rennolds Diary, October 10, 1864, UTK; Smith: Robert Davis Smith, *Confederate Diary of Robert D. Smith*, 75.
87. Sloan: William Sloan Diary, entry dated October 14, 1864, TSLA; Tunnel Hill supply depot abandoned: "Sherman Changes the Seat of War," *Daily Ohio Statesman* (Columbus, OH), October 25, 1864.
88. Hardy: William Hardy to his wife, Sallie Hardy, October 8, 1864, USM; Hood: John Bell Hood, *Advance and Retreat*, 260; TX journalist reporting high morale: "By Wednesday's Mail," *Dallas (TX) Herald*, November 12, 1864; Battle: John Battle to his wife, October 11, 1864, GSA; Lanning: James Lanning Diary, entry dated October 7, 1864, ADAH; Foster: Samuel T. Foster and Norman D. Brown, *One of Cleburne's Command*, 140; Livingston: Archie Livingston to his father, October 9, 1864, in Coski, ed., "I am In for Anything for Success," 77; SC journalist reporting high morale: "From General Hood's Army," *Yorkville (SC) Enquirer*, November 2, 1864; Vann: Samuel King Vann and Nancy Elizabeth Neel Vann, *"Most Lovely Lizzie,"* 54.
89. Shotwell: R. H. Shotwell, "Hood's Campaign Through North Georgia," 312; Rennolds: E. H. Rennolds Diary, entries dated October 16, 17, and 18, 1864, UTK; Dixon: Mumford Dixon Diary, entry dated October 10, 1864, TSLA; Lanning: James Lanning Diary, entry dated October 1, 1864, ADAH; McDermid: Benjamin Rountree, "Letters from a Confederate Soldier," 295;

Howell: Wilson Howell Manuscript, Department of Archives and Manuscripts, BPL.

90. Soldiers' feet worn out: E. H. Rennolds Diary, October 17, 1864, UTK; Crittenden: John Crittenden to his wife, Bettie, October 15, 1864, AUA; Deavenport: Thomas Deavenport Journal, entry dated September 23, 1864, TSLA; Jarman: Robert Jarman, "The History of Company K, 27th Mississippi Infantry," MDAH.
91. Movement of forces of Hood and Wheeler: John Bell Hood, *Advance and Retreat*, 263, 268; position of Jackson's cavalry division: Jefferson Davis, Lynda Lasswell Crist, Barbara J. Rozek, Kenneth H. Williams, and Richard J. Sommers, eds., *The Papers of Jefferson Davis September 1864–May 1865* (Baton Rouge: Louisiana State Univ. Press, 2003), 207; forces of Hood and Sherman separated: R. S. Bevier, *History of the First and Second Missouri Confederate Brigades*, 246.
92. Thomas Deavenport Journal, entry dated October 23, 1864, TSLA.

3. "Everything Looks Like Desolation"

1. John Crittenden to his wife, Bettie, October 31, 1864, AUA.
2. Cold weather as Army of Tennessee entered Alabama and officers pushing the pace: W. W. McMillian, "Reminiscences of War of 1861," ADAH; soldiers starving: E. H. Rennolds Diary, October 25, 1864, UTK; longing for tobacco: R. S. Bevier, *History of the First and Second Missouri Confederate Brigades*, 247.
3. Sherman's instructions to Thomas: W. T. Sherman to General Thomas, October 20, 1864, *OR*, ser. 1, vol. 39, pt. 3, p. 178; forces available to Thomas: Thomas Van Horne and Edward Ruger, *History of the Army of the Cumberland*, 186; Sherman on Hood versus Johnston: W. T. Sherman to General Corse, October 7, 1864, in United States Senate, *Reports of Committees: 30th Congress, 1st Session–48th Congress, 2nd Session*, 219.
4. Murphree: Joel Dyer Murphree, "Autobiography and Civil War Letters of Joel Murphree of Troy, Alabama, 1864–1865," 197; Davis: Newton Davis Papers, Folder 4, 1864 Letters, ADAH; Crittenden: John Crittenden to his wife, Bettie, October 31, 1864, AUA.
5. Localized membership in companies and batteries from Alabama: Margaret E. Wagner, Gary W. Gallagher, and Paul Finkelman, *The Library of Congress Civil War Desk Reference* (New York: Simon and Schuster, 2002), 374; Alabama's regional organization: Edith Ziegler, *Schools in the Landscape: Localism, Cultural Tradition, and the Development of Alabama's Public Education System, 1865–1915* (Tuscaloosa: Univ. of Alabama Press, 2010), 1; percentage of Alabama batteries and companies from counties along the line of march: Willis Brewer, "Brief Historical Sketches of Military Organi-

zations Raised In Alabama During the Civil War," Alabama State Department of Archives and History, accessed on December 10, 2014, http://www.archives.alabama.gov/referenc/alamilor/mil_org.html.

6. Jones: Edgar W. Jones, "History of the 18th Alabama Infantry," ADAH; General French story: "Sammy Keep Your Shirt On," *Confederate Veteran* 1, no. 8 (August 1893): 239.
7. Rest and resupply October 20–21: Francis Shoup, "Journal of Francis A. Shoup, C.S. Army, Chief of Staff," *OR*, ser. 1, vol. 39, pt. 1, p. 807; men grateful for rest: Samuel Oswald Conley Diary, entry dated October 15, 1864, GSA; gathering food: George Little and James Robert Maxwell, *A History of Lumsden's Battery, C.S.A* (Tuscaloosa, AL: R. E. Rhodes Chapter, United Daughters of the Confederacy, 1905), 18; and James Robert Maxwell, *Autobiography of James Robert Maxwell of Tuskaloosa, Alabama* (New York: Greenberg, 1926), 253; Murphree: Joel Dyer Murphree, "Autobiography and Civil War Letters of Joel Murphree of Troy, Alabama, 1864–1865," 197; newly arrived recuperated men posing supply problems: E. H. Rennolds Diary, October 20, 1864, UTK; Sparkman: John W. Sparkman, *The Diary of Sergt. John W. Sparkman*, 76; McDermid: Benjamin Rountree, "Letters from a Confederate Soldier," 296.
8. Crittenden's wound: Carded Records Showing Military Service of Soldiers Who Fought in Confederate Organizations, compiled 1903–1927, documenting the period 1861–1865, Record Group 109, National Archives and Records Administration; Crittenden's third child: United States Census, 1880.
9. John Crittenden to his wife, Bettie, October 15, 1864, AUA.
10. Jones's attempt to visit family: Edgar W. Jones, "History of the 18th Alabama Infantry," ADAH; Confederate troops under constant threat from Union cavalry: Memoir of J. W. Preston, ADAH.
11. Wyeth: John A. Wyeth, *With Sabre and Scalpel: The Autobiography of a Soldier and Surgeon*, 316; Pillow: Gid. J. Pillow, "HDQRS. Vol. and Conscript Bureau, No. 2," July 23, 1863, *OR*, ser. 4, vol. 2, 680; and Gid. J. Pillow, "Brigadier-General Mackall," *OR*, ser. 4, vol. 2, 638; request to Wheeler: James Saunders, "Maj. Gen. Joseph Wheeler," January 30, 1864, *OR*, ser. 1, vol. 52, pt. 2, p. 614; 72nd Indiana Infantry: B. F. McGee and Wm. R. Jewell, *History of the 72d Indiana Volunteer Infantry*, 445.
12. On Alabamians loyal to the federal government, see, for example, *OR*, ser. 1, vol. 38, pt. 4, pp. 280, 307; Goodloe: Albert Theodore Goodloe, *Confederate Echoes*, 293; Etter: Diary of Risenar Etter, entry dated October 5, 1864, SRNBP; Dodge: *OR*, ser. 1, vol. 32, pt. 3, p. 274; Ridge: George Ridge, Testimony to the Southern Claims Commission.
13. Strict orders against straggling: W. E. Preston, "Memoir of W. E. Preston," ADAH; Kelley: Samuel Kelley Letters, ADAH; Higgins: George Washington

Higgins to his wife, October 21, 1864, Corinth National Park; Porcher: John Porcher, dictated to his daughter Elinor Porcher, "Father's War Story," *Recollections and Reminiscences*, 383, Southern History Collection, BPL; Smith: Daniel P. Smith and Jim D. Moody, *Company K First Alabama Regiment, or, Three Years in the Confederate Service* (Gaithersburg, MD: Butternut Press, 1984), 112, 118.

14. Rennolds: Edwin Hansford Rennolds, *A History of the Henry County Commands*, 102; 6th Alabama Cavalry: C. T. Hardman to his wife, October 24, 1864, BPL; Crittenden: John Crittenden Letters, AUA; Maxwell: James Robert Maxwell, *Autobiography of James Robert Maxwell*, 257; Roane: Larry J. Daniel, *Soldiering in the Army of Tennessee*, 36.
15. F. B., "A Nice Pair of Moccasins," *Southern Bivouac* 2 (1884–1885): 453.
16. Hood's rendezvous plans with Forrest: John Bell Hood, *Advance and Retreat*, 270; Federal defenders at Guntersville, AL: Michael Thomas Smith, *The 1864 Franklin-Nashville Campaign*, 26; Sherman on Hood's decision not to cross: W. T. Sherman, "Major-General Thomas," *OR*, ser. 1, vol. 39, pt. 3, p. 448; McDill: W. J. McDilll to his sister, [the letter is dated "Oct. 3rd./64," but this is clearly a misprint; based on information in the letter, it was written sometime between the Army of Tennessee's arrival in Florence in October 31, 1864, and McDill's death at the Battle of Franklin on November 30, 1864], *Civil War Letters*, vol. 1, West Tennessee, Southern History Collection, BPL; Hood's decision to cross at Decatur, AL: Alfred Roman, *The Military Operations of General Beauregard*, 293.
17. Major roads crossing in Decatur, AL: James Veatch, "Report of Brig. Gen. James C Veatch, U.S. Army," *OR*, ser. 1, vol. 32, pt. 1, p. 685; Decatur Road: T. A. Deland and A. Davis Smith, *Northern Alabama*, 427; railroads crossing in Decatur, AL: David M. Owens, *The Devil's Topographer: Ambrose Bierce and the American War Story*, 50; pontoon bridge over Tennessee River at Decatur, AL: Michael Thomas Smith, *Nashville Campaign*, 26; Hood's belief that Decatur could be easily captured: Alfred Roman, *The Military Operations of General Beauregard*, 293.
18. Position of Stewart's, Cheatham's, and Lee's Corps approaching Decatur: Noel Carpenter, *A Slight Demonstration: Decatur, October 1864*, 34; Gordon: G. W. Gordon, "Eleventh Tennessee Infantry," in *Military Annals of Tennessee. First Series*, 300.
19. Arrival near Decatur on October 26: Daniel P. Smith and Jim D. Moody, *Company K First Alabama Regiment*, 112; Littlejohn: Elbridge Littlejohn, "The Civil War Letters of Elbridge Littlejohn," pt. 2, p. 32; Smith: Daniel P. Smith and Jim D. Moody, *Company K First Alabama Regiment*, 113; Warrick: Thomas Warrick Papers, ADAH; 3rd Florida Infantry: J. W. Kellum, "Third Florida Regiment," *Confederate Veteran* 14, no. 12 (December

1906): 554; Clark: Walter A. Clark, *Under the Stars and Bars*, 153; 33rd Alabama Infantry: Memoir of J. W. Preston, ADAH.

20. James McNeilly, "Andersonville," *Confederate Veteran* 15, no. 1 (January 1907): 16.
21. Edgar W. Jones, "History of the 18th Alabama Infantry," ADAH.
22. Description of Union defenses at Decatur: Charles C. Doolittle, "The Defense of Decatur, Alabama," in Robert Hunter and W. H. Chamberlin, *Sketches of War History, 1861–1865: Papers Read Before the Ohio Commandery of the Military Order of the Loyal Legion of the United States* (Cincinnati: R. Clark, 1888), 266; Union gunboats near Decatur: Official Records of the Union and Confederate Navies, ser. 1, vol. 26, p. 573.
23. 10th Indiana Cavalry reports approaching Confederate army: Michigan Adjutant-General's Department and John Robertson, *Michigan in the War*, 387; Doolittle verifies report: Charles Doolittle, "Report of Col. Charles C. Doolittle, Eighteenth Michigan Infantry," *OR*, ser. 1, vol. 39, pt. 1, p. 700; and Robert Dunnavant, *Decatur, Alabama: Yankee Foothold in Dixie, 1861–1865*, 119.
24. Albert Theodore Goodloe, *Confederate Echoes*, 292.
25. 2nd Tennessee Union Cavalry: Robert Dunnavant, *Decatur, Alabama*, 119; Confederate skirmish line: Albert Theodore Goodloe, *Confederate Echoes*, 292; Spence: Alexander Spence to his sweetheart Amanda Wilson, November 3, 1864, Spence Family Collection, FU; Shannon: Isaac Shannon, "Sharpshooters with Hood's Army," *Confederate Veteran* 15, no. 3 (March 1907): 123.
26. Charles Doolittle, "Report of Col. Charles C. Doolittle," *OR*, ser. 1, vol. 39, pt. 1, p. 701.
27. Reinforcements arrive and sustain 2nd Tennessee Union Cavalry: Charles Doolittle, "Report of Col. Charles C. Doolittle," *OR*, ser. 1, vol. 39, pt. 1, p. 700; Sanders: Diary of L. Jackson Sanders, entry dated October 26, 1864, SRNBP.
28. Robert Dunnavant, *Decatur, Alabama*, 120.
29. Isaac Shannon, "Sharpshooter's with Hood's Army," 123.
30. Union infantrymen falling back: Robert Dunnavant, *Decatur, Alabama*, 120; Confederates waiting for reinforcements: Albert Theodore Goodloe, *Confederate Echoes*, 293.
31. Confederate artillery from Stewart's Corps opening fire on Union line: Edward Noyes, "Excerpts from the Civil War Diary of E. T. Eggleston," 353; Lumsden's Battery and Tarrant's Alabama Battery: Edward Tarrant, "After Action Report November 2, 1864," Joseph Jones Collection, TU; James Robert Maxwell, *Autobiography of James Robert Maxwell*, 258.
32. 5th Tennessee Infantry unhappy at Hood's orders to assault: Edwin Hansford Rennolds, *A History of the Henry County Commands*, 102; French:

Samuel Gibbs French, *Two Wars: An Autobiography of General Samuel G. French*, 288.

33. Doolittle reinforcing eastern flank of Union defenses: Charles Doolittle, "Report of Col. Charles C. Doolittle, Eighteenth Michigan Infantry," *OR*, ser. 1, vol. 39, pt. 1, p. 701; 19th Tennessee Infantry's failed advance: W. J. Worsham and C. W. Heiskell, *Old Nineteenth Tennessee Regiment*, 136; Miller: Noel Carpenter, *A Slight Demonstration*, 55; Ozanne: Isaac Shannon, "Sharpshooter's With Hood's Army," 123.
34. Arrival of Union reinforcements and General Granger: Charles Doolittle, "Report of Col. Charles C. Doolittle," *OR*, ser. 1, vol. 39, pt. 1, p. 701; Lt. Col. Williams ordering Tarrant's Battery forward: Edward Tarrant, "After Action Report November 2, 1864," Joseph Jones Collection, TU.
35. Positions of Confederate forces around Decatur: Francis Shoup, "Journal of Francis A. Shoup, C.S. Army, Chief of Staff," *OR*, ser. 1, vol. 39, pt. 1, p. 807; Confederates unprotected from rain: R. S. Granger to Major-General Thomas, October 27, 1864, *OR*, ser. 1, vol. 39, pt. 3, p. 469; Confederates falling into flooded rifle pits: John W. Lavender and Ted R. Worley, *The War Memoirs of Captain John W. Lavender*, 104; Union soldiers better protected from weather: R. S. Granger to Major-General Thomas, October 27, 1864, *OR*, ser. 1, vol. 39, pt. 3, p. 469.
36. Lavender: John W. Lavender and Ted R. Worley, *The War Memoirs of Captain John W. Lavender*, 104; dueling bands: Noel Carpenter, *A Slight Demonstration*, 65; Cheatham's men advancing through fog: R. S. Granger to Major-General Thomas, October 27, 1864, *OR*, ser. 1, vol. 39, pt. 3, p. 469.
37. Thomas's order and Union garrison confidence: Geo. Thomas to General Granger, October 27, 1864, *OR*, ser. 1, vol. 39, pt. 3, p. 469; and R. S. Granger to Major-General Thomas, October 27, 1864, *OR*, ser. 1, vol. 39, pt. 3, p. 469; more Federal reinforcements arrive and join fighting: Charles Doolittle, "Report of Col. Charles C. Doolittle," *OR*, ser. 1, vol. 39, pt. 1, p. 701; 14th Colored Infantry: Joseph T. Wilson, *The Black Phalanx*, 299; Given: George Schmutz, *History of the 102d Regiment*, 171.
38. Confederates continuing to push forward unsuccessfully: Francis Shoup, "Journal of Francis A. Shoup," *OR*, ser. 1, vol. 39, pt. 1, p. 807; rain storms reducing visibility: Samuel T. Foster and Norman D. Brown, *One of Cleburne's Command*, 142; Tarrant: Edward Tarrant, "After Action Report November 2, 1864," Joseph Jones Collection, TU.
39. Confederate soldiers digging in: George H. Thomas "Report of Operations," *OR*, series 1, vol. 39, pt. 1, p. 588; men without entrenching tools using cups: Daniel P. Smith and Jim D. Moody, *Company K First Alabama Regiment*, 113.
40. Gen. P. G. T. Beauregard at Hood's headquarters: Francis Shoup, "Journal of Francis A. Shoup, C.S. Army, Chief of Staff," *OR*, ser. 1, vol. 39, pt. 1, p.

807; Gen. Beauregard's critique of Hood's campaign: Alfred Roman, *The Military Operations of General Beauregard in the War*, 293.

41. Charles Doolittle, "Report of Col. Charles C. Doolittle, Eighteenth Michigan Infantry," *OR*, ser. 1, vol. 39, pt. 1, p. 702.

42. Movement of the 1st Alabama Infantry: Daniel P. Smith and Jim D. Moody, *Company K First Alabama Regiment*, 113; Federals capturing prisoners: R. S. Granger to Major-General Thomas, October 28, 1864, *OR*, ser. 1, vol. 39, pt. 3, p. 487; position of Stewart's, Cheatham's and Lee's Corps: Francis Shoup, "Journal of Francis A. Shoup, C.S. Army, Chief of Staff," *OR*, ser. 1, vol. 39, pt. 1, p. 807.

43. Number of Union troops at the garrison: Charles Doolittle, "Report of Col. Charles C. Doolittle, Eighteenth Michigan Infantry," *OR*, ser. 1, vol. 39, pt. 1, p. 702; number of Confederate soldiers: John Bell Hood and Stephen M. Hood, *The Lost Papers of Confederate General John Bell Hood*, 100; Federals preparing to attack on Oct. 28: George H. Thomas "Report of Operations," *OR*, series 1, vol. 39, pt. 1, p. 588; Federal officers gathering noncombatants: Charles Doolittle, "Report of Col. Charles C. Doolittle, Eighteenth Michigan Infantry," *OR*, ser. 1, vol. 39, pt. 1, p. 702; Gen. Granger positioning artillery and infantry: Robert Granger, "Report of Brig. Gen. Robert S. Granger U.S. Army, Commanding District of Northern Alabama," *OR*, ser. 1, vol. 39, pt. 1, p. 697.

44. Forty Confederates from 3rd Confederate Infantry taken prisoner: Mumford Dixon Diary, entry dated October 26, 1864, TSLA; Cooper: James Cooper, "Memoir of James Cooper, 20th Tennessee Infantry," NTPL; Pettus and Harlan: Albert Theodore Goodloe, *Confederate Echoes*, 292.

45. Fourteenth Colored Infantry attack and resulting casualties: Joseph T. Wilson, *The Black Phalanx*, 299; 2nd Tennessee counterattack and Union infantry disabling cannons: Robert Davis Smith, *Confederate Diary of Robert D. Smith*, 79.

46. Darlene Clark Hine and Earnestine Jenkins, *A Question of Manhood*, vol. 1, p. 557; Tennessee Civil War Centennial Commission, *Tennesseans in the Civil War: A Military History of Confederate and Union Units with Available Rosters of Personnel*, 176.

47. Union soldiers in high spirits: Joseph T. Wilson, *The Black Phalanx*, 299; Granger: General R. S. Granger to General Thomas, October 28, 1864, *OR*, ser. 1, vol. 39, pt. 3, p. 487; Thomas: Major-General Thomas to General R. S. Granger, October 28, 1864, *OR*, ser. 1, vol. 39, pt. 3, p. 487.

48. Confederates engaging Union gunboats and Eggleston: Edward Noyes, "Excerpts from the Civil War Diary of E. T. Eggleston," 353; Granger: Robert Granger, "Report of Brig. Gen. Robert S. Granger U. S. Army, Commanding District of Northern Alabama," *OR*, ser. 1, vol. 39, pt. 1, p. 698.

49. Hood's army scouting alternate river crossing: A. P. Mason, "Headquarters" *OR*, ser. 1, vol. 39, pt. 3, p. 865; distance between Confederate army and Union line: Noel Carpenter, *A Slight Demonstration*, 121; Granger: Robert Granger, "Decatur, Ala., October 29, 1864," *OR*, ser. 1, vol. 39, pt. 3, pp. 504, 505.
50. Doolittle: Charles Doolittle, "Report of Col. Charles C. Doolittle," *OR*, ser. 1, vol. 39, pt. 1, p. 703; McDill: W. J. McDilll to his sister, [the letter is dated "Oct. 3rd./64.," but this is clearly a misprint; based on information in the letter, it was written sometime between the Army of Tennessee's arrival in Florence in October 31, 1864, and McDill's death at the Battle of Franklin on November 30, 1864], *Civil War Letters*, vol. 1, West Tennessee, Southern History Collection, BPL; for Union newspaper accounts, see, for example, "Hood Repulsed at Decatur—Capture of Guns and Prisoners," *Evening Star* (Washington, DC), October 31, 1864; and "Good News from Decatur!" *Brownlow's Knoxville (TN) Whig and Rebel Ventilator*, November 2, 1864; for concern about another Confederate attack, see, for example, "Hood's Destination in Middle Tennessee," *Cleveland (OH) Morning Leader*, November 10, 1864.
51. For Confederate newspaper accounts, see, for example, "From Gen. Hood's Army," *Weekly Standard* (Raleigh, NC), November 23, 1864; position of Hood's headquarters and Lee's, Stewart's, and Cheatham's Corps: Francis Shoup, "Journal of Francis A. Shoup," *OR*, ser. 1, vol. 39, pt. 1, p. 807; wounded left behind and Murphree: Joel Dyer Murphree, "Autobiography and Civil War Letters of Joel Murphree of Troy, Alabama, 1864–1865," 197; relative numbers of Union and Confederate forces participating at Decatur: Charles Doolittle, "Report of Col. Charles C. Doolittle," *OR*, ser. 1, vol. 39, pt. 1, pp. 701, 703; Confederates forced west: "Hood's Destination in Middle Tennessee," *Cleveland (OH) Morning Leader*, November 10, 1864.
52. Lavender: John W. Lavender and Ted R. Worley, *The War Memoirs of Captain John W. Lavender*, 106; estimate of Union versus Confederate casualties at Decatur: Union Army, *A History of Military Affairs in the Loyal States*, 351; Sykes: John Collins, "Sad Story of the War," *Confederate Veteran* 6, no. 3 (March 1898): 116.
53. Hood: John Bell Hood, *Advance and Retreat*, 271; Spence: Alexander Spence to his sweetheart Amanda Wilson, November 3, 1864, Spence Family Collection, FU; Bates: James C. Bates and Richard G. Lowe, *A Texas Cavalry Officer's Civil War*, 327; Confederate journalist on Hood's intent: "From General Hood's Army," *Daily Dispatch* (Richmond, VA), November 16, 1864.
54. Smith: Daniel P. Smith and Jim D. Moody, *Company K First Alabama Regiment*, 113; extreme hunger and stealing corn from horses: Edwin Hansford Rennolds, *A History of the Henry County Commands*, 102; Nelson: H. K.

Nelson, "Tennessee, A Grave or a Free Home," 508; Spence: Alexander Spence to his sweetheart Amanda Wilson, November 3, 1864, Spence Family Collection, FU.

55. D. W. Sanders, "Hood's Tennessee Campaign," 251, Southern History Collection, BPL.
56. Smith: Daniel P. Smith and Jim D. Moody, *Company K First Alabama Regiment*, 113; Etter: Diary of Risenar Etter, entry dated October 5, 1864, SRNBP; Higgins: George Washington Higgins to his wife, November 1, 1864, Corinth National Park; Foster: Samuel T. Foster and Norman D. Brown, *One of Cleburne's Command*, 143; Davis: Newton Davis Papers, ADAH.
57. Sparkman: John W. Sparkman, *The Diary of Sergt. John W. Sparkman*, 77; Rennolds: E. H. Rennolds Diary, October 31, 1864, UTK; Key: Wirt Armistead Cate, *Two Soldiers*, 145; Hood's circular: *OR*, ser. 1, vol. 45, pt. 1, p. 735.
58. Jesse Henderson Diary, entry dated October 25, 1864, UM.
59. Confederates arriving at Muscle Shoals, AL: Daniel P. Smith and Jim D. Moody, *Company K First Alabama Regiment*, 113; Head: Thomas A. Head, *Campaigns and Battles of the Sixteenth Regiment*, 147; Confederate soldiers setting up camp: J. P. Cannon, *Inside of Rebeldom*, 257.
60. Union cavalry occupying Florence, AL: Stephen D. Lee, "Report of Lieut. Gen. Stephen D. Lee, C. S. Army, Commanding a Corps," *OR*, ser. 1, vol. 39, pt. 1, p. 811; Confederate soldiers lamenting Union control of crossing and shelling town: Edgar W. Jones, "History of the 18th Alabama Infantry," ADAH; Lindsay: R. H. Lindsay, "Capture of Florence, ALA., Under Hood," *Confederate Veteran* 4, no. 12 (December 1896): 423; Dicks: John Dicks, "More About the Capture of Florence, ALA.," *Confederate Veteran* 5, no. 5 (May 1897): 214.
61. Lee ordering attack: Stephen D. Lee, "Report of Lieut. Gen. Stephen D. Lee, C. S. Army, Commanding a Corps," *OR*, ser. 1, vol. 39, pt. 1, p. 811; Jones quotations on view of Florence and painting, engineers setting up pontoon bridge, and torches in boats: Edgar W. Jones, "History of the 18th Alabama Infantry," ADAH; Confederates using scrap wood as oars and Lindsay: R. H. Lindsay, "Capture of Florence, ALA., Under Hood," 423; Lanning: John Dicks, "More About the Capture of Florence, ALA.," 214; Confederate shell killing Andrew Devilbliss: Lieutenant A. T. Martin to Mary Devilbliss, November 15, 1864, TU.
62. Civilians providing information leading to the Confederate capture of Florence: R. H. Lindsay, "Capture of Florence, ALA., Under Hood," 423; Federals quick withdrawal from Florence: *OR*, ser. 1, vol. 39, p. 870; shallow river preventing Union gunboats from engaging Confederates: *OR*, ser. 1, vol. 39, p. 395; Davis: Newton Davis Papers, ADAH; Henderson: W. H. Henderson to his father and mother, November 18, 1864, PMNC.

63. Lindsay: R. H. Lindsay, "Capture of Florence, ALA., Under Hood," 423; Davis: Newton Davis Papers, ADAH; Crittenden: John Crittenden Letters, AUA; 12th US Colored Troops: *OR*, ser. 3, vol. 4, p. 763.
64. Kelley: Samuel Kelley Letters, ADAH; Crane: Daniel Cone, *Last to Join the Fight*, 151.
65. Union patrol repelled on Nov. 1: Wirt Armistead Cate, *Two Soldiers*, 146; Union attempt to destroy pontoon bridge on Nov. 4: Robert M. Magill and Brenda D. Phillips, *Personal Reminiscences of a Confederate Soldier Boy*, 66; Union cavalry advance on Nov. 5: John Crittenden Letters, AUA; Confederate soldiers abandon advance to gather food and blankets: James Lanning Diary, ADAH; twenty Union prisoners: Newton Davis Papers, ADAH; Vann: Samuel King Vann and Nancy Elizabeth Neel Vann, *"Most Lovely Lizzie,"* 60.
66. For information provided by Union scouts, see, for example, "Hood's Army," *Independent* (Oskaloosa, KS), October 22, 1864; and "The War in Georgia," *Highland Weekly News* (Hillsboro, OH), October 27, 1864; Confederate forces on the picket line and improving defenses: John Crittenden Letters, AUA; freezing rain: William McLeod Diary, entry dated November 15E. H, FSA; Hood ordering destruction of houses: *OR*, ser. 1, vol. 39, pt. 3, p. 877.
67. Generals promising supplies in Florence: W. J. Worsham and C. W. Heiskell, *Old Nineteenth Tennessee Regiment*, 134; Littlejohn: Elbridge Littlejohn, "The Civil War Letters of Elbridge Littlejohn," pt. 2, p. 31; Smith: Daniel P. Smith and Jim D. Moody, *Company K First Alabama Regiment*, 114; men eating parched corn and unseasoned greens: Edgar W. Jones, "History of the 18th Alabama Infantry," ADAH; men eating mule: James Robert Maxwell, *Autobiography of James Robert Maxwell*, 258; Crittenden: John Crittenden Letters, AUA; Rennolds: E. H. Rennolds Diary, November 5, 1864, UTK; Key: Wirt Armistead Cate, *Two Soldiers*, 148; men stealing food from horses and eating acorns: H. K. Nelson, "Tennessee, A Grave or a Free Home," 508; soldiers lacking clothing and shoes: Daniel P. Smith and Jim D. Moody, *Company K First Alabama Regiment*, 114.
68. McDill: W. J. McDilll to his sister, [the letter is dated "Oct. 3rd./64," but this is clearly a misprint; based on information in the letter, it was written sometime between the Army of Tennessee's arrival in Florence in October 31, 1864, and McDill's death at the Battle of Franklin on November 30, 1864], Civil War Letters, vol. 1, West Tennessee, Southern History Collection, BPL; Hood requesting supplies: *OR*, ser. 1, vol. 39, pp. 870–71, 888–89; and John Bell Hood, *Advance and Retreat*, 272; Collins: R. M. Collins, *Chapters from the Unwritten History of the War between the States*, 239; Hood requesting ammunition from Josiah Gorgas: *OR*, ser. 1, vol. 39, pt. 2, p. 865.
69. Attempts to extend rail line: *OR*, ser. 1, vol. 39, pt. 3, p. 864; impressing civilian workers: *OR*, ser. 1, vol. 39, pt. 3, p. 877; transferring personal

baggage wagons to supply trains: *OR*, ser. 1, vol. 39, pt. 3, p. 888; news story reporting delivery of food: "Reports from General Hood's Army," *Daily Dispatch* (Richmond, VA), November 23, 1864; Gen. Forrest's cavalry seizing supplies: *OR*, ser. 1, vol. 39, pt. 3, p. 868.

70. Hood: John Bell Hood, *Advance and Retreat*, 253; slow Confederate progress giving Union time to prepare: *OR*, ser. 1, vol. 45, pt. 2, p. 3; Union supplying and training troops while Confederates starved: Andrew F. Smith, *Starving the South: How the North Won the Civil War* (New York: St. Martin's Press, 2011), 27; McMurray: William McMurray, *History of the Twentieth Tennessee Regiment Volunteer Infantry*, 328.
71. Distribution and preparation of rations: Daniel P. Smith and Jim D. Moody, *Company K First Alabama Regiment*, 114; gristmills lacking: John Crittenden Letters, AUA.
72. Smith: Daniel P. Smith and Jim D. Moody, *Company K First Alabama Regiment*, 115; Crittenden: John Crittenden Letters, AUA; Etter: Diary of Risenar Etter, entry dated November 16, 1864, SRNBP; contributions of Robert Patton: Smith and De Land, *Northern Alabama: Historical and Biographical*, 307; Patton feeding Confederate soldiers in fall of 1864: Edgar W. Jones, "History of the 18th Alabama Infantry," ADAH.
73. Confederate army leaders denying discontent: D. W. Sanders, "Hood's Tennessee Campaign," 290, Southern History Collection, BPL; Key: Wirt Armistead Cate, *Two Soldiers*, 149; McCleary: A. C. McLeary "Humorous Incidents of the Civil War," UNCSHC, 10; efforts to arrest misbehaving soldiers: Edgar W. Jones, "History of the 18th Alabama Infantry," ADAH; Crittenden: John Crittenden Letters, AUA; theft of Gen. States Rights Gist's cow: H. K. Nelson, "'Tennessee, A Grave or a Free Home," 508.
74. Continued foraging despite strict discipline: John Crittenden Letters, AUA; Smith: Daniel P. Smith and Jim D. Moody, *Company K First Alabama Regiment*, 115; officers refusing to forage but accepting food: Memoir of J. W. Preston, ADAH; Foster: Samuel T. Foster and Norman D. Brown, *One of Cleburne's Command*, 143; Little: George Little and James Robert Maxwell, *A History of Lumsden's Battery*, 51.
75. Failure to pay Confederate soldiers: Daniel P. Smith and Jim D. Moody, *Company K First Alabama Regiment*, 114; Higgins: George Washington Higgins to his wife, October 21, 1864, Corinth National Park; Murphree: Joel Dyer Murphree, "Autobiography and Civil War Letters of Joel Murphree of Troy, Alabama, 1864–1865," 198.
76. Time near Florence providing rest and relaxation: R. H. Lindsay, "Capture of Florence, ALA., Under Hood," 423; mingling at plays and dances: Diary of William Brown, entries dated November 11 and November 17, 1864, SRNBP; medical treatment during time near Florence: Samuel T. Foster and Norman

D. Brown, *One of Cleburne's Command*, 143; Key: Wirt Armistead Cate, *Two Soldiers*, 145–46; Davis: Newton Davis Papers, ADAH; Morton: John Watson Morton, *The Artillery of Nathan Bedford Forrest's Cavalry*, 268.

77. Tillman: J. A. Tillman to his sister Maggie Tillman, November 1, 1864, *Recollections and Reminiscences*, 397, Southern History Collection, BPL; Fleming: George C. Bittle, "Fighting Men View the Western War, 1862–1864," 32.
78. Henderson: W. H. Henderson to his father and mother, November 18, 1864, William Henry Henderson Papers, PMNC; Eggleston: Edward Noyes, "Excerpts from the Civil War Diary of E. T. Eggleston," 353; Sparkman: John W. Sparkman, *The Diary of Sergt. John W. Sparkman*, 77; Smith: Robert Davis Smith, *Confederate Diary of Robert D. Smith*, 82.
79. Crittenden: John Crittenden Letters, AUA; Key: Wirt Armistead Cate, *Two Soldiers*, 151; Lanning: James Lanning Diary, ADAH.
80. Crittenden: John Crittenden Letters, AUA; Vann: Samuel King Vann and Nancy Elizabeth Neel Vann, *"Most Lovely Lizzie,"* 59; Lanning: James Lanning Diary, ADAH; Warrick: Thomas Warrick Papers, ADAH; Davis: Newton Davis Papers, ADAH.
81. Official report on soldiers present for duty: *OR*, ser. 1, vol. 39, pt. 3, p. 893; editorial on men present for duty: James T. McCormick, "The Weakness of Our Armies Explained," *Jacksonville (AL) Alabama Republican*, October 27, 1864; Lockhart's estimate: *OR*, ser. 1, vol. 3, p. 880; AL legislature's appeal to deserters: W. H. Crenshaw and Thomas A. Walker, "Address to Alabama Soldiers Absent from the Army Without Leave and Joint Resolution in Relation Thereto," *Jacksonville (AL) Alabama Republican*, November 17, 1864; Cannon: J. P. Cannon, *Inside of Rebeldom*, 257; Key: Wirt Armistead Cate, *Two Soldiers*, 147.
82. Confederate deserters joining the Union army offered jobs and bonuses: T. S. Bowers, "Special Orders, No. 126," *Daily National Republican* (Washington, DC), November 25, 1864; deserters providing Union army with information: "Southern News," *Cleveland (OH) Morning Leader*, October 19, 1864; Lanning: James Lanning Diary, ADAH; desertion crippling the Confederate war effort: Mark A. Weitz, *More Damning Than Slaughter*, 276.
83. Confederate manpower exhausted: Steven H. Newton, *Lost for the Cause*, 2; Hill: Andrew Hill, "Personal Recollections of Andrew Malone Hill," ADAH; Livingston: Archie Livingston to his sisters, November 13, 1864, in Coski, ed., "I am In for Anything for Success," 77; Cleburne suggesting arming slaves: James M. McPherson, *The Illustrated Battle Cry of Freedom*, 732; Davis: Jefferson Davis, "Richmond, VA.," January 13, 1864, *OR*, ser. 1, vol. 52, pt. 2, p. 596; Cobb: Michael A. Bellesiles, *A People's History of the U.S. Military*, 111.
84. Smith: Robert Davis Smith, *Confederate Diary of Robert D. Smith*, 79;

heavy rains hampering delivery of provisions: Wirt Armistead Cate, *Two Soldiers*, 148; Union troops preventing supply transport across the Tennessee River: "From Cairo and Below," *Daily Intelligencer* (Wheeling, VA), November 15, 1864.

85. Smith: Robert Davis Smith, *Confederate Diary of Robert D. Smith*, 78; McDill: W. J. McDilll to his sister, [The letter is dated "Oct. 3rd./64.," but this is clearly a misprint; based on information in the letter, it was written sometime between the Army of Tennessee's arrival in Florence in October 31, 1864, and McDill's death at the Battle of Franklin on November 30, 1864.], *Civil War Letters, vol. 1, West Tennessee*, Southern History Collection, BPL; Etter: Diary of Risenar Etter, entry dated November 3, 1864, SRNBP; Preston: Memoir of J. W. Preston, ADAH; Higgins: George Washington Higgins to his wife, October 21, 1864, Corinth National Park; Rennolds: E. H. Rennolds Diary, entries dated October 31–November 1, 1864, UTK; Collins: R. M. Collins, *Chapters from the Unwritten History of the War between the States*, 239; soldiers suffering from mange: William Hardy to his wife, Sallie Hardy, November 20, 1864, William H. and Sallie J. Hardy Papers, USM.

86. Foster: Samuel T. Foster and Norman D. Brown, *One of Cleburne's Command*, 144; Dent: Stouten Dent to his wife, Anna, November 7, 1864, S. H. Dent Papers, AUA; Littlejohn: Elbridge Littlejohn, "The Civil War Letters of Elbridge Littlejohn," pt. 2, p. 31; Lanning: James Lanning Diary, ADAH; questioning Hood's planned advance into Tennessee: Wiley Sword, *The Confederacy's Last Hurrah*, 210.

87. For Unionists and Federal troops in North Alabama, see for example, "Latest News By Telegraph," *St. Cloud (MN) Democrat*, November 24, 1864; and *Montana Post* (Virginia City, Montana Territory), December 10, 1864; Jarman: Robert Jarman, "The History of Company K, 27th Mississippi Infantry," MDAH; Crittenden: John Crittenden Letters, AUA; Kelly: Samuel Kelley Letters, ADAH; Ross's Brigade engaging with Union forces: Lawrence Ross, "Report of Brig. Gen. Lawrence S. Ross, C. S. Army, Commanding Ross' Brigade, of Operations October 24, 1864–December 27, 1864," *OR*, ser. 1, vol. 45, pt. 1, p. 768; Confederate prisoners providing information: Edward Hatch, "Headquarters Cavalry Division," *OR*, ser. 1, vol. 45, pt. 1, p. 887.

88. On rebels confronting hunger and lack of clothing and equipment, see, for example, "A Panoramic View of Hood's Army," *Daily Ohio Statesman* (Columbus, OH), October 27, 1864; "Late Rebel Papers," *Daily Wabash Express* (Terre-Haute, IN), November 5, 1864; and "Hood's Movements," *Cleveland (OH) Morning Leader*, November 5, 1864; on inability of Hood's army to acquire supplies, see *OR*, ser. 1, vol. 39, pt. 3, pp. 864, 888.

89. Confederate army overstaying its welcome: Edgar W. Jones, "History of the 18th Alabama Infantry," ADAH; and John Crittenden Letters, AUA; Key:

Wirt Armistead Cate, *Two Soldiers*, 148–49; Rennolds: E. H. Rennolds Diary, November 8, 1864, UTK; Smith: Daniel P. Smith and Jim D. Moody, *Company K First Alabama Regiment*, 114; Davis: Newton Davis Papers, ADAH; lack of tents and blankets: "A Panoramic View of Hood's Army," *Daily Ohio Statesman* (Columbus, OH), October 27, 1864; Crittenden: John Crittenden Letters, AUA.

90. Weakness of Confederacy necessitating movement: John Bell Hood, *Advance and Retreat*, 253; soldier from SC: J. Roderick Heller, *The Confederacy Is on Her Way Up the Spout*, 86.

91. Hardy: William Hardy to his wife, Sallie Hardy, November 20, 1864, William H. and Sallie J. Hardy Papers, USM; Cooper: James Litton Cooper, "The Civil War Diary of Captain James Litton Cooper, September 30, 1861 to January 1865," ed. William T. Alderson, *Tennessee Historical Quarterly* 15 (June 1956): 166; Henderson: W. H. Henderson to his father and mother, November 18, 1864, William Henry Henderson Papers, PMNC; newspaper mocking Hood: "The Richmond Papers on Gen. Sherman," *Bedford (PA) Inquirer*, December 9, 1864; Jones: Edgar W. Jones, "History of the 18th Alabama Infantry," ADAH; Crittenden: John Crittenden Letters, AUA; Confederate prisoners on Hood's motives for movement: "From Hood's Army," *Cleveland (OH) Morning Leader*, November 8, 1864; Scott: John Thomas Scott to his sweetheart Miss Philo, September 5, 1864, AUA; Higgins: George Washington Higgins to his wife, November 17, 1864, Corinth National Park.

92. Arrival of Gen. Forrest's cavalry: *OR*, ser. 1, vol. 39, pt. 1, p. 808; Forrest becoming commander of all cavalry: John Watson Morton, *The Artillery of Nathan Bedford Forrest's Cavalry*, 268.

93. Newton Cannon and Campbell H. Brown, *The Reminiscences of Sergeant Newton Cannon*, 58.

94. Number and condition of cavalry troopers under Forrest's command: Nathan Forrest, "Report of Maj. Gen. Nathan B. Forrest," OR, ser. 1, vol. 45, pt. 1, p. 752; Forrest losing wagon train to Union: James Chalmers, "Report of Big. Gen. James R. Chalmers," *OR*, ser. 1, vol. 45, pt. 1, p. 763.

95. Foster: Samuel T. Foster and Norman D. Brown, *One of Cleburne's Command*, 144; Key: Wirt Armistead Cate, *Two Soldiers*, 150; Crittenden: John Crittenden to his wife, Bettie, November 18, 1864, AUA.

96. Army of Tennessee leaving Alabama: *OR*, ser. 1, vol. 45, pt. 1, p. 669; Young: John Preston Young, *The Seventh Tennessee Cavalry*, 103; time of sunrise: Thomas P. Ashmore, F. H. Singer, and Thos. R. Rhodes, *Grier's Southern Almanac, for the Year of Our Lord 1864*, 17; description of morning: William McLeod Diary, entry dated November 20, 1864, FSA; incessant rain: Thomas A. Head, *Campaigns and Battles of the Sixteenth Regiment, Tennessee Volunteers*, 147; men marching through mud: Joseph Boyce, "Mis-

sourians in the Battle of Franklin," 102; Shannon: Isaac Shannon, "Sharpshooter's with Hood's Army," 123; Foster: Samuel T. Foster and Norman D. Brown, *One of Cleburne's Command*, 144; snow and frozen ground: Daniel P. Smith and Jim D. Moody, *Company K First Alabama Regiment*, 117; McMorrics: Edward Young McMorrics, "History of the First Alabama Volunteer Infantry CSA," ADAH.

4. "By Some Misunderstanding"

1. Edwin Hansford Rennolds, *A History of the Henry County Commands*, 103.
2. Hood's plan of attack: John Bell Hood, *Advance and Retreat*, 281; officers instructing men not to straggle: H. K. Nelson, "Tennessee, A Grave or a Free Home," 508; trustworthy men assigned to provost guard: E. H. Rennolds Diary, entry dated November 19, 1864, UTK; Hood's rhetoric about the advance: Ephraim Anderson, *Memoirs*, 395; Foster: Samuel T. Foster and Norman D. Brown, *One of Cleburne's Command*, 145.
3. Cannon: Newton Cannon and Campbell H. Brown, *The Reminiscences of Sergeant Newton Cannon*, 58; Forrest's troopers screening Confederate forces: "Journal of the Army of Tennessee," *OR*, ser. 1, vol. 45, pt. 1, p. 669; position of Forrest's divisions: Nathan Forrest, "Report of Maj. Gen. Nathan B. Forrest," *OR*, ser. 1, vol. 45, pt. 1, p. 752; cavalry advancing rapidly: Diary of Stephen Jordan, entry dated November 24, 1864, TSLA; and John Watson Morton, *The Artillery of Nathan Bedford Forrest's Cavalry*, 271; position of Cheatham's, Lee's, and Stewart's Corps: David Williamson, *The Third Battalion Mississippi Infantry and the 45th Mississippi Regiment*, 252.
4. Hood as unpredictable opponent: W. T. Sherman to General Corse, October 7, 1864, in United States Senate, *Reports of Committees: 30th Congress, 1st Session–48th Congress, 2nd Session* (Washington, DC: GPO, 1866), 219; Shellenberger: John K. Shellenberger, *The Battle of Spring Hill*, 5; Federal commanders concerned but hoping to force a fight: Jacob D. Cox, *The Battle of Franklin, Tennessee, November 30, 1864: A Monograph*, 21; Avery: W. H. H. Avery to his father, November 30, 1864, HHS.
5. Gen. Thomas moving forces to prepare for Hood's offensive: Thomas B. Van Horne and Edward Ruger, *History of the Army of the Cumberland* 165: troops moving toward Nashville from Pulaski, TN: Jacob D. Cox, *The Battle of Franklin, Tennessee, November 30, 1864*, 21.
6. Nelson: H. K. Nelson, "Tennessee, A Grave or a Free Home," 508; Rennolds: Edwin Hansford Rennolds, *A History of the Henry County Commands*, 103; Boyce: Joseph Boyce, "Missourians in the Battle of Franklin," 102.
7. Union supporters in TN: Diary of Risenar Etter, entry dated November 16, 1864, SRNBP; numerous bushwackers: E. H. Rennolds Diary, entry dated November 22, 1864, UTK; Tennessee Unionists terrorizing Confederate

troops: Edward Young McMorries, "History of the First Alabama Volunteer Infantry CSA," ADAH; Murphree: Joel Dyer Murphree, "Autobiography and Civil War Letters of Joel Murphree of Troy, Alabama, 1864–1865," 200; Henderson: Jesse Henderson Diary, entry dated November 21, 1864, UM.

8. Etter: Diary of Risenar Etter, entry dated November 24, 1864, SRNBP; Key: Wirt Armistead Cate, *Two Soldiers*, 158.
9. Confederate soldiers going days without food: Diary of Risenar Etter, entry dated November 25, 1864, SRNBP; Hood allowing quartermasters to confiscate grain: Robert Jarman, "The History of Company K, 27th Mississippi Infantry," MDAH; limited daily rations: Edgar W. Jones, "History of the 18th Alabama Infantry," ADAH; men frustrated by lack of food: Edward Young McMorries, "History of the First Alabama Volunteer Infantry CSA," ADAH; Anthony: Jeff Toalson, *No Soap, No Pay, Diarrhea, Dysentery & Desertion*, 255; Ritter: William Ritter, "Sketch of the Third Battery of Maryland Artillery," 538.
10. Troops continuing to steal food: Edgar W. Jones, "History of the 18th Alabama Infantry," ADAH; men stealing from Gen. Cheatham: H. K. Nelson, "Tennessee, A Grave or a Free Home," 508; Jarman: Robert Jarman, "The History of Company K, 27th Mississippi Infantry," MDAH.
11. Edgar W. Jones, "History of the 18th Alabama Infantry," ADAH.
12. Failure of plans to recruit Tennesseans: Isham Harris, "Tuscumbia, ALA.," *OR*, ser. 1, vol. 57, pt. 2, p. 732; Gen. Lee ordering men to enforce conscription laws: J. W. Ratchford, Assistant Adjutant-General, "General Orders No. 66," *OR*, ser. 1, vol. 45, pt. 1, p. 1245; Whittler: Samuel R. Watkins, *"Co. Aytch,"* 205; Hotze: Peter Hotze, "Memoir," Hotze Family Papers, ASA; McMurray: William McMurray, *History of the Twentieth Tennessee Regiment Volunteer Infantry*, 340.
13. Nathan Forrest, "Report of Maj. Gen. Nathan B. Forrest, C. S. Army, Commanding Cavalry, of Operations November 16, 1864–January 23, 1865," *OR*, ser. 1, vol. 45, pt. 1, p. 752.
14. Lawrence Ross, "Report of Brig. Gen. Lawrence S. Ross, C. S. Army, Commanding Ross' Brigade, of Operations October 24, 1864–December 27, 1864," *OR*, ser. 1, vol. 45, pt. 1, p. 768.
15. Murphree: Joel Dyer Murphree, "Autobiography and Civil War Letters of Joel Murphree of Troy, Alabama, 1864–1865," 200; Cooper: James Litton Cooper, "The Civil War Diary of Captain James Litton Cooper, September 30, 1861 to January 1865," 166; Collins: R. M. Collins, *Chapters from the Unwritten History of the War between the States*, 239.
16. Joy: Charles Gore Joy, "The Stampede at La Fayette, Ga.," 475; Ross: Lawrence Ross, "Report of Brig. Gen. Lawrence S. Ross, C. S. Army, Commanding Ross' Brigade, of Operations October 24, 1864–December 27, 1864," *OR*,

ser. 1, vol. 45, pt. 1, p. 768; Anderson: Ephraim Anderson, *Memoirs*, 395; Collins: R. M. Collins, *Chapters from the Unwritten History of the War between the States*, 239; Walker: T. J. Walker, "Reminiscences of the Civil War," 68; Copley: John M. Copley, *A Sketch of the Battle of Franklin, Tenn.*, 30.

17. Key: Wirt Armistead Cate, *Two Soldiers*, 158; Clark: Walter A. Clark, *Under the Stars and Bars*, 168.

18. Lanning: James Lanning Diary, entry dated November 22, 1864, ADAH; Nelson: H. K. Nelson, "Tennessee, A Grave or a Free Home," 508; Etter: Diary of Risenar Etter, entry dated November 22, 1864, SRNBP; Cooper: James Cooper, "Memoir of James Cooper, 20th Tennessee Infantry," Special Collections Division, NTPL; Cooke: Bill O'Neal and Samuel Alonza Cooke, "The Civil War Memories of Samuel Alonza Cooke," *Southwestern Historical Quarterly* 74, no. 4 (April 1971): 545; Black: John Preston Young, *The Seventh Tennessee Cavalry*, 117; Missourians cheering for snow: Joseph Boyce, "Missourians in the Battle of Franklin," 102; Dicks: John Dicks, "Capt. John A. Dicks, Natchez, Miss.," *Confederate Veteran* 3, no. 1 (January 1895): 14.

19. Jones: Edgar W. Jones, "History of the 18th Alabama Infantry," ADAH; Clark and laundress: Walter A. Clark, *Under the Stars and Bars*, 175, 176.

20. Sparkman: John W. Sparkman, *The Diary of Sergt. John W. Sparkman*, 76; cannons and wagons slowed by mud: Joel Dyer Murphree, "Autobiography and Civil War Letters of Joel Murphree of Troy, Alabama, 1864–1865," 200; Hood ordering regiments to push wagons: B. F. Weathers, "B. F. Weathers Papers," ADAH; pushing wagons as only solution: R. W. Banks, *The Battle of Franklin, November 30, 1864*, 24; wagons falling into pond: Wirt Armistead Cate, *Two Soldiers*, 154.

21. Crude moccasins from cow hides: Edgar W. Jones, "History of the 18th Alabama Infantry," ADAH; Jarman: Robert Jarman, "The History of Company K, 27th Mississippi Infantry," MDAH.

22. Forrest's cavalry skirmishing: Thomas P. Ashmore, F. H. Singer, and Thos. R. Rhodes, *Grier's Southern Almanac, for the Year of Our Lord 1864*, 17; Black: John Preston Young, *The Seventh Tennessee Cavalry*, 117; Bleecker: James Dinkins, *1861 to 1865, by an Old Johnnie*, 226.

23. Union troops gathering near Columbia: W. J. Worsham and C. W. Heiskell, *Old Nineteenth Tennessee Regiment*, 139; Union troops involved and Confederate cavalry attempting to advance: R. R. Hancock, *Hancock's Diary: Or, A History of the Second Tennessee Confederate Cavalry*, 513, 514.

24. Position of Confederate corps around Columbia: "Journal of the Army of Tennessee," *OR*, ser. 1, vol. 45, pt. 1, p. 670; veteran soldiers anticipating action: J. P. Cannon, *Inside of Rebeldom*, 258.

25. John W. Sparkman, *The Diary of Sergt. John W. Sparkman*, 78.

26. Hood ordering flanking maneuver: Edgar W. Jones, "History of the 18th Alabama Infantry," ADAH; Hood moving Forrest's cavalry and ordering pontoon bridge: R. R. Hancock, *Hancock's Diary*, 513; Hood positioning Lee's, Cheatham's, and Stewart's Corps: R. M. Collins, *Chapters from the Unwritten History of the War between the States*, 241.
27. Gen. Thomas ordering Gen. Schofield to hold bridges at Columbia: Benson Bobrick, *Master of War: The Life of General George H. Thomas*, 269; Schofield deciding to pull back: James R. Knight, *Hood's Tennessee Campaign*, 32; Schofield sending word to Thomas: Jacob D. Cox, *The Army in the Civil War*, 232.
28. Columbia abandoned: "Journal of the Army of Tennessee," *OR*, ser. 1, vol. 45, pt. 1, p. 670; Confederate soldiers' cautious approach: J. P. Cannon, *Inside of Rebeldom*, 258; railroad bridge across Duck River destroyed: Carter Stevenson, "Report of Maj. Gen. Carter L. Stevenson, C. S. Army, Commanding Division, of Operations September 29–December 17, 1864," *OR*, ser. 1, vol. 45, pt. 1, p. 693; Copley: John M. Copley, *A Sketch of the Battle of Franklin, Tenn.*, 30; Preston: W. E. Preston, "Memoir of W. E. Preston," ADAH.
29. James Lanning Diary, entry dated November 28, 1864, ADAH.
30. Murphree: Joel Dyer Murphree, "Autobiography and Civil War Letters of Joel Murphree of Troy, Alabama, 1864–1865," 200; Cannon: J. P. Cannon, *Inside of Rebeldom*, 258.
31. Hood issuing General Orders No. 37: J. P. Cannon, *Inside of Rebeldom*, 258; order ignored: James R. Knight, *Hood's Tennessee Campaign*, 32; Murphree: Joel Dyer Murphree, "Autobiography and Civil War Letters of Joel Murphree of Troy, Alabama, 1864–1865," 200; Johnston: John Johnston, "Personal Reminiscences of the Civil War 1861–1865," TSLA; guns and ammunition captured: Carter Stevenson, "Report of Maj. Gen. Carter L. Stevenson, C. S. Army, Commanding Division, of Operations September 29–December 17, 1864," *OR*, ser. 1, vol. 45, pt. 1, p. 693; Union prisoners: Edward Noyes, "Excerpts from the Civil War Diary of E. T. Eggleston," 353.
32. Union forces targeting Confederates from north of river: Edgar W. Jones, "History of the 18th Alabama Infantry," ADAH; gunfire: John Johnston, "Personal Reminiscences of the Civil War 1861–1865," TSLA; Cannon: Newton Cannon and Campbell H. Brown, *The Reminiscences of Sergeant Newton Cannon, from Holograph Material Provided by His Grandson, Samuel M. Fleming, Jr.* (Franklin, TN: Carter House Association, 1963), 58.
33. Gen. Lee commanding forces on south bank of river: "Journal of the Army of Tennessee," *OR*, ser. 1, vol. 45, pt. 1, p. 670; Union and Confederate forces battling across river: Stephen D. Lee, "Report of Lieut. Gen. Stephen D. Lee, C. S. Army, Commanding Army Corps, of Operations November 2–December 17, 1864," *OR*, ser. 1, vol. 45, pt. 1, p. 687; casualties among Con-

federate artillery: William Ritter, "Sketch of the Third Battery of Maryland Artillery," 538; Magill: Robert M. Magill and Brenda D. Phillips, *Personal Reminiscences of a Confederate Soldier Boy*, 66.

34. Hood ordering forces across Duck River: "Journal of the Army of Tennessee," *OR*, ser. 1, vol. 45, pt. 1, p. 670; Stephen D. Lee, "Report of Lieut. Gen. Stephen D. Lee, C. S. Army, Commanding Army Corps, of Operations November 2–December 17, 1864," *OR*, ser. 1, vol. 45, pt. 1, p. 687; Carter Stevenson, "Report of Maj. Gen. Carter L. Stevenson, C. S. Army, Commanding Division, of Operations September 29–December 17, 1864," *OR*, ser. 1, vol. 45, pt. 1, p. 693.
35. R. R. Hancock, *Hancock's Diary*, 579.
36. Confederates take log fort at river crossing: R. R. Hancock, *Hancock's Diary*, 514; exhausted horses prevent capture of Union forces: Diary of Robert Battle, entry dated November 29, 1864, SRNBP.
37. Pontoon bridges: R. R. Hancock, *Hancock's Diary*, 514; Hood sending men north after Schofield's forces: James R. Knight, *Hood's Tennessee Campaign*, 41; orders distributed explaining Hood's intention: J. P. Cannon, *Inside of Rebeldom*, 258; Maxwell: George Little and James Robert Maxwell, *A History of Lumsden's Battery*, 18; and James Robert Maxwell, *Autobiography of James Robert Maxwell*, 262; Hood's expectations for exhausted men: W. J. Worsham and C. W. Heiskell, *Old Nineteenth Tennessee Regiment*, 139.
38. Confederates advancing with Cheatham's Corps in the lead: W. J. Worsham and C. W. Heiskell, *Old Nineteenth Tennessee Regiment*, 139; muddy roads and troops traversing fields: Edward Young McMorries, "History of the First Alabama Volunteer Infantry CSA," ADAH; Collins: R. M. Collins, *Chapters from the Unwritten History of the War between the States*, 239; Copley: John M. Copley, *A Sketch of the Battle of Franklin, Tenn.*, 32; Dunlap: Sam Dunlap, "Hard Times on Hood's Retreat," *Confederate Veteran* 7, no. 6 (June 1899): 266; Jarman: Robert Jarman, "The History of Company K, 27th Mississippi Infantry," MDAH.
39. Young: John Preston Young, *The Seventh Tennessee Cavalry*, 117; Forrest attempting a series of assaults: Nathan Forrest, "Report of Maj. Gen. Nathan B. Forrest, C. S. Army, Commanding Cavalry, of Operations November 16, 1864–January 23, 1865," *OR*, ser. 1, vol. 45, pt. 1, p. 753.
40. Arrival of Confederate divisions and Hood's orders to Cheatham: Ben Cheatham, Benjamin F. Cheatham, "The Lost Opportunity at Spring Hill, Tenn. General Cheatham's Reply to General Hood," *Southern Historical Society Papers* 9 (1881): 524, 528.; Dodd: W. O. Dodd, "Reminiscences of Hood's Tennessee Campaign," *Southern Historical Society Papers* 9 (1881): 520.
41. Position of Cleburne's forces: James R. Knight, *Hood's Tennessee Campaign*, 43; dismounted Confederate cavalry joining infantry to take

steep hill: John Johnston, "Personal Reminiscences of the Civil War 1861–1865," TSLA.

42. Luther Bradley, "Report of Brig. Gen. Luther P. Bradley," *OR*, ser. 1, vol. 45, pt. 1, p. 267.
43. John Johnston, "Personal Reminiscences of the Civil War 1861–1865," TSLA.
44. Confederate infantry pursuing Union forces and dividing plunder: A. J. Batchelor, "On Hood's Campaign to Franklin," *Confederate Veteran* 18, no. 9 (September 1910): 426; 33rd Alabama Infantry: W. A. Drennan, Inspection of Featherston's Brigade, September 14, 1864; exhausted Confederates resting in full gear: W. E. Preston, "Memoir of W. E. Preston," ADAH; and John Tate, Inspection of Cantey's Brigade, September 18, 1864.
45. Collins: R. M. Collins, *Chapters from the Unwritten History of the War between the States*, 242; McMorries: Edward Young McMorries, "History of the First Alabama Volunteer Infantry CSA," ADAH; Copley: John M. Copley, *A Sketch of the Battle of Franklin, Tenn.*, 32.
46. Hood concluding that Union forces refused to attack: John Bell Hood, *Advance and Retreat*, 285; Cheatham opposed to night attacks: William Old to John Bell Hood, September 10, 1877, in John Bell Hood and Stephen M. Hood, *The Lost Papers of Confederate General John Bell Hood*, 120; Gen. Cleburne supporting Cheatham: S. D. Lee to John Bell Hood, August 25, 1875, in Hood and Hood, *Lost Papers*, 115; Hood agreeing to send Stewart's Corps: John Bell Hood, *Advance and Retreat*, 287.
47. Alexander P. Stewart, "Reports of Lieut. Gen. Alexander P. Stewart, C. S. Army, Commanding Army Corps, of Operations November 29–January 20, 1864," *OR*, ser. 1, vol. 45, pt. 1, p. 713.
48. Meeting of Forrest, Stewart, and Hood: "Journal of the Army of Tennessee," *OR*, ser. 1, vol. 45, pt. 1, p. 670; Stephen M. Hood, *John Bell Hood: The Rise, Fall, and Resurrection of a Confederate General*, 114; Sam Davis Elliot, *Isham G. Harris of Tennessee*, 172.
49. Ross's Brigade ordered to block the road: Stephen M. Hood, *John Bell Hood*, 114; Ross's Brigade engaging Federal cavalry and ultimately withdrawing: Lawrence Ross, "Report of Brig. Gen. Lawrence S. Ross," *OR*, ser. 1, vol. 45, pt. 1, p. 769; Union troops forcing Ross's Brigade to withdraw: Nathan Forrest, "Report of Maj. Gen. Nathan B. Forrest," *OR*, ser. 1, vol. 45, pt. 1, p. 753; Hood unaware that road was open: Stephen M. Hood, *John Bell Hood*, 114.
50. L. M. Graham: "Inquiries by and About Veterans," *Confederate Veteran* 7, no. 10 (September 1899): 454; Batchelor: A. J. Batchelor, "On Hood's Campaign to Franklin," 426; Rennolds: Edwin Hansford Rennolds, *A History of the Henry County Commands*, 103; Collins: R. M. Collins, *Chapters from the Unwritten History of the War between the States*, 244.

51. Jarman: Robert Jarman, "The History of Company K, 27th Mississippi Infantry," MDAH; Lee: Stephen D. Lee, "Report of Lieut. Gen. Stephen D. Lee," *OR*, ser. 1, vol. 45, pt. 1, p. 687.
52. Sunrise on Nov. 29: Thomas P. Ashmore, F. H. Singer, and Thos. R. Rhodes, *Grier's Southern Almanac*, 17; cavalry in need of ammunition: Nathan Forrest, "Report of Maj. Gen. Nathan B. Forrest," *OR*, ser. 1, vol. 45, pt. 1, p. 753.
53. Hood blaming Cheatham for Federal escape: John Bell Hood, *Advance and Retreat*, 284, 287; Hood initially demanding Cheatham's removal then relenting: John Bell Hood, "Headquarters Army of Tennessee," *OR*, ser. 1, vol. 45, pt. 1, p. 657; Hood quotation: John Bell Hood, *Advance and Retreat*, 287.
54. Cheatham, "The Lost Opportunity at Spring Hill," *Southern Historical Society Papers*: 526, 527.
55. Isham G. Harris, "Narrative of Gov. Isham G. Harris as Told to Col. Brown—Hood's Campaign," Special Collections Division, NTPL.
56. Copley: John M. Copley, *A Sketch of the Battle of Franklin, Tenn.*, 34; Collins: R. M. Collins, *Chapters from the Unwritten History of the War between the States*, 244; Ritter: William Ritter, "Sketch of the Third Battery of Maryland Artillery," 539; Duncan: Thomas D. Duncan, *Recollections of Thomas D. Duncan*, 181.
57. T. J. Walker, "Reminiscences of the Civil War," 68.
58. Lee: Stephen M. Hood, *John Bell Hood*, 136; French: Samuel French, *Two Wars*, 292; Cheairs: James R. Knight, *Hood's Tennessee Campaign*, 53; Vaulx: J. P. Young, "Hood's Failure at Spring Hill," *Confederate Veteran* 16, no. 1 (January 1908): 36.
59. Hood suggesting he could have destroyed Federal army: John Bell Hood, *Advance and Retreat*, 284, 287; alternative escape routes for Federal forces: Thomas Connelly, *Autumn of Glory*, 501; Schofield's troops concentrated near Spring Hill: Stanley Horn, "The Spring Hill Legend," *Civil War Times Illustrated* 8, no. 4 (April 1969): 32; night attacks poorly regarded: E. P. Alexander, *The American Civil War: A Critical Narrative*, 467; Gen. Schofield's record: Terry Jones, *Historical Dictionary of the Civil War*, 1270; Cox: Jacob D. Cox, *The Battle of Franklin, Tennessee*, 33; competence of Union forces near Spring Hill: Eric Jacobson and Richard A. Rupp, *For Cause & for Country*, 182.

5. "Victory Is Ours but Very Dearly Bought"

1. James Lanning Diary, entry dated November 30, 1864, ADAH.
2. Confederate cavalry engaging Union rear guard: Nathan Forrest, "Report of Maj. Gen. Nathan B. Forrest," *OR*, ser. 1, vol. 45, pt. 1, p. 753; Stewart's Corps: Alexander P. Stewart, "Reports of Lieut. Gen. Alexander P. Stewart," *OR*, ser. 1, vol. 45, pt. 1, p. 708; Cheatham's Corps, Lee's infantrymen, and

artillery: "Itinerary of the Army of Tennessee," *OR*, ser. 1, vol. 45, pt. 1, p. 670; Hood: William Ritter, "Sketch of the Third Battery of Maryland Artillery," 539.

3. Cannon: J. P. Cannon, *Inside of Rebeldom*, 239; Capers: Ellison Capers, "Report of Col. Ellison Capers," *OR*, ser. 1, vol. 45, pt. 1, p. 736; Boyce: Joseph Boyce, "Missourians in the Battle of Franklin," 102.
4. Jones: Edgar W. Jones, "History of the 18th Alabama Infantry," ADAH; Collins: R. M. Collins, *Chapters from the Unwritten History of the War between the States*, 246; Flatau: Mamie Yeary, *Reminiscences of the Boys in Gray*, 227.
5. Union corps arriving in Franklin: Jacob Cox, *The Battle of Franklin, Tennessee*, 37; description of Franklin: John M. Copley, *A Sketch of the Battle of Franklin*, 36; and Joe Johnston, *Franklin*, 7; population of Franklin and description of Union fortifications: W. F. Prosser, "A Remarkable Episode of the Late War," *United Service* (December 1889): 620.
6. Jacob Cox, *The Battle of Franklin*, Tennessee, 39.
7. Schofield's plans for the Union escape: John Schofield, *Forty-Six Years in the Army*, 177; Union troops improving fortifications: Jacob Cox, *The Battle of Franklin, Tennessee*, 45.
8. Forrest's cavalry encountering Federal troops: Nathan Forrest, "Report of Maj. Gen. Nathan B. Forrest," *OR*, ser. 1, vol. 45, pt. 1, p. 753; earlier ruse by Union forces: J. P. Cannon, *Inside of Rebeldom*, 239; Federal forces engaging Confederates: Frederick Fout and Albert E. Fout, *Die schwersten Tage des Bürgerkrieges von 1864 und 1865*, 36; and W. R. Carter, *History of the First Regiment of Tennessee Volunteer Cavalry*, 214; Capers: Ellison Capers, "Report of Col. Ellison Capers," *OR*, ser. 1, vol. 45, pt. 1, p. 736; Federal rear guard withdrawing: Edward Walthall, "Reports of Maj. Gen. Edward C. Walthall," *OR*, ser. 1, vol. 45, pt. 1, p. 720; and W. R. Carter, *History of the First Regiment of Tennessee Volunteer Cavalry*, 214.
9. Hood's arrival: Irving A. Buck, *Cleburne and His Command*, 328; Copley: John M. Copley, *A Sketch of the Battle of Franklin*, 46.
10. Nathan Forrest, "Report of Maj. Gen. Nathan B. Forrest," *OR*, ser. 1, vol. 45, pt. 1, p. 753.
11. Position of Stewart's divisions and initial engagement with Union cavalry: J. P. Cannon, *Inside of Rebeldom*, 259; absence of artillery: Alexander P. Stewart, "Reports of Lieut. Gen. Alexander P. Stewart," *OR*, ser. 1, vol. 45, pt. 1, p. 708; Maxwell: George Little and James Robert Maxwell, *A History of Lumsden's Battery*, 262; position of Stewart's infantry: Edward Walthall, "Reports of Maj. Gen. Edward C. Walthall," *OR*, ser. 1, vol. 45, pt. 1, p. 720.
12. Position of Cheatham's and Stewart's Corps: Alexander P. Stewart, "Reports of Lieut. Gen. Alexander P. Stewart," *OR*, ser. 1, vol. 45, pt. 1, p. 708; and

William Bate, "Report of Maj. Gen. C. S. Army," *OR*, ser. 1, vol. 45, pt. 1, p. 742; position of Cleburne's, Brown's, and Bate's Divisions: Ellison Capers, "Report of Col. Ellison Capers," *OR*, ser. 1, vol. 45, pt. 1, p. 736; Cheatham's order to Bate: William Bate, "Report of Maj. Gen. C. S. Army," *OR*, ser. 1, vol. 45, pt. 1, p. 742.

13. W. A. Gallaway, "Explosion Before the Battle of Franklin," *Confederate Veteran* 15, no. 12 (December 1907): 569.
14. Biography of States Rights Gist: Spencer Tucker et al., *American Civil War*, 780; recollections of Gist's slave: Wilson Gee, *The Gist Family of South Carolina*, 85.
15. Position of Federal line: Ellison Capers, "Report of Col. Ellison Capers," *OR*, ser. 1, vol. 45, pt. 1, p. 736; and Edward Young McMorries, "History of the First Alabama Volunteer Infantry CSA," ADAH; Collins: R. M. Collins, *Chapters from the Unwritten History of the War between the States*, 246; Boyce: Joseph Boyce, "Missourians in the Battle of Franklin," 102; Athey: George Athey to his father, December, n.d., 1864, George Athey Letters, SRNBP.
16. Union works and Schofield's orders: Jacob Cox, *The Battle of Franklin, Tennessee*, 67; Wagner's orders, Opdycke's refusal, and Shellenberger: John Shellenberger, *The Battle of Franklin, Tennessee*, 3.
17. Second line of Federal defenses: Ellison Capers, "Report of Col. Ellison Capers," *OR*, ser. 1, vol. 45, pt. 1, p. 736; Edward Young McMorries, "History of the First Alabama Volunteer Infantry CSA," ADAH; and John M. Copley, *A Sketch of the Battle of Franklin, Tenn.*, 42.
18. Position of buildings belonging to Fountain Carter: John M. Copley, *A Sketch of the Battle of Franklin, Tenn.*, 42; Tod Carter: Rosalie Carter, "Capt. Tod Carter of the Confederate States Army," National Park Service website, accessed March 25, 2016, https://www.nps.gov/stri/learn/historyculture/upload/TN_Carter%20Bio_20th%20Infantry.pdf; Cox's headquarters, Reilly's Brigade, and Opdycke's Brigade: Jacob Cox, *The Battle of Franklin, Tennessee*, 52, 53, 80.
19. Wilson's position and plan to defeat Forrest: James Wilson, *Under the Old Flag*, 48, 49; Schofield's doubts about Wilson: J. M. Schofield, "Franklin, November 30, 1864–9:50 a.m.," *OR*, ser. 1, vol. 45, pt. 1, p. 1169.
20. Schofield's headquarters: W. F. Prosser, "A Remarkable Episode of the Late War," 620; 1st Ohio Light Artillery: Jacob Cox, *The Battle of Franklin, Tennessee*, 123; Herman Hattaway, *Reflections of a Civil War Historian*, 25; and Spencer Tucker et al., *American Civil War*, 87.
21. G. C. Phillips, "Witness to the Battle of Franklin," *Confederate Veteran* 14, no. 6 (June 1906): 261.
22. Stanley: David Stanley, "Report of Maj. Gen. David S. Stanley," *OR*, ser.

1, vol. 45, pt. 1, p. 115; approximate numbers of opposing forces: Spencer Tucker et al., *American Civil War*, 705; McMurray: William McMurray, *History of the Twentieth Tennessee Regiment Volunteer Infantry*, 328; Union artillery advantage: James R. Knight, *Hood's Tennessee Campaign*, 146; Cheatham's and Forrest's objections to frontal assault and Hood's response: Irving A. Buck, *Cleburne and His Command*, 327, 328; Schofield's fear: J. M. Schofield, "Franklin, November 30, 1864–9:50 a.m.," *OR*, ser. 1, vol. 45, pt. 1, p. 1169.

23. Hood reiterating order for frontal assault: Irving A. Buck, *Cleburne and His Command*, 328; Hood's battle plan: Thomas A. Head, *Campaigns and Battles of the Sixteenth Regiment*, 376.
24. Boyce: Joseph Boyce, "Cockrell's Brigade Band at Franklin," *Confederate Veteran* 19, no. 6 (June 1911): 271; Pulliam: Mamie Yeary, *Reminiscences of the Boys in Gray*, 623; Worsham and Heiskell: W. J. Worsham and C. W. Heiskell, *Old Nineteenth Tennessee Regiment*, 140.
25. Edward Young McMorries, "History of the First Alabama Volunteer Infantry CSA," ADAH.
26. R. N. Rea, "Mississippi Soldier of the Confederacy," 287.
27. While most sources state that the Confederate assault began at 4:00 p.m., some disagree. For example, the "Itinerary of the Army of Tennessee," *OR*, ser. 1, vol. 45, pt. 1, p. 675, states that "Franklin was attacked at about 3 o'clock." General Stewart, meanwhile, reported that he only received the order to attack at "about 4 p.m." Alexander P. Stewart, "Reports of Lieut. Gen. Alexander P. Stewart, C. S. Army, Commanding Army Corps, of Operations November 29–January 20, 1864," *OR*, ser. 1, vol. 45, pt. 1, p. 708. The exact moment was probably unknown and at this point is impossible to pin down with absolute certainty.
28. Position of Forrest's cavalry: Nathan Forrest, "Report of Maj. Gen. Nathan B. Forrest, C. S. Army, Commanding Cavalry, of Operations November 16, 1864–January 23, 1865," *OR*, ser. 1, vol. 45, pt. 1, p. 753; McMorries: Edward Young McMorries, "History of the First Alabama Volunteer Infantry CSA," ADAH; Copley: John M. Copley, *A Sketch of the Battle of Franklin, Tenn.*, 48.
29. W. J. Worsham and C. W. Heiskell, *Old Nineteenth Tennessee Regiment*, 141.
30. John Johnston, "Personal Reminiscences of the Civil War 1861–1865, TSLA.
31. R. M. Collins, *Chapters from the Unwritten History of the War between the States*, 246.
32. Boyce: Joseph Boyce, "Cockrell's Brigade Band at Franklin," 271.
33. Mamie Yeary, *Reminiscences of the Boys in Gray*, 227.
34. Stewart's and Cheatham's Corps advancing: Alexander P. Stewart, "Reports of Lieut. Gen. Alexander P. Stewart," *OR*, ser. 1, vol. 45, pt. 1, p. 708; and Edward Young McMorries, "History of the First Alabama Volunteer

Infantry CSA," ADAH; Carter: Carole Robinson, "Capt. Tod Carter's Tragic Death, A Life Lost Too Soon," *Williamson Herald*, Franklin, TN, November 15, 2014.

35. D. W. Sanders, "Hood's Tennessee Campaign," 8, Southern History Collection, BPL.
36. W. D. Mintz, CHA, quoted in David Logsdon, *Eyewitnesses at the Battle of Franklin*, 9.
37. Edwin Hansford Rennolds, *A History of the Henry County Commands*, 104.
38. T. J. Walker, "Reminiscences of the Civil War," 68.
39. Joseph Boyce, "Cockrell's Brigade Band at Franklin," 271.
40. G. C. Phillips, "Witness to the Battle of Franklin," 262.
41. Ellison Capers, "Report of Col. Ellison Capers," *OR*, ser. 1, vol. 45, pt. 1, p. 737.
42. John Johnston, "Personal Reminiscences of the Civil War 1861–1865," TSLA.
43. Roberts: B. T. Roberts, "Vivid Reminiscences of Franklin," *Confederate Veteran* 1, no. 11 (November 1913): 339; Hockersmith: P. E. Hockersmith, "Seeing the Battle of Franklin," *Confederate Veteran* 12, no. 5 (May 1904): 227; Banks: R. W. Banks, *The Battle of Franklin*, 50; Morton: John Watson Morton, *The Artillery of Nathan Bedford Forrest's Cavalry*, 273.
44. Confederate artillery absent and Hood's plans: "Itinerary of the Army of Tennessee," *OR*, ser. 1, vol. 45, pt. 1, p. 670; William Bate, "Report of Maj. Gen. C. S. Army," *OR*, ser. 1, vol. 45, pt. 1, p. 743; and Edward Walthall, "Reports of Maj. Gen. Edward C. Walthall," *OR*, ser. 1, vol. 45, pt. 1, p. 721; Union artillery firing with little Confederate response: James Dinkins, *1861 to 1865, by an Old Johnnie*, 236; and R. W. Banks, *The Battle of Franklin*, 50.
45. Preston: W. E. Preston, "Memoir of W. E. Preston," ADAH; Hotze: Peter Hotze, "Memoir," Hotze Family Papers, ASA; Confederates preserving line during advance: Mumford Dixon Diary, entry dated November 30, 1864, TSLA; Confederate infantry in high spirits: Alexander P. Stewart, "Reports of Lieut. Gen. Alexander P. Stewart," *OR*, ser. 1, vol. 45, pt. 1, p. 708; Confederate infantry resisting firing: Samuel T. Foster and Norman D. Brown, *One of Cleburne's Command*, 147; Collins: R. M. Collins, *Chapters from the Unwritten History of the War between the States*, 246.
46. John M. Copley, *A Sketch of the Battle of Franklin*, 49.
47. Walthall: Edward Walthall, "Reports of Maj. Gen. Edward C. Walthall," *OR*, ser. 1, vol. 45, pt. 1, p. 720; capture of the Union outer works raises Confederate spirits: John M. Copley, *A Sketch of the Battle of Franklin*, 50; Confederates continuing toward second Union line: Samuel T. Foster and Norman D. Brown, *One of Cleburne's Command*, 147; Boyce: Joseph Boyce, "Cockrell's Brigade Band at Franklin," 271.

48. Ellison Capers, "Report of Col. Ellison Capers," *OR*, ser. 1, vol. 45, pt. 1, p. 737.
49. Better fortifications at second Union line: Thomas A. Head, *Campaigns and Battles of the Sixteenth Regiment*, 150; Federal line firing again: John M. Copley, *A Sketch of the Battle of Franklin*, 52; Federal artillery firing from across the river: Edward Walthall, "Reports of Maj. Gen. Edward C. Walthall," *OR*, ser. 1, vol. 45, pt. 1, p. 720.
50. B. T. Roberts, "Vivid Reminiscences of Franklin," 339.
51. McMorries: Edward Young McMorries, "History of the First Alabama Volunteer Infantry CSA," ADAH; Preston: W. E. Preston, "Memoir of W. E. Preston," ADAH; Copley: John M. Copley, *A Sketch of the Battle of Franklin*, 53; Walker: T. J. Walker, "Reminiscences of the Civil War," 69.
52. Buck: Irving A. Buck, *Cleburne and His Command*, 328; Morton: John Watson Morton, *The Artillery of Nathan Bedford Forrest's Cavalry*, 276; Rennolds: Edwin Hansford Rennolds, *A History of the Henry County Commands*, 105; Dixon: Mumford Dixon Diary, entry dated November 30, 1864, TSLA.
53. Confederates continuing forward under heavy Union fire: Edward Walthall, "Reports of Maj. Gen. Edward C. Walthall," *OR*, ser. 1, vol. 45, pt. 1, p. 720; Head: Thomas A. Head, *Campaigns and Battles of the Sixteenth Regiment*, 150; Ward: John H. Ward, "The Eleventh Tennessee Infantry," *Confederate Veteran* 16, no. 8 (August 1908): 420.
54. Walker: T. J. Walker, "Reminiscences of the Civil War," 69; Etter: Diary of Risenar Etter, entry dated November 30, 1864, SRNBP; Hickey: "A Hero in the Strife," *Confederate Veteran* 2, no. 9 (September 1894): 282; Rennolds: Edwin Hansford Rennolds, *A History of the Henry County Commands*, 106.
55. Men from Gist's and Gordon's Brigades taking a portion of the second line: Ellison Capers, "Report of Col. Ellison Capers," *OR*, ser. 1, vol. 45, pt. 1, p. 737; Foster: Samuel T. Foster and Norman D. Brown, *One of Cleburne's Command*, 148; Flowers: Edwin Hansford Rennolds, *A History of the Henry County Commands*, 106; Synnamon: James Synnamon, "A Veteran with Many Wounds," *Confederate Veteran* 21, no. 12 (December 1913): 582; Roberts: B. T. Roberts, "Vivid Reminiscences of Franklin," 339.
56. Irving A. Buck, *Cleburne and His Command*, 331; and Levi Tucker Scofield, *The Retreat from Pulaski to Nashville*, 37.
57. Opdycke's men retake broken portion of Union second line: Irving A. Buck, *Cleburne and His Command*, 331; Opdycke as savior of Union army: John Shellenberger, *The Battle of Franklin*, 3.
58. Confederates stuck in front of cotton gin: Samuel T. Foster and Norman D. Brown, *One of Cleburne's Command*, 150; Rea: R. N. Rea, "Mississippi Soldier of the Confederacy," 287.

59. Worsham and Heiskell: W. J. Worsham and C. W. Heiskell, *Old Nineteenth Tennessee Regiment*, 143; Confederate soldiers using dead comrades as shields: James Dinkins, *1861 to 1865, by an Old Johnnie*, 236; Rennolds and death of Gen. Strahl: Edwin Hansford Rennolds, *A History of the Henry County Commands*, 106, 107; Morton: John Watson Morton, *The Artillery of Nathan Bedford Forrest's Cavalry*, 276.
60. Rennolds: Edwin Hansford Rennolds, *A History of the Henry County Commands*, 108; Ward: John H. Ward, "The Eleventh Tennessee Infantry," 420; Mims: Mamie Yeary, *Reminiscences of the Boys in Gray*, 521; Hotze: Peter Hotze, "Memoir," Hotze Family Papers, ASA.
61. William Bate, "Report of Maj. Gen. C. S. Army," *OR*, ser. 1, vol. 45, pt. 1, pp. 742, 743.
62. Gist's horse shot: Gene C. Armistead, *Horses and Mules in the Civil War*, 145; Gist continuing on foot: Wilson Gee, *The Gist Family of South Carolina*, 85; and Ellison Capers, "Report of Col. Ellison Capers," *OR*, ser. 1, vol. 45, pt. 1, p. 737; Gist shot in thigh: W. Scott Poole, *South Carolina's Civil War*, 127; death of Gist: Ellison Capers, "Report of Col. Ellison Capers," *OR*, ser. 1, vol. 45, pt. 1, p. 737; and W. Scott Poole, *South Carolina's Civil War*, 127; artillery shells: James Dinkins, *1861 to 1865, by an Old Johnnie*, 236.
63. Description of Federal second line: William Bate, "Report of Maj. Gen. C. S. Army," *OR*, ser. 1, vol. 45, pt. 1, p. 742; Yeatman: William Yeatman, "My Military Life," SRNBP; Tennesseans slaughtered trying to break through: Charles Gore Joy, "The Stampede at La Fayette, Ga.," 476.
64. Bate's Division: William Bate, "Report of Maj. Gen. C. S. Army," *OR*, ser. 1, vol. 45, pt. 1, p. 742; Chalmers's Division: James Chalmers, "Report of Big. Gen. James R. Chalmers," *OR*, ser. 1, vol. 45, pt. 1, p. 764; Reddick: H. W. Reddick, *Seventy-Seven Years in Dixie*, 58; Carter: Rosalie Carter, "Capt. Tod Carter of the Confederate States Army," National Park Service website, accessed March 25, 2016, https://www.nps.gov/stri/learn/historyculture/upload/TN_Carter%20Bio_20th%20Infantry.pdf; Confederates unable to capture inner line of Union breastworks: Alexander P. Stewart, "Reports of Lieut. Gen. Alexander P. Stewart," *OR*, ser. 1, vol. 45, pt. 1, p. 708.
65. Lee's arrival and attempt to aid Cheatham: Stephen D. Lee, "Report of Lieut. Gen. Stephen D. Lee," *OR*, ser. 1, vol. 45, pt. 1, p. 687; and Henry Clayton, "Report of Maj. Gen. Henry D. Clayton," *OR*, ser. 1, vol. 45, pt. 1, p. 697; Lee's troops connect with Bate's Division: William Bate, "Report of Maj. Gen. C. S. Army," *OR*, ser. 1, vol. 45, pt. 1, p. 743.
66. C. Irvine Walker, "Sketch of the Career of the 10th and 19th South Carolina," *Recollections and Reminiscences*, 367, Southern History Collection, BPL.
67. Robert Jarman, "The History of Company K, 27th Mississippi Infantry," MDAH.

68. Second line of Union works near Carter's Creek Pike supported by battery: William Bate, "Report of Maj. Gen. C. S. Army," *OR*, ser. 1, vol. 45, pt. 1, p. 742; Jarman: Robert Jarman, "The History of Company K, 27th Mississippi Infantry," MDAH; Baumer: Joseph Baumer Memoir, ADAH.
69. James Cooper, "Memoir of James Cooper, 20th Tennessee Infantry," NTPL.
70. Copley: John M. Copley, *A Sketch of the Battle of Franklin*, 49; Confederates defeating Union cavalry: Alexander P. Stewart, "Reports of Lieut. Gen. Alexander P. Stewart," *OR*, ser. 1, vol. 45, pt. 1, p. 708; Buford's Division proceeding dismounted: Nathan Forrest, "Report of Maj. Gen. Nathan B. Forrest," *OR*, ser. 1, vol. 45, pt. 1, p. 754; Confederate right flank taking fire from two directions: J. P. Cannon, *Inside of Rebeldom*, 259.
71. Walthall ordering Reynolds around thicket and replacing him with Cantey: Edward Walthall, "Reports of Maj. Gen. Edward C. Walthall," *OR*, ser. 1, vol. 45, pt. 1, p. 720; McMorries: Edward Young McMorries, "History of the First Alabama Volunteer Infantry CSA," ADAH; 1st Alabama within rifle range: J. P. Cannon, *Inside of Rebeldom*, 259.
72. Nesbitt: N. B. Nesbitt, "The Grand Old Veteran," *Confederate Veteran* 3, no. 2 (February 1895): 50; Boyce: Joseph Boyce, "Cockrell's Brigade Band at Franklin," 271; Anderson: Ephraim Anderson, *Memoirs*, 396.
73. Forrest ordering Jackson's Division across river: Nathan Forrest, "Report of Maj. Gen. Nathan B. Forrest," *OR*, ser. 1, vol. 45, pt. 1, p. 754; Hancock: R. R. Hancock, *Hancock's Diary*, 520.
74. Pulliam: Mamie Yeary, *Reminiscences of the Boys in Gray*, 623; Weathers: B. F. Weathers, "B. F. Weathers Papers," ADAH; McMillan: W. W. McMillan, "Reminiscences of War of 1861," ADAH.
75. J. P. Cannon, *Inside of Rebeldom*, 259.
76. D. C. Marshall to the Bost Family, January 22, 1865, BCAS.
77. Joseph Boyce, "Cockrell's Brigade Band at Franklin," 271.
78. Stephen A. Cowley, Inspection of Quarles's Brigade, September 15, 1864; Edward Young McMorries, "History of the First Alabama Volunteer Infantry CSA," ADAH.
79. Confederates repulsed with huge losses: B. F. Weathers, "B. F. Weathers Papers," ADAH; Pulliam: Mamie Yeary, *Reminiscences of the Boys in Gray*, 623; Copley: John M. Copley, *A Sketch of the Battle of Franklin, Tenn.*, 53; Stephens: M. D. L. Stephens, "Diary of M. D. L. Stephens," CHA, quoted in David Logsdon, *Eyewitnesses at the Battle of Franklin*, 46.
80. John M. Copley, *A Sketch of the Battle of Franklin*, 55.
81. Boyce: Joseph Boyce, "Cockrell's Brigade Band at Franklin," 271; Stephens: M. D. L. Stephens, "Diary of M. D. L. Stephens," CHA, quoted in David Logsdon, *Eyewitnesses at the Battle of Franklin*, 46.
82. Copley: John M. Copley, *A Sketch of the Battle of Franklin*, 56; Cannon: J. P. Cannon, *Inside of Rebeldom*, 259.

83. W. W. McMillan, "Reminiscences of War of 1861," ADAH.
84. Weathers: B. F. Weathers, "B. F. Weathers Papers," ADAH; Morton: John Watson Morton, *The Artillery of Nathan Bedford Forrest's Cavalry*, 275.
85. Clayton: Henry Clayton, "Report of Maj. Gen. Henry D. Clayton," *OR*, ser. 1, vol. 45, pt. 1, p. 697; death of Tod Carter: Rosalie Carter, "Capt. Tod Carter of the Confederate States Army," National Park Service website, accessed March 25, 2016, https://www.nps.gov/stri/learn/historyculture/upload/TN_Carter%20Bio_20th%20Infantry.pdf.
86. Stovall's Brigade: Marcellus Stovall, "Report of Brig. Gen. Marcellus A. Stovall," OR, ser. 1, vol. 45, pt. 1, p. 701; Tillman and the 24th South Carolina: Ellison Capers, "Report of Col. Ellison Capers," *OR*, ser. 1, vol. 45, pt. 1, p. 737; cavalry in Jackson's Division: Nathan Forrest, "Report of Maj. Gen. Nathan B. Forrest," *OR*, ser. 1, vol. 45, pt. 1, p. 754; Lanning: James Lanning Diary, entry dated November 30, 1864, ADAH; McMorries: Edward Young McMorries, "History of the First Alabama Volunteer Infantry CSA," ADAH; Marshall: D. C. Marshall to the Bost Family, January 22, 1865, BCAS; Bevier: R. S. Bevier, *History of the First and Second Missouri Confederate Brigades*, 255.
87. James Dinkins, *1861 to 1865, by an Old Johnnie*, 236.
88. Hood's plans: Edward Walthall, "Reports of Maj. Gen. Edward C. Walthall," *OR*, ser. 1, vol. 45, pt. 1, p. 721.
89. Diary of William Brown, entry dated November 30, 1864, SRNBP.
90. Cox displeased with order to retreat, Schofield's response, and Cox's order to withdraw: John Shellenberger, *The Battle of Franklin*, 41; Cox's preference to counterattack: Frederick Fout, *Die Schwersten Tage Des Burgerkrieges Von 1864 Und 1865*, 107; and Levi Tucker Scofield, *The Retreat from Pulaski to Nashville*, 52; Schofield's rationale for withdrawing from Franklin: John Schofield, *Forty-Six Years in the Army* (New York: Century Co., 1897), 187.
91. 19th Tennessee: W. J. Worsham and C. W. Heiskell, *Old Nineteenth Tennessee Regiment*, 143; Henderson: Jesse Henderson Diary, entry dated December 1, 1864, UM; Hood's dawn assault cancelled: Edward Walthall, "Reports of Maj. Gen. Edward C. Walthall, C. S. Army, Commanding Division and Rear Guard of Infantry, of Operations November 20, 1864–January 8, 1865," *OR*, ser. 1, vol. 45, pt. 1, p. 721; Joy: Charles Gore Joy, "The Stampede at La Fayette, Ga.," 476; Rennolds: E. H. Rennolds Diary, entry dated December 1, 1864, UTK.
92. Hood's estimate of Confederate casualties at Franklin: John Hood, "Reports of General John B. Hood, C.S. Army, Commanding Army of Tennessee," *OR*, ser. 1, vol. 45, pt. 1, p. 654; Union casualties at Franklin: Jacob Cox, *The Battle of Franklin*, 215; Union estimates of Confederate casualties at Franklin: John Schofield, "Report of Maj. Gen. John M. Schofield, U. S. Army, Commanding Army of the Ohio," *OR*, ser. 1, vol. 45, pt. 1, p. 344.

93. Actual Confederate casualties at Franklin: Wiley Sword, *The Confederacy's Last Hurrah*, 269; losses of Confederate officers at Franklin: "List of Division, Brigade, and Regimental Commanders Killed, Wounded, Missing and Captured in the Battle of November 30, at Franklin, Tenn.," *OR*, ser. 1, vol. 45, pt. 1, p. 686; period with hardest fighting and greatest losses: John M. Copley, *A Sketch of the Battle of Franklin*, 64; Hill: Andrew Hill, "Personal Recollections of Andrew Malone Hill," ADAH.
94. Hood arguing Franklin proved Army of Tennessee unstoppable: A. P. Mason, by Command of General Hood, "General Field Orders No. 38," *OR*, ser. 1, vol. 45, pt. 2, p. 638; Lanning: James Lanning Diary, entry dated November 30, 1864, ADAH; Ritter: William Ritter, "Sketch of the Third Battery of Maryland Artillery," 538; Boyce: Joseph Boyce, "Cockrell's Brigade Band at Franklin," 271.
95. Rozell: George Rozell, "General Joseph E. Johnston," 429; Hockersmith: P. E. Hockersmith, "Seeing the Battle of Franklin," 227; Dunlap: Sam Dunlap, "Hard Times on Hood's Retreat," 266; Foster: Samuel T. Foster and Norman D. Brown, *One of Cleburne's Command*, 150, 151; Jones: Edgar W. Jones, "History of the 18th Alabama Infantry," ADAH.

6. "Frozen Out"

1. W. J. Worsham and C. W. Heiskell, *Old Nineteenth Tennessee Regiment*, 152.
2. Position of Forrest's cavalry divisions and hundreds of Union prisoners taken en route to Nashville: R. R. Hancock, *Hancock's Diary*, 522, 523; Confederate cavalry encountering Union troops: John Watson Morton, *The Artillery of Nathan Bedford Forrest's Cavalry*, 277.
3. Confederate casualties at Franklin: "List of Division, Brigade, and Regimental Commanders," *OR*, ser. 1, vol. 45, pt. 1, p. 686; men separated from their units: Levi Tucker Scofield, *The Retreat from Pulaski to Nashville*, 49; Joy: Charles Gore Joy, "The Stampede at La Fayette, Ga.," 476; Ward: John H. Ward, "The Eleventh Tennessee Infantry," 420; Foster: Samuel T. Foster and Norman D. Brown, *One of Cleburne's Command*, 150.
4. Confederates reorganizing and burying their dead: John S. Holland to his friend Dr. William Farell, January 1, 1865, John S. Holland Civil War Letter, KRC, AHC; Kellum: J. W. Kellum, "Third Florida Regiment," 554; burying men in trenches: George Brewer, "History of the 46th Alabama Regiment Volunteer Infantry," ADAH; Bell: Mamie Yeary, *Reminiscences of the Boys in Gray*, 53; Etter: Diary of Risenar Etter, entry dated December 1, 1864, SRNBP; Boone: Mamie Yeary, *Reminiscences of the Boys in Gray*, 66; Harris: "Historical Sketch of Selden – Lovelace Battery," ADAH; Cooper: James Cooper, "Memoir of James Cooper, 20th Tennessee Infantry," Special Collections Division, NTPL.

5. A. P. Mason, by Command of General Hood, "General Field Orders No. 38," *OR*, ser. 1, vol. 45, pt. 2, p. 638.
6. Army of Tennessee moving north, position of infantry and artillery: "Itinerary of the Army of Tennessee," *OR*, ser. 1, vol. 45, pt. 1, p. 671; cavalry in the lead: John Watson Morton, *The Artillery of Nathan Bedford Forrest's Cavalry*, 277.
7. Nashville at the start of the war: James L. McDonough, *Nashville: The Western Confederacy's Final Gamble*, 123; Nashville's importance as a crossroads of road, rail, and river traffic: Kevin Comer, *Louisville & Nashville Railroad in South Central Kentucky*, 11; Union capturing and fortifying Nashville: William Morel Moxley, *Oh, What a Loansome* [sic] *Time I Had*, 116.
8. Brown: Diary of William Brown, entry dated November 30, 1864, SRNBP; Lanning: James Lanning Diary, entry dated December 1, 1864, ADAH; Maxwell: James Robert Maxwell, *Autobiography of James Robert Maxwell*, 262.
9. Hood's claim of higher morale: John Bell Hood, *Advance and Retreat*, 297; Jones: Edgar W. Jones, "History of the 18th Alabama Infantry," ADAH; Vann: Samuel King Vann and Nancy Elizabeth Neel Vann, *"Most Lovely Lizzie,"* 63; Crook: W. Jere Crook to his cousin Hattie Crook, December 10, 1864, W. Jere Crook Letters, TSLA; Dent: Stouten Dent to his wife, Anna, December 4, 1864, S. H. Dent Papers, AUA; Rape: A. D. Rape, "Some Thrilling War Experiences," *Confederate Veteran* 35, no. 5 (May 1927): 179.
10. Joy: Charles Gore Joy, "The Stampede at La Fayette, Ga.," 476; Boone: Mamie Yeary, *Reminiscences of the Boys in Gray*, 66; Gale: William Gale to his wife, January 19, 1864, William Gale Letters, TSLA; men feeling Hood was foolish to march on Nashville: W. J. Worsham and C. W. Heiskell, *Old Nineteenth Tennessee Regiment*, 151; Arnold: James Arnold to Thomas M. Owen, February 4, 1911, ADAH; Lavender: John W. Lavender, *The War Memoirs of Captain John W. Lavender*, 110; Dinkins: James Dinkins, *1861 to 1865, by an Old Johnnie*, 238; Jones: Joseph Jones, "Sketch of My Army Life from 1861 to 1865," ASA.
11. Scofield: Levi Tucker Scofield, *The Retreat from Pulaski to Nashville*, 49; Hotze: Peter Hotze, "Memoir," Hotze Family Papers, ASA; Copley: John M. Copley, *A Sketch of the Battle of Franklin*, 64.
12. Holland Thompson, *Edward Lyman Munson*, 256, 258, 260, 262.
13. Bevier: R. S. Bevier, *History of the First and Second Missouri Confederate Brigades*, 255; civilians providing housing and food: Holland Thompson, *The Photographic History of the Civil War*, 260; Davis: James Sherrod to Bettie Davis, December 13, 1864, Newton N. Davis Papers, ADAH; Key: Wirt Armistead Cate, *Two Soldiers*, 161.
14. Army of Tennessee moving toward Nashville: "Itinerary of the Army of Tennessee," OR, ser. 1, vol. 45, pt. 1, p. 671; Forrest's cavalry within three

miles of Nashville: R. R. Hancock, *Hancock's Diary*, 523; positions of Confederate cavalry and artillery around Nashville: John Watson Morton, *The Artillery of Nathan Bedford Forrest's Cavalry*, 277, 278.

15. Battle: Diary of Robert Battle, entry dated December 2, 1864, SRNBP; Cooper and Litton: James Cooper, "Memoir of James Cooper, 20th Tennessee Infantry," NTPL; Head: Thomas A. Head, *Campaigns and Battles of the Sixteenth Regiment*, 155.
16. R. R. Hancock, *Hancock's Diary*, 523, 534.
17. Additional Confederate forces south of Nashville on Dec. 2: "Itinerary of the Army of Tennessee," *OR*, ser. 1, vol. 45, pt. 1, p. 671; Union bombardment: Diary of Risenar Etter, entry dated December 3, 1864, SRNBP; and Thomas A. Head, *Campaigns and Battles of the Sixteenth Regiment*, 151; Confederate units forced back: Edward Noyes, "Excerpts from the Civil War Diary of E. T. Eggleston," 355; Holland: John S. Holland to his friend Dr. William Farell, January 1, 1865, John S. Holland Civil War Letters, KRC, AHC; Jones: Edgar W. Jones, "History of the 18th Alabama Infantry," ADAH.
18. Cullens: G. T. Cullens, "Our Second Campaign to Nashville," *Confederate Veteran* 12, no. 9 (September 1904): 436; Walker: C. Irvine Walker, "Sketch of the Career of the 10th and 19th South Carolina," *Recollections and Reminiscences*, 367, Southern History Collection, BPL; Gen. Thomas's forces: James R. Knight, *Hood's Tennessee Campaign*, 91; Hood's forces: John Bell Hood, *Advance and Retreat*, 298.
19. John Bell Hood, *Advance and Retreat*, 299.
20. Position of Hood's troops around Nashville and location of Hood's headquarters: "Itinerary of the Army of Tennessee," *OR*, ser. 1, vol. 45, pt. 1, p. 671; cavalry providing screens: Irving A. Buck, *Cleburne and His Command*, 347; Hood's hopes for fighting at Nashville: John Bell Hood, *Advance and Retreat*, 299; "Itinerary of the Army of Tennessee," *OR*, ser. 1, vol. 45, pt. 1, p. 671.
21. Buck: Irving A. Buck, *Cleburne and His Command*, 347; Bevier: R. S. Bevier, *History of the First and Second Missouri Confederate Brigades*, 255; Bonaparte: Michael Eggleston, *The White Man's Fight*, 73.
22. Christopher Einolf, "George H. Thomas," *Encyclopedia of Virginia*, accessed April 5, 2016, http://www.encyclopediavirginia.org/Thomas_George_H_1816–1870#start_entry; J. Watts De Peyster, *Major-General George H. Thomas*, 14.
23. Stanton urging Thomas to attack: Edwin Stanton, "Letter to General Grant," *OR*, ser. 1, vol. 45, pt. 2, p. 84; Grant demanding that Thomas attack: Ulysses S. Grant, *Personal Memoirs of U. S. Grant*, 566; Grant threatening to remove Thomas: Ulysses Grant, "Letter to Edwin Stanton," *OR*, ser. 1, vol. 45, pt. 2, p. 84.

24. Thomas's eclectic troops: Thomas Van Horne and Edward Ruger, *History of the Army of the Cumberland*, 186; Thomas promising an assault: George Thomas, "Letter to General Grant," *OR*, ser. 1, vol. 45, pt. 1, p. 1034; Stanton on Thomas: Edwin Stanton, "Letter to General Grant," *OR*, ser. 1, vol. 45, pt. 2, p. 84.
25. Union well positioned versus the Confederate forces at Nashville: "The Situation in Tennessee," *Daily Intelligencer* (Wheeling, VA), December 7, 1864; "The War," *Xenia (OH) Sentinel*, December 16, 1864.
26. Sparkman: John W. Sparkman, *The Diary of Sergt. John W. Sparkman*, 70; Vann: Samuel King Vann and Nancy Elizabeth Neel Vann, *"Most Lovely Lizzie,"* 64; Harris: "Historical Sketch of Selden – Lovelace Battery," ADAH.
27. Improvised shelters: R. M. Collins, *Chapters from the Unwritten History of the War between the States*, 251; sleeping pits and Jones quotation: Edgar W. Jones, "History of the 18th Alabama Infantry," ADAH; Meadows: Memoir of R. B. Meadows, CHA, quoted in David Logsdon, *Eyewitnesses at the Battle of Franklin*, 27.
28. Chalmers's Confederate cavalry capturing transports: "Itinerary of the Army of Tennessee," *OR*, ser. 1, vol. 45, pt. 1, p. 671; Union retaking transports: John Watson Morton, *The Artillery of Nathan Bedford Forrest's Cavalry*, 279; McCleary: A. C. McLeary, "Humorous Incidents of the Civil War," UNCSHC, 6.
29. John Watson Morton, *The Artillery of Nathan Bedford Forrest's Cavalry*, 279, 280.
30. Morton: John Watson Morton, *The Artillery of Nathan Bedford Forrest's Cavalry*, 280; Henderson: Diary of F. E. Henderson, entry dated December 5, 1864, RCHS.
31. Hood sending reinforcements to Forrest: "Itinerary of the Army of Tennessee," *OR*, ser. 1, vol. 45, pt. 1, p. 671; McLeod: William McLeod Diary, entry dated December 7, 1864, FSA; plans to capture Murfreesboro: R. R. Hancock, *Hancock's Diary*, 525.
32. Federal forces around Murfreesboro: "Itinerary of the Army of Tennessee," *OR*, ser. 1, vol. 45, pt. 1, p. 671; Forrest's troops: R. R. Hancock, *Hancock's Diary*, 526; Forrest's troops skirmishing with Union around Murfreesboro and Barteau wounded: Hancock, *Hancock's Diary*, 524; Union troops refusing to attack: John Watson Morton, *The Artillery of Nathan Bedford Forrest's Cavalry*, 281.
33. Copley: John M. Copley, *A Sketch of the Battle of Franklin*, 70; Nashville residents unimpressed: "The Situation Yesterday," *Nashville (TN) Daily Union*, December 7, 1864; Federal response to shelling: "Itinerary of the Army of Tennessee," *OR*, ser. 1, vol. 45, pt. 1, p. 671; Union gunboats shelling Confederate lines: Wirt Armistead Cate, *Two Soldiers*, 164.

34. Position of Confederates around Murfreesboro and assault of Federal troops: R. R. Hancock, *Hancock's Diary*, 526, 527; Confederate cavalry attempted attack on Murfreesboro: John Watson Morton, *The Artillery of Nathan Bedford Forrest's Cavalry*, 281.
35. Gen. Milroy's counterattack: John Watson Morton, *The Artillery of Nathan Bedford Forrest's Cavalry*, 282; James Cooper, "Memoir of James Cooper, 20th Tennessee Infantry," NTPL.
36. Forrest unable to hold the Confederate line: John Watson Morton, *The Artillery of Nathan Bedford Forrest's Cavalry*, 283; failing Confederate right causing retreat: R. R. Hancock, *Hancock's Diary*, 527; Milroy's withdrawal: John Watson Morton, *The Artillery of Nathan Bedford Forrest's Cavalry*, 284; Cooper: James Cooper, "Memoir of James Cooper, 20th Tennessee Infantry," NTPL; Yeatman: William Yeatman, "My Military Life," SRNBP.
37. Hardy: William Hardy to his wife, Sallie Hardy, December 14, 1864, William H. and Sallie J. Hardy Papers, USM; Hancock: R. R. Hancock, *Hancock's Diary*, 528.
38. Key, advance by Lee's Corps, and Union artillery firing on Confederates: Wirt Armistead Cate, *Two Soldiers*, 161, 164; rebels occupying abandoned Union rifle pits: "Itinerary of the Army of Tennessee," *OR*, ser. 1, vol. 45, pt. 1, p. 672.
39. McLeod: William McLeod Diary, entry dated December 7, 1864, FSA; Cooper: James Cooper, "Memoir of James Cooper, 20th Tennessee Infantry," NTPL; Head: Thomas A. Head, *Campaigns and Battles of the Sixteenth Regiment*, 152.
40. Stewart's and Lee's Corps in new position: "Itinerary of the Army of Tennessee," *OR*, ser. 1, vol. 45, pt. 1, p. 672; desperate need for wood: Edwin Hansford Rennolds, *A History of the Henry County Commands*, 110; wood shortage causing suffering: E. H. Rennolds Diary, entry dated December 7, 1864, UTK; Rape: A. D. Rape, "Some Thrilling War Experiences," 179; Magill: Robert M. Magill, *Personal Reminiscences of a Confederate Soldier Boy*, 69; Collins: R. M. Collins, *Chapters from the Unwritten History of the War between the States*, 251; McWhirter: George McWhirter, "Soldier in the Western Army," *Confederate Veteran* 5, no. 12 (December 1897): 623.
41. Hood's instructions for constructing defensive works: "Itinerary of the Army of Tennessee," *OR*, ser. 1, vol. 45, pt. 1, p. 672; McMorries: Edward Young McMorries, "History of the First Alabama Volunteer Infantry CSA," ADAH.
42. Scofield: Levi Tucker Scofield, *The Retreat from Pulaski to Nashville*, 56, 62; Miller: John Miller, letters dated December 4 and December 14, 1864, John Miller Civil War Letters, private collection of Mike Northway, accessed September 28, 2015, http://www.civilwararchive.com/; Federal cav-

alry concentrating at Edgefield: "Itinerary of the Army of Tennessee," *OR*, ser. 1, vol. 45, pt. 1, p. 672; Union scouting parties: William Ritter, "Sketch of the Third Battery of Maryland Artillery," 541; Maley: H. H. Maley to his father and mother, December 13, 1864, Henry H. Maley Letters, UND.

43. Clark: Walter A. Clark, *Under the Stars and Bars*, 154; McWhirter: George McWhirter, "Soldier in the Western Army," 623; Joy: Charles Gore Joy, "The Stampede at La Fayette, Ga.," 476; Mims: Mamie Yeary, *Reminiscences of the Boys in Gray*, 521; Crook: W. Jere Crook to his cousin Hattie Crook, December 10, 1864, W. Jere Crook Letters, TSLA; McLeod: William McLeod Diary, entry dated December 12, 1864, FSA; Pettus: Edmund Pettus to his wife, December 14, 1864, Edmund Pettus Letters, ADAH; Worsham and Heiskell: W. J. Worsham and C. W. Heiskell, *Old Nineteenth Tennessee Regiment*, 152; Knight: Mamie Yeary, *Reminiscences of the Boys in Gray*, 409.

44. Etter: Diary of Risenar Etter, entry dated December 10, 1864, SRNBP; Mims: Mamie Yeary, *Reminiscences of the Boys in Gray*, 521; Thompson: Jeff Toalson, *No Soap, No Pay, Diarrhea, Dysentery & Desertion*, 263; raiding supply wagons: Robert Jarman, "The History of Company K, 27th Mississippi Infantry," MDAH; Maxwell: James Robert Maxwell, *Autobiography of James Robert Maxwell*, 266; Harmon: James Harmon, "Memoir of J. W. Harmon," TSLA.

45. Growing number of Confederate soldiers without shoes: Edgar W. Jones, "History of the 18th Alabama Infantry," ADAH; McMorries: Edward Young McMorries, "History of the First Alabama Volunteer Infantry CSA," ADAH; Collins: R. M. Collins, *Chapters from the Unwritten History of the War between the States*, 251; Moose: David Logsdon, *Eyewitnesses at the Battle of Franklin*, 43.

46. Hood begging for troops: "Itinerary of the Army of Tennessee," *OR*, ser. 1, vol. 45, pt. 1, p. 672; Hood asking for railroad repair: "Itinerary of the Army of Tennessee," *OR*, ser. 1, vol. 45, pt. 1, p. 671.

47. Few supplies remaining in Middle Tennessee: "The Situation Yesterday," *Nashville (TN) Daily Union*, December 7, 1864; locals fleeing from foraging Confederates: "The Franklin Fight," *Wilmington (NC) Journal*, December 8, 1864; Porcher: John Porcher, dictated to his daughter Elinor Porcher, "Father's War Story," *Recollections and Reminiscences*, 386, Southern History Collection, BPL; Confederates taking supplies at gunpoint: Edward Young McMorries, "History of the First Alabama Volunteer Infantry CSA," ADAH; Hardy: William Hardy to his wife, Sallie Hardy, December 14, 1864, William H. and Sallie J. Hardy Papers, USM.

48. Pettus: Edmund Pettus to his wife, December 14, 1864, Edmund Pettus Letters, ADAH; Hardy: William Hardy to his wife, Sallie Hardy, December 14,

1864, William H. and Sallie J. Hardy Papers, USM; Hood seeking to conscript reinforcements from surrounding counties: "Itinerary of the Army of Tennessee," *OR*, ser. 1, vol. 45, pt. 1, p. 672; Hood requesting prisoner exchange: "Itinerary of the Army of Tennessee," *OR*, ser. 1, vol. 45, pt. 1, p. 671.

49. Rennolds: E. H. Rennolds Diary, entry dated December 8, 1864, UTK; Battle: Diary of Robert Battle, entry dated December 3, 1864, SRNBP; Henderson: F. E. Henderson Diary, entry dated December 9, 1864, RCHS; Lanning: James Lanning Diary, entry dated December 1, 1864, ADAH; Dinkins: James Dinkins, *1861 to 1865, by an Old Johnnie*, 238.
50. Hood pressuring cavalry to capture supplies: "Itinerary of the Army of Tennessee," *OR*, ser. 1, vol. 45, pt. 1, p. 671; army giving furloughs in hopes of supplies, little pay for Confederate soldiers: E. H. Rennolds Diary, entries dated December 8 and December 12, 1864, UTK; soldiers scavenging for wild game: George McWhirter, "Soldier in the Western Army," 623; officers ignoring trade with the enemy: Mamie Yeary, *Reminiscences of the Boys in Gray*, 53.
51. Union forces stealing firewood: Wirt Armistead Cate, *Two Soldiers*, 159; Worsham and Heiskell: W. J. Worsham and C. W. Heiskell, *Old Nineteenth Tennessee Regiment*, 151; Harris: "Historical Sketch of Selde—Lovelace Battery," ADAH; Arnold: James Arnold to Thomas M. Owen, February 4, 1911, ADAH.
52. Samuel T. Foster and Norman D. Brown, *One of Cleburne's Command*, 154.
53. Coleman: John Coleman to his sweetheart Virginia Adkins, December 4, 1864, John and Virginia Adkins Coleman Paper, Texas Collection, BUL, Waco, TX; Lanning: James Lanning Diary, entry dated December 6, 1864, ADAH; Pettus: Edmund Pettus to his wife, December 14, 1864, Edmund Pettus Letters, ADAH; Boone: Mamie Yeary, *Reminiscences of the Boys in Gray*, 66; Cooper: James Cooper, "Memoir of James Cooper, 20th Tennessee Infantry," NTPL.
54. Numbers of Confederate deserters: J. G. Parkhurst, "Report of Rebel Deserters," *OR*, ser. 1, vol. 45, pt. 1, p. 48; slaves joining the Union army: Robert Jarman, "The History of Company K, 27th Mississippi Infantry," MDAH.
55. Hardy: William Hardy to his wife, Sallie Hardy, December 14, 1864, William H. and Sallie J. Hardy Papers, USM; Key: Wirt Armistead Cate, *Two Soldiers*, 166; Bevier: R. S. Bevier, *History of the First and Second Missouri Confederate Brigades*, 255; Etter: Diary of Risenar Etter, entry dated December 11, 1864, SRNBP; Yeatman: William Yeatman, "My Military Life," SRNBP.
56. Number of Confederates able for duty: "Abstract from Field Return of the Army of Tennessee," *OR*, ser. 1, vol. 45, pt. 1, p. 678; Hayden: S. A. Hayden to his sister Beck, n.d., S. A. Hayden Letters, Louisiana and Lower Mississippi Valley Collections, LSU.

57. Weather warming: E. H. Rennolds Diary, entry dated December 14, 1864, UTK; Cameron: Maxwell Cameron to his sister, December 14, 1864, Cameron Papers, UA; Etter: Diary of Risenar Etter, entry dated December 14, 1864, SRNBP; Cannon: J. P. Cannon, *Inside of Rebeldom*, 263.
58. Federal forces preparing for attack: Levi Tucker Scofield, *The Retreat from Pulaski to Nashville*, 63; Lavender: John W. Lavender and Ted R. Worley, *The War Memoirs of Captain John W. Lavender*, 112.

7. "Put an End to Them"

1. Edgar W. Jones, "History of the 18th Alabama Infantry," ADAH.
2. Grant urging Thomas to advance: Ulysses S. Grant, *Personal Memoirs of U. S. Grant*, 566; Grant traveling to Nashville to remove Thomas: Charles F. Ritter and Jon L. Wakelyn, *Leaders of the American Civil War*, 421.
3. Weather improving and Thomas preparing to move: Thomas Van Horne, *History of the Army of the Cumberland*, 258; Union troop numbers: Louise Littleton Davis, *Nashville Tales*, 134; Thomas's plan of attack: Thomas B. Vane Home, *The Life of Major-General George H. Thomas*, 322; Union cavalry troopers carrying Spencer carbines: Derek Smith, *In the Lion's Mouth: Hood's Tragic Retreat from Nashville*, 48.
4. Elijah Evan Edwards Journal, entry dated December 15, 1864, MHS.
5. Elijah Evan Edwards Journal, entry dated December 15, 1864, MHS
6. Confederates preparing for battle: John Bell Hood, *Advance and Retreat*, 298; Sanders: D. W. Sanders, "Hood's Tennessee Campaign," 170, Southern History Collection, BPL; sounds of rifle and cannon fire: Elijah Evan Edwards Journal, entry dated December 15, 1864, MHS; Battle: Diary of Robert Battle, entry dated December 15, 1864, SRNBP; Johnston: John Johnston, "Personal Reminiscences of the Civil War 1861–1865," TSLA; Hayden: S. A. Hayden to his sister Beck, n.d., S. A. Hayden Letters, Louisiana and Lower Mississippi Valley Collections, LSU.
7. Division of former slaves advancing: John F. Fisher, *They Rode with Forrest and Wheeler*, 167; division of black Union soldiers advancing, attempting retreat, then advancing again: W. J. Worsham and C. W. Heiskell, *Old Nineteenth Tennessee Regiment*, 152; McMurray quotation and description of Union casualties in pond: William McMurray, *History of the Twentieth Tennessee Regiment Volunteer Infantry*, 347; "no quarter" for black troops: Bill O'Neal and Samuel Alonza Cooke, "The Civil War Memories of Samuel Alonza Cooke," 546; artillery firing: Wirt Armistead Cate, *Two Soldiers*, 167.
8. Charles Martin, "Jackson's Brigade in the Battle of Nashville," *Confederate Veteran* 17, no. 1 (January 1909): 12.
9. Hood sending brigades to Confederate right: William McMurray, *History of the Twentieth Tennessee Regiment Volunteer Infantry*, 346; Jarman: Robert

Jarman, "The History of Company K, 27th Mississippi Infantry," MDAH. Although Jarman did not explicitly explain, his original rifle was probably a two-banded model 1858 Enfield rifle, roughly fifty inches long and weighing about eight and a half pounds. His newly acquired weapon was most likely a fifty-five-inch-long, three-banded model 1853 Enfield rifle musket, which weighed about nine and a half pounds.

10. George H. Thomas, "Report of Maj. Gen. George H. Thomas," *OR*, ser. 1, vol. 45, pt. 1, p. 38.
11. William Gale to his wife, January 19, 1865, William Gale Letters, TSLA.
12. James Dinkins, *1861 to 1865, by an Old Johnnie*, 245.
13. John Johnston, "Personal Reminiscences of the Civil War 1861–1865," TSLA.
14. J. T. Tunnell, "Ector's Brigade in Battle of Nashville," *Confederate Veteran* 12, no. 7 (July 1904): 348.
15. James Robert Maxwell, *Autobiography of James Robert Maxwell*, 267.
16. "Report of Maj. Gen. George H. Thomas," *OR*, ser. 1, vol. 45, pt. 1, p. 38.
17. Wirt Armistead Cate, *Two Soldiers*, 168.
18. John Johnston, "Personal Reminiscences of the Civil War 1861–1865," TSLA.
19. David Logsdon, *Eyewitnesses at the Battle of Franklin*, 58.
20. Jesse Henderson Diary, entry dated December 15, 1864, UM.
21. Robert H. Dacus, *Reminiscences of Company "H,"* 20.
22. James Robert Maxwell, *Autobiography of James Robert Maxwell*, 267.
23. C. Irvine Walker, "Sketch of the Career of the 10th and 19th South Carolina," *Recollections and Reminiscences*, 367, Southern History Collection, BPL.
24. Confederate reinforcements too late to hold Redoubt No. 5: William Gale to his wife, January 19, 1865, William Gale Letters, TSLA; wedge driven between Confederates and Cumberland River: Edwin Hansford Rennolds, *A History of the Henry County Commands*, 110.
25. Richard Harris, "Historical Sketch of Selden – Lovelace Battery," ADAH.
26. Wirt Armistead Cate, *Two Soldiers*, 168.
27. Portions of Cheatham's Corps sent to reinforce retreating men from Stewart's Corps: W. J. Worsham and C. W. Heiskell, *Old Nineteenth Tennessee Regiment*, 152; and Thomas A. Head, *Campaigns and Battles of the Sixteenth Regiment*, 152; Union advance briefly stopped: Richard Harris, "Historical Sketch of Selden – Lovelace Battery," ADAH.
28. James Cooper, "Memoir of James Cooper, 20th Tennessee Infantry," Special Collections Division, NTPL.
29. Edward Young McMorries, "History of the First Alabama Volunteer Infantry CSA," ADAH.
30. James Robert Maxwell, *Autobiography of James Robert Maxwell*, 269.
31. Robert M. Magill and Brenda D. Phillips, *Personal Reminiscences of a Confederate Soldier Boy*, 69.

32. G. W. Garrett, "The First Day's Battle at Nashville," *Confederate Veteran* 18, no. 10 (October 1910): 470.
33. John Johnston, "Personal Reminiscences of the Civil War 1861–1865," TSLA.
34. S. A. Hayden to his sister Beck, n.d., S. A. Hayden Letters, Louisiana and Lower Mississippi Valley Collections, LSU.
35. Confederate army battered but intact: James Lanning Diary, entry dated December 15, 1864, ADAH; Gen. Chalmers leading a fighting retreat: James Dinkins, *1861 to 1865, by an Old Johnnie*, 246.
36. James Robert Maxwell, *Autobiography of James Robert Maxwell*, 270.
37. John Johnston, "Personal Reminiscences of the Civil War 1861–1865," TSLA.
38. William Gale to his wife, January 19, 1865, William Gale Letters, TSLA.
39. Garrett: G. W. Garrett, "The First Day's Battle at Nashville," 470; Lord: John Lord and Natalie Shipman, *Frontier Dust*, 14; Edwards: Elijah Evan Edwards Journal, entry dated December 15, 1864, MHS.
40. Hood: John Bell Hood, *Advance and Retreat*, 302; Buck: Irving A. Buck, *Cleburne and His Command*, 349; Holland: John S. Holland to his friend Dr. William Farell, January 1, 1865, John S. Holland Civil War Letter, KRC, AHC; Jordan: Stephen Jordan Diary, entry dated December 15, 1864, TSLA.
41. George H. Thomas, "Report of Maj. Gen. George H. Thomas," *OR*, ser. 1, vol. 45, pt. 1, p. 39.
42. Christopher J. Einolf, *George Thomas*, 274.
43. Army of Tennessee's new position: Edward Young McMorries, "History of the First Alabama Volunteer Infantry CSA," ADAH; new positions for Cheatham's, Lee's, and Stewart's Corps, and army entrenching on new line: John Bell Hood, *Advance and Retreat*, 302; Gale: William Gale to his wife, January 19, 1865, William Gale Letters, TSLA.
44. 19th Tennessee Infantry: W. J. Worsham and C. W. Heiskell, *Old Nineteenth Tennessee Regiment*, 152; 20th Tennessee Infantry: James Cooper, "Memoir of James Cooper, 20th Tennessee Infantry," NTPL; McMorries: Edward Young McMorries, "History of the First Alabama Volunteer Infantry CSA," ADAH; 10th South Carolina Infantry: C. Irvine Walker, "Sketch of the Career of the 10th and 19th South Carolina," *Recollections and Reminiscences*, 367, Southern History Collection, BPL; Walker: T. J. Walker, "Reminiscences of the Civil War," 68; 3rd Maryland Artillery: William Ritter, "Sketch of the Third Battery of Maryland Artillery," 541; occasion firing by Union troops during the night: James Cooper, "Memoir of James Cooper, 20th Tennessee Infantry," NTPL; relative figures for Union and Confederate troops and equipment: James L. McDonough, *Nashville*, 238.
45. Cooper: James Cooper, "Memoir of James Cooper, 20th Tennessee Infantry," NTPL; Harmon: James Harmon, "Memoir of J. W. Harmon," TSLA; Worsham and Heiskell: W. J. Worsham and C. W. Heiskell, *Old Nineteenth*

Tennessee Regiment, 154; Smith: Ed Smith, "Douglas's Battery in Battle of Nashville," *Confederate Veteran* 12, no. 11 (November 1904): 531; Jarman: Robert Jarman, "The History of Company K, 27th Mississippi Infantry," MDAH; Kelley: Samuel Kelly letter dated January 1, 1864, Samuel Kelley Letters, ADAH; Finley's Florida Brigade: Edwin Hansford Rennolds, *A History of the Henry County Commands*, 110; McLeod: William McLeod Diary, entry dated December 7, 1864, FSA; Seldon's Alabama Battery: Richard Harris Memoir, ADAH; Federal skirmishers: Elijah Evan Edwards Journal, entry dated December 16, 1864, MHS.

46. Thomas launching diversionary attack and Union infantry defeating Confederate skirmishers: George H. Thomas, "Report of Maj. Gen. George H. Thomas," *OR*, ser. 1, vol. 45, pt. 1, p. 39; Harmon: James Harmon, "Memoir of J. W. Harmon," TSLA; Head: Thomas A. Head, *Campaigns and Battles of the Sixteenth Regiment*, 152; Smith's description of Union advance and Union troops wavering under Confederate fire but continuing assault: Ed Smith, "Douglas's Battery in Battle of Nashville," 531; Confederate infantry firing on Union troops: Samuel Kelly letter dated January 1, 1864, Samuel Kelley Letters, ADAH; Moose: David Logsdon, *Eyewitnesses at the Battle of Franklin*, 86; first wave of Union attackers under intense Confederate fire: James Arnold to Thomas M. Owen, February 4, 1911, ADAH; Confederate troops driving back Union forces: George Brewer, "History of the 46th Alabama Regiment Volunteer Infantry," ADAH.
47. Union plan of attack: George H. Thomas, "Report of Maj. Gen. George H. Thomas," *OR*, ser. 1, vol. 45, pt. 1, p. 39; Gale: William Gale to his wife, January 19, 1865, William Gale Letters, TSLA.
48. Cooper: James Cooper, "Memoir of James Cooper, 20th Tennessee Infantry," NTPL; Union troops continuing advance: Elijah Evan Edwards Journal, entry dated December 16, 1864, MHS.
49. Edgar W. Jones, "History of the 18th Alabama Infantry," ADAH.
50. Cullens: G. T. Cullens, "Our Second Campaign to Nashville," 436; Harris: "Historical Sketch of Selden – Lovelace Battery," ADAH; McMorries: Edward Young McMorries, "History of the First Alabama Volunteer Infantry CSA," ADAH; Cannon: J. P. Cannon, *Inside of Rebeldom*, 263; Battle: Diary of Robert Battle, entry dated December 16, 1864, SRNBP.
51. Conley: Samuel Conley Diary, entry dated December 17, 1864, GSA; Wilson's cavalry wrapping around Confederate line: Edward Young McMorries, "History of the First Alabama Volunteer Infantry CSA," ADAH; and Thomas A. Head, *Campaigns and Battles of the Sixteenth Regiment*, 153; Rennolds: Edwin Hansford Rennolds, *A History of the Henry County Commands*, 111; Federals unleashing crossfire: William B. Bate, "The Campaign in Tennessee," *Annals of the Army of Tennessee* 1, no. 9 (December 1878): 399; Moose: David Logsdon, *Eyewitnesses at the Battle of Franklin*, 43.

52. Finley's Brigade collapsing: William McLeod Diary, entry dated December 7, 1864, FSA; Key: Wirt Armistead Cate, *Two Soldiers*, 168; Dunlap: Sam Dunlap, "Hard Times on Hood's Retreat," 266; Holland: John S. Holland to his friend Dr. William Farell, January 1, 1865, John S. Holland Civil War Letters, KRC, AHC; Kellum: J. W. Kellum, "Third Florida Regiment," 554.
53. William B. Bate, "The Campaign in Tennessee," *Annals of the Army of Tennessee* 1, no. 9, 399; Park Marshall, "Shy's Hill—Whence the Name?" *Confederate Veteran* 20, no. 11 (November 1912): 522. William Shy became more famous in death than he was in life. In 1977 police found the body of an oddly dressed, apparently recently deceased murder victim with no identification. In desperation they asked forensic anthropologist Dr. William Bass of the University of Tennessee for help. Bass estimated that the man was killed roughly one year before. After further study, investigators determined that the corpse belonged to Shy and that grave robbers had unearthed the departed colonel looking for valuables. Shy's sealed iron coffin had done an excellent job of preserving the body. Bass later quipped that he only missed the time of death by 113 years. In the aftermath of the discovery, Bass realized that scientists knew very little about human decomposition. To remedy this deficiency, he founded the University of Tennessee's Anthropology Research Facility, better known as the Body Farm. On this little patch of Tennessee soil, experts expose human corpses to every conceivable condition, carefully documenting human decomposition and providing investigators with priceless knowledge.
54. Gale: William Gale to his wife, January 19, 1865, William Gale Letters, TSLA; Conley: Samuel Oswald Conley Diary, entry dated December 1, 1864, GSA; Collins: R. M. Collins, *Chapters from the Unwritten History of the War between the States*, 254.
55. Richard Harris, "Historical Sketch of Selden – Lovelace Battery," ADAH.
56. Edward Young McMorries, "History of the First Alabama Volunteer Infantry CSA," ADAH.
57. Memoir of R. B. Meadows, CHA, quoted in David Logsdon, *Eyewitnesses at the Battle of Franklin*, 97.
58. Robert H. Dacus, *Reminiscences of Company "H,"* 21.
59. Thomas A. Head, *Campaigns and Battles of the Sixteenth Regiment*, 152.
60. Ed Smith, "Douglas's Battery in Battle of Nashville," 531.
61. Edgar W. Jones, "History of the 18th Alabama Infantry," ADAH.
62. Thomas Fowler, "Autobiography of Thomas Fowler," *Recollections and Reminiscences*, 301, Southern History Collection, BPL.
63. Memoir of R. B. Meadows, CHA, quoted in David Logsdon, *Eyewitnesses at the Battle of Franklin*, 98.
64. Samuel Kelly letter dated January 1, 1864, Samuel Kelley Letters, ADAH.
65. George Rozell, "General Joseph E. Johnston," 429.

66. George Brewer, "History of the 46th Alabama Regiment Volunteer Infantry," ADAH.
67. A. D. Rape, "Some Thrilling War Experiences," 179.
68. Memoir of James Ratchford, quoted in David Logsdon, *Eyewitnesses at the Battle of Franklin*, 102.
69. C. Irvine Walker, "Sketch of the Career of the 10th and 19th South Carolina," *Recollections and Reminiscences*, 368, Southern History Collection, BPL.
70. Edward Young McMorries, "History of the First Alabama Volunteer Infantry CSA," ADAH.
71. Magill: Robert M. Magill and Brenda D. Phillips, *Personal Reminiscences of a Confederate Soldier Boy*, 69; Ridley: B. L. Ridley, "Heroines of the South," *Confederate Veteran* 4, no. 4 (April 1896): 106.
72. Edwin Hansford Rennolds, *A History of the Henry County Commands*, 111; E. H. Rennolds Diary, entry dated December 16, 1864, UTK.
73. James Cooper, "Memoir of James Cooper, 20th Tennessee Infantry," NTPL.
74. Memoir of R. B. Meadows, CHA, quoted in David Logsdon, *Eyewitnesses at the Battle of Franklin*, 99.
75. J. P. Cannon, *Inside of Rebeldom*, 265.
76. T. J. Walker, "Reminiscences of the Civil War," 68.
77. Edwin Hansford Rennolds, *A History of the Henry County Commands*, 111.
78. R. M. Collins, *Chapters from the Unwritten History of the War between the States*, 256.
79. H. W. Reddick, *Seventy-Seven Years in Dixie*, 48.
80. James Tanner, "A Soldier Who Lost His Nerve," *Confederate Veteran* 19, no. 7 (July 1911): 355.
81. Edgar W. Jones, "History of the 18th Alabama Infantry," ADAH.
82. "Anniversary of the Battle of Nashville," *Christian Advocate* (Nashville, TN), February 10, 1922.
83. Arnold: James Arnold to Thomas M. Owen, February 4, 1911, ADAH; Douglas's Texas Battery: Ed Smith, "Douglas's Battery in Battle of Nashville," 532; Rape: A. D. Rape, "Some Thrilling War Experiences," 180.
84. James Dinkins, *1861 to 1865, by an Old Johnnie*, 248.
85. William Yeatman, "My Military Life," SRNBP.
86. W. J. Worsham and C. W. Heiskell, *Old Nineteenth Tennessee Regiment*, 154.
87. James Cooper, "Memoir of James Cooper, 20th Tennessee Infantry," Special Collections Division, NTPL.
88. Hood sending Chalmers's cavalry against Union cavalry: John Johnston, "Personal Reminiscences of the Civil War 1861–1865," TSLA; Polk: W. A. Polk, "Gallant Col. William F. Taylor," *Confederate Veteran* 16, no. 3 (March 1908): 124; Meadows: A. J. Meadows, "The 4th Tennessee Infantry," *Confederate Veteran* 14, no. 6 (July 1906): 312.

89. Figures for Confederate casualties and captured soldiers: Steven E. Woodworth and Kenneth J. Winkle, *Atlas of the Civil War*, 362; for press coverage, see, for example, "From General Thomas," *Daily Intelligencer* (Wheeling, VA), December 23, 1864; and "Deplorable Condition of Hood's Army," *Dayton (OH) Daily Empire*, December 23, 1864; desertion numbers: J. G. Parkhurst, "Report of Rebel Deserters," *OR*, ser. 1, vol. 45, pt. 1, p. 48.
90. T. B. Childress to Robert Crittenden, December 13, 1865, AUA; United States Census, 1870, 1880, 1890, 1900, "Bettie Browning Crittenden."
91. Charles Swett, "Abstract from Inspection Report of Artillery," *OR*, ser. 1, vol. 45, pt. 1, p. 682; "Report of Ordnance Material Captured," *OR*, ser. 1, vol. 45, pt. 1, p. 49.
92. "Report of Ordnance Material Captured," *OR*, ser. 1, vol. 45, pt. 1, p. 48.
93. Confederate infantry participation at the Battle of Nashville: "Abstract from Field Return of the Army of Tennessee," *OR*, ser. 1, vol. 45, pt. 1, p. 679; captured infantry weapons: Steven E. Woodworth and Kenneth J. Winkle, *Atlas of the Civil War*, 362.

8. "Ragamuffins Fleeing in Disgrace"

1. James Cooper, "Memoir of James Cooper, 20th Tennessee Infantry," NTPL.
2. Sounds of battle's aftermath: Elijah Evan Edwards Journal, entry dated December 16, 1864, MHS; Maley: H. H. Maley to his mother and father, December 21 and 25, 1864, Henry H. Maley Letters, UND.
3. Survivors camped near Brentwood: Edwin Hansford Rennolds, *A History of the Henry County Commands*, 112; men calling out instructions to new arrivals: Robert M. Magill and Brenda D. Phillips, *Personal Reminiscences of a Confederate Soldier Boy*, 69; Cannon: J. P. Cannon, *Inside of Rebeldom*, 265; Jones: Edgar W. Jones, "History of the 18th Alabama Infantry," ADAH; Joy: Charles Gore Joy, "The Stampede at La Fayette, Ga.," 476.
4. R. M. Collins, *Chapters from the Unwritten History of the War between the States*, 258.
5. P. T. Martin, "Recollections of a Confederate," *Confederate Veteran* 15 No. 5 (May 1907) 232.
6. Gen. Lee commanding men near Brentwood: Irving A. Buck, *Cleburne and His Command*, 350; Jones: Edgar W. Jones, "History of the 18th Alabama Infantry," ADAH.
7. Duncan: Thomas D. Duncan, *Recollections of Thomas D. Duncan*, 181; Clark: Walter A. Clark, *Under the Stars and Bars*, 155; Battle: Diary of Robert Battle, entry dated December 16, 1864, SRNBP; Banks: R. W. Banks, *The Battle of Franklin*, 25.
8. Clinton: Daniel Cone, *Last to Join the Fight*, 161; Etter: Diary of Risenar

Etter, entry dated December 16, 1864, SRNBP; Maxwell: James Robert Maxwell, *Autobiography of James Robert Maxwell*, 272.

9. Charles D. Dreux, "First Volunteers from Louisiana" *Confederate Veteran* 3 No. 5 (May 1895) 146.
10. Collins: R. M. Collins, *Chapters from the Unwritten History of the War between the States*, 261; Company C, 27th Alabama Infantry: J. P. Cannon, *Inside of Rebeldom*, 268; Jordan: Stephen Jordan Diary, entry dated December 18, 1864, TSLA; Battle: Diary of Robert Battle, entry dated December 16, 1864, SRNBP; Woodson: Agatha A. Woodson, "Whipped and Demoralized, But Not Scattered," *Recollections and Reminiscences*, 437, Southern History Collection, BPL.
11. Confederates traveling through Franklin: William McLeod Diary, entry dated December 17, 1864, FSA; Johnston: John Johnston, "Personal Reminiscences of the Civil War 1861–1865," TSLA.
12. W. A. Polk, "Gallant Col. William F. Taylor," 124.
13. McWhirter: George McWhirter, "Soldier in the Western Army," 623; Brewer: George Brewer, "History of the 46th Alabama Regiment Volunteer Infantry," ADAH.
14. Robert M. Magill and Brenda D. Phillips, *Personal Reminiscences of a Confederate Soldier Boy*, 63.
15. Edgar W. Jones, "History of the 18th Alabama Infantry," ADAH.
16. F. G. Terry, "Buford's Division in Hood's Rear," *Confederate Veteran* 13, no. 4 (April 1905): 161.
17. Dunlap: Sam Dunlap, "Hard Times on Hood's Retreat," 266; Moose: David Logsdon, *Eyewitnesses at the Battle of Franklin*, 43; Key: Wirt Armistead Cate, *Two Soldiers*, 170; Hancock: R. R. Hancock, *Hancock's Diary*, 534; Vann: Samuel King Vann and Nancy Elizabeth Neel Vann, *"Most Lovely Lizzie,"* 68; Dacus: Robert H. Dacus, *Reminiscences of Company "H,"* 23; Sparkman: John W. Sparkman, *The Diary of Sergt. John W. Sparkman*, 80.
18. Davis: Henrietta Short to Nancy Davis, December 29, 1864, Newton Davis Papers, ADAH; "Captain Samuel Brown," *Confederate Veteran* 15, no. 7 (September 1907): 420.
19. Army of Tennessee continuing south: Edwin Hansford Rennolds, *A History of the Henry County*, 112; McNeilly: James McNeilly, "The Retreat from Nashville Tennessee," *Confederate Veteran* 26, no. 7 (July 1918): 305; Forrest warning Hood: John Johnston, "Personal Reminiscences of the Civil War 1861–1865," TSLA; Conley: Samuel Oswald Conley Diary, entry dated December 26, 1864, GSA; Key: Wirt Armistead Cate, *Two Soldiers*, 170.
20. McWhirter: George McWhirter, "Soldier in the Western Army," 623; Forrest's response to Walthall: Michael Thomas Smith, *The 1864 Franklin-Nashville Campaign*, 96–97.

21. 18th Alabama Infantry in rear guard fight: Edgar W. Jones, "History of the 18th Alabama Infantry," ADAH; Rennolds: Edwin Hansford Rennolds, *A History of the Henry County Commands*, 113; Collins: R. M. Collins, *Chapters from the Unwritten History of the War between the States*, 258; Joy: Charles Gore Joy, "The Stampede at La Fayette, Ga.," 475; Rape: A. D. Rape, "Some Thrilling War Experiences," 180.
22. Campbell: Henry Campbell, "Three Years in the Saddle," Henry Campbell Papers, Robert T. Ramsay Jr. Archival Center of WC, Crawfordsville, IN; Thomas: George H. Thomas, "George H. Thomas to the Soldiers," December 29, 1864, *OR*, ser. 1, vol. 45, pt. 1, p. 50.
23. Collins: R. M. Collins, *Chapters from the Unwritten History of the War between the States*, 263; Cooper: James Cooper, "Memoir of James Cooper, 20th Tennessee Infantry," Special Collections Division, NTPL.
24. W. J. Worsham and C. W. Heiskell, *Old Nineteenth Tennessee Regiment*, 152.
25. John Johnston, "Personal Reminiscences of the Civil War 1861–1865," TSLA.
26. Etter: Diary of Risenar Etter, entry dated December 17, 1864, SRNBP; bloody footprints: Edward Young McMorries, "History of the First Alabama Volunteer Infantry CSA," ADAH; men pausing in Columbia, raiding chicken coops: Robert Jarman, "The History of Company K, 27th Mississippi Infantry," MDAH; Joy: Charles Gore Joy, "The Stampede at La Fayette, Ga.," 477.
27. Memoir of J. W. Preston, ADAH.
28. John Dicks, "Capt. John A. Dicks, Natchez, Miss.," 14.
29. Improvised rear guard near Pulaski: R. M. Collins, *Chapters from the Unwritten History of the War between the States*, 263; Jones: Edgar W. Jones, "History of the 18th Alabama Infantry," ADAH; Cooper: James Cooper, "Memoir of James Cooper, 20th Tennessee Infantry," Special Collections Division, NTPL.
30. Dunlap: Sam Dunlap, "Hard Times on Hood's Retreat," 266; Key: Wirt Armistead Cate, *Two Soldiers*, 173.
31. Quarreling over cowhides: "Southern Crosses of Honor Bestowed," *Confederate Veteran* 9, no. 2 (February 1901): 72; Jones: Edgar W. Jones, "History of the 18th Alabama Infantry," ADAH; Collins: R. M. Collins, *Chapters from the Unwritten History of the War between the States*, 265.
32. Furloughs granted to men from TN: John Bell Hood, *Advance and Retreat*, 307; Etter: Diary of Risenar Etter, entry dated December 20, 1864, SRNBP; Cannon: J. P. Cannon, *Inside of Rebeldom*, 269.
33. Johnston: John Johnston, "Personal Reminiscences of the Civil War 1861–1865," TSLA; fear of bushwackers: R. M. Collins, *Chapters from the Unwritten History of the War between the States*, 264; Jones: Edgar W.

Jones, "History of the 18th Alabama Infantry," ADAH; Rennolds: E. H. Rennolds Diary, December 23, 1864, UTK.

34. Burning pontoons: E. H. Rennolds Diary, December 24, 1864, UTK; Gale: William Gale to his wife, January 19, 1865, William Gale Letters, TSLA.
35. Jarman: Robert Jarman, "The History of Company K, 27th Mississippi Infantry," MDAH; artillery struggling to cross Shoal Creek: Wirt Armistead Cate, *Two Soldiers*, 172.
36. Cooper: James Cooper, "Memoir of James Cooper, 20th Tennessee Infantry," NTPL; Magill: Robert M. Magill and Brenda D. Phillips, *Personal Reminiscences of a Confederate Soldier Boy*, 70; Clark: Walter A. Clark, *Under the Stars and Bars*, 160.
37. Gale: William Gale to his wife, January 19, 1865, William Gale Letters, TSLA; men lashing pontoons together: Robert Jarman, "The History of Company K, 27th Mississippi Infantry," MDAH.
38. "Captains R. L. Cobb and F. P. Gracey,"*Confederate Veteran* 3, no. 8 (August 1895): 249.
39. Cooper: James Cooper, "Memoir of James Cooper, 20th Tennessee Infantry," NTPL; Boaz: Mamie Yeary, *Reminiscences of the Boys in Gray*, 63; rebel batteries: John Porcher, dictated to his daughter Elinor Porcher, "Father's War Story," *Recollections and Reminiscences*, 387, Southern History Collection, BPL; Reddick: H. W. Reddick, *Seventy-Seven Years in Dixie*, 48.
40. Collins: R. M. Collins, *Chapters from the Unwritten History of the War between the States*, 266; Joy: Charles Gore Joy, "The Stampede at La Fayette, Ga.," 477; Jones: Edgar W. Jones, "History of the 18th Alabama Infantry," ADAH.
41. Roland Gooch, "Special Department," *Confederate Veteran* 6, no. 3 (March 1898): 134.
42. P. T. Martin, "Recollections of a Confederate," 232.
43. Maxwell: James Robert Maxwell, *Autobiography of James Robert Maxwell*, 272; Preston: Memoir of J. W. Preston, ADAH; Morton: John Watson Morton, *The Artillery of Nathan Bedford Forrest's Cavalry*, 280.
44. Littlejohn: Elbridge Littlejohn, "The Civil War Letters of Elbridge Littlejohn," pt. 2, p. 34; Kelley: Samuel Kelley Letters Home, January 13 and 14, 1865, ADAH.
45. Soldiers spent wages on luxuries rather than equipment: Joseph Baumer Memoir, ADAH; Magill: Robert M. Magill and Brenda D. Phillips, *Personal Reminiscences of a Confederate Soldier Boy*, 72; Cooper: James Cooper, "Memoir of James Cooper, 20th Tennessee Infantry," NTPL; Holland: John S. Holland to his friend Dr. William Farell, January 1, 1865, John S. Holland Civil War Letter, KRC, AHC; Hall: Alex Hall to his father, January 12, 1864, Alex Hall Letters, ADAH.

46. Brewer: George Brewer, "History of the 46th Alabama Regiment Volunteer Infantry," ADAH; Dacus: Robert H. Dacus, *Reminiscences of Company "H,"* 24; Murphree: Joel Dyer Murphree, "Autobiography and Civil War Letters of Joel Murphree of Troy, Alabama, 1864–1865," 209; Gale: William Gale to his wife, January 19, 1865, William Gale Letters, TSLA.
47. Magill: Robert M. Magill and Brenda D. Phillips, *Personal Reminiscences of a Confederate Soldier Boy*, 72; conflicting identities of southern men: Larry Johnson, "16th Regiment Tennessee Infantry, CSA," SRNBP; Murphree: Joel Dyer Murphree, "Autobiography and Civil War Letters of Joel Murphree of Troy, Alabama, 1864–1865," 201.
48. Hood sending men home on furloughs: John Bell Hood, *Advance and Retreat*, 307; Rennolds: Edwin Hansford Rennolds, *A History of the Henry County Commands*, 110; Rea: R. N. Rea, "Mississippi Soldier of the Confederacy," 288; Cooke: Bill O'Neal and Samuel Alonza Cooke, "The Civil War Memories of Samuel Alonza Cooke," 548; Cooper: James Cooper, "Memoir of James Cooper, 20th Tennessee Infantry," NTPL; Jarman: Robert Jarman, "The History of Company K, 27th Mississippi Infantry," MDAH; Johnson: Larry Johnson, "16th Regiment Tennessee Infantry, CSA," SRNBP.
49. Hood resigning: John Bell Hood, *Advance and Retreat*, 311; Arnold: James Arnold to Thomas M. Owen, February 4, 1911, ADAH; Littlejohn: Elbridge Littlejohn, "The Civil War Letters of Elbridge Littlejohn," pt. 2, p. 34; Dent: Stouten Dent to his wife, Anna, February 1, 1864, S. H. Dent Papers, AUA; Chambers: W. P. Chambers, *Chamber's Confederate Journal*, 87; Bevier: R. S. Bevier, *History of the First and Second Missouri Confederate Brigades*, 260.

Conclusion

1. R. S. Bevier, *History of the First and Second Missouri Confederate Brigades*, 260.
2. Mark L. Bradley, *The Civil War Ends, 1865*, 14.
3. For examples of conflict between protecting men and sending them into combat, see James Cooper Nisbet, *Four Years on the Firing Line*, 307; and Edwin Hansford Rennolds, *A History of the Henry County Commands*, 104. For examples of conflict between causing civilians pain and protecting them, see Watson Landingham to his mother, July 14, 1864, Irenus Watson Landingham Collection, AUA; Hiram Smith Williams, Lewis Nicholas Wynne, and Robert A. Taylor, *This War So Horrible*, 106; and Samuel T. Foster and Norman D. Brown, *One of Cleburne's Command*, 143. For examples of soldiers loathing young and old in the ranks while lamenting dwindling numbers, see Benjamin Rountree, "Letters from a Confederate Soldier," 285; and James Robert Maxwell, *Autobiography of James Robert*

Maxwell, 244. For examples of soldiers torn between desire to go home and duty to army, see Hugh Black to his wife, July 20, 1864, Hugh Black Papers, FSUA; John W. Sparkman, *The Diary of Sergt. John W. Sparkman*, 78; Larry Johnson, "16th Regiment Tennessee Infantry, CSA," SRNBP; Hosea Garret to his uncle, August 1st, 1864, Hosea Garrett Jr. Civil War Letters, KRC, AHC; and James Lanning Diary, entry dated November 28, 1864, ADAH.

4. Mark A. Weitz, *More Damning Than Slaughter*, 30.
5. Ted Ownby, *Subduing Satan*.
6. For the quote "lean and hungry set of wolves see Shelby Foote, The Civil War: A Narrative, Fort Sumter to Perryville, 663.
7. Nevil Shute, *On the Beach* (1957), frontispiece.

Appendix

1. Note: A version of this report appeared as Thrasher, Christopher. "Ragged Rebels Sure Enough" The Army of Tennessee in September 1864." *Tennessee Historical Quarterly* 75, no. 1 (2016): 2-27. Thomas Lawrence Connelly, *Autumn of Glory*, 508; Wiley Sword, *The Confederacy's Last Hurrah: Spring Hill, Franklin, and Nashville* (Lawrence, KS: Univ. Press of Kansas, 1993), 65, 68–70.
2. Leslie D. Jensen, "A Survey of Confederate Central Government Quartermaster Issue Jackets, Part 1," *Military Collector and Historian* (Fall and Winter 1989); Harold S. Wilson, *Confederate Industry Manufacturers and Quartermasters in the Civil War* (Jackson: Univ. Press of Mississippi, 2002), 127.
3. I used a very simple method of analyzing these sources. I set up an Excel spreadsheet that mimicked the preprinted forms used in the original inspections, listing units as named by the inspectors and filling in their information on each category. When I found particularly interesting notes or comments left by the inspecting officers, I recorded those as well. When inspectors left out information, I recorded it as blank. When their writing was illegible, I noted that as well. After compiling all of the information I used various Excel functions to calculate and graph the data. This was an imperfect process and I hope that other scholars will examine these reports in an effort to either verify or correct my findings.
4. For inspection reports, see, Inspection Reports and Related Records Received by the Inspector Branch in the Confederate Adjutant and Inspector General's Office, Microfilm M935, US National Archives and Records Administration; for Confederate regulations, see, Confederate States of America and James A. Seddon, *Regulations for the Army of the Confederate States, 1864. Revised and Enlarged with a New and Copious Index* (Richmond, VA: J. W. Randolph, 1864), 29.

5. In an effort to better understand the men completing these inspection reports, I attempted to assemble as much information as possible on each inspecting officer. I began by looking at each inspection report and attempted to read the name of the inspecting officer. I cross-referenced these names against the names listed in United States, *List of Staff Officers of the Confederate States Army, 1861–1865* (Washington, DC: GPO, 1891), which often, although not always, provided confirmation regarding the name and dates of service of these inspectors. I cross-checked their names against the database provided online by the National Park Service (http://www.nps.gov/civilwar/search-soldiers.htm). I discovered additional information in the Compiled Service Records of Confederate Soldiers held by the National Archives, which I accessed through www.fold3.com. I compiled the data into an Excel spreadsheet for ease of display and to help me graph the information. This was an imperfect process, but one that provided unprecedented insights into the inspection reports and the daily operations of the Confederate Army of Tennessee.
6. Gould: General Edmund Pettus to General Samuel Cooper, June 26, 1864, Compiled Service Record of John McKee Gould, National Archives; Ramsey: United States, *List of Staff Officers of the Confederate States Army, 1861–1865* (Washington, DC: GPO, 1891), 135; Army of Tennessee's professionalism: Herman Hattaway and Archer Jones, *How the North Won: A Military History of the Civil War* (Urbana: Univ. of Illinois Press, 1983).
7. See, for example, F.W. Ragland, Inspection of Reynolds's Brigade, September 18, 1864; Stephen A. Cowley, Inspection of Quarles's Brigade, September 15, 1864; and Patrick Henry, Inspection of Adams's Brigade, September 17, 1864.
8. See, for example, Henry Tupper, Inspection of Brantley's Brigade, September 18, 1864.
9. Joseph Flanagan, Inspection of Cockrell's Brigade, September 20, 1864.
10. Oladowski: *OR*, ser. 1, vol. 23, pt. 2, p. 763; Lawton: *OR*, ser. 4, vol. 3, pp. 1039–40; Flanagan: Joseph Flanagan, Inspection of Cockrell's Brigade, September 20, 1864.
11. This figure was calculated by the author based on the figures from the September 1864 brigade-level infantry inspection reports.
12. John Tate, Inspection of Cantey's Brigade, September 18, 1864.
13. *OR*, ser. 1, vol. 23, pt. 2, p. 762; Stephen M. Hood, *John Bell Hood*, 91.
14. *OR*, ser. 1, vol. 23, pt. 2, p. 762.
15. This figure was calculated by the author based on the figures from the September 1864 brigade-level infantry inspection reports.
16. See, for example, "The Importance of a Careful Medical Inspection of Recruits," *Lancet*, published in London, England, Vol. I, No. VII, February 18, 1854, 191.

17. Repairing broken civilian weapons: *OR*, ser. 1, vol. 6, pt. 2, p. 833; mix of smoothbore muskets and flintlocks in A. P. Stewart's Division: Larry J. Daniel, *Soldiering in the Army of Tennessee: A Portrait of Life in a Confederate Army* (Chapel Hill: Univ. of North Carolina Press, 1991), 42; number of smoothbore muskets in March 1863: *OR*, ser. 1, vol. 23, pt. 2, p. 762.
18. These figures were calculated by the author based on the figures from the September 1864 brigade-level infantry inspection reports.
19. John Tate, Inspection of Cantey's Brigade, September 18, 1864.
20. These figures were calculated by the author based on the figures from the September 1864 brigade-level infantry inspection reports.
21. Arthur James Lyon Fremantle, *Three Months in the Southern States* (New York: J. Bradburn, 1864), 157.
22. These figures were calculated by the author based on the figures from the September 1864 brigade-level infantry inspection reports.
23. John Tate, Inspection of Cantey's Brigade, September 18, 1864.
24. Gorgas: Josiah Gorgas, "Notes on the Ordnance Department of the Confederate Government," *Southern Historical Society Papers* 12, no. 1 (January 1884): 68; surrender of Fort Donelson due to depleted ammunition: Bromfield Lewis Ridley, *Battles and Sketches of the Army of Tennessee* (Mexico, MO: Missouri Print. & Pub. Co., 1906), 52; Oladowski: *OR*, ser. 1, vol. 23, pt. 2, p. 758.
25. These figures were calculated by the author based on the figures from the September 1864 brigade-level infantry inspection reports.
26. H. L. Scott, *Military Dictionary* (New York: Can Nostrand, 1861) 24.
27. These figures were calculated by the author based on the figures from the September 1864 brigade-level infantry inspection reports.
28. George Williams, Inspection of Govan's Brigade, September 14, 1864.
29. On bayonets and bayonet scabbards generally, see, for example, Arthur Fremantle, *Three Months in the Southern States*, 157; "The Gallant 13th Indiana," *Holmes County Farmer*, April 10, 1862, Tennessee State Library and Archives; and "Delusions as to Bayonet Wounds," *Portage Sentinel*, Ravenna, OH, February 1, 1862; on using bayonets as pothooks, see Samuel R. Watkins, *"Company Aytch,"* 75.
30. *OR*, ser. 3, vol. 2, p. 753.
31. These figures were calculated by the author based on the figures from the September 1864 brigade-level infantry inspection reports.
32. Griffith: Paddy Griffith, *Battle Tactics of the Civil War* (New Haven, CT: Yale Univ. Press, 1989), 77; Fremantle: Arthur James Lyon Fremantle, *Three Months in the Southern States*, 225; prevalence of smoothbore muskets: *OR*, ser. 1, vol. 23, pt. 2, p. 762.
33. Army of Northern Virginia better positioned to capture Union material:

Stanley F. Horn, *The Army of Tennessee* (Norman: Univ. of Oklahoma Press, 1941), vii; numbers of captured weapons and sets of accouterments: William C. Davis and Russ A. Pritchard, *The Fighting Men of the Civil War* (New York: Gallery Books, 1989), 58.

34. *Regulations for the Army of the Confederate States*, 106.
35. George Williams, Inspection of Govan's Brigade, September 14, 1864.
36. Captured Confederates lacking blankets: "News from the South," *Evening Telegraph*, Philadelphia, PA, November 4, 1864; less than 25 percent of Confederate soldiers with blankets: "Is It True," *Southern Watchman*, Athens, GA, November 23, 1864, Georgia State Archives; Union POW noting absence of blankets: "A Panoramic View of Hood's Army," *Daily Ohio Statesmen*, Columbus, OH, October 27, 1864.
37. *Regulations for the Army of the Confederate States*, 10.
38. Lawton: *OR*, ser. 4, vol. 3, pp. 1039–40; Tupper: Henry Tupper, Inspection of Brantley's Brigade, September 18, 1864.
39. *Regulations for the Army of the Confederate States*, 107, 406, 407.
40. Fremantle: Arthur Fremantle, *Three Months in the Southern States*, 156, 164; Henry Tupper, Inspection of Brantley's Brigade, September 18, 1864; Flanagan: Joseph Flanagan, Inspection of Cockrell's Brigade, September 20, 1864; Sneed: Sebron Sneed to his wife, June 7, 1864, Briscoe Center for American History, Univ. of Texas at Austin; Cantey's Brigade: John Tate, Inspection of Cantey's Brigade, September 18, 1864.
41. *Regulations for the Army of the Confederate States*, 10, 410.
42. These figures were calculated by the author based on the figures from the September 1864 brigade-level infantry inspection reports.
43. *OR*, ser. 4, vol. 3, p. 1040.
44. United States War Department, Revised United States Army Regulations of 1861 (Washington, DC, Government Printing Office, 1863) 517.
45. *Regulations for the Army of the Confederate States*, 408; Arthur Fremantle, *Three Months in the Southern States*, 157
46. This figure was calculated by the author based on adding up all of the figures from the September 1864 brigade-level infantry inspection reports.
47. McGee: "Georgia," *Semi Weekly Standard*, (Raleigh, NC) October 21, 1864; Confederate prisoners from Atlanta lacking shoes: "News from the South," *Evening Telegraph* (Philadelphia, PA) November 4, 1864; Union POW on barefoot Confederates: "A Panoramic View of Hood's Army," *Daily Ohio Statesmen* (Columbus, OH) October 27, 1864; defenders of the nation lacking clothes and shoes: "What's the News," *Chattanooga (TN) Daily Rebel*, July 27, 1864.
48. This figure was calculated by the author based on adding up all of the figures from the September 1864 brigade-level infantry inspections.

49. See, for example, Samuel R. Watkins, *"Company Aytch,"* 66; *OR*, ser. 1, vol. 20, p. 416; *OR*, ser. 1, vol. 23, p. 757; and *OR*, ser. 1, vol. 32, p. 508.
50. Soldiers without shoes told to wait by rail lines: *OR*, ser. 1, vol. 20, pt. 2, p. 416; Atlanta depot producing shoes for soldiers: *OR*, ser. 1, vol. 20, pt. 2, p. 759.
51. For the February 1864 figure, see *OR*, ser. 1, vol. 52, pt. 2, p. 697. The September 1864 figure was calculated by the author based on adding up all of the figures from the September 1864 brigade-level infantry inspection reports.
52. Pickett's Division inspection and large quantities of shoes at Richmond depot: Jeff Toalson, *No Soap, No Pay, Diarrhea, Dysentery & Desertion*, 211, 272; McClellan: William Cowan McClellan, *Welcome the Hour of Conflict: William Cowan McClellan and the 9th Alabama*, ed. John C. Carter (Tuscaloosa: Univ. of Alabama Press, 2007), 273; soldier sending extra clothing home: Philip Katcher and Michael Youens, *The Army of Northern Virginia* (Reading, PA: Osprey Pub, 1975), 11.
53. This figure was calculated by the author based on adding up all of the figures from the September 1864 brigade-level infantry inspections.
54. See for example: the inspection of Sears's Brigade which lists the condition of the brigade's arms as "clean" and the condition of accoutrements as "in good order" but leaves the section on condition of clothing blank. Also see for example: inspection of Maney's brigade which lists the brigade's arms as "clean" and the condition of accoutrements as "good" but leaves the section on condition of clothing blank.
55. S. Bertram Browne, *A Companion to the New Rifle Musket* (London: Allen, 1859), 3.
56. *Regulations for the Army of the Confederate States*, 10.
57. Davis to Gorgas: Josiah Gorgas, "Notes on the Ordnance Department of the Confederate Government," 78; men furnishing their own uniforms: *OR*, ser. 4, vol. 1, p. 232; proud claims of privately provided army clothing: *Southern Recorder* (Milledgeville, GA), January 28, 1862; failed attempts to keep up with army's clothing needs: E. Merton Coulter, *The Confederate States of America, 1861–1865* (Baton Rouge: Louisiana State Univ. Press, 1950), 445.
58. Frank Everson Vandiver, *Ploughshares into Swords: Josiah Gorgas and Confederate Ordnance* (Austin: Univ. of Texas Press, 1952), 115.
59. On loss of depots, see Spencer Tucker, Paul G. Pierpaoli, and William E. White, *The Civil War Naval Encyclopedia* (Santa Barbara, CA: ABC-CLIO, 2011), 476; Thomas Lawrence Connelly, *Army of the Heartland: The Army of Tennessee, 1861–1862* (Baton Rouge: Louisiana State Univ. Press, 1967), 136; and Andrew F. Smith, *Starving the South*, 169; on Selma, AL, depot, see Vandiver, *Ploughshares into Swords*, 148, 219.
60. Craig L. Symonds and William J. Clipson, *The Naval Institute Historical*

Atlas of the U.S. Navy (Annapolis, MD: Naval Institute Press, 1995), 90, 98, 100.

61. *OR*, ser. 1, vol. 3, p. 593; Vandiver, *Ploughshares into Swords*, 115.
62. Hood, *Advance and Retreat*, 253.
63. *OR*, ser. 4, vol. 3, pp. 1039–40.
64. Wilson, *Confederate Industry*, 127.
65. See, for example, "Bank's Retreat," *Daily Intelligencer*, (Wheeling, VA) May 30, 1862.
66. Flanagan: Joseph Flanagan, Inspection of Cockrell's Brigade, September 20, 1864; soldier willing his clothing and blanket: Samuel R. Watkins, *"Company Aytch,"* 88.
67. *Regulations for the Army of the Confederate States*, 10.
68. For an example of Confederate authorities encouraging women to send clothing, see "Quartermasters' Stores," *Opelousas Courier*, (Opelousas, LA) July 30, 1864; for Confederate soldiers depending on friends and family for winter clothing, see letter from Archibald D. Norris, Co. K, 7th Tennessee Infantry Regiment CSA, August 28, 1861, Tennessee State Library and Archives, Nashville, TN; on request for immediate supply of clothing for men who could not receive it from home, see Joseph Flanagan, Inspection of Cockrell's Brigade, September 20, 1864.
69. For examples of Confederates using captured Union equipment, see Fremantle, *Three Months in the Southern States*, 157; Samuel R. Watkins, *"Company Aytch,"* 66; Confederate soldiers ordering Union prisoners to relinquish overcoats: *OR*, ser. 2, vol. 7, p. 60; Confederates wearing captured Union shoes: "Shoes," *Memphis (TN) Daily Appeal*, September 20, 1862; Union soldiers expecting and feeling sympathy for Confederates stripping dead and captured Union troops: Marshall Thatcher, *A Hundred Battles in the West, St. Louis to Atlanta, 1861 65* (Detroit, MI: self-published, 1884), 312.
70. This figure was calculated by the author based on adding up all of the figures from the September 1864 brigade-level infantry inspections.
71. John Tate, Inspection of Cantey's Brigade, September 18, 1864.
72. Captain [illegible first name] Pickens, Inspection of Holtzclaw's Brigade, September 10, 1864.
73. James Jones, Inspection of Smith's (Also Known as Tyler's) Brigade, September 18, 1864.
74. William Simms, Inspection of Tucker's (Also Known as Sharp's) Brigade, September, 18, 1864.
75. Andrew Haughton, *Training, Tactics, and Leadership in the Confederate Army of Tennessee*, 57.
76. Lucy Virginia French Diary, Tennessee State Library and Archives, Nashville, TN.

BIBLIOGRAPHY

Abbreviations

ADAH	Alabama Department of Archives and History
ASA	Arkansas State Archives
AHC	Atlanta History Center
AUA	Auburn University Archives
BUL	Baylor University Library
BPL	Birmingham Public Library, Southern History Collection
BCAS	Butler Center for Arkansas Studies, Central Arkansas Library System
CHA	Carter House Archives
CNBP	Corinth National Battlefield Park
EU	Emory Univrsity, Manuscript, Archives, and Rare Book Library
FU	Fisk University Archives
FSA	Florida State Archives
FSUA	Florida State University Archives
GHS	Georgia Historical Society
GSA	Georgia State Archives
GVSUA	Grand Valley State University Archives
HHS	Hartselle Historical Society, Hartselle, Alabama
KRC	Kenan Research Center, Atlanta History Center
LSU	Louisiana State University
MHS	Minnesota Historical Society
MDAH	Mississippi Department of Archives and History
NTPL	Nashville, Tennessee, Public Library
NARA	National Archives and Records Administration
OR	*The War of the Rebellion: A Compilation of the Official Records of the Union and Confederate Armies*
PMNC	Pearce Museum at Navarro College
RU	Rice University
RCHS	Rutherford County Historical Society

SRNBP	Stones River National Battlefield Park
TSLA	Tennessee State Library and Archives
TU	Tulane University
UA	University of Alabama Libraries
UG	University of Georgia, Hargrett Rare Book and Manuscript Library
UM	University of Mississippi
UNCSHC	University of North Carolina, Southern Historical Collection
UND	University of Notre Dame, Rare Books and Special Collections
USM	University of Southern Mississippi
UTK	University of Tennessee at Knoxville
UT	University of Texas, Briscoe Center for American History
WC	Wabash College

Manuscript Collections

Alabama Department of Archives and History (Montgomery, AL)
- Andrew Hill, "Personal Recollections of Andrew Malone Hill."
- B. F. Weathers Papers
- Edgar W. Jones Papers
- Edward McMorries, "History of the First Regiment Alabama Volunteer Infantry."
- George Brewer, "History of the 46th Alabama Regiment Volunteer Infantry."
- James Lanning Diary
- Joseph Baumer Memoir
- Newton Davis Papers
- Richard Harris "Historical Sketch of Selden—Lovelace Battery."
- Samuel Kelly Letters
- Thomas Warrick Papers
- W. E. Matthews Memoir
- W. E. Preston, "Unit History 33rd Alabama Infantry."
- W. W. McMillian, "Reminiscences of War of 1861."

Arkansas State Archives (Little Rock, Arkansas)
- Hotze Family Papers
- Joseph Jones, "Sketch of My Army Life from 1861 to 1865."
- Patrick Cleburne Papers
- Thomas Hardin Letters

Atlanta History Center (Atlanta, Georgia)
- Barkley and King Family Civil War Correspondence
- Hosea Garrett Jr. Civil War Letters
- John S. Holland Letters

Auburn University Archives (Auburn, Alabama)
Stouten Hubert Dent Letters
Irenus Watson Landingham Collection
John Crittenden Collection
John Thomas Scott Letters
Baylor University Library (Waco, Texas)
John and Virginia Adkins Coleman Papers, Texas Collection
Birmingham Public Library, Southern History Collection (Birmingham, Alabama)
Dick Harris Letters
Frank Millican Letters
Hardman Family Letters
John Porcher Papers
T. G. Baker, "Sketch of T. G. Baker."
Wilson Howell Manuscript
Butler Center for Arkansas Studies, Central Arkansas Library System (Little Rock, Arkansas)
Bost Family Civil War Letters
Carter House Archives (Franklin, Tennessee)
Memoir of R. B. Meadows
Papers of Lieutenant W. D. Mintz
Diary of M. D. L. Stephens
Corinth National Battlefield Park (Corinth, Mississippi)
George Washington Higgins Letters
EU, Manuscript, Archives, and Rare Book Library
Andrew Jackson Neal Papers
Fisk University Archives (Nashville, Tennessee)
Spence Family Collection
Florida State Archives (Tallahassee, Florida)
William McLeod Diary
Florida State University Archives (Tallahassee, Florida)
Hugh Black Papers
Georgia Historical Society (Savannah, Georgia)
Alva Sinks Letters
Georgia State Archives (Morrow, Georgia)
John Battle Letters
Samuel Oswald Conley Diary
Grand Valley State University Archives (Allendale, Michigan)
John Bennitt Diary
Hartselle Historical Society (Hartselle, Alabama)
W. H. H. Avery Letters

Kenan Research Center, Atlanta History Center (Atlanta, Georgia)
- Benjamin T. Hunter Papers
- Colin Dunlop Civil War Letters

Louisiana State University (Baton Rouge, Louisiana)
- S. A. Hayden Letters

Minnesota Historical Society (St. Paul, Minnesota)
- Elijah Evan Edwards Journals

Mississippi Department of Archives and History (Jackson, Mississippi)
- Robert Jarman, "The History of Company K, 27th Mississippi Infantry and its First and Last Muster Rolls."

Nashville Public Library (Nashville, Tennessee)
- Isham G. Harris, "Narrative of Gov. Isham G. Harris as Told to Col. Brown."
- James Cooper Memoir

National Archives and Records Administration (Washington, District of Columbia)
- Compiled Service Records
- Confederate Inspection Reports
- Southern Claims Commission Records

Pearce Museum at Navarro College (Corsicana, Texas)
- William Henry Henderson Papers

Rice University (Houston, Texas)
- Jefferson Davis Papers

Rutherford County Historical Society (Murfreesboro, Tennessee)
- F. E. Henderson Diary

Stones River National Battlefield Park (Murfreesboro, Tennessee)
- Diary of L. Jackson Sanders
- Diary of Risenar Etter
- Diary of Robert Battle
- Diary of William Brown
- George Athey Letters
- Larry G. Thompson, "16th Regiment Tennessee Infantry, CSA."
- Wilbur F. Mims, "War History of the Prattville Dragoons."
- William Yeatman, "My Military Life."

Tennessee State Library and Archives (Nashville, Tennessee)
- Memoir of J. W. Harmon
- John Johnston, "Personal Reminiscences of the Civil War 1861–1865."
- M. H. Dixon Diary
- Stephen Jordan Diary
- Thomas Deavenport Journal
- William Gale Letters

William Sloan Diary
William. J. Watson Diary
W. Jere Crook Letters
Tulane University (New Orleans, Louisiana)
Andrew Devilbliss Letters
Joseph Jones Collection
University of Alabama Libraries (Tuscaloosa, Alabama)
Henry De Lamar Clayton Sr. Papers
Samuel D. Cameron and Maxwell A. Cameron Papers
University of Georgia, Hargrett Rare Book and Manuscript Library
E. Merton Coulter Manuscript Collection (Athens, Georgia)
University of Mississippi (University, Mississippi)
Charles Roberts Collection
Jesse Henderson Diary
University of North Carolina, Southern Historical Collection (Chapel Hill, North Carolina)
A. C. McLeary, "Humorous Incidents of the Civil War."
Richard Wharton Papers
University of Notre Dame, Rare Books and Special Collections (Notre Dame, Indiana)
Henry H. Maley Letters
University of Southern Mississippi (Hattiesburg, Mississippi)
William H. and Sallie J. Hardy Papers
University of Tennessee, Knoxville (Knoxville, Tennessee)
E. H. Rennolds Diary, Civil War Collection
University of Texas, Briscoe Center for American History (Austin, Texas)
Sebron Sneed Letters
Wabash College (Crawfordsville, Indiana)
Henry Campbell Papers

Newspapers and Periodicals

Alexandria Gazette, Alexandria, District of Columbia
Brownlow's Knoxville Whig and Rebel Ventilator, Knoxville, Tennessee
Chattanooga Rebel, Griffin, Georgia
Christian Advocate, Nashville, Tennessee
Cleveland Morning Leader, Cleveland, Ohio
Confederate Chronicles of Tennessee
Confederate Veteran, Nashville, Tennessee
Daily Dispatch, Richmond, Virginia
Daily Intelligencer, Wheeling, West Virginia
Daily National Republican, Washington, DC

Daily Ohio Statesmen, Columbus, Ohio
Daily Wabash Express, Terre-Haute, Indiana
Dayton Daily Empire, Dayton, Ohio
Edgefield Advertiser, Edgefield, South Carolina
Evening Telegraph, Philadelphia, Pennsylvania
Harper's New Monthly Magazine, New York, New York
Jacksonville Alabama Republican, Jacksonville, Alabama
Lancet, London, England
Nashville Daily Union, Nashville, Tennessee
North Carolina Standard, Raleigh, North Carolina
Semi Weekly Standard, Raleigh, North Carolina
Southern Historical Society Papers, Richmond, Virginia
Southern Recorder, Milledgeville, Georgia
Southern Watchman, Athens, Georgia
United Service
Weekly Standard, Raleigh, North Carolina
Western Democrat, Charlotte, North Carolina
Wilmington Journal, Wilmington, North Carolina
Yorkville Enquirer, Yorkville, South Carolina

Government Publications

Candler, Allen D. *The Confederate Records of the State of Georgia*. Vol. 2. Atlanta, GA: C. P. Byrd, State Printer, 1909.

Confederate States of America. *Army Regulations, Adopted for the Use of the Army of the Confederate States, in Accordance with Late Acts of Congress*. New Orleans: Bloomfield and Steel, 1861.

Confederate States of America. *Laws of Congress in Regard to Taxes, Currency and Conscription, Passed February 1864*. Richmond: James E. Goode, 1864.

Tennessee. *Tennesseans in the Civil War: A Military History of Confederate and Union Units with Available Rosters of Personnel*. Nashville, TN: Civil War Centennial Commission, 1964.

Union Army. *A History of Military Affairs in the Loyal States, 1861–65—Records of the Regiments in the Union Army—Cyclopedia of Battles—Memoirs of Commanders and Soldiers*. Madison, WI: Federal Pub. Co., 1908.

United States. *Revised United States Army Regulations of 1861*. Washington, DC: Government Printing Office, 1863.

United States, B. F. Wade, and Daniel Wheelwright Gooch. *Report of the Joint Committee on the Conduct of the War at the Second Session, Thirty-Eighth Congress*. Vol. 1. Washington, DC: Government Printing Office, 1865.

United States. *The War of the Rebellion: Official Records of the Union and Confederate Armies*. Washington, DC: Government Printing Office, 1899.

United States. *The Census of 1860.* Washington, DC: Government Printing Office, 1899.

Published Primary Sources

Anderson, Ephraim. *Memoirs: Historical and Personal; Including the Campaigns of the First Missouri Confederate Brigade.* St. Louis: Times Printing Company, 1868.

Ashmore, Thomas P., F. H. Singer, and Thos. R. Rhodes. *Grier's Southern Almanac, for the Year of Our Lord 1864: Being Bissextile or Leap Year, and the Fourth of the War for Separation, and (Until the Fourth of July,) the Eighty-Eighth of the Independence of the United States: Calculated for the Latitude and Meridian of Augusta, Ga. . . . and Will Serve for All Adjacent States.* Augusta, GA: Published for the trade by F. H. Singer, 1863.

Austin, J. P. *The Blue and the Gray; Sketches of a Portion of the Unwritten History of the Great American Civil War, a Truthful Narrative of Adventure, with Thrilling Reminiscences of the Great Struggle on Land and Sea.* Atlanta, GA: Franklin Print. and Pub. Co., 1899.

Banks, R. W. *The Battle of Franklin, November 30, 1864, The Bloodiest Engagement of the War Between the States.* New York: Neale Publishing Company, 1908.

Bates, James C., and Richard G. Lowe. *A Texas Cavalry Officer's Civil War: The Diary and Letters of James C. Bates.* Baton Rouge: Louisiana State University Press, 1999.

Beard, Richard. "To the Editor." *Military Essays and Recollections: Papers Read Before the Commandery of the State of Illinois, Military Order of the Loyal Legion of the United States.* Vol. 1. Chicago: A. C. McClurg and Company, 1891.

Bevier, R. S. *History of the First and Second Missouri Confederate Brigades. 1861–1865. And, From Wakarusa to Appomattox, a Military Anagraph.* St. Louis: Bryan, Brand and Co., 1879.

Browne, S. Bertram. *A Companion to the New Rifle Musket.* London: Allen, 1859.

Buck, Irving. *Cleburne and His Command.* New York: Neale Pub. Co., 1908.

Candler, Allen D. *The Confederate Records of the State of Georgia.* Atlanta, GA: C. P. Byrd, State Printer, 1909.

Cannon, J. P. *Inside of Rebeldom: The Daily Life of a Private in the Confederate Army.* Washington, DC: National Tribune, 1900.

Cannon, J. P., Noel Crowson, and John V. Brogden. *Bloody Banners and Barefoot Boys: A History of the 27th Regiment Alabama Infantry CSA: The Civil War Memoirs and Diary Entries of J.P. Cannon, M.D.* Shippensburg, PA: Burd Street Press, 1997.

Cannon, Newton, and Campbell H. Brown. *The Reminiscences of Sergeant Newton Cannon, from Holograph Material Provided by His Grandson, Samuel M. Fleming, Jr.* Franklin, TN: Carter House Association, 1963.

Carter, W. R. *History of the First Regiment of Tennessee Volunteer Cavalry in the Great War of the Rebellion, With the Armies of the Ohio and Cumberland, Under Generals Morgan, Rosecrans, Thomas, Stanley and Wilson. 1862–1865.* Knoxville, TN: Gaut-Ogden Co., Printers, 1902.

Cate, Wirt Armistead, Thomas J. Key, and Robert J. Campbell. *Two Soldiers: The Campaign Diaries of Thomas J. Key, C.S.A., December 7, 1863–May 17, 1865, and Robert J. Campbell, U.S.A., January 1, 1864–July 21, 1864.* Chapel Hill: UNCSHC Press, 1938.

Chambers, W. P. *Chamber's [sic] Confederate Journal.* Carrollton, MS: Pioneer Pub., 2002.

Chesnutt, Mary Boykin, Isabella D. Martin, and Myrta Lockett Avary. *A Diary from Dixie: The Civil War's Most Celebrated Journal, Written 1860–1865 by the Wife of James Chesnutt, Jr., an Aide to President Jefferson Davis and a Brigadier-General in the Confederate Army.* New York: Portland House, 1997.

Chester, William. "Notes and Documents: The Diary of Captain Elisha Tompkins Hollis." *West Tennessee Historical Papers* 39 (1985): 82 – 118.

Christ, Mark. *Getting Used to Being Shot At: The Spence Family Civil War Letters.* Fayetteville, AR: University of Arkansas Press, 2010.

Clark, Walter A. *Under the Stars and Bars; Or, Memories of Four Years Service with the Oglethorpes, of Augusta, Georgia.* Augusta, GA: Chronicle Print. Co., 1900.

Collins, R. M. *Chapters from the Unwritten History of the War between the States: or, The Incidents in the Life of a Confederate Soldier in Camp, on the March, in the Great Battles, and in Prison.* St. Louis: Nixon-Jones Printing Co., 1893.

Cone, Daniel. *Last to Join the Fight: The 66TH Georgia Infantry.* Macon, GA: Mercer University 2014.

Cooper, James Litton. "The Civil War Diary of Captain James Litton Cooper, September 30, 1861 to January 1865." Edited by William T. Alderson. *Tennessee Historical Quarterly* 15 (June 1956): 141 - 173.

Copley, John M. *A Sketch of the Battle of Franklin, Tenn. With Reminiscences of Camp Douglas.* Chapel Hill, NC: Academic Affairs Library, UNCSHC at Chapel Hill, 1998.

Coski, John. "I am In for Anything for Success: The Letters of Sergeant Archie Livingston, 3rd Florida Infantry." *North and South* 6, no. 3 (April 2003): 76 – 86.

Cox, Jacob D. *The Army in the Civil War.* Vol. 10, *The March to the Sea, Franklin and Nashville.* New York: Charles Scribner's Sons, 1882.

Cox, Jacob D. *The Battle of Franklin, Tennessee, November 30, 1864: A Monograph.* New York: C. Scribner's Sons, 1897.

Cumming, Kate. *A Journal of Hospital Life in the Confederate Army of Tennessee: From the Battle of Shiloh to the End of the War: with Sketches of Life and Character, and Brief Notices of Current Events During That Period.* Louisville, KY: John P. Morton and Co., 1866.

Dacus, Robert H. *Reminiscences of Company "H," First Arkansas Mounted Rifles.* Dardanelle, AR: Post-Dispatch Print., 1897.

Davis, Jefferson. *The Papers of Jefferson Davis.* Vol. 10, *October 1863–August 1864.* Edited by Lynda Lasswell Crist. Baton Rouge: Louisiana State University Press, 1999.

Davis, Jefferson. *The Rise and Fall of the Confederate Government.* New York: D. Appleton and Co., 1881.

Dinkins, James. *1861 to 1865, by an Old Johnnie. Personal Recollections and Experiences in the Confederate Army.* Cincinnati: R. Clarke Co., 1897.

Doolittle, Charles C. "The Defense of Decatur, Alabama." In *Sketches of War History, 1861–1865: Papers Read Before the Ohio Commandery of the Military Order of the Loyal Legion of the United States,* by Robert Hunter and W. H. Chamberlin. Cincinnati: R. Clark, 1888.

Duncan, Thomas D. *Recollections of Thomas D. Duncan: A Confederate Soldier.* Nashville, TN: McQuiddy Print. Co., 1922.

F. B. "A Nice Pair of Moccasins." *Southern Bivouac* 2 (1884–1885): 452 – 457.

Fout, Fredrick, and Albert E. Fout. *Die schwersten Tage des Bürgerkrieges von 1864 und 1865. Der Feldzug unter Schofield und Thomas gegen Hood in Tennessee.—Die Schlachten von Franklin und Nashville.* Chicago: Erinnerungen von Fred'k W. Fout, 1902.

Foster, Samuel T., and Norman D. Brown. *One of Cleburne's Command: The Civil War Reminiscences and Diary of Capt. Samuel T. Foster, Granbury's Texas Brigade, CSA.* Austin: University of Texas Press, 1980.

Fremantle, Arthur, and James, Lyon. *Three Months in the Southern States.* New York: J. Bradburn, 1864.

French, Samuel Gibbs. *Two Wars: An Autobiography of General Samuel G. French . . . Mexican War; War between the States, a Diary; Reconstruction Period, His Experience; Incidents, Reminiscences, Etc.* Nashville, TN: Confederate Veteran, 1901.

Goodloe, Albert Theodore. *Confederate Echoes: A Soldier's Personal Story of Life in the Confederate Army from the Mississippi to the Carolinas.* Nashville: Smith and Lamar, 1907.

Grant, Ulysses. *Personal Memoirs of U. S. Grant, Two Volumes in One.* New York: C. L. Webster, 1894.

Guild, George. *A Brief Narrative of the Fourth Tennessee Cavalry Regiment, Wheeler's Corps, Army of Tennessee.* Nashville: Cornell, 1913.

Hadaway, Claude Lee. "With Loyalty and Honor as a Patriot: Recollections of a Confederate Soldier." Edited by Royce Shingleton. *Alabama Historical Quarterly* 33 (Fall/Winter 1971): 240 - 263.

Hager, George. "Second Tennessee Cavalry." In *The Military Annals of Tennessee. First Series: Embracing a Review of Military Operations, with Regimental Histories and Memorial Rolls*, by John Berrien Lindsley. Nashville: J. M. Lindsley and Co., 1886.

Hancock, R. R. *Hancock's Diary: Or, A History of the Second Tennessee Confederate Cavalry*. Nashville: Brandon Print. Co., 1887.

Head, Thomas A. *Campaigns and Battles of the Sixteenth Regiment, Tennessee Volunteers, in the War between the States, With Incidental Sketches of the Part Performed by Other Tennessee Troops in the Same War, 1861–1865*. Nashville, TN: Cumberland Presbyterian Pub. House, 1885.

Heller, J. Roderick, Carolynn Ayres Heller, and Milton Barrett. *The Confederacy Is on Her Way Up the Spout: Letters to South Carolina, 1861–1864*. Athens: University of Georgia Press, 1992.

Hood, John Bell. *Advance and Retreat: Personal Experiences in the United States and Confederate States Armies*. New Orleans: Published for the Hood Orphan Memorial Fund, 1880.

Hood, John Bell, and Stephen M. Hood. *The Lost Papers of Confederate General John Bell Hood*. El Dorado Hills, CA: Savas Beatie, 2015.

Jackman, John S., and William C. Davis. *Diary of a Confederate Soldier: John S. Jackman of the Orphan Brigade*. Columbia, SC: University of South Carolina Press, 1997.

Johnston, Bradley. *A Memoir of the Life and Public Service of Joseph E. Johnston: Once the Quartermaster General of the Army of the United States, and a General in the Army of the Confederate States of America*. Baltimore: R.H. Woodward and Company, 1891.

Johnston, Willis Fletcher, and O. O. Howard. *Life of Wm. Tecumseh Sherman. Late Retired General, U.S.A.: A Graphic History of His Career in War and Peace; His Romantic Youth; His Stern and Patriotic Manhood; His Calm and Beautiful Old Age; a Marvelous March from the Mountain of Time to the Sea of Eternity*. Philadelphia, PA: Edgewood Publishing Company, 1891.

Kagan, Neil, and Stephen G. Hyslop. *Eyewitness to the Civil War: The Complete History from Secession to Reconstruction*. Washington, DC: National Geographic, 2006.

Kirwan, A. D., ed. *Johnny Green of the Orphan Brigade—Journal of a Confederate Soldier.* Lexington, KY: University of Kentucky Press, 1956.

Lavender, John W., and Ted R. Worley. *The War Memoirs of Captain John W. Lavender, C.S.A. [They Never Came Back: The Story of Co. F. Fourth*

Arks. Infantry. C.S.A., Originally Known as the Montgomery Hunters, As Told by Their Commanding Officer]. Pine Bluff, AR: W. M. Hackett and D. R. Perdue, 1957.

Little, George, and James Robert Maxwell. *A History of Lumsden's Battery, C.S.A.* Tuscaloosa, AL: R. E. Rhodes Chapter, United Daughters of the Confederacy, 1905.

Littlejohn, Elbridge. "The Civil War Letters of Elbridge Littlejohn." Part 2, edited by Vicki Betts. *Chronicles of Smith County, Texas* 18 (Summer 1979): 11 - 50.

Lord, John, and Natalie Shipman. *Frontier Dust.* Hartford, CT: Edwin Valentine Mitchell, 1926.

Ludlow, William. *The Battle of Allatoona.* Detroit: Winn and Hammond, Printers, 1891.

Magill, Robert, and Brenda D. Phillips. *Personal Reminiscences of a Confederate Soldier Boy.* Milledgeville, GA: Boyd, 1993.

Maxwell, James Robert. *Autobiography of James Robert Maxwell of Tuscaloosa, Alabama.* Baltimore: Gateway Press, 1996.

McGee, B. F., and Wm. R. Jewell. *History of the 72d Indiana Volunteer Infantry of the Mounted Lightning Brigade . . . Especially Devoted to Giving the Reader a Definite Knowledge of the Service of the Common Soldier. With an Appendix Containing Complete Roster of Officers and Men.* Lafayette, IN: S. Vater and Co., Printers, 1882.

McMurray, William. *History of the Twentieth Tennessee Regiment Volunteer Infantry, C.S.A.* Nashville: Publication Committee, consisting of W. J. McMurray, D. J. Roberts, and R. J. Neal, 1904.

Miller, George Knox, and Richard M. McMurry. *An Uncompromising Secessionist: The Civil War of George Knox Miller, Eighth (Wade's) Confederate Cavalry.* Tuscaloosa: University of Alabama Press, 2007.

Morton, John Watson. *The Artillery of Nathan Bedford Forrest's Cavalry, "the Wizard of the Saddle."* Nashville: Publishing House of the M. E. Church, South, Smith and Lamar, Agents, 1909.

Moxley, William Morel, Emily Beck Moxley, and Thomas W. Cuter. Oh, *What a Loansome Time I Had: The Civil War Letters of Major William Morel Moxley, Eighteenth Alabama Infantry, and Emily Beck Moxley.* Tuscaloosa: University of Alabama Press, 2002.

Murphree, Joel Dyer. "Autobiography and Civil War Letters of Joel Murphree of Troy, Alabama, 1864 1865." *Alabama Historical Quarterly* 19 (Spring 1957): 170 - 208.

Nisbet, James Cooper. *Four Years on the Firing Line.* Chattanooga: Imperial Press, 1914.

Noyes, Edward. "Excerpts from the Civil War Diary of E. T. Eggleston." *Tennessee Historical Quarterly* 17 (December 1958): 170–208.

Oake, William Royal, and Stacy D. Allen. *On the Skirmish Line Behind a Friendly Tree: The Civil War Memoirs of William Royal Oake, 26th Iowa Volunteers*. Helena, MT: Farcountry Press, 2006.

O'Neal, Bill, and Samuel Alonza Cooke. "The Civil War Memories of Samuel Alonza Cooke." *Southwestern Historical Quarterly* 74, no. 4 (April 1971): 535–48.

Patrick, Robert. *Reluctant Rebel: The Secret Diary of Robert Patrick, 1861–1865*. Edited by F. Jay Taylor. Baton Rouge: Louisiana State University Press, 1959.

Reddick, H. W. *Seventy-Seven Years in Dixie: The Boys in Gray of 61–65*. Santa Rosa, FL: H. W. Reddick, 1910.

Rennolds, Edwin Hansford. *A History of the Henry County Commands Which Served in the Confederate States Army, Including Rosters of the Various Companies Enlisted in Henry County, Tenn.* Jacksonville, FL: Sun Publishing Company, 1904.

Ridley, Broomfield. *Battles and Sketches of the Army of Tennessee.* Mexico, MO: Missouri Print. and Pub. Co., 1906.

Roman, Alfred. *The Military Operations of General Beauregard in the War between the States 1861 to 1865: Including a Brief Personal Sketch and a Narrative of His Services in the War with Mexico, 1846–8*. Vol. 2. New York: Harper, 1884.

Rountree, Benjamin. "Letters from a Confederate Soldier." *Georgia Review* 18, no. 3 (Fall 1964): 267 - 297.

Sanders, D. W. "Hood's Tennessee Campaign." *Southern Bivouac* 4 (1884–1885): 66, 357.

Schellenberger, John. *The Battle of Franklin, Tennessee: November 30, 1864; a Statement of the Erroneous Claims Made by General Schofield, and an Exposition of the Blunder Which Opened the Battle.* Cleveland: Priv. Print. for the author by the Arthur H. Clark Company, 1916.

Schellenberger, John K. *The Battle of Spring Hill, Tennessee Read After the Stated Meeting Held February 2d, 1907.* Saint Louis: Commandery of the State of Missouri, 1907.

Schmutz, George. *History of the 102d Regiment, O.V.I.* Wooster, OH: self-published, 1907.

Schofield, John. *Forty-Six Years in the Army.* New York: Century Co., 1897.

Scofield, Levi Tucker. *The Retreat from Pulaski to Nashville, Tenn.; Battle of Franklin, Tennessee, November 30th, 1864.* Cleveland: Press of the Caxton Co., 1909.

Scott, H. L. *Military Dictionary.* New York: Can Nostrand, 1861.

Sorrel, G. Moxley. *Recollections of a Confederate Staff Officer.* Jackson, TN: McCowat Mercer Press, 1958.

Sherman, William T. *Memoirs of General William T. Sherman*. Vol. 2. New York: D. Appleton, 1876.

Sherman, William T., Brooks D. Simpson, and Jean V. Berlin, *Sherman's Civil War: Selected Correspondence of William T. Sherman, 1860–1865*. Chapel Hill: UNCSHC Press, 1999.

Smith, Daniel P., and Jim D. Moody. *Company K First Alabama Regiment, or, Three Years in the Confederate Service*. Gaithersburg, MD: Butternut Press, 1984.

Smith, Robert Davis, Virginia Wood Alexander, and Jill Knight Garrett. *Confederate Diary of Robert D. Smith*. Columbia, TN: Capt. James Madison Sparkman Chapter, UDC, 1997.

Society of the Confederate Chronicles. *Confederate Chronicles of Tennessee*. Covington, TN: Society of the Confederate Chronicles, Tennessee Division, Sons of Confederate Veterans, 1986.

Sparkman, John W. *The Diary of Sergt. John W. Sparkman, Sr., of the Quartermaster's Department: 48th Tennessee Regiment, C.S.A., 1881–1865*. Birmingham, AL: Library, 1940.

Toalson, Jeff. *No Soap, No Pay, Diarrhea, Dysentery & Desertion: A Composite Diary of the Last 16 Months of the Confederacy from 1864 to 1865 As Seen by the Soldiers, Farmers, Clerks, Nurses, Sailors, Farm Girls, Merchants, Nuns, Surgeons, Chaplains and Wives*. Lincoln, NE: iUniverse, 2006.

United Daughters of the Confederacy. *Recollections and Reminiscences 1861–1865 through World War I*. Columbia: South Carolina Division United Daughters of the Confederacy, 1990.

Van Horne, Thomas, and Edward Ruger. *History of the Army of the Cumberland: Its Organization, Campaigns, and Battles, written at the Request of Major-General George H. Thomas Chiefly from His Private Military Journal and Official and Other Documents Furnished by Him*. Cincinnati: R. Clarke and Co., 1875.

Vann, Samuel, and Nancy Elizabeth Neel Vann. *"Most Lovely Lizzie": Love Letters of a Young Confederate Soldier*. Birmingham, AL: Privately Mimeographed, 1958.

Watkins, Samuel R. *"Co. Aytch": Maury Grays, First Tennessee Regiment, or, a Side Show of the Big Show*. Chattanooga, TN: Times Print. Co., 1900.

Wiley, Bell Irvin. "The Confederate Letters of John W. Hagan." *Georgia Historical Quarterly* 38, no. 3 (September 1954): 170 – 200.

Williams, Hiram Smith, Lewis Nicholas Wynne, and Robert A. Taylor. *This War So Horrible: The Civil War Diary of Hiram Smith Williams*. Tuscaloosa: University of Alabama Press, 2017.

Wilson, James. *Under the Old Flag; Recollections of Military Operations in the*

War for the Union, the Spanish War, the Boxer Rebellion, Etc. Vol. 2. New York: D. Appleton and Co., 1912.

Worsham, W. J., and C. W. Heiskell. *Old Nineteenth Tennessee Regiment, C.S.A. June, 1861–April 1865.* Knoxville, TN: Press of Paragon Print. Co., 1902.

Wyeth, John A. *Life of General Nathan Bedford Forrest.* New York: Harper and Brothers, 1899.

———. *With Sabre and Scalpel; The Autobiography of a Soldier and Surgeon.* New York and London: Harper and Bros., 1914.

Yeary, Mamie. *Reminiscences of the Boys in Gray, 1861–1865.* Dallas, TX: For the Author by Smith and Lamar, Pub. House, M.E. Church, South, 1912.

Young, John Preston. *The Seventh Tennessee Cavalry (Confederate): A History.* Nashville: For the author by Publishing House of the M.E. Church, South, Barbee and Smith, Agents, 1890.

Young, Lot D. *Reminiscences of a Soldier of the Orphan Brigade.* Louisville: Courier-Journal Job Print. Co., 1918.

Secondary Sources

Alexander, E. P. *The American Civil War: A Critical Narrative.* London: Siegle, Hill and Co., 1908.

Armistead, Gene C. *Horses and Mules in the Civil War: A Complete History with a Roster of More Than 700 War Horses.* Jefferson, NC: McFarland and Company, 2013.

Arnold, James R., and Roberta Wiener. *American Civil War: The Essential Reference Guide.* Santa Barbara, CA: ABC-CLIO, 2011.

Bailey, Anne. *The Chessboard of War: Sherman and Hood in the Autumn Campaigns of 1864.* Lincoln: University of Nebraska Press, 2000.

Barney, William L. *The Oxford Encyclopedia of the Civil War.* New York: Oxford University Press, 2011.

Bobrick, Benson. *Master of War: The Life of General George H. Thomas.* New York: Simon and Schuster, 2009.

Bonds, Russell S. *War Like the Thunderbolt: The Battle and Burning of Atlanta.* Yardley, PA: Westholme, 2009.

Carpenter, Noel. *A Slight Demonstration: Decatur, October 1864: Clumsy Beginning of Gen. John Hood's Tennessee Campaign.* Austin, TX: Legacy Books and Letters, 2007.

Comer, Kevin. *Louisville & Nashville Railroad in South Central Kentucky.* Charleston, SC: Arcadia Pub., 2012.

Connelly, Thomas Lawrence. *Autumn of Glory: The Army of Tennessee, 1862–1865.* Baton Rouge: Louisiana State University Press, 1971.

Coulter, E. Merton. *The Confederate States of America, 1861–1865.* Baton Rouge: Louisiana State University Press, 1950.

Daniel, Larry J. *Soldiering in the Army of Tennessee: A Portrait of Life in a Confederate Army*. Chapel Hill: UNCSHC Press, 1991.

Davis, Louise Littleton. *Nashville Tales*. Gretna, LA: Pelican Pub. Co., 1981.

Davis, Robert Scott. *Civil War Atlanta*. Charleston, SC: History Press, 2011.

Davis, Stephen. *Atlanta Will Fall: Sherman, Joe Johnston, and the Yankee Heavy Battalions*. Wilmington, DE: Scholarly Resources, 2001.

Deland, T. A., and A. Davis Smith. *Northern Alabama, Historical and Biographical*. Birmingham, AL: Smith and De Land, 1888.

Dunnavant, Robert. *Decatur, Alabama: Yankee Foothold in Dixie, 1861–1865*. Athens, AL: Pea Ridge Press, 1995.

Eggleston, Michael. *The White Man's Fight: How African Americans in the Civil War Won the Confidence of the Nation and the Price They Paid*. Bloomington, IN: AuthorHouse, 2012.

Fisher, John F. *They Rode with Forrest and Wheeler: A Chronicle of Five Tennessee Brothers' Service in the Confederate Western Cavalry*. Jefferson, NC: McFarland and Co., 1995.

Gallman, Matthew J., and Gary W. Gallagher. *Lens of War: Exploring Iconic Photographs of the Civil War*. Athens: University of Georgia Press, 2015.

Gee, Wilson. *The Gist Family of South Carolina and Its Maryland Antecedents*. Charlottesville, VA: Privately printed for the author by Jarman's, 1934.

Hahn, Barbara. Making Tobacco Bright. Baltimore, MD: Johns Hopkins University Press, 2011.

Hattaway, Herman, and Archer Jones. *How the North Won: A Military History of the Civil War*. Urbana: University of Illinois Press, 1983.

Haughton, Andrew. *Training, Tactics, and Leadership in the Confederate Army of Tennessee: Seeds of Failure*. London: Frank Cass, 2000.

Hine, Darlene Clark, and Earnestine Jenkins. *A Question of Manhood: A Reader in U.S. Black Men's History and Masculinity*. Bloomington: Indiana University Press, 1999.

Hood, Stephen. *John Bell Hood: The Rise, Fall, and Resurrection of a Confederate General*. El Dorado Hills, CA: Savas, 2013.

Horn, Stanley F. *The Army of Tennessee*. Norman: University of Oklahoma Press, 1941.

———. "The Spring Hill Legend." *Civil War Times Illustrated* 8, no. 4 (April 1969): 21–33.

Jacobson, Eric, and Richard A. Rupp. *For Cause and for Country: A Study of the Affair at Spring Hill and the Battle of Franklin*. Franklin, TN: O'More Publishing, 2007.

Johnston, Joe. *Franklin*. Charleston, SC: Arcadia Publishing, 2014.

Jones, Terry. *Historical Dictionary of the Civil War*. Lanham, MD: Scarecrow Press, 2011.

Kaufman, David R. *Peachtree Creek: A Natural and Unnatural History of Atlanta's Watershed.* Athens: University of Georgia Press, in cooperation with the AHC, 2007.

Knight, James R. *Hood's Tennessee Campaign: The Desperate Venture of a Desperate Man.* Charleston, SC: History Press, 2014.

Livermore, Thomas Leonard. *Numbers and Losses in the Civil War in America, 1861–1865.* Boston: Houghton, Mifflin, 1901.

McDonough, James. *Nashville: The Western Confederacy's Final Gamble.* Knoxville: University of Tennessee Press, 2004.

McDonough, James, and Thomas Lawrence Connelly. *Five Tragic Hours: The Battle of Franklin.* Knoxville: University of Tennessee Press, 1983.

McMurry, Richard M. "Confederate Morale in the Atlanta Campaign of 1864." *Georgia Historical Quarterly* 54, no. 2 (Summer 1970): 226 – 243.

McPherson, James. *Battle Cry of Freedom: The Civil War Era.* New York: Oxford University Press, 1988.

McWhiney, Grady, and Perry D. Jamieson. *Attack and Die: Civil War Military Tactics and the Southern Heritage.* University, AL: University of Alabama Press, 1982.

Mendoza, Alexander. *Chickamauga 1863 Rebel Breakthrough.* Santa Barbara, CA: ABC-CLIO, LLC, 2013.

———. *Confederate Struggle for Command: General James Longstreet and the First Corps in the West.* College Station: Texas A & M University Press, 2008.

Mendoza, Alexander, and Charles D. Grear. Texans and War New Interpretations of the States Military History. College Station: Texas A & M University Press, 2012.

Newton, Steven H. *Lost for the Cause: The Confederate Army in 1864.* New York: Da Capo Press, 2000.

Owens, David, M. *The Devil's Topographer: Ambrose Bierce and the American War Story.* Knoxville: University of Tennessee Press, 2006.

Ownby, Ted. *Subduing Satan: Religion, Recreation, and Manhood in the Rural South, 1865–1920.* Chapel Hill and London: University of North Carolina Press, 2014.

Perello, Chris. *The Quest for Annihilation: The Role and Mechanics of Battle in the American Civil War.* Bakersfield, CA: Strategy and Tactics Press, 2009.

Poole, W. Scott. *South Carolina's Civil War: A Narrative History.* Macon, GA: Mercer University Press, 2005.

Power, J. Tracy. Lee's Miserables: Life in the Army of Northern Virginia from the Wilderness to Appomattox. Chapel Hill : University of North Carolina Press, 1998.

Ritter, Charles, and Jon L. Wakelyn. *Leaders of the American Civil War: A Biographical and Historiographical Dictionary*. Westport, CT: Greenwood Press, 1998.

Sheehan-Dean, Aaron Charles. *The Civil War: The Final Year Told by Those Who Lived It*. New York: Library of America, 2014.

Smith, Derek. *In the Lion's Mouth: Hood's Tragic Retreat from Nashville, 1864*. Mechanicsburg, PA: Stackpole Books, 2011.

Smith, Michael Thomas. *The 1864 Franklin-Nashville Campaign. The Finishing Stroke*. Santa Barbara, CA: Praeger, 2014.

Springer, Paul J., and Glenn Robins. *Transforming Civil War Prisons: Lincoln, Lieber, and the Politics of Captivity*. New York: Routledge, 2014.

Sword, Wiley. *The Confederacy's Last Hurrah: Spring Hill, Franklin, and Nashville*. Lawrence, KS: University Press of Kansas, 1993.

Thompson, Holland, Edward Lyman Munson, and Deering J. Roberts. *The Photographic History of the Civil War: In Ten Volumes: Semi-Centennial Memorial: Thousands of Scenes Photographed 1861–65, with Text by Many Special Authorities*. Vol. 7. New York: Review of Reviews, 1911.

Tucker, Spencer, James R. Arnold, Roberta Wiener, Paul G. Pierpaoli, and David Coffey. *American Civil War: The Definitive Encyclopedia and Document Collection*. Santa Barbara, CA: ABC-CLIO, 2013.

Wagner, Margaret, Gary W. Gallagher, and Paul Finkelman. *The Library of Congress Civil War Desk Reference*. New York: Simon and Schuster, 2002.

Walker, Scott. *Hell's Broke Loose in Georgia: Survival in a Civil War Regiment*. Athens: University of Georgia Press, 2005.

Weitz, Mark A. *More Damning Than Slaughter: Desertion in the Confederate Army*. Lincoln: University of Nebraska Press, 2005.

Wilson, Joseph T. *The Black Phalanx; A History of the Negro Soldiers of the United States in the Wars of 1775–1812, 1861–'65*. Hartford, CT: American Pub. Co., 1890.

Woodworth, Steven E., and Kenneth J. Winkle. *Atlas of the Civil War*. New York: Oxford University Press, 2004.

Yearns, W. Buck. *The Confederate Congress*. Athens: University of Georgia Press, 1960.

Young, John Russell. *Around the World with General Grant: A Narrative of the Visit of General U.S. Grant, Ex-President of the United States, to Various Countries in Europe, Asia, and Africa, in 1877, 1878, 1879, To Which Are Added Certain Conversations with General Grant on Questions Connected with American Politics and History*. New York: American News Co., 1879.

Ziegler, Edith. *Schools in the Landscape Localism, Cultural Tradition, and the Development of Alabama's Public Education System, 1865–1915*. Tuscaloosa: University of Alabama Press, 2010.

INDEX